# Case Studies in Lifespan Development

*to*
*Jim Kalat and Jim Luginbuhl*
*for showing me how to teach and showing me why it's important*

*and to*
*Carson, Ellie, and Zelda*
*for showing me everything else*

Sara Miller McCune founded SAGE Publishing in 1965 to support the dissemination of usable knowledge and educate a global community. SAGE publishes more than 1000 journals and over 800 new books each year, spanning a wide range of subject areas. Our growing selection of library products includes archives, data, case studies and video. SAGE remains majority owned by our founder and after her lifetime will become owned by a charitable trust that secures the company's continued independence.

Los Angeles | London | New Delhi | Singapore | Washington DC | Melbourne

# Case Studies in Lifespan Development

## Stephanie M. Wright
Georgia Gwinnett College

**$SAGE**

Los Angeles | London | New Delhi
Singapore | Washington DC | Melbourne

**SAGE**

FOR INFORMATION:

SAGE Publications, Inc.
2455 Teller Road
Thousand Oaks, California 91320
E-mail: order@sagepub.com

SAGE Publications Ltd.
1 Oliver's Yard
55 City Road
London, EC1Y 1SP
United Kingdom

SAGE Publications India Pvt. Ltd.
B 1/I 1 Mohan Cooperative Industrial Area
Mathura Road, New Delhi 110 044
India

SAGE Publications Asia-Pacific Pte. Ltd.
18 Cross Street #10-10/11/12
China Square Central
Singapore 048423

Acquisitions Editor: Lara Parra
Marketing Manager: Katherine Hepburn
Production Editor: Veronica Stapleton Hooper
Copy Editor: Pam Schroeder
Typesetter: Hurix Digital
Proofreader: Wendy Jo Dymond
Cover Designer: Candice Harman

Copyright © 2020 by SAGE Publications, Inc.

All rights reserved. Except as permitted by U.S. copyright law, no part of this work may be reproduced or distributed in any form or by any means, or stored in a database or retrieval system, without permission in writing from the publisher.

All third party trademarks referenced or depicted herein are included solely for the purpose of illustration and are the property of their respective owners. Reference to these trademarks in no way indicates any relationship with, or endorsement by, the trademark owner.

Printed in the United States of America

ISBN: 978-1-5443-6186-4

This book is printed on acid-free paper.

19 20 21 22 23 10 9 8 7 6 5 4 3 2 1

# Brief Contents

Preface — xiv
Acknowledgments — xvi
About the Author — xviii

## PART I: THE CASES — 2

**1** Jamal Jones — 2
**2** Naomi Rowe — 24
**3** James Albert — 44
**4** Riley Everett — 70
**5** Leonardo Ramirez — 96
**6** London Dennel — 118
**7** Edward Archer — 142
**8** Aiza Morris — 164
**9** Zack Park — 186
**10** Bliss McCallen — 212
**11** Poppy Bell — 234
**12** Aminah Mohammed — 262

## PART II: APPENDIX

Appendix A: Student Research Kit — 287

## PART III: DIGITAL-ONLY APPENDICES

Appendix A: Domain Mapping

Appendix B: Alternate Cases With Moderate Outcomes

Appendix C: Alternate Cases With Negative Outcomes

# Detailed Contents

| | | | |
|---|---|---|---|
| **Preface** | xiv | Digital Tools | xv |
| For Instructors | xiv | **Acknowledgments** | xvi |
| Purpose | xiv | **About the Author** | xviii |
| Learning Objectives | xiv | | |
| Pedagogy | xiv | | |

## PART I: THE CASES     2

## 1    Jamal Jones     2

| | | | |
|---|---|---|---|
| Overview | 2 | 11. Physical and Cognitive Development in Late Childhood | 12 |
| Introduction | 2 | 12. Socioemotional Development in Late Childhood | 13 |
| Meet Jamal Jones | 3 | | |
| 1. Development and Its Influences | 3 | 13. Physical and Cognitive Development in Adolescence | 13 |
| 2. Biological and Environmental Foundations | 4 | 14. Socioemotional Development in Adolescence | 14 |
| 3. Prenatal Development, Birth, and Newborn Experience | 5 | 15. Physical and Cognitive Development in Emerging/Early Adulthood | 15 |
| 4. Physical Development in Infancy and Toddlerhood | 6 | 16. Socioemotional Development in Emerging/Early Adulthood | 16 |
| 5. Cognitive Development in Infancy and Toddlerhood | 7 | 17. Physical and Cognitive Development in Middle Adulthood | 17 |
| 6. Socioemotional Development in Infancy and Toddlerhood | 8 | 18. Socioemotional Development in Middle Adulthood | 18 |
| 7. Physical and Cognitive Development in Early Childhood | 9 | 19. Physical and Cognitive Development in Late Adulthood | 19 |
| 8. Socioemotional Development in Early Childhood | 10 | 20. Socioemotional Development in Late Adulthood | 20 |
| 9. Physical and Cognitive Development in Middle Childhood | 10 | 21. Experience With Death and Dying | 21 |
| 10. Socioemotional Development in Middle Childhood | 11 | Case Discussion Questions | 22 |

## 2    Naomi Rowe     24

| | | | |
|---|---|---|---|
| Introduction | 24 | 1. Development and Its Influences | 25 |
| Meet Naomi Rowe | 24 | 2. Biological and Environmental Foundations | 26 |

| | |
|---|---|
| 3. Prenatal Development, Birth, and Newborn Experience | 27 |
| 4. Physical Development in Infancy and Toddlerhood | 28 |
| 5. Cognitive Development in Infancy and Toddlerhood | 29 |
| 6. Socioemotional Development in Infancy and Toddlerhood | 30 |
| 7. Physical and Cognitive Development in Early Childhood | 31 |
| 8. Socioemotional Development in Early Childhood | 31 |
| 9. Physical and Cognitive Development in Middle Childhood | 32 |
| 10. Socioemotional Development in Middle Childhood | 33 |
| 11. Physical and Cognitive Development in Late Childhood | 34 |
| 12. Socioemotional Development in Late Childhood | 34 |
| 13. Physical and Cognitive Development in Adolescence | 35 |
| 14. Socioemotional Development in Adolescence | 36 |
| 15. Physical and Cognitive Development in Emerging/Early Adulthood | 37 |
| 16. Socioemotional Development in Emerging/Early Adulthood | 38 |
| 17. Physical and Cognitive Development in Middle Adulthood | 39 |
| 18. Socioemotional Development in Middle Adulthood | 40 |
| 19. Physical and Cognitive Development in Late Adulthood | 41 |
| 20. Socioemotional Development in Late Adulthood | 42 |
| 21. Experience With Death and Dying | 43 |
| Case Discussion Questions | 43 |

# 3  James Albert 44

| | |
|---|---|
| Introduction | 44 |
| Meet James Albert | 44 |
| 1. Development and Its Influences | 45 |
| 2. Biological and Environmental Foundations | 46 |
| 3. Prenatal Development, Birth, and Newborn Experience | 47 |
| 4. Physical Development in Infancy and Toddlerhood | 49 |
| 5. Cognitive Development in Infancy and Toddlerhood | 50 |
| 6. James's Socioemotional Development in Infancy and Toddlerhood | 51 |
| 7. Physical and Cognitive Development in Early Childhood | 52 |
| 8. Socioemotional Development in Early Childhood | 53 |
| 9. Physical and Cognitive Development in Middle Childhood | 54 |
| 10. Socioemotional Development in Middle Childhood | 55 |
| 11. Physical and Cognitive Development in Late Childhood | 56 |
| 12. Socioemotional Development in Late Childhood | 57 |
| 13. Physical and Cognitive Development in Adolescence | 58 |
| 14. Socioemotional Development in Adolescence | 59 |
| 15. Physical and Cognitive Development in Emerging/Early Adulthood | 61 |
| 16. Socioemotional Development in Emerging/Early Adulthood | 62 |
| 17. Physical and Cognitive Development in Middle Adulthood | 63 |
| 18. Socioemotional Development in Middle Adulthood | 64 |
| 19. Physical and Cognitive Development in Late Adulthood | 66 |
| 20. Socioemotional Development in Late Adulthood | 67 |
| 21. Experience With Death and Dying | 68 |
| Case Discussion Questions | 69 |

# 4  Riley Everett — 70

Introduction — 70
Meet Riley Everett — 70
1. Development and Its Influences — 71
2. Biological and Environmental Foundations — 72
3. Prenatal Development, Birth, and Newborn Experience — 72
4. Physical Development in Infancy and Toddlerhood — 73
5. Cognitive Development in Infancy and Toddlerhood — 74
6. Socioemotional Development in Infancy and Toddlerhood — 75
7. Physical and Cognitive Development in Early Childhood — 76
8. Socioemotional Development in Early Childhood — 78
9. Physical and Cognitive Development in Middle Childhood — 79
10. Socioemotional Development in Middle Childhood — 79
11. Physical and Cognitive Development in Late Childhood — 81
12. Socioemotional Development in Late Childhood — 81
13. Physical and Cognitive Development in Adolescence — 82
14. Socioemotional Development in Adolescence — 84
15. Physical and Cognitive Development in Emerging/Early Adulthood — 84
16. Socioemotional Development in Emerging/Early Adulthood — 86
17. Physical and Cognitive Development in Middle Adulthood — 88
18. Socioemotional Development in Middle Adulthood — 89
19. Physical and Cognitive Development in Late Adulthood — 92
20. Socioemotional Development in Late Adulthood — 93
21. Experience With Death and Dying — 94
Case Discussion Questions — 95

# 5  Leonardo Ramirez — 96

Introduction — 96
Meet Leonardo Ramirez — 96
1. Development and Its Influences — 97
2. Biological and Environmental Foundations — 98
3. Prenatal Development, Birth, and Newborn Experience — 98
4. Physical Development in Infancy and Toddlerhood — 99
5. Cognitive Development in Infancy and Toddlerhood — 101
6. Socioemotional Development in Infancy and Toddlerhood — 102
7. Physical and Cognitive Development in Early Childhood — 103
8. Socioemotional Development in Early Childhood — 104
9. Physical and Cognitive Development in Middle Childhood — 105
10. Socioemotional Development in Middle Childhood — 105
11. Physical and Cognitive Development in Late Childhood — 106
12. Socioemotional Development in Late Childhood — 107
13. Physical and Cognitive Development in Adolescence — 108
14. Socioemotional Development in Adolescence — 109
15. Physical and Cognitive Development in Emerging/Early Adulthood — 110
16. Socioemotional Development in Emerging/Early Adulthood — 111

| | |
|---|---|
| 17. Physical and Cognitive Development in Middle Adulthood | 112 |
| 18. Socioemotional Development in Middle Adulthood | 113 |
| 19. Physical and Cognitive Development in Late Adulthood | 115 |
| 20. Socioemotional Development in Late Adulthood | 116 |
| 21. Experience With Death and Dying | 116 |
| Case Discussion Questions | 117 |

# 6  London Dennel 118

| | |
|---|---|
| Introduction | 118 |
| Meet London Dennel | 118 |
| 1. Development and Its Influences | 119 |
| 2. Biological and Environmental Foundations | 120 |
| 3. Prenatal Development, Birth, and Newborn Experience | 121 |
| 4. Physical Development in Infancy and Toddlerhood | 122 |
| 5. Cognitive Development in Infancy and Toddlerhood | 124 |
| 6. Socioemotional Development in Infancy and Toddlerhood | 125 |
| 7. Physical and Cognitive Development in Early Childhood | 126 |
| 8. Socioemotional Development in Early Childhood | 127 |
| 9. Physical and Cognitive Development in Middle Childhood | 128 |
| 10. Socioemotional Development in Middle Childhood | 129 |
| 11. Physical and Cognitive Development in Late Childhood | 130 |
| 12. Socioemotional Development in Late Childhood | 130 |
| 13. Physical and Cognitive Development in Adolescence | 131 |
| 14. Socioemotional Development in Adolescence | 132 |
| 15. Physical and Cognitive Development in Emerging/Early Adulthood | 133 |
| 16. Socioemotional Development in Emerging/Early Adulthood | 135 |
| 17. Physical and Cognitive Development in Middle Adulthood | 135 |
| 18. Socioemotional Development in Middle Adulthood | 136 |
| 19. Physical and Cognitive Development in Late Adulthood | 137 |
| 20. Socioemotional Development in Late Adulthood | 138 |
| 21. Experience With Death and Dying | 139 |
| Case Discussion Questions | 140 |

# 7  Edward Archer 142

| | |
|---|---|
| Introduction | 142 |
| Meet Edward Archer | 142 |
| 1. Development and Its Influences | 143 |
| 2. Biological and Environmental Foundations | 144 |
| 3. Prenatal Development, Birth, and Newborn Experience | 144 |
| 4. Physical Development in Infancy and Toddlerhood | 145 |
| 5. Cognitive Development in Infancy and Toddlerhood | 146 |
| 6. Socioemotional Development in Infancy and Toddlerhood | 147 |
| 7. Physical and Cognitive Development in Early Childhood | 148 |
| 8. Socioemotional Development in Early Childhood | 151 |

| | |
|---|---|
| 9. Physical and Cognitive Development in Middle Childhood | 152 |
| 10. Socioemotional Development in Middle Childhood | 152 |
| 11. Physical and Cognitive Development in Late Childhood | 153 |
| 12. Socioemotional Development in Late Childhood | 154 |
| 13. Physical and Cognitive Development in Adolescence | 154 |
| 14. Socioemotional Development in Adolescence | 155 |
| 15. Physical and Cognitive Development in Emerging/Early Adulthood | 156 |
| 16. Socioemotional Development in Emerging/Early Adulthood | 157 |
| 17. Physical and Cognitive Development in Middle Adulthood | 158 |
| 18. Socioemotional Development in Middle Adulthood | 159 |
| 19. Physical and Cognitive Development in Late Adulthood | 160 |
| 20. Socioemotional Development in Late Adulthood | 160 |
| 21. Experience With Death and Dying | 162 |
| Case Discussion Questions | 163 |

# 8  Aiza Morris — 164

| | |
|---|---|
| Introduction | 164 |
| Meet Aiza Morris | 164 |
| 1. Development and Its Influences | 165 |
| 2. Biological and Environmental Foundations | 165 |
| 3. Aiza's Prenatal Development, Birth, and Newborn Experience | 166 |
| 4. Physical Development in Infancy and Toddlerhood | 167 |
| 5. Cognitive Development in Infancy and Toddlerhood | 168 |
| 6. Socioemotional Development in Infancy and Toddlerhood | 168 |
| 7. Physical and Cognitive Development in Early Childhood | 169 |
| 8. Socioemotional Development in Early Childhood | 170 |
| 9. Physical and Cognitive Development in Middle Childhood | 171 |
| 10. Socioemotional Development in Middle Childhood | 172 |
| 11. Physical and Cognitive Development in Late Childhood | 172 |
| 12. Socioemotional Development in Late Childhood | 173 |
| 13. Physical and Cognitive Development in Adolescence | 174 |
| 14. Socioemotional Development in Adolescence | 175 |
| 15. Physical and Cognitive Development in Emerging/Early Adulthood | 177 |
| 16. Socioemotional Development in Emerging/Early Adulthood | 179 |
| 17. Physical and Cognitive Development in Middle Adulthood | 180 |
| 18. Socioemotional Development in Middle Adulthood | 181 |
| 19. Physical and Cognitive Development in Late Adulthood | 182 |
| 20. Socioemotional Development in Late Adulthood | 183 |
| 21. Experience With Death and Dying | 184 |
| Case Discussion Questions | 185 |

# 9  Zack Park — 186

| | |
|---|---|
| Introduction | 186 |
| Meet Zack Park | 186 |
| 1. Development and Its Influences | 187 |
| 2. Biological and Environmental Foundations | 188 |

| | | | |
|---|---|---|---|
| 3. Prenatal Development, Birth, and Newborn Experience | 189 | 13. Physical and Cognitive Development in Adolescence | 200 |
| 4. Physical Development in Infancy and Toddlerhood | 191 | 14. Socioemotional Development in Adolescence | 201 |
| 5. Cognitive Development in Infancy and Toddlerhood | 193 | 15. Physical and Cognitive Development in Emerging/Early Adulthood | 203 |
| 6. Socioemotional Development in Infancy and Toddlerhood | 193 | 16. Socioemotional Development in Emerging/Early Adulthood | 204 |
| 7. Physical and Cognitive Development in Early Childhood | 194 | 17. Physical and Cognitive Development in Middle Adulthood | 206 |
| 8. Socioemotional Development in Early Childhood | 195 | 18. Socioemotional Development in Middle Adulthood | 207 |
| 9. Physical and Cognitive Development in Middle Childhood | 196 | 19. Physical and Cognitive Development in Late Adulthood | 208 |
| 10. Socioemotional Development in Middle Childhood | 197 | 20. Socioemotional Development in Late Adulthood | 209 |
| 11. Physical and Cognitive Development in Late Childhood | 198 | 21. Experience With Death and Dying | 210 |
| 12. Socioemotional Development in Late Childhood | 199 | Case Discussion Questions | 211 |

# 10 Bliss McCallen 212

| | | | |
|---|---|---|---|
| Introduction | 212 | 12. Socioemotional Development in Late Childhood | 223 |
| Meet Bliss McCallen | 212 | | |
| 1. Development and Its Influences | 213 | 13. Physical and Cognitive Development in Adolescence | 224 |
| 2. Biological and Environmental Foundations | 214 | 14. Socioemotional Development in Adolescence | 225 |
| 3. Prenatal Development, Birth, and Newborn Experience | 215 | 15. Physical and Cognitive Development in Emerging/Early Adulthood | 226 |
| 4. Physical Development in Infancy and Toddlerhood | 216 | 16. Socioemotional Development in Emerging/Early Adulthood | 227 |
| 5. Cognitive Development in Infancy and Toddlerhood | 217 | 17. Physical and Cognitive Development in Middle Adulthood | 228 |
| 6. Socioemotional Development in Infancy and Toddlerhood | 217 | 18. Socioemotional Development in Middle Adulthood | 228 |
| 7. Physical and Cognitive Development in Early Childhood | 218 | 19. Physical and Cognitive Development in Late Adulthood | 229 |
| 8. Socioemotional Development in Early Childhood | 219 | 20. Socioemotional Development in Late Adulthood | 230 |
| 9. Physical and Cognitive Development in Middle Childhood | 220 | 21. Experience With Death and Dying | 231 |
| 10. Socioemotional Development in Middle Childhood | 221 | Case Discussion Questions | 232 |
| 11. Physical and Cognitive Development in Late Childhood | 222 | | |

# 11 Poppy Bell — 234

| | |
|---|---|
| Introduction | 234 |
| Meet Poppy Bell | 234 |
| 1. Development and Its Influences | 235 |
| 2. Biological and Environmental Foundations | 236 |
| 3. Prenatal Development, Birth, and Newborn Experience | 236 |
| 4. Physical Development in Infancy and Toddlerhood | 237 |
| 5. Cognitive Development in Infancy and Toddlerhood | 239 |
| 6. Socioemotional Development in Infancy and Toddlerhood | 240 |
| 7. Physical and Cognitive Development in Early Childhood | 240 |
| 8. Socioemotional Development in Early Childhood | 242 |
| 9. Physical and Cognitive Development in Middle Childhood | 243 |
| 10. Socioemotional Development in Middle Childhood | 244 |
| 11. Physical and Cognitive Development in Late Childhood | 245 |
| 12. Socioemotional Development in Late Childhood | 246 |
| 13. Physical and Cognitive Development in Adolescence | 247 |
| 14. Socioemotional Development in Adolescence | 249 |
| 15. Physical and Cognitive Development in Emerging/Early Adulthood | 251 |
| 16. Socioemotional Development in Emerging/Early Adulthood | 253 |
| 17. Physical and Cognitive Development in Middle Adulthood | 255 |
| 18. Socioemotional Development in Middle Adulthood | 256 |
| 19. Physical and Cognitive Development in Late Adulthood | 257 |
| 20. Socioemotional Development in Late Adulthood | 259 |
| 21. Experience With Death and Dying | 260 |
| Case Discussion Questions | 261 |

# 12 Aminah Mohammed — 262

| | |
|---|---|
| Introduction | 262 |
| Meet Aminah Mohammed | 262 |
| 1. Development and Its Influences | 263 |
| 2. Biological and Environmental Foundations | 263 |
| 3. Prenatal Development, Birth, and Newborn Experience | 264 |
| 4. Physical Development in Infancy and Toddlerhood | 265 |
| 5. Cognitive Development in Infancy and Toddlerhood | 266 |
| 6. Socioemotional Development in Infancy and Toddlerhood | 267 |
| 7. Physical and Cognitive Development in Early Childhood | 268 |
| 8. Socioemotional Development in Early Childhood | 269 |
| 9. Physical and Cognitive Development in Middle Childhood | 271 |
| 10. Socioemotional Development in Middle Childhood | 272 |
| 11. Physical and Cognitive Development in Late Childhood | 273 |
| 12. Socioemotional Development in Late Childhood | 274 |
| 13. Physical and Cognitive Development in Adolescence | 275 |
| 14. Socioemotional Development in Adolescence | 276 |

15. Physical and Cognitive Development in Emerging/Early Adulthood — 277
16. Socioemotional Development in Emerging/Early Adulthood — 278
17. Physical and Cognitive Development in Middle Adulthood — 279
18. Socioemotional Development in Middle Adulthood — 281
19. Physical and Cognitive Development in Late Adulthood — 283
20. Socioemotional Development in Late Adulthood — 284
21. Experience With Death and Dying — 285
Case Discussion Questions — 286

# PART II APPENDIX

**Appendix A: Domain Mapping** — 287

# PART III DIGITAL-ONLY APPENDICES

**Appendix A: Student Research Kit**

Domain Research
Bioloical Theory
    Freud
Cognitive Theory
    Piaget
    Vygotsky
Socioemotional Theory
    Erickson
    Kohlberg
    Gilligan
General Developmental Domain Impacts
    Cognitive
    Socioemotional
    Cultural

**Appendix B: Alternate Cases With Moderate Outcomes**

Jamal Jones
Naomi Rowe
James Albert
Riley Everett
Leonardo Ramirez
London Dennel
Edward Archer
Azia Morris
Zack Park
Bliss McCallen
Poppy Bell
Aminah Mohammed

**Appendix C: Alternate Cases With Undesirable Outcomes**

Jamal Jones
Naomi Rowe
James Albert
Riley Everett
Leonardo Ramirez
London Dennel
Edward Archer
Azia Morris
Zack Park
Bliss McCallen
Poppy Bell
Aminah Mohammed

# Preface

Several years ago, a colleague and I began reengineering a course in lifespan human development. While I was teaching at a school offering several programs in the health sciences, human development was the yeoman's course of the psychology department. Although I had deep training and field experience in the area, teaching lifespan development always filled me with a sense of grappling for a way to help students deeply connect with the material. As the backbone of our department, this was important. Furthermore, given the programs sending students to us—nursing, human services, and education—the imperative to do more than regurgitate stage theorists and talk about the onset of life events such as puberty and senility seemed to shortchange their purpose in being there. I wanted a course that transcended the ordinary and gave students in the health sciences a firm grounding in the developing human across the lifespan.

## For Instructors

With *Case Studies for Lifespan Development*, SAGE offers instructors a dozen complete, diverse cases from conception through end of life. Online accompaniments include objective and subjective assessment items. Each chapter of each case maps onto learning objectives for companion texts and includes appropriate class assignments in addition to Bloom's Taxonomy–based test items that include true/false, multiple-choice, and essay questions.

## Purpose

Adopting the case study model allows students to safely explore human development within the social context from perspectives that may often be alien to their life experiences. As instructors, we want to impart this knowledge, but doing so can challenge both student and faculty as we work to expand worldviews without pedantry or sophistry. By giving students a case in which to invest themselves, a life that is hopefully different from their own, this learning occurs organically and, thus, more deeply.

## Learning Objectives

Specific learning objectives for each domain and period of development are presented at the beginning of each developmental moment. These learning objectives map to primary text material and are assessed by prepared class assignments and test items instructors can access online through SAGE Edge.

## Pedagogy

Having used a modified Harvard Case Study method previously in a range of courses, I thought to do it again. The principal difference between what this course accomplishes compared to a Harvard Business School course is the introduction of multiple cases simultaneously. However, it is possible to conduct the course with a single case, much more in line with the Harvard model. This multicase model is intended for use across all levels of lifespan development from introductory through the advanced undergraduate and early graduate levels.

## Digital Tools

### Assessment

Combine either Tara Kuther's *Lifespan Development: Lives in Context*, Second Edition, or Laura Levine and Joyce Munsch's *Child Development: From Infancy to Adolescence*, Second Edition, with *Case Studies in Lifespan Development* to connect students to the process of development across the lifespan. Included within the Coursepack offerings for both core textbooks are embedded autograded assessment and open-ended discussion questions tied directly to the 12 cases from *Case Studies in Lifespan Development*.

### Assessment and Instructor's Resources

Additionally, each Coursepack houses the accompanying instructor's manual for the casebook.

### Alternate Case Outcomes

Finally, within each Coursepack you will find 24 alternate case outcomes. For each case there is a complete undesirable and moderate alternate outcome paired with open-ended discussion questions.

### For Students

Each case in this book contains learning objectives that are paired with your primary text (or can stand alone). Each of these learning objectives is carefully designed to ensure you've mastered the course material associated with that portion of the case. Your instructor will provide guidance to you as you progress through your case, and you will have opportunities to test your learning through formal assessment such as essays and multiple-choice tests or classroom assignments. This combination of material and assessment should allow you to enjoy a meaningful learning experience that will deepen your understanding of lifespan development within a real-world context.

# Acknowledgments

A book like this requires the effort of a cadre of people. I am so thankful for Lara Parra at SAGE, who believed in the power of these case studies and their value in the classroom and advocated so fiercely on their behalf. Special thanks, too, to the SAGE team that worked with Lara to bring this book to life, including Emma Newsom, design, marketing, and others. I want to thank Rachel Earl for early review of cases, suggestions for improvement, and for the introduction of new case histories. This volume is richer for her creativity and her consistent review and input. To the students who engaged with early releases of these cases and offered invaluable feedback on both substance and process, I offer my deep gratitude. To those who participated in follow-up assessment on pedagogical efficacy, I remain in your debt. Finally, to the many anonymous reviewers of iteration after iteration of these cases, thank you; your thoughts and input helped create a better book.

We specifically thank the following reviewers:

Carson Anderson, Wake County Public School System

Shannon Coulter, Moorpark College

Michael Cox, Ohio Christian University, Southern New Hampshire University, Argosy University

Elizabeth Dose, Georgia Highlands College

Theresa Garfield, Texas A&M University–San Antonio

Ashley M. Harvey, Colorado State University

Martin Jones, University of New Mexico

Robyn Maitoza, York College of Pennsylvania

Rebecca Witt Meacham, West Liberty University

Wendy Morrison, Montana State University

Tracy Perron, The College of New Jersey

Gary Popoli, Stevenson University

Martha Ravola, Alcorn State University

Richard Sheridan, William Carey University

Stacy Thompson, Southern Illinois University

Margot Underwood, Joliet Junior College

Mary Wilson, Georgia Highlands College

Christina Wolfe, Georgia Highlands College

Finally, I want to acknowledge my family: my daughters, Carson, Ellie, and Zelda, for their constant love and encouragement, especially Zelda whose tolerance for my long working hours is equaled only by her ability to cheerlead me through my doubts; my son-in-law Nick for his ability to be both a solid sounding board and an integral piece of my emotional backbone; and Elaine Wright and Samantha Simons, my mother and my sister, who consistently offer guidance, light, and love as I follow my dreams. You are all stitched into the spine of this book.

# About the Author

**Stephanie M. Wright** is a socio-legal psychologist and associate professor of psychology at Georgia Gwinnett College. She received her Bachelor of Science in Psychology from High Point University and her master's and doctoral degrees from North Carolina State University. Since earning her degree, Stephanie's scholarship has spanned at-risk children and adolescents, survivors of domestic violence and sexual assault, and underrepresented groups navigating the legal system. She has also led institutional effectiveness and research efforts, assisted in professional development of institutional research staff and also of faculty in data-driven pedagogy and decision-making. In the classroom, she focuses on lifespan development with a Harvard Case Study approach, research methodology, and applied psychology from a behavioral economics and health disparities approach. Stephanie grounds all courses in literature that reflects and appreciates the insight of Ecological Systems Theory and the lasting impacts of childhood developments on adult outcomes.

# 1 Jamal Jones

## Overview

Built from a series of cases studies developed and actively used by Stephanie Wright, several colleagues, and a multitude of students, *Cases in Lifespan Development* offers students a fun, comprehensive view into life through key developmental stages. Students themselves have weighed in on the case details and outcomes, sharing their own observations, worries, and moments of triumph to build engrossing examples. By using paired assessment delivered through a SAGE Coursepack, instructors and learners will also have the opportunity to check understanding, spark discussion, and share their experiences as they follow development through a semester.

## Introduction

Welcome to your case study!

Congratulations! You will follow the lifespan of baby boy Jamal Jones. Try to use your best judgment, textbook, classmates, instructor, and supplementary resources to make the best decisions to help him grow.

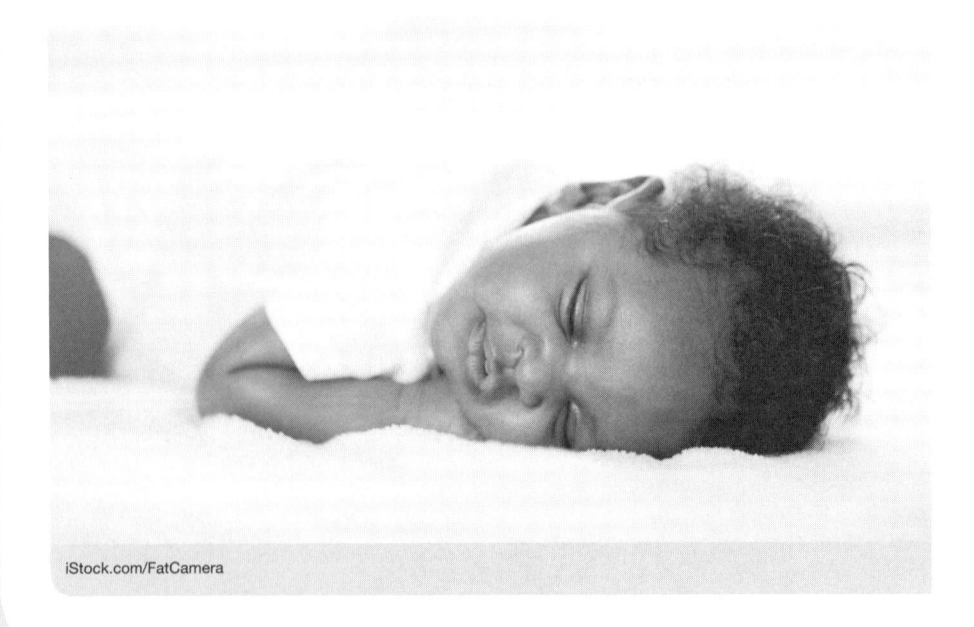

iStock.com/FatCamera

This semester you will observe Jamal as he grows from infant to child to teen to adult. Who will he become in your care? Will you understand and agree with all decisions available within his circumstances? How will you feel about the tough decisions that forever shape his path in life?

## Meet Jamal Jones

Jamal is the third son of a single African American mother. His father is not involved in his development or present in his life. However, Jamal has a father figure—his uncle Malik, who spends a good deal of time with the family. Jamal's mom works two part-time jobs, until she requires bed rest during her pregnancy with Jamal and is fired from one of them. The Joneses are poor, but Jamal's mother, Neka, works hard to support her family. The family lives in subsidized housing, and Jamal's mother has no employer-sponsored health insurance.

Through this case study and your lifespan course you will be asked to consider decisions regarding Jamal's physical, emotional, and cognitive growth and development from several perspectives: his mother Neka's, his uncle Malik's, and his brothers' Kiyon and Keyun as well as those of his spouse, children, other family members, friends, teachers, doctors, and supervisors.

Now let's get started.

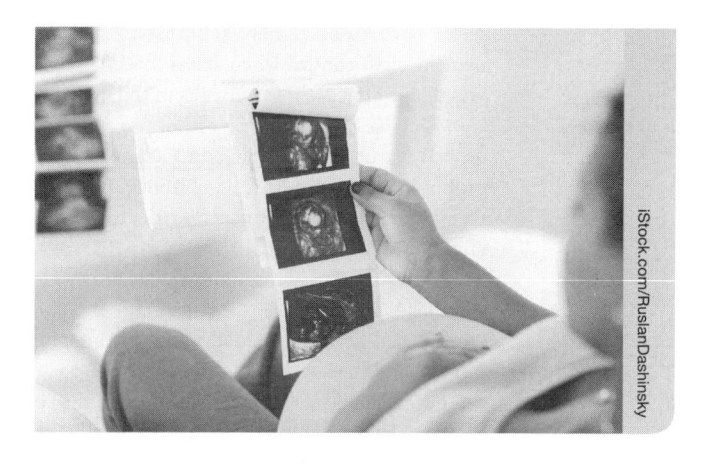

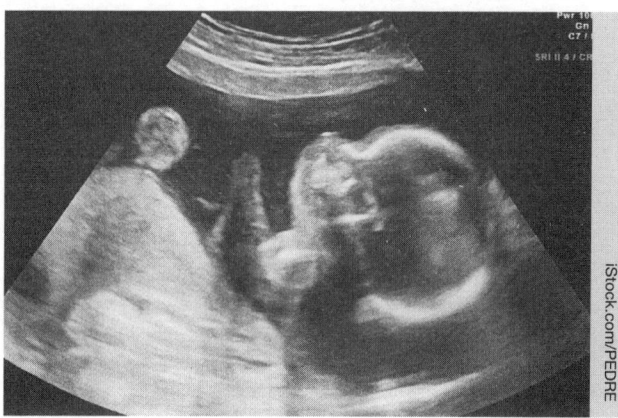

## 1. Development and Its Influences

### Today you will practice the following:

1.1 Outline five principles of the lifespan developmental perspective.

1.2 Explain three theoretical controversies about human development.

1.3 Summarize five theoretical perspectives on human development.

1.4 Describe the methods and research designs used to study human development.

Neka didn't expect to have a third son. In fact, she had been weighing how to afford more permanent birth control when she realized she was pregnant. She learned of her pregnancy with Jamal only after feeling nauseous in the mornings consistently during her first trimester.

During the 24th week of her pregnancy, on a Tuesday, Jamal's mother, Neka, feels very unwell at work. She nearly faints as she is eating her turkey sandwich, chips, and Coke while on her lunch break. At the insistence of her coworker and close friend Janessa she manages to leave early enough to see her doctor, Dr. Coop. Neka has to drive to this appointment alone.

After thoroughly examining Neka, Dr. Coop is concerned about Neka's blood pressure, which is high.

"Neka, given your blood pressure it's highly possible you are suffering from preeclampsia. For you and the baby to be okay, I need you to take it easy for the next two weeks. You'll need to call out sick and stay at home in bed or on the couch. You'll also need help with your other boys. At least you'll get to catch up on TV." Dr. Coop sighs with a soft smile.

Frightened for both her unborn baby's health and her own, Neka follows Dr. Coop's orders. This means she must let not one but two bosses know that she has been ordered to rest in bed. Her boss at the facility where she's worked since high school is understanding, but Neka's second job supervisor, for whom she has only worked a short while, is not. She is fired from her second job.

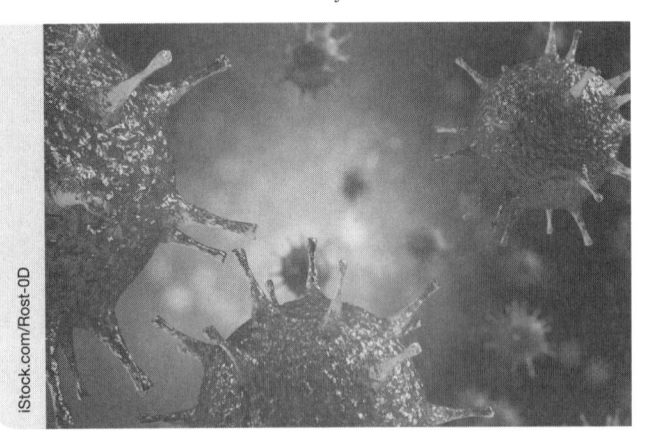

As a result Neka must make sacrifices to manage her spending, which means she must begin choosing carefully who to feed what and when, with her two small children receiving the best food she can afford each day. At the end of her bed rest period, she begins to hunt for another job to replace the one she was fired from. She participates in several interviews, trying to mask her growing belly each time, but she quickly finds that no one is interested in hiring a pregnant woman who will soon need to be absent for a lengthy maternity leave.

## 2. Biological and Environmental Foundations

### Today you will practice the following:

2.1  Discuss the genetic foundations of development.

2.2  Identify examples of genetic disorders and chromosomal abnormalities.

2.3  Discuss the choices available to prospective parents in having healthy children.

2.4  Describe the interaction of heredity and environment, including behavioral genetics and the epigenetic framework.

"Oh, Jamal, you're never going to know your daddy. I didn't either, and I turned out okay," Neka whispers with a smile to her growing abdomen as she brushes her teeth before work. Neka's statement holds true, and Jamal will never know the biological history of his own father. However, he will interact throughout his life with other biological family members, from his Uncle Malik to his mother to his two older brothers, Kiyun and Keyon. His smile will reflect a gap between his front teeth, similar to his shy older brother Kiyun's and the smile of his mother. In fact, this is the same smile Kiyun will show when he greets and holds baby brother Jamal for the first time.

Despite his closeness from the start with Kiyon, as a small child Jamal, with his dimples and his bubbly personality, will reflect that of his heavy-set older brother Keyon. As an infant Jamal is warm, friendly, and a bit tenacious, and he laughs regularly.

The Jones family lives in a low-income housing unit in an urban environment. Because of this the Joneses are close to several neighboring families: the Lewis family, the Milsteins, and the Washburnes. Growing up Jamal can hear the arguments that occur between his teenage neighbor Avi Milstein and his mother, Krista. He spends time as a child with Ms. Lewis, his mother's close friend and support.

"Mom, I'm hungry" is a phrase Jamal will learn to repeat early on from his brothers as Jamal and his family have few resources to spare during his childhood. Jamal's family only rarely enjoys a dinner out together at Kiyon and Keyun's favorite restaurant, McDonald's. These and his other biological and environmental factors will increase Neka's prenatal stress levels. Biologically speaking, this means that greater-than-ideal amounts of corticosteroids will pass the blood-brain barrier during her pregnancy with Jamal.

Neka's preeclampsia, the cause of her needed bed rest in the prior section, puts Jamal at risk for a number of negative outcomes, including preterm birth or being small-for-date, both of which would have cascading effects.

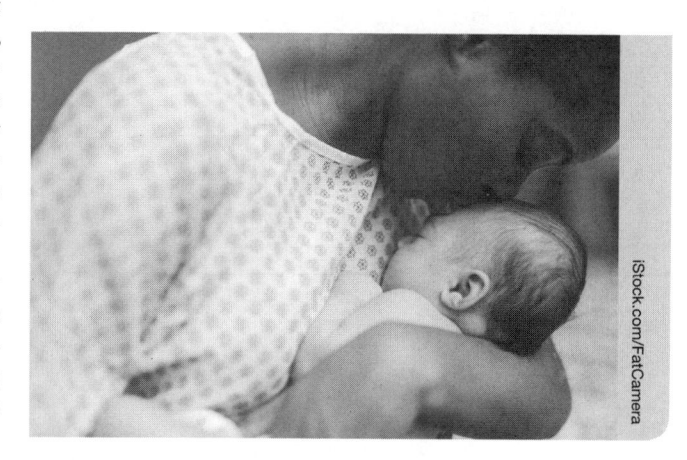

## 3. Prenatal Development, Birth, and Newborn Experience

### Today you will practice the following:

3.1 *Describe the three periods of prenatal development that begin with conception.*

3.2 *Identify how exposure to teratogens can influence the prenatal environment.*

3.3 *Explain the process of childbirth.*

3.4 *Discuss the neonate's physical capacities, including development in low-birth-weight infants.*

"Sis, I hope you got enough rest today. How you feeling? I went to Redbox, snagged the new *Avengers*, and scooped up burgers for us and the boys tonight. I think they put pickles on yours, even though I asked them not to, but you can pick them off, right?" Neka wrinkles her nose, although a beaming smile crosses her face. Jamal's uncle Malik, a handyman, has stepped in to help her provide for the boys for a short time during her bed rest.

After two weeks Neka is able to find short-term, part-time work—caring for her next-door neighbor's vivacious little boy, Bobby—enabling her to work from home while Bobby's parents are at work.

"Mom, I have a hole in my shoe! By my big toe from being too active again!" Keyun shouts as he barrels in the front door after school.

Kiyun looks up from his game on the floor with his friend Bobby. "Geez, good thing I don't think she heard you. Mom says we can't buy new things like shoes right now, Key. Don't tell her. It will make her cry again." As evidenced by the brothers' interaction, the money Neka earns keeping an eye on Bobby doesn't make up for the lost job, but it's a big help and allows her to rest as her doctor recommended.

Thanks to Malik and Neka's second job, Jamal is born full term after 39 weeks and healthy, and his brothers are able to remain healthy, too. Throughout his childhood baby Jamal will soon hear his uncle Malik repeat, "The night you were born, right as I went to bed, your Momma was up pacing around, saying you was banging around in her belly. I knew you were just having batting practice. You batted your way right out of her belly that same night and were home just a couple nights later. Right on time to catch the last game of the series in my arms. You slept through the whole thing, but you've been a baseball fan ever since birth, Bud."

## 4. Physical Development in Infancy and Toddlerhood

### Today you will practice the following:

4.1 Discuss growth and the role of nutrition in development during infancy and toddlerhood.

4.2 Summarize brain development during infancy and toddlerhood.

4.3 Compare infants' early learning capacities for habituation, classical conditioning, operant conditioning, and imitation.

4.4 Describe infants' developing sensory abilities.

4.5 Analyze the roles of maturation and contextual factors in infant and toddler motor development.

Neka is able to continue working from home for a few more weeks, which allows her to spend a bit of time at home with Jamal in his earliest life stages. They bond well, and he is a happy, healthy baby boy. When she does return to working two jobs, she leaves him in the care of a neighbor, Ms. Lewis, who watches children in her home. This saves Neka money and allows Jamal to be in a safe, comfortable setting with other children he already knows. His older brother, Neka's middle son, Kiyun, also stays at this home, too, while Jamal's oldest brother, Keyon, attends the local elementary school. At least twice a week, Uncle Malik continues to join the family for dinner.

"Uncle Malik, cheeseburgers are your favorite food! You always bring them when you come over. They're mine too, but Mom says I need to eat more apples," Keyon states thoughtfully. Looking at Jamal, who is at his mother's feet, he continues: "When can Jamal even eat cheeseburgers like us? All he ever has is milk, French fries, and the boring scrambled eggs Mom usually makes!"

"Keyon! Where are your manners? And say thank you to your uncle for bringing over anything at all for dinner!" Neka chides.

She scoops Jamal up in her arms, moving him to his seat at the small kitchen table as Keyon apologizes. "Sorry, Uncle. Sorry, Mom. Fries and burgers are good, too. Mom, can we draw a story with pictures tonight with you after dinner? Even Kiyun and Jamal like doing that."

Momentarily ignoring Kiyun's question Neka turns to her brother. "Malik, thanks for bringing over burgers again. Lately this kid is always on the move. We really need a baby gate so I can keep him away from the stairs. I'm noticing that he's super curious about them, especially when his brothers run up and down." Fourteen-month-old Jamal gleefully reaches for a handful of French fries as he watches his family gather around the dinner table.

"Fy!" he says, turning to shove a French fry into Neka's nose. She laughs and tells him to eat his own fries. "Fy!" he says again, offering the soggy spears to his uncle Malik. So far, Jamal can say *Momma*, *bo* for brother, *Mee* for Malik . . . and *fy*. Neka figures everyone knows what his favorite food will be.

## 5. Cognitive Development in Infancy and Toddlerhood

### Today you will practice the following:

5.1 *Discuss the cognitive-developmental perspective on infant reasoning.*

5.2 *Describe the information processing system in infants.*

5.3 *Discuss individual differences in infant intelligence.*

5.4 *Summarize the patterns of language development during infancy and toddlerhood.*

Jamal first called Neka *Momma*. Now he can say *fy* for fries and *Key* and *Kie* for his brothers. He can also say *dog* quite well. Ms. Lewis, who takes care of him when Neka works, has a small dog he likes to play with.

With the near-constant presence of his brothers and Neka and Uncle Malik reading to him and playing with him, Jamal will learn more words every day. He already counts on his fingers to three, even though he doesn't say the numbers, and he uses babbling to help go to sleep at night. Third and later children often talk later and less than other children in families, but Jamal is happy and engaging. His family can't help but interact with him, helping facilitate his timely language development.

## 6. Socioemotional Development in Infancy and Toddlerhood

### Today you will practice the following:

6.1 *Summarize the psychosocial tasks of infancy and toddlerhood.*

6.2 *Describe emotional development in infancy, and identify contextual and cultural influences on emotional development in infants and toddlers.*

6.3 *Identify the styles and stability of temperament, including the role of goodness of fit in infant development.*

6.4 *Describe how attachment develops in infancy and toddlerhood.*

6.5 *Differentiate the roles of self-concept, self-recognition, and self-control in infant development.*

Neka notices that going to work has become a particular challenge. Every day now Jamal has a crying jag that lasts from the minute she starts to edge for the door until she can no longer hear him as she walks down the hallway away from Ms. Lewis's door. She went through the same thing with Keyon and Kiyun, so she knows this is perfectly normal. Jamal's dealing with separation anxiety because they have such a close bond. She also knows he stops crying before she even gets to the car. Knowing these things doesn't make it any easier to leave her crying baby for hours and hours when she just wants to hold him and dry his tears.

## 7. Physical and Cognitive Development in Early Childhood

### Today you will practice the following:

7.1 Discuss physical development in early childhood.

7.2 Compare Piaget's cognitive-developmental and Vygotsky's sociocultural perspectives on cognitive development in early childhood.

7.3 Describe information-processing abilities during early childhood.

7.4 Summarize young children's advances in language development.

7.5 Contrast social learning and cognitive-developmental perspectives on moral development in early childhood.

7.6 Identify and explain approaches to early childhood education.

When Jamal approaches preschool age, Neka applies for him to start at the nearby Head Start Pre-K program. Both of his brothers, Kiyun and Keyon, attended the school, and Jamal is accepted into the program. Jamal begins to learn to draw, write his letters, count to 10 on his fingers, understand colors (his favorite is green), describe shapes, and even grasp a small bit of geography and other foundational real-world concepts. Additionally, preschool allows Jamal the opportunity to catch up with his more affluent peers in reading and math.

At the first parent–teacher conference, Neka is dismayed when Jamal's teacher expresses some concerns. Jamal is significantly behind his peers in fine motor development. The teacher lays several pieces of paper on the table between them. They are different shapes like circles, diamonds, and rectangles edged with dotted lines, and Neka sees where Jamal had been instructed to cut around the edges with scissors. His edges are uneven, and often he'd cut into the shape. The teacher suggests that Neka could practice with Jamal at home and says that she is sure with practice Jamal will catch up quickly. Neka agrees and buys safety scissors at the dollar store on her way home. That night, she makes a game of cutting out shapes that she draws on the backs of envelopes from the junk mail pile. Getting all three boys in on the activity, she thinks she can make Jamal feel less targeted and maybe having his brothers there to guide him will help some, too.

## 8. Socioemotional Development in Early Childhood

### Today you will practice the following:

8.1 Discuss young children's emerging sense of initiative, self-concept, and self-esteem.

8.2 Summarize the development of emotional understanding, regulation, and behavior in early childhood.

8.3 Identify four parenting styles and their associations with child outcomes.

8.4 Compare biological, cognitive, and contextual theoretical explanations of gender role development.

8.5 Explain the function of play and the form it takes during early childhood.

In his preschool Jamal also befriends his classmates, beginning to develop some of his social skills before starting kindergarten in a year. Neka knows all the teachers and administrators and feels fortunate that Jamal will be headed to the program in the fall. When Jamal starts the Head Start program, Neka enrolls in a few morning classes at the local state college. She thinks it will be nice to be going to school with her boys even if it means she'll have to work more at night instead of being at home with them.

Even though Jamal and his brothers are all in school during the day now, Ms. Lewis still keeps an eye on them while Neka works. Jamal likes going to Ms. Lewis's because he gets to spend time with one of Ms. Wilson's other charges and a good friend of Jamal's, Zuri, who doesn't go to Head Start with him. They're still good pals, and one of the things Jamal really likes is that he gets to show Zuri all the stuff he's learning. It's almost like he gets to be the teacher when they're together. She doesn't read as fast as he does, and it takes her longer to do some of the math problems he shows her. He doesn't care because when she gets stuck, he can unstick her. He hopes they get to be in the same kindergarten classroom next year.

## 9. Physical and Cognitive Development in Middle Childhood

### Today you will practice the following:

9.1 Identify patterns of physical and motor development during middle childhood and common health issues facing school-age children.

9.2 Discuss school-age children's capacities for reasoning and processing information.

9.3 Summarize views of intelligence including the uses, correlates, and criticisms of intelligence tests.

9.4 *Examine patterns of moral development during middle childhood.*

9.5 *Summarize language development during middle childhood.*

9.6 *Discuss children's learning at school.*

On Jamal's first day of school, his Kindergarten teacher Ms. Anderson asks all of the children in the class to sit on the "reading rug" so she can read them a story. Jamal loves books, and he loves reading. He gets as good a seat as he can near the teacher's feet and sits still, waiting. Once everyone is more or less quiet, she picks up a book with a fish on the cover. He can see that the title says *Rainbow Fish*. Jamal has this book at home and likes it. After Ms. Anderson finishes reading the book and asks the class a few questions, she sends everyone back to their seats. Jamal stands, and the teacher says to him, "Jamal, that was very good sitting. How did you learn to sit so still?" Jamal laughs. "I have two big brothers, Ms. Anderson. Sometimes I have to sit still just so they don't know where I am. If I don't, they either tickle me until I pee or steal my cookies." Ms. Anderson laughs with him. "I think I'd learn to sit still, too."

By the time Jamal is moving through elementary school, he's only a year or so behind Kiyun, and their oldest brother is in middle school. All the boys are doing well academically. The thing Jamal likes best about elementary school is homework. His mom has two years of school left to get a degree in marketing, and she does her homework at the table with Jamal and Kiyun. Jamal loves this time of day because his mom is pretty much the most amazing person he knows.

## 10. Socioemotional Development in Middle Childhood

### Today you will practice the following:

10.1 *Describe school-age children's self-conceptions and motivation.*

10.2 *Examine the roles of friendship, peer acceptance, and peer victimization in school-age children's adjustment.*

10.3 *Discuss family relationships in middle childhood and the influence of family structure on adjustment.*

10.4 *Analyze the role of resilience in promoting adjustment to adversity, including characteristics of children and contexts that promote resilience.*

Jamal has shown a real talent for baseball. His uncle Malik works hard to ensure he has money for Jamal's Little League uniform and cleats, and every year the two establish a tradition: selecting a new glove for Jamal. Jamal's two favorite pastimes are playing baseball with his teammates and watching baseball games with his brothers.

When Jamal is close to finishing elementary school, his family leaves the apartment he's always lived in. His mom has rented a house a few miles away. Her boss hired her full-time when he learned she would be getting her degree in a few months, and she saved as much money as she could until they could afford to move. Jamal's even getting his own room. He can't wrap his head around the idea. When they move in, Uncle Malik helps him hang a shelf for his baseball trophies and then takes him into the backyard to play catch.

In his new neighborhood, Jamal's mom let's him go to the park by himself and with his brothers. It's only two streets away. After a few times at the park, Jamal realizes that he doesn't ever see kids his age, not like when he and Zuri played at their old playground. He does see big boys a lot. His big brothers seem to know them but don't ever speak to them. Uncle Malik brings burgers over one night a few weeks after they move in, and while Jamal munches his fries, his mom talks about the playground and what his brothers have told her. Uncle Malik says it sounds like gang business and they shouldn't go the playground anymore. Jamal knows about gangs, but he doesn't know anyone who is actually in one. Uncle Malik's advice seems pretty good to him, and he promises his mom they won't go anymore ever.

## 11. Physical and Cognitive Development in Late Childhood

### Today you will practice the following:

11.1 Describe school-age children's self-conceptions and motivation.

11.2 Examine the roles of friendship, peer acceptance, and peer victimization in school-age children's adjustment.

11.3 Discuss family relationships in middle childhood and the influence of family structure on adjustment.

11.4 Analyze the role of resilience in promoting adjustment to adversity, including characteristics of children and contexts that promote resilience.

Over the next few years, Jamal develops confidence in his abilities on the ballfield. Uncle Malik makes sure he has the money for uniforms, gloves, and balls. The game helps him focus.

Baseball isn't everything. Jamal's pretty good at school, too. Now that his mom spends so much time in college, he gets to see instead of just hear why learning means so much in their family. Not that he gets everything. He doesn't, for sure, but if his mom can't answer something, usually Keyon or Kiyun can. His mom always reminds him, too, that he can't have "no shame in his game"; if he doesn't understand something and none of them can help him, then he has to ask the teacher. With all these people helping him, he manages pretty well.

## 12. Socioemotional Development in Late Childhood

Today you will practice the following:

*12.1  Summarize the processes by which self-concept, self-esteem, and identity change during adolescence.*

*12.2  Discuss the nature of parent–child relationships in adolescence.*

*12.3  Examine the developmental progression of peer relations in adolescence.*

*12.4  Analyze patterns of adolescent sexual activity including sexual orientation.*

*12.5  Identify common psychological and behavioral problems in adolescence.*

Jamal comes to depend on the annual glove shopping with Uncle Malik. It's their man-to-man time, and he looks forward to each as every season approaches. It's times like this with his uncle that he doesn't even care that his dad isn't around. His uncle helps his mom take care of everything. Who needs a deadbeat dad when he has a real man in his life like Uncle Malik?

If he thinks really, really hard, he can sometimes remember when he was little and how he and his brothers sometimes stayed with a neighbor while their mom worked. Now that they're older, they don't always have a babysitter, but Mom is still gone a lot of the time. She's at work and at school, which makes her twice as busy as before. Jamal misses her a lot. He also thinks it cool that she's in college. He doesn't know anyone whose mom is in college. One day, when he's a lot bigger, he's going to go to college, too. He wants to be smart, just like his mom. One month before his last day of elementary school, his mom graduates from college. Everyone goes to watch her walk across the stage, and then they all go out to dinner to celebrate. Life is just about as good as it gets.

## 13. Physical and Cognitive Development in Adolescence

Today you will practice the following:

*13.1  Evaluate the "storm and stress" perspective on adolescence in light of research evidence.*

*13.2  Summarize the physical changes that occur with puberty and the correlates of pubertal timing.*

*13.3  Discuss brain development during adolescence and its effect on behavior.*

*13.4 Identify ways in which thinking changes in adolescence and how these changes are reflected in adolescent decision-making and behavior.*

*13.5 Discuss moral development and influences on moral reasoning.*

*13.6 Describe the challenges that school transitions pose for adolescents and the role of parents in academic achievement.*

If you ask Jamal, going through puberty is rough. He starts to develop strange feelings for his best friend, Zuri, and now he's glad he moved away from her. It would be ten times worse if he had to ride the bus with her every day. Between vocal changes and the changes in his thoughts and feelings toward girls in his class and normal teasing at the hands of his older brothers, Jamal is lucky to have the support of his uncle, Malik, his friends on the baseball field, and his mom, Neka, in his academics to offset the razzing from his older brothers.

His mom asks him a couple times if he's seen Zuri lately, and he tries to avoid her question. Unfortunately, his brothers notice and correctly guess what's going on. Keyon's been dating for a couple years. There's always a new girl coming over to the house, so much so that their mom and Uncle Malik make jokes about it when Keyon isn't around, but Jamal knows it's his turn now. Keyon starts teasing him about Zuri even though Jamal tells him they're just friends. One day, Zuri bikes over to his house after school to work on a project for social studies, and they watch a little television when they're finished. Jamal finally gets the courage to hold her hand, but his mom's car door slamming in the driveway puts an end to that fast. Zuri leaves quickly after that, and Jamal shuts himself in his room to think about how being so close to her and holding her hand make him feel.

## 14. Socioemotional Development in Adolescence

### Today you will practice the following:

*14.1 Summarize the processes by which self-concept, self-esteem, and identity change during adolescence.*

*14.2 Discuss the nature of parent–child relationships in adolescence.*

*14.3 Examine the developmental progression of peer relations in adolescence.*

*14.4 Analyze patterns of adolescent sexual activity including sexual orientation.*

*14.5 Identify common psychological and behavioral problems in adolescence.*

Jamal is finally in high school. He has become a bit shyer during his middle school and early high school years. Despite his position as a starter on the baseball team, he prefers to spend his lunch hours in a corner or the library reading. Jamal is an honor roll student in the classroom. His older brothers, Kiyun and Keyon, have graduated. Keyon has found a successful career as a manager in a local car dealership. Kiyun just left for college and his freshman year in the dorms. Jamal knows his mom and Uncle Malik expect him to do well, too. After everything his mom did for them, there's no way he's not going to do everything he can to make her proud.

As graduation draws closer, Uncle Malik starts taking Jamal for a weekly burger and fries—their "boys' night" his uncle calls them. Jamal tries to remember if his older brothers had the same sort of one-on-one times with their uncle and thinks maybe they did. When they're at dinner, Uncle Malik always has something he wants to say, and Jamal figures this is the stuff his dad would talk to him about if he had one. Well, he does, Uncle Malik, and he doesn't care that his biological dad isn't around. A lot of what they talk about Jamal learned in sex ed: how not to get a sexually transmitted disease, how not to get a girl pregnant, how not to take advantage of someone. Those were clinical discussions, though, and he likes having someone close to him that he can ask personal questions.

It seems like all his teammates on the baseball team talk about their girlfriends and having sex. Jamal's dated some, but he's still a virgin. Every now and then, he thinks about Zuri, his best friend from the old neighborhood, and wonders what she's doing, but he knows calling her would be the wrong thing to do. He misses being a little kid with her, but he doesn't think hooking up with her would be a good idea. The night Uncle Malik tells him that *not* having sex is normal—good even!—is one of the most reassuring nights he's had in high school. Now he can stop thinking about sex, even if it's just until he's on his next date, and spend time with his uncle talking about other things he worries about sometimes, like how his friends always want him to go partying after they win a game or how so many of his friends do stupid things to look cool. At a party once, Jamal tried smoking with his friends just to fit in, but he ended up looking like a dork when he couldn't stop coughing and he thought he would throw up after he finished the cigarette.

## 15. Physical and Cognitive Development in Emerging/Early Adulthood

### Today you will participate in the following:

15.1 *Describe the features and characteristics of emerging and early adulthood.*

15.2 *Summarize the physical developments of emerging and early adulthood.*

15.3 *Analyze physical and sexual health issues in emerging and early adulthood.*

15.4 *Compare postformal reasoning, pragmatic thought, and cognitive-affective complexity.*

PART I  The Cases

15.5  *Explain how attending college influences young adults' development, and identify challenges faced by first-generation and nontraditional students.*

15.6  *Discuss vocational choice and the transition to work.*

Following in his middle brother's footsteps, Jamal goes to college when he graduates from high school. He's fortunate to receive a partial scholarship for baseball to a state college. Jamal worked a part-time job in high school, just like Keyon and Kiyun, and he always saved half of every paycheck. Because of this and because she's saved a little money when she could since he was a young kid, he and Neka can pay the rest of his tuition. Jamal studies hard, is a good teammate, and manages to graduate only a year late.

When Mom, Uncle Malik, and his brothers move him into his dorm room a couple hours away from home, Jamal is aware of his privilege. His mom is smart, and for more than half his life, she's made a good income even if they were still a single-parent family. She worked hard, and she knew how to keep all of them straight. They also had Uncle Malik standing in as a father. Going to school with lots of kids who started out just like himself but without those advantages, Jamal knew how lucky he was. So many of those kids—kids like Zuri—never even made it out of high school. They dropped out to get jobs and help their parents with bills, or they got pregnant and started families when they were still kids themselves. He doesn't have as much as some of the other kids he knows, never would probably, but he knows how to make the most of what he has, and he knows the value of working hard and staying in school. When he starts college, he figures that gives him an advantage over people who have less. Keeping his old classmates in his mind and never forgetting the goals he has for himself—a college degree, a good job, and a home of his own one day—he is able to focus on what matters. He doesn't party like some of his teammates, and he never once lets himself slack off in his classes. Jamal isn't a straight-A student, but he gives everything he has to everything he does, and in the end, that is enough.

## 16. Socioemotional Development in Emerging/Early Adulthood

### Today you will practice the following:

16.1  *Summarize psychosocial development in emerging and early adulthood.*

16.2  *Discuss influences on friendship and mate selection and interactions in emerging and early adulthood.*

16.3  *Analyze the diverse romantic situations that may characterize emerging and early adulthood, including singlehood, cohabitation, marriage, and divorce.*

16.4  *Compare the experiences of young adults as stepparents, never-married parents, and same-sex parents.*

As he makes his way through college, he falls in love (a couple of times). His freshman year, he's so busy with class and baseball that he doesn't even look at girls much even though they look at him. One, a girl named Sarah, tries to talk to him a few times, but he tells her as politely as he can that he's just too busy for a relationship. When he runs into her again in the fall of his sophomore year, she tries again, and he asks her out. They date for a while, and Jamal kicks himself for waiting so long. Sarah is gorgeous and smart. She's funny and likes all the same things he does. After a few months, they have sex, and at 19, he's finally not a virgin anymore. A few weeks later, Sarah stops taking his calls, and when he finally shows up at her dorm to ask what's going on, she tells him she's met someone else. Devastated, Jamal spends a week in his bed skipping class, practice, and even meals, although the opportunity to eat is the one thing he rarely misses. Eventually, his roommate and teammate Sam pulls him out of bed and down to the dining hall. He eats three cheeseburgers and a plate of fries and ignores Sarah when she comes in with her new boyfriend. He does meet another girl a couple weeks later, and he dates Kaila through the spring until he decides she's not the one for him. Over the next three years, he continues to meet, and date, different girls, but no one is the perfect match.

After five years of college, Jamal graduates. Having not been drafted by any baseball league—not that he really expected it—he gets a job copyediting for a small entertainment e-zine published online once a week. He meets a girl in his department, Erica, and they find they have a lot in common, including similar childhood stories, and they go out for dinner one Friday after a long workweek. Jamal is trying to decide whether or not to apply for an opening in the marketing department (he does, and he gets the job), and Erica is getting ready to pitch their boss on a new section for the magazine (she does, and the boss loves her idea). Eventually—after many road trips, adventures, and a series of long discussions with Neka and Uncle Malik and asking Erica's father for her hand—Jamal will propose to and marry Erica.

## 17. Physical and Cognitive Development in Middle Adulthood

### Today you will practice the following:

17.1 Summarize age-related physical changes during middle adulthood.

17.2 Discuss common health conditions and illnesses and the roles of stress and hardiness on health during middle adulthood.

17.3 Contrast the findings of cross-sectional and longitudinal studies of crystallized and fluid intelligence over adulthood.

17.4 Analyze changes in cognitive capacities during middle adulthood, including attention, memory, processing speed, and expertise.

After successfully managing the marketing department at the e-zine, Jamal makes a big career move. He takes a position as the marketing director for the local A-league baseball team. He and Erica talk about the possibility for a long time before the job is even available, and they both agree that he will be happiest doing that kind of work. When the team needs the leadership Jamal knows he can give, he goes for it. After a number of years with the team, he's offered another position, COO of a well-known technology firm (his company creates sleek, streamlined smartphones). His mother, Neka, who is just retiring from her own role in a public relations firm, is very proud.

## 18. Socioemotional Development in Middle Adulthood

### Today you will practice the following:

18.1 Summarize the theories and research on psychosocial development during middle adulthood.

18.2 Describe the changes that occur in self-concept, identity, and personality during middle adulthood.

18.3 Analyze relationships in middle adulthood, including friend, spousal, parent–child, and grandparent relationships.

18.4 Discuss influences on job satisfaction and retirement planning during middle adulthood.

Erica and Jamal have a stable, loving marriage from their earliest days well into middle age. The two of them, despite their busy careers and lives, have two creative, energetic little girls, Amelia and Alexis, who keep them busy, including Jamal getting to coach the girls' softball teams throughout their childhood. When he looks back to his own childhood, Jamal doesn't think about how far he's come; he thinks about how lucky his whole family is.

He and Erica bought a house on a street in the same neighborhood as Neka, Jamal's mother, and she is able to care for Jamal and Erica's young children as they grow. Jamal is also able to support and care for his mother as she ages. Often, in the evenings when it's time to take the girls home, Neka comes with them and stays for dinner. Jamal likes these nights because it gives his mom a chance to reminisce, which he senses she needs. As Amelia grows older and Erica starts to talk about college for their oldest child, Neka takes Jamal's hand and warns him of the empty nest and how quiet the house will be with the children gone. "I thought I would relish the quiet," she admits, "but once you were gone, I realized how wrong I was."

He and his family routinely see Kiyun, Keyon, and their two families as well. Theirs is close-knit family, which is why Jamal finds himself struck to the core when Uncle Malik dies suddenly of a stroke a few months before Amelia graduates from high school. Neka withdraws and grieves for her brother, who was such a support all of Jamal's life, and he lets her have this time to herself while he tries to figure out how to let go of the uncle who was the only father he ever knew.

They all miss Uncle Malik so much. After a few months pass and the world starts to right itself again, Jamal reaches out to his mom and to his daughters. Amelia has held them all together after the funeral, but Alexis is as withdrawn as Neka has been. Erica expresses her concern to him one night. "Do you think she's doing drugs? Or, Jamal, you don't think she's cutting, do you?" Jamal shakes his head. "I don't know, but we'll find out, and we'll handle it together."

Alexis has been drinking and smoking weed with friends whenever she gets the chance. Erica and Jamal are mortified by the discovery but determined to keep their family together and get Alexis the help she needs. Neka steps in with firm, no-nonsense advice, too. For the first time in his life, Jamal looks to an uncertain future without the confidence that he has whatever is necessary to take care of anything that happens.

## 19. Physical and Cognitive Development in Late Adulthood

### Today you will practice the following:

*19.1 Discuss age-related changes in brain and body systems in late adulthood, and identify ways that older adults may compensate for changes.*

*19.2 Identify risk and protective factors for health in late adulthood.*

*19.3 Summarize common dementias including characteristics, risk and protective factors, and treatment.*

*19.4 Analyze patterns of cognitive change in late adulthood.*

As Jamal ages, he experiences a range of normal declinations based on his genetic makeup, from weight gain to gray hair. Each time he goes to the doctor for a checkup, he's reminded of his mother's aging, which was complex and difficult to watch. Neka remained healthy for her entire life, not developing any major illnesses like heart disease or suffering any severe injuries like a broken hip. In her late 60s, however, she began to show signs of forgetfulness that were more than not knowing where she left her keys. She always knew where her keys were, but sometimes she would forget what exactly she was meant to use them for, or she would get to the grocery store and not know what she was supposed to buy there or how to find her way home. The family doctor diagnosed her with Alzheimer's disease and said that although there was no one cause for the disease, Neka's long struggles with the chronic acute stress from being poor and working two jobs while raising the boys and trying to attend school probably resulted in excess secretions of corticosteroids over a number of years. This, he told them, may be at least partially responsible.

Jamal, however, remains cognitively sound, enjoying a fine memory and routinely beating his wife and daughters when they play *Jeopardy!* after dinner. Watching game shows and continuing to read his favorite books does become more difficult after a while, and like his mother, Jamal is eventually fitted for a pair of bifocals to see better both at a distance due to myopia and up close because of hyperopia. For a while, he thinks failing eyesight will be the worst of it, especially because his mom was so healthy. Uncle Malik did pass away younger than his mom of a hypertension-related stroke, but he had that unhealthy habit of eating only cheeseburgers and fries. Jamal eats well, always has, and he's physically active. So, he's surprised when he learns at a checkup that he's developed type II diabetes. His doctor tells him she believes he probably inherited the predisposition from his biological father. For several years, he's able to manage his diabetes with careful diet and exercise, but eventually, he requires a combination of medications to help. In his last few years, he needs insulin shots as well.

## 20. Socioemotional Development in Late Adulthood

### Today you will practice the following:

*20.1 Examine the contributions of self-concept, personality, and religiosity to older adults' well-being.*

*20.2 Identify social contexts in which older adults live and their influence on development.*

*20.3 Summarize features of older adults' relationships with friends, spouses, children, and grandchildren, and identify how these relationships affect older adults' functioning.*

*20.4 Discuss influences on the timing of retirement and adaptation to retirement.*

As he nears his own retirement, Jamal becomes a grandfather. His first grandchild, a little girl named Addison, is the light of his life. He and Erica both continue to work well into their 60s, and they share the challenges associated with caring for their aging parents. Erica's parents still live independently, but Jamal convinces Neka she will be more comfortable and happier in a nearby assisted-living facility that specializes in the care of patients with dementia. He sees her every day on his way to work or on the way home. Erica is visiting her one evening, and Neka decides she's tired and needs a nap. It's been a difficult day of not remembering who she is or who her family are, and her anger drains both of them. Just before she falls asleep, Neka returns to herself, looks at Erica lucidly, and tells her she loves her and she's been a wonderful daughter. She passes away while she sleeps.

Jamal and his brothers struggle with Neka's death. Although the family has always been close, losing her draws them all a little closer, and Keyon and Kiyun begin hosting a weekly barbeque, alternating houses. Jamal is only too glad to offer his house, too. Erica talks to Jamal. She's worried about Alexis and how she's handling Neka's death. They remember all too well how she bottomed out after Malik died, and she's worried about what will happen now that her beloved grandmother is gone. She and Jamal agree to talk to her—every day if they need to—and make sure she has all the support she needs to grieve in a healthy way.

Even through the deaths of his mother and much later his two older brothers, both Jamal and Erica are able to maintain a healthy, vibrant lifestyle. They are loved and cared for by their supportive network of children and the grandchildren they thoroughly enjoy.

## 21. Experience With Death and Dying

### Today you will practice the following:

*21.1 Identify ways in which death has been defined and end-of-life issues that may arise.*

*21.2 Contrast children's, adolescents', and adults' understanding of death.*

*21.3 Discuss the physical and emotional process of dying as it is experienced over the lifespan.*

*21.4 Summarize typical grief reactions to the loss of loved ones and the influence of development on bereavement.*

Erica outlives Jamal. He dies in his sleep at the age of 89. Erica remains in their family home, which is located in the neighborhood where Jamal grew up and where their oldest daughter, their son-in-law, and their granddaughters Addison and Sidney live.

Jamal's death is neither expected nor unexpected. At his age, both Jamal and Erica understand that death is inevitable but doesn't have to be imminent. He's lived a long, healthy, and full life, and when he passes away, he's been ready to do so. Erica isn't ready. Often, she and Jamal talked about who should go first, and she always hoped she would. Living in a world that didn't contain her lifetime partner was a change she couldn't contemplate. Jamal joked and told her she was a hot tamale even in her 80s and could find someone new. Now, with him really gone, she knows she was right. The house is so empty, and that's just how she feels. The children, Alexis and Amelia, need her to be strong for them even though they're hardly children anymore. Their own children will be making them grandchildren soon enough. Sometimes, that thought makes her almost smile. She will be a great-grandmother. Then she remembers; Jamal will never be a great-grandfather.

They want her to talk about it—of course, the girls do—and she tries. As she zips the black dress and pins on the black hat for Jamal's funeral, Erica acknowledges to herself that she'll want to talk, probably sooner than later, just not yet. Right now she wants to be alone in her house with her grief and her memories. She reaches out and touches his face in a photograph on her dresser. She read somewhere that losing a spouse is the most devastating loss a person can endure. Well, she figures that's true.

## CASE DISCUSSION QUESTIONS

1. Why is Jamal's mother Neka's choice to spend two weeks in bed like the doctor strongly suggests not a no-brainer as it might seem it should be?

2. Neka never marries, spending all her time and resources on her children. What positive and negative effects might have been felt in Jamal's life across any or all domains (biological, cognitive, and socioemotional) if she'd found a good man she loved and married him, allowing this new person to help her parent the boys?

3. In early adulthood, Jamal might've made other choice than he did. What if he began running with a gang to which his brother Keyon belonged, and both he and his brother were killed in a shooting in middle adulthood? What factors in Jamal's case could've led to this outcome? Why?

4. Jamal's entire life occurs over many decades that are, loosely, contemporary. Cars, telephones, televisions, and so on exist, and Jamal does work for a company that manufactures cell phones. However, other technology (e.g., artificial intelligence, the international space station) aren't mentioned. Would Jamal's life have been different if he were born in a specific period, earlier or later? If so, how? Be specific.

# 2 Naomi Rowe

## Introduction

Welcome to your case study!

Congratulations! You will follow the lifespan of baby girl Naomi Rowe. Try to use your best judgment, textbook, classmates, instructor, and supplementary resources to make the best decisions to help her grow.

This semester you will observe Naomi as she grows from infant to child to teen to adult. Who will she become in your care? Will you understand and agree with all decisions available within her circumstances? How will you feel about the tough decisions that forever shape her path in life?

## Meet Naomi Rowe

Naomi is the first daughter of Alicia and Justin Rowe, a biracial couple who've been married for two years. Justin is Caucasian, and Naomi identifies as African American, although she, too, is

iStock.com/Rawpixel

the child of an African American mother and Caucasian father. The Rowes are middle income. Justin is active duty with the army and attending college part time on tuition assistance, pursuing a degree in computer science. Alicia has taken some college classes, but with Naomi on the way, she has suspended her studies. Shortly before Naomi is born, Justin is deployed with his unit. He will be gone for two years, making Alicia a de facto single mother for this time. When he gets home, he'll be granted 10 days of paternity leave.

Through this case study and your lifespan course you will be asked to consider decisions regarding Naomi's physical, emotional, and cognitive growth and development from several perspectives: her mother Alicia's, her father Justin's, and her grandparents' as well as those of her spouse, children, other family member, friends, teachers, doctors, and supervisors.

Now let's get started.

## 1. Development and Its Influences

### Today you will practice the following:

*1.1  Outline five principles of the lifespan developmental perspective.*

*1.2  Explain three theoretical controversies about human development.*

*1.3  Summarize five theoretical perspectives on human development.*

*1.4  Describe the methods and research designs used to study human development.*

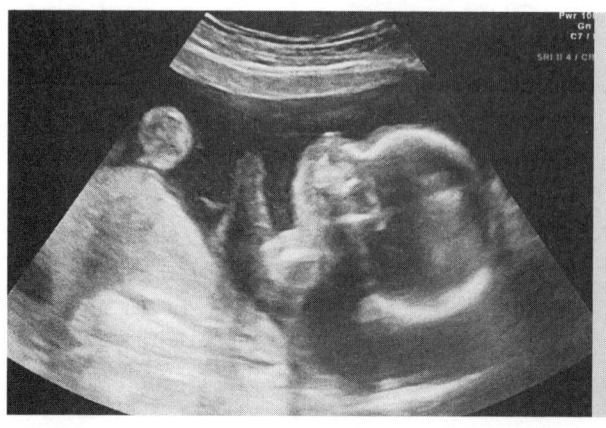

Alicia and Justin were happy to learn they'd be having their first child. Sometime after their first anniversary, they decided they wanted to start a family, and even though they knew Justin would likely be deployed before a baby would be born, they decided this was the time. Justin's military status gives them TriCare insurance, which means Alicia and the baby will have excellent prenatal and perinatal care. Alicia won't have to be worried about anything—well, almost anything. Not long after she was married, Alicia suffered the double blow of both her parents dying. It saddens her every time she thinks about her parents not becoming grandparents and her baby not knowing half of her grandparents. But Justin's parents live somewhat close by, and they are loving people. Alicia knows the baby won't have a lack of grandparent attention.

## 2. Biological and Environmental Foundations

### Today you will practice the following:

2.1 *Discuss the genetic foundations of development.*

2.2 *Identify examples of genetic disorders and chromosomal abnormalities.*

2.3 *Discuss the choices available to prospective parents in having healthy children.*

2.4 *Describe the interaction of heredity and environment, including behavioral genetics and the epigenetic framework.*

Alicia and Justin spend time decorating the second bedroom in their modest-but-comfortable apartment off base before Justin gets his orders to deploy. This gives him the opportunity to participate in as much of the pre-birth nesting as he can. They also spend hours recording Justin reading baby books and taking pictures to make into photo albums so that their baby will know the sound of Daddy's voice and the look of Daddy's face when he finally returns home.

Once Justin leaves, Alicia faces several long, lonely months of pregnancy without him. As her belly grows, she rocks in the chair they put in the nursery and talks to their developing daughter. "Oh, Naomi, it's going to be so long before you meet your daddy. I wish he could be there when you're born to hold you and see you take your first breath. He's going to miss all of your first-firsts . . . rolling over, sitting up, first steps." Alicia sheds a few tears at the thought.

Because the Rowes live modestly and Justin works for the army, they have good health care and access to excellent foods like fresh produce and free-range beef and chicken. Alicia can see her midwife whenever she wants to, and she doesn't have to worry about having money for tests or prenatal medications. Her husband, however, is gone. Not only is he gone; he's very gone and isn't coming back for 24 months as well. Sometimes the loneliness is overwhelming. Sometimes the thought of having a child when she still feels like a child at 22 and raising that child for two years by herself feels overwhelming. There are days when Alicia wishes she didn't have to go anywhere or see anyone. These and other biological and environmental factors may increase her prenatal stress levels. Biologically speaking, this means that greater-than-ideal amounts of corticosteroids will pass the blood-brain barrier during her pregnancy with Naomi. If she's depressed, Naomi may also experience an excess of serotonin production during her prenatal development. Either or both of these may have long-term consequences for her development across all domains.

## 3. Prenatal Development, Birth, and Newborn Experience

> Today you will practice the following:
>
> 3.1  Describe the three periods of prenatal development that begin with conception.
> 3.2  Identify how exposure to teratogens can influence the prenatal environment.
> 3.3  Explain the process of childbirth.
> 3.4  Discuss the neonate's physical capacities, including development in low-birth-weight infants.

"Alicia," Justin's mother says a few weeks before Naomi's due date, "I have a treat for us today. Get dressed, and I'll pick you up in an hour." Alicia doesn't want to go anywhere. Her back aches, and she misses Justin. His mother's only being nice, and she doesn't want to hurt her feelings. So, she gets dressed, brushes her teeth, and gets in the car when her mother-in-law Sarah arrives.

They spend a lovely day at the spa, where Alicia is treated to a special suite of services just for pregnant women. She even gets a pedicure. She can hardly see her toes anymore, but it feels great, and Sarah tells her the pink nail polish she picked out is perfect. After she's home and alone again, she admits to herself that it was a good day, and she's glad she went. She's going to try to make a point to go out somewhere, even if it's just to walk down the street once each day.

Naomi is born without complications at 38 weeks. She is healthy and scores highly on her one- and five-minute APGARS. This is due, in large part, to the excellent care Alicia took of herself during her pregnancy and the extras afforded to her from Justin's job, like TriCare insurance and on-demand medical care.

Naomi will grow accustomed to the stories of her birth, stories told by her mom and by Grandma Sarah and Grandpa Joe. They all had their own versions, but they start and end the same. Mom called Grandma Sarah to say her back hurt so badly that she couldn't sleep, and her grandparents took Mom to the hospital. In the end, only Mom and Grandma Sarah were in the room with the midwife when Naomi was born. Naomi loves this part because her mom says that three generations of strong Rowe women were in that room in the best way at that moment.

## 4. Physical Development in Infancy and Toddlerhood

> Today you will practice the following:
>
> 4.1 Discuss growth and the role of nutrition in development during infancy and toddlerhood.
>
> 4.2 Summarize brain development during infancy and toddlerhood.
>
> 4.3 Compare infants' early learning capacities for habituation, classical conditioning, operant conditioning, and imitation.
>
> 4.4 Describe infants' developing sensory abilities.
>
> 4.5 Analyze the roles of maturation and contextual factors in infant and toddler motor development.

Naomi spends her first months at home alone with Alicia. She is a happy, easy baby. In the beginning weeks, Alicia is happy for the quiet. Her mother-in-law, Sarah, comes over every couple of days to give Alicia a break but not so often as to intrude, and the arrangement works well. However, after a few months pass, Alicia begins to experience postpartum depression. She becomes easily irritated, impatient with Naomi, and often resentful. She feels her bond with Naomi weakening, and even though she wants that to change, she feels powerless to make things better.

At Naomi's one-year checkup, the pediatrician asks a series of routine questions about Naomi's behavior and about her interactions with Alicia. Noting Alicia's halfhearted responses, the pediatrician stops her and puts her hand on Alicia's arm. "Alicia, what's bothering you?"

With no warning, Alicia feels tears welling in her eyes. She nods, then shakes her head, and nods again. Patting Naomi's knee, she says, "Everything's fine. It's all fine."

"Doesn't look fine," the doctor says.

Alicia shakes her head. "Really it is. I'm sorry to be so much trouble. I've just been a little blue lately."

"Sounds like postpartum depression to me," the pediatrician tells her and, seeing Alicia's confusion, adds, "the baby blues. Don't worry. It's very common. I'm going to ask that you call your midwife and make an appointment for this week. Can you do that?"

Alicia nods. "You think it will help?"

"I do."

When Alicia leaves Naomi's checkup—with a perfect report on Naomi—she feels lighter for the first time in months.

Despite Alicia's struggle with postpartum depression, Naomi has an active and stimulating infancy. Sarah and Joe are involved in her life and buy her a number of educational toys. Alicia joins a Mommy and Me playgroup that has playdates twice each week. Being around other children offers Naomi the opportunity to learn new words and practice communicating with others. She's outside so often that blue becomes her favorite color (because she loves the bigness of the sky so much), and she develops a fascination for how the natural world operates, like how flowers grow and why butterflies like flower gardens.

## 5. Cognitive Development in Infancy and Toddlerhood

### Today you will practice the following:

5.1 *Discuss the cognitive-developmental perspective on infant reasoning.*

5.2 *Describe the information processing system in infants.*

5.3 *Discuss individual differences in infant intelligence.*

5.4 *Summarize the patterns of language development during infancy and toddlerhood.*

Most of the time, Alicia takes Naomi to story time at the library or to play with other children in the park, but sometimes Grandma Sarah takes her. Alicia likes it when Grandma Sarah takes her because she always gets ice cream for a treat on the way home. Mommy taking her is the very best, though, because she gets on the ground and plays with Naomi in the sandbox building sandcastles and making up stories when they play. Naomi's favorite stories are the ones when Mommy starts by saying there's a poor, trapped prince in the high tower of the castle, and Princess Naomi must ride on her valiant steed to rescue him. Naomi isn't quite sure what a valiant steed is, but it sounds fun.

When they play The Princess Saves the Prince, Mommy does silly things. She makes Naomi run around the sandbox counting to funny numbers like 11 or 13 or she makes Naomi figure out a riddle like what letter comes between H and J in the alphabet. When Naomi can get the right answer, then she saves the prince! She's a good rescuer. Other children at the park try to figure out Mommy's riddles, too. Sometimes, they're faster than she is (but Mommy always lets Princess Naomi do the rescuing anyway), but mostly Naomi figures out the answers first. Mommy says she's clever. Naomi isn't sure, but she thinks that word means she's smart.

## 6. Socioemotional Development in Infancy and Toddlerhood

### Today you will practice the following:

6.1 *Summarize the psychosocial tasks of infancy and toddlerhood.*

6.2 *Describe emotional development in infancy and identify contextual and cultural influences on emotional development in infants and toddlers.*

6.3 *Identify the styles and stability of temperament, including the role of goodness of fit in infant development.*

6.4 *Describe how attachment develops in infancy and toddlerhood.*

6.5 *Differentiate the roles of self-concept, self-recognition, and self-control in infant development.*

Alicia and Naomi have a difficult time during Alicia's postpartum depression, and Naomi's attachment process with her mother is interrupted. Thanks to the pediatrician's intervention, Alicia is able to get help after only a few months, and she and Naomi get their relationship back on track. By the time she's 18 months old, Naomi has biweekly playdates with her "friends," usually at a public park or story time at the public library. Naomi prefers the park.

Just before her second birthday, her mother makes fish sticks and tater tots for dinner one night. Naomi has two fish sticks in her mouth and is singing her ABCs around them when the door to their apartment opens. Sometimes Grandma Sarah and Grandpa Joe come over for a surprise, and she turns around in her chair to wave to them. It isn't her grandparents. In the doorway stands a man she doesn't know. He looks sort of familiar, but she doesn't know him. "Mommy!" she calls to Alicia, who's in the bedroom folding clothes. "Mommy!"

Alicia calls back to her, "Coming. Just a minute, sweetheart!"

The man comes into the apartment and closes the door. "Naomi?"

Naomi isn't certain about the man, but she nods and swallows her fish sticks. "Yes."

"Naomi," he says as he get on his knees, "it's Daddy."

She climbs off her chair and walks over to him. He does look a little like the pictures in her room. She pokes at his arm and takes off his hat. Without his hat, he looks more like the picture. "Daddy?"

"Yes, it's Daddy. Can I hug you?"

"Yes, Daddy."

While Naomi gets her first hug from her daddy, who seems to be happy but is crying, Mommy comes back into the room. She yells, "Oh! Justin!" Daddy stands up, still holding Naomi, and hugs Mommy, too. "Why didn't you tell me you were coming today?"

"I wanted to surprise my girls," Daddy said.

Naomi pulls on his ear. "Want some fish sticks, Daddy?"

## 7. Physical and Cognitive Development in Early Childhood

### Today you will practice the following:

7.1 Discuss physical development in early childhood.

7.2 Compare Piaget's cognitive-developmental and Vygotsky's sociocultural perspectives on cognitive development in early childhood.

7.3 Describe information-processing abilities during early childhood.

7.4 Summarize young children's advances in language development.

7.5 Contrast social learning and cognitive-developmental perspectives on moral development in early childhood.

7.6 Identify and explain approaches to early childhood education.

Naomi is so excited for preschool. Her father took her shopping for new tennis shoes, and her mother took her to visit the school where she would spend part of every day with her friends learning to read and write. She has a blue book bag with white stripes, and her mother is going to pack her lunches in a matching lunchbox. She's going to have so much fun!

Alicia and Justin go to Naomi's first parent–teacher conference together. The conference is student led, and Naomi goes through a folder of work she selected to show her parents while her teacher tells them how she's doing in different tasks. She is especially proud when her teacher tells them how well she's doing writing her ABCs. Naomi works hard at writing.

## 8. Socioemotional Development in Early Childhood

### Today you will practice the following:

8.1 Discuss young children's emerging sense of initiative, self-concept, and self-esteem.

8.2 Summarize the development of emotional understanding, regulation, and behavior in early childhood.

8.3 Identify four parenting styles and their associations with child outcomes.

8.4 Compare biological, cognitive, and contextual theoretical explanations of gender role development.

8.5 Explain the function of play and the form it takes during early childhood.

Naomi sits at the table with her mother and father during the parent–teacher conference, while her teacher tells her parents that she has something called "good leadership potential." Her teacher says she likes to help her friends in the class, and Naomi nods. This is true. Then her teacher says that sometimes Naomi can talk a little loudly or a little too much and not give other children a chance to speak in class. She frowns. She doesn't think she does this. Mommy looks at her with a funny face. Naomi can tell she isn't angry, but she isn't happy either. She wonders if she's still going to get ice cream on the way home.

## 9. Physical and Cognitive Development in Middle Childhood

### Today you will practice the following:

9.1 Identify patterns of physical and motor development during middle childhood and common health issues facing school-age children.

9.2 Discuss school-age children's capacities for reasoning and processing information.

9.3 Summarize views of intelligence, including the uses, correlates, and criticisms of intelligence tests.

9.4 Examine patterns of moral development during middle childhood.

9.5 Summarize language development during middle childhood.

9.6 Discuss children's learning at school.

In elementary school, Naomi does well academically. She also shows a talent for soccer, and her father signs her up to play on the community rec team. She gets new cleats, her own ball, and a team jersey. She loves playing on a team with other girls and looks forward to her Wednesday afternoon practices and Saturday games. Her parents tell her that as long as she's doing well in school, she can play as much soccer as she wants to. Pretty soon, Naomi's playing in all her spare hours. Her mom has to chase her down in the park close to where they live most evenings just so she can come home to eat and do her homework. "Girl, you and that ball'll be the death of me," Mommy scolds, but Naomi has the feeling that she isn't really mad.

## 10. Socioemotional Development in Middle Childhood

Today you will practice the following:

10.1  Describe school-age children's self-conceptions and motivation.

10.2  Examine the roles of friendship, peer acceptance, and peer victimization in school-age children's adjustment.

10.3  Discuss family relationships in middle childhood and the influence of family structure on adjustment.

10.4  Analyze the role of resilience in promoting adjustment to adversity, including characteristics of children and contexts that promote resilience.

When Naomi is in the second grade, her father is deployed again. He has to go away sometimes but usually only for a month or so. Her mom explains that this is because she and Daddy decided it would be better if Naomi lived as much as she could in one place. So, she and Mommy don't follow Daddy all the time when he goes different places in the United States (a place she's learning about in school). But when he leaves for a long time a long way away, she knows because he takes her out for a special Daddy–Naomi dinner and explains why he's going away and where he'll be. He's going to a base on the other side of the world in a country called Turkey. Naomi laughs and tells him that's a silly name for a country. Daddy agrees. Then he explains how important Turkey is to a lot of different people from other countries right now, and she tries to understand. She feels bad for the children he tells her about, the ones living there in big tents and warehouses because they had to run away from their own houses in another country, but she's not sure why other kids get to have Daddy before she does. That doesn't seem fair at all.

"Will you send me pictures?"

"All the time, my little north star."

She likes it when he calls her a "star," because she feels special. "I wish you didn't have to go, Daddy."

"So does Mommy," her mother says as she joins them in Naomi's room, "but we'll be all right. Won't we, kiddo?"

"I know you'll take care of each other, and I'll be back before you know it," Daddy says, but Naomi is pretty sure that last part isn't true.

## 11. Physical and Cognitive Development in Late Childhood

### Today you will practice the following:

*11.1* Describe school-age children's self-conceptions and motivation.

*11.2* Examine the roles of friendship, peer acceptance, and peer victimization in school-age children's adjustment.

*11.3* Discuss family relationships in middle childhood and the influence of family structure on adjustment.

*11.4* Analyze the role of resilience in promoting adjustment to adversity, including characteristics of children and contexts that promote resilience.

By the end of elementary school, Naomi is a star on her community league soccer team. She loves playing. Sometimes, when she's alone on the field near her apartment and she's practicing dribbling, she thinks about learning to play when she was little. She misses her dad and how they took that Saturday to pick out her cleats and a brand-new ball. She still practices with the same ball even though it's just a little smaller than regulation. She calls it her lucky ball because her dad bought it for her. If she had her choice, she would go to school on the soccer field!

She likes school well enough, and she does great in most of her classes. She doesn't do poorly in any of them. Mr. Cooper in her fifth grade science class likes her because she's good at all that plant stuff like photosynthesis. Her mom tells her this is to be expected, that she always loved being outside and learning about nature when she was a little girl. She even keeps all of their house plants healthy and green. Her mom has a black thumb. She likes plants in the house but can't keep them alive. Naomi seems to have a touch. She tries to show her mom how easy it is, but Alicia loses interest quickly and says, "Honey, you know that's your thing. As long as I don't have to throw them out dead, we're doing great." "We're" not doing anything, Naomi thinks, but she doesn't say it.

## 12. Socioemotional Development in Late Childhood

### Today you will practice the following:

*12.1* Summarize the processes by which self-concept, self-esteem, and identity change during adolescence.

*12.2* Discuss the nature of parent–child relationships in adolescence.

*12.3* Examine the developmental progression of peer relations in adolescence.

*12.4* Analyze patterns of adolescent sexual activity including sexual orientation.

*12.5* Identify common psychological and behavioral problems in adolescence.

"Will we always live here?" she asks her mom one night as they eat dinner. They're having tomato soup and grilled cheese sandwiches. Her mom makes the best grilled cheese sandwiches in the world, and Naomi has a lot of friends whose moms have given her grilled cheese sandwiches. She considers herself something of an expert.

"What do you mean 'here,' Naomi?" Mom asks. "Do you mean in this town or in this apartment?"

"Either, I guess."

"Well," her mom says with a big sigh, "we'll probably always live in the town or close by. Your grandparents are getting older, and it will be important to be close to them as they age. As for this apartment? I hope not. I wouldn't want a house with all the upkeep by myself when your dad is gone, but maybe when he gets back, we'll talk about moving to a bigger place."

Naomi would like that. It's hard to have sleepovers with more than one or two girls in their tiny apartment. If they're loud at night, it bothers her mom, and sometimes she yells at Naomi to be quiet. Sometimes her mom yells at her to be quiet even when she's alone and not making much noise. Naomi's dad is on his third deployment in her life, and she's figured out that Mom gets sad—like big sad—when he goes away for a long time. Mom calls it "depression," and she takes special medicine to help her feel better. Her mom usually takes longer to notice her depression than Naomi does, though, and Naomi has to live with a few weeks of missed soccer games, extra yelling, and a lot of crying—a lot of crying. It scares her, but mostly it makes her feel nervous because she doesn't want her mom to be so sad. She thinks she should be able to make her mom happy, but when she tries, she only seems to make it worse. That's when her mom figures out she needs to see the doctor most of the time. Naomi's always glad when that happens because then she doesn't have to make up reasons why her mom isn't at a game or why she forgot to send cupcakes for the class field trip or something else she didn't do.

## 13. Physical and Cognitive Development in Adolescence

### Today you will practice the following:

13.1 *Evaluate the "storm and stress" perspective on adolescence in light of research evidence.*

13.2 *Summarize the physical changes that occur with puberty and the correlates of pubertal timing.*

13.3 *Discuss brain development during adolescence and its effect on behavior.*

13.4 *Identify ways in which thinking changes in adolescence and how these changes are reflected in adolescent decision-making and behavior.*

13.5 *Discuss moral development and influences on moral reasoning.*

13.6 *Describe the challenges that school transitions pose for adolescents and the role of parents in academic achievement.*

Naomi stands with her foot on top of her lucky soccer ball, staring into the bleachers. She's trying to practice, but there's Bradley Carter again, sitting there all alone watching her. He is so annoying. Even if sometimes he does look a little cute, she's busy trying to study or play her way into a college scholarship. It's bad enough she's a girl with the periods and the hormones and the pimples. She doesn't need to add boys on top of all that.

Her parents seem to always be asking her if she likes someone—anyone. No, I don't, she yells in her head, but she just shakes her head no. Bradley Carter's face sometimes leaps into her mind then, but she pushes it right back out again. No, thank you. "It's okay if you do," her mom assures her, but her dad's expression says otherwise. She keeps quiet and wonders if she might score more goals—or less!—if Bradley comes to one of her games.

## 14. Socioemotional Development in Adolescence

### Today you will practice the following:

*14.1 Summarize the processes by which self-concept, self-esteem, and identity change during adolescence.*

*14.2 Discuss the nature of parent–child relationships in adolescence.*

*14.3 Examine the developmental progression of peer relations in adolescence.*

*14.4 Analyze patterns of adolescent sexual activity, including sexual orientation.*

*14.5 Identify common psychological and behavioral problems in adolescence.*

"Mom," Naomi asks one night as they make dough for a homemade pizza, "when you were my age, did you have trouble with your friends?"

Her mom frowns but doesn't look at her. Naomi sees her lips turn down before she asks, "What kind of trouble?"

"I always had so many friends in elementary school, even in middle school. But now . . ." She doesn't finish the sentence, but her mom picks it up for her. She knows she will because her mom is like her, biracial. It shouldn't, but it makes a difference.

"Oh, that. Well," she says, kneading dough, "it's normal for all kids to have fewer and fewer friends as they get older but to have those friends become more intimate, to be more important to your life—like Erica and Sydney are to you," she adds.

Erica and Sydney are Naomi's best friends. Sydney is white, but Erica's also mixed. Her mom is black, and her dad is Japanese. She doesn't know what she would do without them. They are the Three Musketeers. Sometimes, their parents call them the triplets.

"I guess."

"What's bothering you, Naomi?"

"I guess I feel sort of . . ." She struggles for the right word. "Clan-less. When I try to hang out with the white kids, like when I'm just with Sydney, they want me to act 'whiter,' whatever that is, and when I'm with Erica and the black kids, they want me to act 'blacker.' I don't want to be one or the other. I want to be both."

Her mom nods. "I understand. You know, I'm biracial just like you, but when I'm asked what my race is, I say African American."

"I didn't understand that before, but I'm starting to."

"At some point, it was just easier to be one or the other."

Naomi hugs her mom's waist, covering them both in flour. "Do you ever feel like you turned you back on your white heritage?"

"Pretty much every day."

Naomi struggles to be true to both sides of her family, especially because her only living grandparents are white, and her only black living relative is her mom. It's hard, but she feels like she manages most of the time. Her parents help her by making sure she has opportunities to explore her history—both sides of it. As graduation approaches, so does Bradley Carter, who among other wonderful things, is also of mixed race and really gets her. She wishes she'd known that sooner.

Bradley attends all of Naomi's soccer games. He takes her out to dinner or the movies but only one night each week, which is what she tells him she has time for. He hangs out with her parents for family game night. She pokes at him a lot, trying to find the flaw. He doesn't even pressure her to have sex, and everyone she knows is having sex. Eventually, she starts to wonder if something's wrong with her.

"Don't you think I'm pretty?" she asks him.

"I think you're gorgeous."

"Then I think we should do it."

Bradley squeezes her hand, but he also laughs. "I think we can manage a way to be a little more romantic than that. But, Nae, you're leaving for college in a few months. Are you sure you want to do this? Like now and with me?"

She is sure.

## 15. Physical and Cognitive Development in Emerging/Early Adulthood

### Today you will practice the following:

15.1 *Describe the features and characteristics of emerging and early adulthood.*

15.2 *Summarize the physical developments of emerging and early adulthood.*

15.3 *Analyze physical and sexual health issues in emerging and early adulthood.*

15.4 *Compare postformal reasoning, pragmatic thought, and cognitive-affective complexity.*

15.5 *Explain how attending college influences young adults' development, and identify challenges faced by first-generation and nontraditional students.*

15.6 *Discuss vocational choice and the transition to work.*

Naomi's parents drive her to college with a tiny U-Haul attached to the back of their SUV. She's nervous, excited, and just a little scared. She and Erica are going to room together. That's a lucky break for her because she thought the university would make her room with one of the other soccer players—not that she isn't looking forward to being good friends with the team. She is. It just feels safe somehow living with one of her two best friends. Plus, Erica knows Naomi's personal weaknesses. She'll keep her on track so she doesn't screw up and lose her soccer scholarship.

After unloading all her boxes and setting up a lot of her things, she looks around her dorm room, terrified. Her dad asks what's wrong, and she tells him she's scared. When he tells her she'll be fine, she asks, "How do you know?"

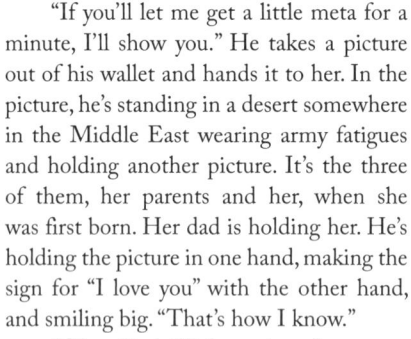

"If you'll let me get a little meta for a minute, I'll show you." He takes a picture out of his wallet and hands it to her. In the picture, he's standing in a desert somewhere in the Middle East wearing army fatigues and holding another picture. It's the three of them, her parents and her, when she was first born. Her dad is holding her. He's holding the picture in one hand, making the sign for "I love you" with the other hand, and smiling big. "That's how I know."

"Okay, Dad. I'll do my best."

"That's all anyone can do."

## 16. Socioemotional Development in Emerging/Early Adulthood

### Today you will practice the following:

16.1  Summarize psychosocial development in emerging and early adulthood.

16.2  Discuss influences on friendship and mate selection and interactions in emerging and early adulthood.

16.3  Analyze the diverse romantic situations that may characterize emerging and early adulthood, including singlehood, cohabitation, marriage, and divorce.

16.4  Compare the experiences of young adults as stepparents, never-married parents, and same-sex parents.

Her dad takes a trip to the dumpster to throw away packing trash, while Naomi and her mom unpack some clothes. When he returns, they hear him enter the room with a booming, "Guess who I found wandering around outside?"

Naomi assumes it's Erica, and she's glad that her best friend will be with her when her parents leave.

"Surprise," Bradley says softly from the doorway, and despite herself, Naomi is overjoyed at seeing him. She gives him a hug and a quick kiss before asking him why he's there. "Turns out they had room for me after all," he tells her, referring to his previous status on the university's wait list.

"Wait!" she yells. "You're going here?"

"I am."

"That's great!"

Naomi knows she's supposed to go to college and experience new things—and she will—but taking her best friend and her sort of boyfriend can't be all bad. With Bradley's arm around her, she wonders how soon she can get rid of her parents.

For four years, Naomi is single-minded. She plays hard on the field, contributing to her team's success but never trying to outdo her teammates. She wins the annual Best Team Player award all four years and scores the winning goal for the state championship in her junior year. She loves almost every minute. In class, she's just as devoted. Majoring in botany, she works hard to finish her degree a semester early, near the end of which she applies to and is accepted in the university's master's program. She's almost able to complete this degree by the end of her soccer eligibility. Her parents gladly pay for her last year of school. After graduation, she takes a job working for the state's agricultural department.

She and Bradley have a tumultuous relationship. He's focused on his own studies in the history department, but he tries to make all of Naomi's home games and most of her closer road games. However, they both get busy, and by sophomore year, Naomi asks for a break from their relationship. Bradley agrees, and she wonders if he already has his eye on someone else. She does. For almost a year, they date other people—in her case, several other people. Naomi decides by junior year as she nears the completion of her first degree, that she's had enough looking around. She calls Bradley and asks him if he wants to get coffee one Saturday morning. When he agrees, she goes prepared to grovel, but so does he. They laugh and agree that they both needed to grow up before they could settle down, and they're ready to do that now.

## 17. Physical and Cognitive Development in Middle Adulthood

### Today you will practice the following:

17.1 *Summarize age-related physical changes during middle adulthood.*

17.2 *Discuss common health conditions and illnesses and the roles of stress and hardiness on health during middle adulthood.*

17.3 *Contrast the findings of cross-sectional and longitudinal studies of crystallized and fluid intelligence over adulthood.*

17.4 *Analyze changes in cognitive capacities during middle adulthood, including attention, memory, processing speed, and expertise.*

After working for several years in the Department of Agriculture, Naomi resigns her position to begin a start-up small business. She decides to open a company that will produce organic fertilizer and pest retardant for the agricultural industry. It's a leap of faith in herself, but she feels like this is the time and she has the skills to make it work. She's never failed at much to speak of, but if this doesn't work out, at least she tried.

## 18. Socioemotional Development in Middle Adulthood

### Today you will practice the following:

18.1  Summarize the theories and research on psychosocial development during middle adulthood.

18.2  Describe the changes that occur in self-concept, identity, and personality during middle adulthood.

18.3  Analyze relationships in middle adulthood, including friend, spousal, parent–child, and grandparent relationships.

18.4  Discuss influences on job satisfaction and retirement planning during middle adulthood.

Just when Naomi decides to start her business, she accepts Bradley's marriage proposal. They've had a standing date—every six months—when he asks, and she always tells him she loves only him and to come back in six months. He always does, and this time, she says yes. Her dad is thrilled because she and Bradley have been living together since college. Now at least they won't be "living in sin." Bradley jokes and accuses her of saying yes right when she's ready to make a risky financial move. She looks at him and says, "But of course," causing both of them to laugh so hard they cry.

Bradley, who got a teaching certificate while finishing his history degree, teaches at the local high school, and Naomi structures her day around his to maximize their time together. She knows how lucky they are. She knows how lucky she is having her parents and her grandparents as role models for how to have a healthy relationship. When Bradley surprises her with flowers and chocolate cake—her favorite—one night and asks her, "So . . . want to make a baby," she nods and says, "Let's do it." She gives birth to Claire 15 months later and Robert 24 months after that. Since Naomi is 35 when Robert is born, she and Bradley decide two is the right number for them, and Naomi has a tubal ligation after delivering their son.

As the children grow, so does Naomi's business. She works hard, and she works long hours, often gathering the children from school and taking them to the office with her until Bradley finishes at the high school and picks them up. One day, Robert sees Naomi's lucky soccer ball sitting on the bookshelf where she always keeps it in her office and asks her what it is. She tells him it's her lucky soccer ball. Then she gives it to him to play with. Although both children take turns kicking and trying to dribble, it's clear from the beginning that Robert has a natural talent. When Bradley walks in and sees their children playing, he says to Naomi, "Like mother, like son. And so it begins." And so it begins as Naomi gets Robert signed up for rec league soccer and volunteers to coach his team.

Bradley and Naomi's is a strong and openly affectionate marriage that supports them through the loss of Naomi's grandparents and, later, Naomi's mother. Alicia had been quietly ailing for some time, and during her last winter she caught the flu and never recovered. Naomi misses her mother terribly, but she thinks about her childhood and coping with her mother's depression. She doesn't want that for her own children and works through her grief with Bradley and a local support group. She finds it helpful, too, that her dad spends more time with them now, eating dinner two or three nights each week at the house they bought across town. Seeing her dad so much keeps her connected to her mom in positive, not sad, ways.

## 19. Physical and Cognitive Development in Late Adulthood

### Today you will practice the following:

*19.1* Discuss age-related changes in brain and body systems in late adulthood, and identify ways that older adults may compensate for changes.

*19.2* Identify risk and protective factors for health in late adulthood.

*19.3* Summarize common dementias, including characteristics, risk and protective factors, and treatment.

*19.4* Analyze patterns of cognitive change in late adulthood.

Naomi makes time to visit the doctor every year, a leftover habit from being an athlete, she tells herself. General checkup, PAP smear, mammogram—every year, she expects good results but is glad to get them anyway. She has children—who seem prepared to give her grandchildren at any moment—and a husband and a growing business. What she doesn't have is time to get seriously ill. The doctor always tells her the same thing: She's in remarkable health for someone her age, which Naomi chalks up to all the years on the field.

After one checkup, she receives a callback that something looks suspicious on her mammogram and the doctor would like to do a needle biopsy. She tells Bradley but not Claire and Robert, who will only worry needlessly. She'll tell them when there's something to tell them. Bradley goes with her to the biopsy, which hurts far more than she's told it will, and afterward they have a quiet lunch at their favorite restaurant. Naomi wonders if they should've chosen someplace they like less in case the news is bad so they don't taint this one. When the office calls two days later, she and Bradley are relieved to hear that the shadow on the mammogram was just a shadow, and Naomi has nothing to worry about.

Naomi continues running three to five miles each day well into her 60s and even in her 70s walks more than two miles each day. When asked about her vitality, she winks at Bradley and says, "He keeps me young." She annoys herself if she happens to forget an appointment or where she placed her glasses. When she worries and asks the doctor, she dismisses Naomi's concern. "You're fine. Forgetting your keys is a natural part of aging. Forgetting what they're for is troubling. You're the healthiest octogenarian I've ever seen, Naomi."

## 20. Socioemotional Development in Late Adulthood

### Today you will practice the following:

20.1 *Examine the contributions of self-concept, personality, and religiosity to older adults' well-being.*

20.2 *Identify social contexts in which older adults live and their influence on development.*

20.3 *Summarize features of older adults' relationships with friends, spouses, children, and grandchildren, and identify how these relationships affect older adults' functioning.*

20.4 *Discuss influences on the timing of retirement and adaptation to retirement.*

Just about the time Naomi is ready to retire, her dad Justin agrees to come and live with her and Bradley. Naomi is relieved. She worries about her dad all alone. Plus, having Dad around will give Bradley someone to talk to when she isn't around. How to retire is another matter. Robert coaches the soccer team at the same high school Bradley retired from, and Claire . . . well, Claire could manage the business, with her degrees in biology and geology, but would she? Naomi thinks maybe she should just sell.

"Mom, don't be ridiculous," Claire tells her over lunch one day. "Of course, I'll help out. How much help do you want?"

"Do you want it?" Naomi asks her. "The business?"

"Want like—"

"Do you want to be the CEO?"

"I . . . Yes."

Claire is never indecisive, like Naomi herself. Good, Naomi thinks, Claire can run the business instead of running her, Naomi. She knows that both children will be there when they really need them.

## 21. Experience With Death and Dying

### Today you will practice the following:

*21.1* Identify ways in which death has been defined and end-of-life issues that may arise.

*21.2* Contrast children's, adolescents', and adults' understanding of death.

*21.3* Discuss the physical and emotional process of dying as it is experienced over the lifespan.

*21.4* Summarize typical grief reactions to the loss of loved ones and the influence of development on bereavement.

Justin and Bradley pass away within a year of one another, giving Naomi two large blows. Her dad dies of a heart attack, and Bradley has a stroke while on a run with her one morning. She does everything she can to save him, but it's hopeless. The children and her three grandchildren circle around her to support her grieving, but Naomi never really recovers. Whether isolation or broken heart or simple age, she passes away in her sleep from undetermined but natural causes at the age of 84.

## CASE DISCUSSION QUESTIONS

1. Naomi's mother, Alicia, struggles with periodic depression when her husband, Naomi's father, Justin, is deployed with the army. How does Alicia's ongoing depression affect Naomi's development across any and all domains (biological, cognitive, and socioemotional)? Be specific.

2. In early childhood, Justin takes Naomi shopping for supplies and signs her up for rec league soccer, a small act that will impact the rest of her life and one of her children's. Create a map of how Naomi's life is impacted across any and all domains (biological, cognitive, and socioemotional) because she began playing soccer and was an exceptional player.

3. Naomi's childhood love of flowers and other plants she saw outdoors leads her to a degree in botany, a job with the Department of Agriculture, and eventually her own brand. What childhood experiences across any and all domains (biological, cognitive, and socioemotional) help explain her choices and her drive?

4. Naomi's entire life occurs over many decades that are, loosely, contemporary. Cars, telephones, televisions, and so on exist, but era-specific technology isn't presented (e.g., cell phones, space shuttles, or artificial intelligence). Would Naomi's life have been different if she were born in a specific period, earlier or later? If so, how? Be specific.

# 3 James Albert

## Introduction

Welcome to your case study!

Congratulations! You will follow the lifespan of baby boy James Albert. Try to use your best judgment, textbook, classmates, instructor, and supplementary resources to make the best decisions to help him grow.

This semester you will observe James as he grows from infant to child to teen to adult. Who will he become in your care? Will you understand and agree with all decisions available within his circumstances? How will you feel about the tough decisions that forever shape his path in life?

## Meet James Albert

James is the first son of Rosslyn and Joss Albert, a Caucasian couple who've been married for a few years. The Alberts are middle income. Joss is 32 years old, holds a bachelor's degree, and

iStock.com/tayana_tomsickova

works a full-time job. Rosslyn, 30 years old, also holds a bachelor's degree and holds a full-time job. The couple own their home in a middle-class, suburban neighborhood, and Joss's employer provides the family's health insurance. Rosslyn's employer is too small to afford offering coverage, although the company does provide a monthly supplement to full-time employees so that they can participate in the health insurance exchange if they wish to. When Rosslyn is 13 weeks into her pregnancy with James, Joss loses his job due to the company's need to downsize; they've been underperforming and decide to cut some higher-salary employees. This is a triple blow to the Alberts, who need both incomes to pay for their home and get ready for Rosslyn's unpaid maternity leave but who also need Joss's employer-sponsored health insurance.

Through this case study and your lifespan course, you will be asked to consider decisions regarding James's physical, emotional, and cognitive growth and development from several perspectives: his mother Rosslyn's, his father Joss's, and his grandparents' as well as those of his siblings, his spouse, his children, other family members, friends, teachers, doctors, and supervisors.

Now let's get started.

## 1. Development and Its Influences

### Today you will practice the following:

*1.1 Outline five principles of the lifespan developmental perspective.*

*1.2 Explain three theoretical controversies about human development.*

*1.3 Summarize five theoretical perspectives on human development.*

*1.4 Describe the methods and research designs used to study human development.*

Rosslyn and Joss have been looking forward to starting a family almost since the day they got married. In some ways, Rosslyn thinks, every move they've made has prepared them to have this baby. She knows she maybe sacrificed a little when she took the job she has so that they could stay close to Joss's mother and her parents. All through college, she thought she'd end up working for a big, glossy magazine in New York, but she'd settled for the weekly newspaper in a town halfway between the soon-to-be grandparents' cities. Journalism is journalism, she tells herself, and Joss helps by doing things like framing her first article in the same fancy frame as their diplomas hang in. He really is the best, a sentiment with which he readily agrees when he flips burgers on their new grill and puts a slice of American cheese on hers. She gets the buns ready, and he smiles at her, thinking how lucky he is that she ever agreed to marry him. True, it took him three years in college and after to convince her, but here they are in their own home, cooking burgers on a beautiful Saturday afternoon, with their baby on the way. He's a little worried about losing his job, but they have money in the bank—not a lot but enough for a while—and they'll figure things out. No one ever said the American dream didn't have potholes along the road.

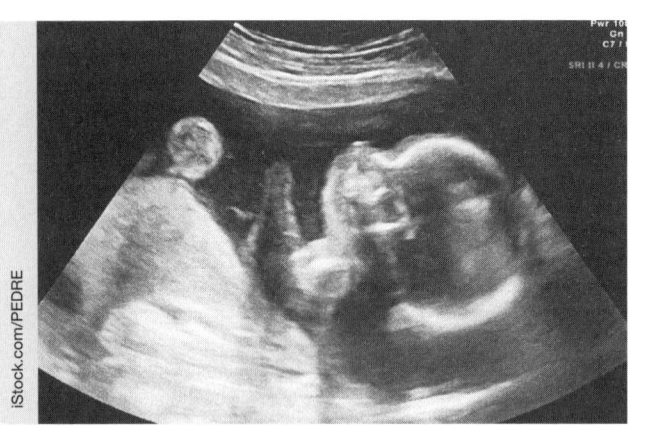

## 2. Biological and Environmental Foundations

> Today you will practice the following:
>
> 2.1 Discuss the genetic foundations of development.
>
> 2.2 Identify examples of genetic disorders and chromosomal abnormalities.
>
> 2.3 Discuss the choices available to prospective parents in having healthy children.
>
> 2.4 Describe the interaction of heredity and environment, including behavioral genetics and the epigenetic framework.

Rosslyn and Joss spend a lot of time together in the evenings looking at the budget. They assess how much money they have saved, how much they need to pay their bills (and what they can cut), and how much Rosslyn can contribute. Then they look at the big ticket item. Joss can choose to continue his insurance through his employer for up to 18 months, but he has to bear the full cost of doing so. It's a lot of money. They run some scenarios through the marketplace to see what the best option is for them. Rosslyn's supplement isn't a lot, but it might be better to use that and some savings to buy a cheaper plan.

In the end, they decide to cut back on all nonessentials—Joss assures Rosslyn that pistachio ice cream is an essential—and pay for the insurance through Joss's employer. It's going to hurt, but they physically have the money, and Joss is going to try hard to get a job as fast as he can, even if it's a step down from his last one. The insurance and a less-than-ideal job—both are temporary stopgap measures to tide them over. Besides, they have each other.

Cutting back means a number of things for Rosslyn (and James) during the remainder of her pregnancy. She's used to buying whatever food she wants to buy at the grocery store. Their hamburgers are made with free-range beef, and every Sunday she roasts a free-range chicken. Organic vegetables, high-end dairy, bakery fresh bread—Joss doesn't tell her what to buy, but they decide that the grocery bill needs to be cut in half. Rosslyn doesn't want to sacrifice all quality, but she knows a lot of her choices have to change. She decides good meat and dairy from the grocery store are the most important. Learning to bake her own bread, she begins buying vegetables from the local growers at the weekend farmers' market. It takes her a couple weeks, but eventually she cuts the food bill almost by half. Joss is impressed, and they agree that her bread is better than the bakery's anyway.

What really hurts are the changes they make at the house. They turn the air-conditioner up to 74 and the heat back to 67. Such small changes, Joss thinks, but, wow, they make a difference in comfort levels. In January, he looks at Rosslyn curled up in the corner of the sofa with wool socks, a book, and hot cocoa. She's not complaining, so neither does he. It's hard, though, he thinks, as he goes to the kitchen for another cup of coffee—anything to feel warmer. It's been four months. Two more months until the baby gets there, and Joss is no closer to a new job. He needs to find something soon because they're going to need new, expensive essentials like diapers, vaccinations, car seats, and baby food. To be fair, Rosslyn has said she'd make the baby food, but with no job, Joss is looking more and more like a stay-at-home dad, and that means he needs to be learning some of this stuff. Even if he does stay home, there's not enough money. The baby's going to have to eat something. Joss can't make baby food from air. He just hopes the kid looks like Rosslyn. He'll learn to stretch a dollar further if the baby has her blue eyes, instead of his green ones, and her curly brown hair. He sincerely hopes he doesn't pass along a gene for the receding hairline that seems to be so prevalent in his family.

Rosslyn looks at him over her book and says, "I hope he has your red hair."

"Me, too," Joss agrees. "I was just thinking that."

"Really?"

"No. Of course not. I hope he looks just like you. Go back to your book, silly."

## 3. Prenatal Development, Birth, and Newborn Experience

### Today you will practice the following:

3.1  *Describe the three periods of prenatal development that begin with conception.*

3.2  *Identify how exposure to teratogens can influence the prenatal environment.*

3.3  *Explain the process of childbirth.*

3.4  *Discuss the neonate's physical capacities, including development in low-birth-weight infants.*

Rosslyn takes good care of herself during the pregnancy. She attends every scheduled prenatal appointment and the recommended prenatal and childbirth classes with Joss. Because they are conscious about the money they spend, she's a little more hesitant than she might otherwise be to telephone the OB-GYN if she feels under the weather or if she has a concern about the baby or the pregnancy. She tends to wait things out and see if they resolve themselves. This is especially true if she's close to a scheduled prenatal appointment. She can always ask then, she figures, or the doctor will probably find anything that's wrong anyway. She convinces herself she's a worrier anyway and there's no reason to run to the doctor over every little thing. Joss tries to be reassuring, too. Every time she sees the doctor and explains a recent worry, the doctor says two things: (1) she and the baby are fine, and (2) she should always call if there's any concern. Better safe than sorry.

"And speaking of better safe than sorry," Dr. Gibson tells her late in the pregnancy, "I'm going to send you for another sonogram today."

Alarmed, Rosslyn asks, "What's wrong?"

He assures her nothing is wrong. "I want to get an estimate of the baby's size. I think we're looking at a pretty big boy. Babies tend to mirror Mom's birth size at delivery. How big were you, Rosslyn?"

Rosslyn laughs, remembering all the stories. "Big," she admits. "Like eight, eight and a half pounds."

"I think this little guy is, too, but I'm not sure your pelvic structure will support a vaginal delivery of a child that size. I could be wrong. Let's get him measured and—"

"But I want a natural birth," Rosslyn protests.

"And we'll give you one if we can. I just want to be prepared."

Figuring he is the doctor for a reason, Rosslyn lets the ultrasound tech measure the baby, explaining how she's doing it as she makes lines all across the image of Rosslyn's fat little boy. "The best estimation will come from the length of his femur," she says. She makes her calculations, consults with the doctor, and returns to Rosslyn with a smile. "Looks like you and Dr. Gibson were in the right ball park. We're going to estimate eight and a half with a half-pound margin on either side if you go to 40 weeks."

"God, I hope I don't," Rosslyn whispers, and they both laugh.

In her 39th week, Rosslyn feels ill at work. Her back aches badly. She's irritable and tired. She also wants to pee all morning long. After lunch, she tells her boss she needs to go home and rest, which is exactly what she does. An hour or so after lying down, she realizes no position is comfortable and reaches for the telephone. Joss is with his mother helping her paint the shutters, but it's probably nothing anyway. She dials the number for the doctor, not caring for once if she wastes money.

"Dr. Gibson's office," the receptionist says when she answers the phone. Her cheery voice annoys Rosslyn.

"This is Rosslyn Albert. I'm a patient of Dr. Gibson. I'm 39 weeks pregnant, and I do not feel well."

When requested by a nurse, she recites her symptoms. She says that, no, she doesn't have anyone who can drive her to the hospital just then, but she's perfectly capable of driving herself. Protesting, she declines the offer of an ambulance (thinking of the cost) and agrees to meet Dr. Gibson in the women's wing. After she hangs up, she calls Joss and tells him she's leaving for the hospital and will he please call her parents and then meet her there?

He sounds much less calm than she does, she thinks, when he agrees.

An hour or so after arriving at the hospital, checking herself in, and climbing mostly undressed into the hospital bed, Dr. Gibson arrives to check her out. Yes, she is definitely in labor. She tells the doctor that it doesn't feel nearly as terrible as she was led to believe it would.

"It will," he tells her before he breaks her water.

Half an hour later, Joss and all the parents arrive at one time, and Rosslyn realizes Dr. Gibson was right. As Joss bends down to kiss her, she whispers, "Get. Me. Drugs."

Some uncounted amount of time later, an anesthesiologist administers an epidural, and Rosslyn's told she still has several hours of labor before she'll transition into the second stage and be ready to push her baby into the world. When James is born—a healthy, beautiful nine-pound baby she delivered vaginally to Dr. Gibson's awed surprise—seven hours later, Rosslyn forgets about her earlier boredom. All the months of waiting, sacrificing, and worrying were absolutely worth it. His first lusty cries as he greets the world please the doctor and call to her. She raises her arms, and the nurse hands him to her. As she strokes his cheek, he turns his head to root and finds her breast, and then he nurses while Joss tickles his feet. James flexes them and then curls his toes. They laugh. She puts a finger to his palm, and he grasps hold of her finger and holds on so tightly she thinks he'll never let go. All the clichés are not cliché at all. He is perfect.

## 4. Physical Development in Infancy and Toddlerhood

### Today you will practice the following:

4.1 *Discuss growth and the role of nutrition in development during infancy and toddlerhood.*

4.2 *Summarize brain development during infancy and toddlerhood.*

4.3 *Compare infants' early learning capacities for habituation, classical conditioning, operant conditioning, and imitation.*

4.4 *Describe infants' developing sensory abilities.*

4.5 *Analyze the roles of maturation and contextual factors in infant and toddler motor development.*

In the first few weeks of his life, James is at home with Joss and Rosslyn, both of whom care for him equally. They share all duties except breast-feeding, and Rosslyn jokes that she knows Joss would do that, too, if he could. Joss—not joking—agrees. It's a magical time for the little family of three. James is an easy baby, going to bed without fuss in the cradle kept at the end of his parents' bed, nursing quietly at night, and falling back to sleep when he finishes.

At the end of Rosslyn's six weeks of maternity leave, she reluctantly returns to work. Before Joss lost his job, they'd discussed the possibility of Rosslyn taking advantage of the federal Family Medical Leave Act and staying with James another six weeks, but the leave is unpaid. They can't do that now. Although she cries from the moment she gets out of bed until the moment she gets to work, Rosslyn returns to work on the seventh Monday after James is born. She calls home every hour and manages to leave work two hours early. When she gets home, James is sitting on Joss's lap, sucking his father's thumb and drooling all over Joss's hand and his own shirt. Joss is using his other hand to look at job ads. She kisses them both.

"Everything go okay?" she asks.

"Since you asked an hour ago? Just fine."

"I'm sorry, but it's so hard to leave him."

"I know, Roz. We missed you, too. Didn't we, James?" he asks, smiling when the baby hears his name and looks up at his father with shining eyes.

When James registers Rosslyn's presence, he furrows his brow and reaches for her. Joss lifts him in the air under his armpits and hands him over to his waiting mother.

"Rosslyn, this kid needs some toys other than stuffed animals. I mean, I knew before that babies put things in their mouths, but all you gotta do is watch him closely to see that he's doing more than shoving things in there. He's *examining* them. He needs stuff he can feel and compare, like those books with fur and sandpaper and rubber and whatever."

"I know what you mean. We can go shopping this weekend."

"Good." Smiling, he says, "And I asked Mom to come tomorrow morning while you're at work. I have a job interview."

## 5. Cognitive Development in Infancy and Toddlerhood

### Today you will practice the following:

5.1 Discuss the cognitive-developmental perspective on infant reasoning.

5.2 Describe the information processing system in infants.

5.3 Discuss individual differences in infant intelligence.

5.4 Summarize the patterns of language development during infancy and toddlerhood.

Rosslyn and Joss take turns reading bedtime stories to James from the beginning of his young life. They received a lot of children's books, especially story books, as baby gifts, and they also buy copies of some of their own childhood favorites. After a couple weeks, Joss starts videoing some of the readings, too, although Rosslyn has no idea why he does it. This is their end-of-the-day quiet time with their son, and with a dim light and lots of cuddling, they make the most of it.

Very soon, post-grabbing phase, James begins asserting his own will on reading time. There are two or three books he seems to dislike, and if Rosslyn or Joss selects one of these, James pushes it away and turns his head to the side, whining. His parents find the behavior amusing but usually select another book as well.

By the time James is a year old, he babbles along with both his parents when they read his favorite stories, often using the same cadence and rhythm they do even if he doesn't use words. When a story contains one of the 15 or so words he does know, he shouts it out just after Rosslyn or Joss speaks the word; he's proud of himself. By the time he's two years old, James can "read" two or three of his shorter story books by having memorized their content. He knows the words, their meanings, and their place in the book based on tying the words to the images on their pages. Even if not all the words are intelligible when his parents hear them, he knows them. His spoken vocabulary is exponentially larger than it was just one year before, and his receptive vocabulary contains enough words now that he understands most of the stories his parents read to him.

## 6. James's Socioemotional Development in Infancy and Toddlerhood

> Today you will practice the following:
>
> 6.1 Summarize the psychosocial tasks of infancy and toddlerhood.
>
> 6.2 Describe emotional development in infancy, and identify contextual and cultural influences on emotional development in infants and toddlers.
>
> 6.3 Identify the styles and stability of temperament, including the role of goodness of fit in infant development.
>
> 6.4 Describe how attachment develops in infancy and toddlerhood.
>
> 6.5 Differentiate the roles of self-concept, self-recognition, and self-control in infant development.

James has a fairly easy transition from being cared for at home to his new daycare routine. In the beginning, he dislikes the whole affair, crying when Joss or Rosslyn drops him off and pushing away from his teacher, Miss Tina. He doesn't want to drink the milk Rosslyn pumped and bottled the night before and fusses loudly when the teacher tries to give it to him. Eventually, she gives up, kisses his wet cheek, and says, "You'll eat when you're hungry, I guess," which he does when Rosslyn picks him up. He grabs at her blouse and bumps her chest with his head, grunting. Laughing, Rosslyn asks if she can borrow the rocking chair, and while she watches other mothers and fathers collect their children, she gently rocks James as he nurses like he hasn't eaten in a year.

"Some babies are like that," Miss Tina tells her. "They just don't like the bottle and wait all day for their mamas to get here and feed them."

"Is there anything I can do?" Rosslyn asks.

Miss Tina shrugs. "Days when it's not too busy, maybe I can try getting him to eat a little from a spoon or a straw. Sometimes it's just the bottle they don't like. We could try a sippy cup, too."

Rosslyn feels a little relief. "That would be great. I'm sorry he's a bother."

"No bother. He's a sweet boy. Just misses you. That's a good thing."

The pediatrician agrees at James's three-month checkup. Dr. Morris squeezes James's fat legs and makes him giggle while he drools around his first tooth.

"He looks just great."

"But he only sips at pumped breastmilk during the day when I'm at work," Rosslyn worries. "Won't he get dehydrated?"

"Unlikely. Many babies who're exclusively breast-fed save it up for those hours. I've seen babies of working mothers who don't start any food until they're ready for table food, and they never take a bottle. They just wait it out at daycare. Trust him, Rosslyn. If he gets really hungry or thirsty, he'll take the bottle."

Reassured, Rosslyn reworks her schedule at work so she can take an extra 15 minutes at lunch. This allows her to run to the daycare and feed James midday. She feels better about that, and he does seem to be thriving. He also seems to have bonded well with Miss

Tina, who tells her secretly one day that she can't help holding him just a little bit more than the other babies. "He's just so lovable," she says, "and he likes playing with my braids."

"I'm sure he does," Rosslyn tells her with a smile, "and we kind of like him at home, too."

Miss Tina laughs and hands the 17 pounds of squirming baby over. "There you go, buddy. I know you're hungry."

James smiles and reaches for Rosslyn. "Little weirdo," she whispers. "Want to eat?"

## 7. Physical and Cognitive Development in Early Childhood

### Today you will practice the following:

7.1 Discuss physical development in early childhood.

7.2 Compare Piaget's cognitive-developmental and Vygotsky's sociocultural perspectives on cognitive development in early childhood.

7.3 Describe information-processing abilities during early childhood.

7.4 Summarize young children's advances in language development.

7.5 Contrast social learning and cognitive-developmental perspectives on moral development in early childhood.

7.6 Identify and explain approaches to early childhood education.

James is tall for his age—a little thin, Dr. Morris said at his last checkup, but healthy as a horse, whatever that means. Sometimes, adults say things he doesn't understand and he has to ask Mom or Dad what they mean. Why is a horse healthier than a boy? Because it only eats apples and not ice cream? If that's the case, James thinks, he'll keep the lesser status of healthy as a boy, thank you.

He's doing great in preschool. He knows all of his letters and how to write his name. The class is working on how to read some simple books, but it's hard for James because he knows all the books by heart. They've all been read to him a million times by his mom or dad, so he can't tell if he's reading or remembering. It's frustrating. Sometimes, he gets mad when he's frustrated. Mom calls it "temper." He's not sure what that means either except that when she uses the word, she seems to be mad, too.

Today, he's working on a practice letter sheet, tracing over the dotted letters slowly so he gets them just right. His best friend Zack is sitting beside him. Zack's already finished and has his head bent over his paper drawing funny lines in the margins. James likes Zack. They like to play the same things and are exactly the same size. They also have birthdays one week apart. That's so cool! Zack wears a neat little hat on his head. He told James it's called a kippah, and because he's Jewish he wears it all the time.

"Even in the bath?" James asked one day.

"Not in the bath." Zack laughed. "That would be dumb."

James likes the lines Zack draws. They're something Zack says is Hebrew, which sounds exotic. "What's that?" he whispers today.

"Letters," Zack whispers back. "I'm trying to remember how to write all the Hebrew letters that are like the English ones we're writing."

James is amazed. "You mean Hebrew is a *language*?"

"Of course. It's the language Jewish people speak."

This concept is almost too much for James to take in, and he nearly forgets to keep whispering. Trying hard not to catch the teacher's attention, he asks Zack, "You speak *two* languages?"

Zack lifts his shoulders. "Sure. Three. My *halmeoni* taught me Korean. Want me to teach you something?"

"Yes! Teach me some Hebrew! But what's a *halmeoni*?" He thinks a long time for something he has worthy of this gift. "I'll give you my Darth Vader thermos."

"She's my grandma. You don't have to give me anything. What do you want to learn to say first?"

James knows the answer to this one. "Friend."

Zack waves his pencil hand. "Ah, that one's easy. *Yedida*."

James has to repeat the word several times before he sounds almost like Zack, but eventually he has it.

"*Yedida*."

## 8. Socioemotional Development in Early Childhood

> ## Today you will practice the following:
>
> 8.1 *Discuss young children's emerging sense of initiative, self-concept, and self-esteem.*
>
> 8.2 *Summarize the development of emotional understanding, regulation, and behavior in early childhood.*
>
> 8.3 *Identify four parenting styles and their associations with child outcomes.*
>
> 8.4 *Compare biological, cognitive, and contextual theoretical explanations of gender role development.*
>
> 8.5 *Explain the function of play and the form it takes during early childhood.*

James's friend Zack looks funny. It's not just the hat. He's half-Korean, and almost everyone else in their class is plain white. Sometimes, other kids call Zack names, but James doesn't mind that he looks different. His mom and his *halmeoni* send the most delicious foods with him for lunch, and James gets to try them all. He especially loves chocolate babka and the *manju halmeoni* makes.

Having a *yedida* like Zack is the best. James tries hard to be a good friend back. Mom makes the best chocolate chip cookies anywhere in the whole world, and he always shares with Zack.

Sometimes Dad packs his sandwiches in plastic bags that he draws little pictures on to make James smile. When he thinks about asking his dad to, his dad includes Zack in the pictures. Zack laughs and points to the kippah.

One day on the playground, James takes turns on the big slide with other kids in his class, landing with a *whoosh* into leaves that crackle at the bottom. Laughing with his friends, he doesn't hear Zack at first, but when he does, his *yedida* is calling for help. James looks for the teacher, but she's not outside with them. He wipes the leaves off his butt and rushes to the circle of boys around Zack and asks what's going on.

"Nothing," Zack says, but James can see he's been crying.

A big boy named Keith pushes Zack and says, "Liar! Tell 'em why you're crying, gook!"

James doesn't know what a "gook" is, but he can tell it's bad. Zack's face gets red, and he bites his lip. James turns to Keith and pushes him back. "Kook! Spook! Took! Zook!" he yells as he keeps pushing. "You're a big bully, and I'm telling Miss Thompson as soon as I see her. You better leave Zack alone." James points at all the boys around them. "All of you better leave Zack alone!"

All across the playground, his friends stop playing and stand staring at him. When Keith and the other bullies walk over to some of them, they turn their backs. Even the girls, usually afraid of Keith, move to a different part of the playground and ignore him. James smiles. He feels good for about five seconds until Miss Thompson's shadow falls over him, all tall and scary.

"Mr. Albert," she says with that voice none of the kids liked, "did I see you bullying Keith Meadows?"

"No! No, ma'am. Keith was bullying Zack, and I only stopped him."

"Hmm." She puts her hands on her hips and looks at both boys. "Let's go inside and have a talk. We have to get to the bottom of what happened so I know what to tell your parents at the end of the day."

James wonders if this is what his grandmother means when she says no good deed goes unpunished.

## 9. Physical and Cognitive Development in Middle Childhood

### Today you will practice the following:

9.1 *Identify patterns of physical and motor development during middle childhood and common health issues facing school-age children.*

9.2 *Discuss school-age children's capacities for reasoning and processing information.*

9.3 *Summarize views of intelligence including the uses, correlates, and criticisms of intelligence tests.*

9.4 *Examine patterns of moral development during middle childhood.*

9.5 *Summarize language development during middle childhood.*

9.6 *Discuss children's learning at school.*

James's parents shove food at him all the time, but he's still skinny. Dr. Morris finally tells his mom not to worry, and that's a big relief for James. He can only eat so much spaghetti and meatballs! Dr. Morris says he'll probably just be tall and thin like Dad. Dad jokes that James can use that to get a basketball scholarship to college. James hates basketball.

What James does like is school. He likes drawing, and all his school worksheets have little drawings in the margins. His mother complains about his doodles, but his teachers tell her it's okay. He's pretty sure they know he's not doodling, and his math teacher even tells his mom and dad that he's noticed some of James's drawings are interesting and make him wish he had more time to talk to James about them. Finally, Dad says, "As long as you're not goofing off, I don't care when and where you draw."

"Joss," his mom says with a funny look at his dad.

"Okay, don't draw on the ceiling. I'd hate to have to pay for broken bones, and you wouldn't find it easy to hold a pencil if your arm was in a cast."

James laughs. He understands the hyperbole. "I get it. Thanks, Dad." Even though he knows she doesn't agree, James says, "Thanks, Mom," too, and she shakes her head before laughing.

## 10. Socioemotional Development in Middle Childhood

### Today you will practice the following:

10.1 *Describe school-age children's self-conceptions and motivation.*

10.2 *Examine the roles of friendship, peer acceptance, and peer victimization in school-age children's adjustment.*

10.3 *Discuss family relationships in middle childhood and the influence of family structure on adjustment.*

10.4 *Analyze the role of resilience in promoting adjustment to adversity, including characteristics of children and contexts that promote resilience.*

James and his *yedida* Zack form a club in third grade. They meet during recess on the playground, and their club has four members. They call the club Words Can Hurt and spend their time thinking of ways to stop bullying. They have specific rules, like everyone's ideas are as good as everyone else's, and there's no leader in the group because everyone is equally important. They meet for a couple of weeks before their teacher Mr. Miller asks them if they'd like their club to become an official club at the school. James doesn't understand what this means, and Mr. Miller explains that the four boys would teach other students the principles of Words Can Hurt, and those students would train other students, and those would train . . . and James understands after that. Their teacher says that he and other teachers would think of students who would be good peer leaders and good candidates for messages about bullying, and the group could meet during lunch as often as they wanted to.

James is so excited! His friends seem excited, too! They already have so many ideas they want to share, and they tumble over each other talking to Mr. Miller.

"Mr. Miller, did you know," James asks him, "that a lot of the things that bullies make fun of other people for are things they can say about themselves?"

Mr. Miller nods. "I did know that. Did you boys figure that out yourselves?" James tells him they did. "That's good, James. I'm glad you've decided there's a way to deal with bullying that doesn't require more bullying. I'm proud of all of you."

## 11. Physical and Cognitive Development in Late Childhood

### Today you will practice the following:

11.1 *Describe school-age children's self-conceptions and motivation.*

11.2 *Examine the roles of friendship, peer acceptance, and peer victimization in school-age children's adjustment.*

11.3 *Discuss family relationships in middle childhood and the influence of family structure on adjustment.*

11.4 *Analyze the role of resilience in promoting adjustment to adversity, including characteristics of children and contexts that promote resilience.*

In fifth grade, James enters a contest hosted by his school district. Students are allowed to submit art in drawing, painting, photography, and sculpture categories. James draws a sketch of the library in Alexandria with a vellum overlay of modern restoration. He gets the idea from a History Channel special on the library, and even though he doesn't win the contest, he gets a yellow ribbon. He enjoys the contest so much he keeps drawing famous world buildings that are so old they're halfway falling down. His dad thinks his drawings are pretty cool, but his friends don't get it.

## 12. Socioemotional Development in Late Childhood

### Today you will practice the following:

*12.1  Summarize the processes by which self-concept, self-esteem, and identity change during adolescence.*

*12.2  Discuss the nature of parent–child relationships in adolescence.*

*12.3  Examine the developmental progression of peer relations in adolescence.*

*12.4  Analyze patterns of adolescent sexual activity including sexual orientation.*

*12.5  Identify common psychological and behavioral problems in adolescence.*

In late elementary school, James sits at the kitchen table every night before dinner to complete his homework. This way, his mom or dad (whoever cooks that night) can answer questions he has, and he's almost always finished before they eat. Then he can do his reading after dinner. It's a good system. He's completing a worksheet on weather systems when he realizes both of his parents are cooking. This is unusual. Whoever doesn't cook gets "alone time" before dinner.

"Why are you both in here?" he asks.

"Noticed that, did you?" Dad asks. "Actually, Mom and I wanted to talk to you when you're done with your homework."

Suspicious, James looks at them. "Did I do something bad?"

"Not at all," his mom tells him, laughing.

"Okay. Hold on then." He answers two more questions about clouds before matching six terms to their definitions. After putting the worksheet in the right folder, he sticks the folder in his book bag and zips it closed. "Done! What's up?"

Mom turns off the stove and pours a pot of pasta into the drainy thing in the sink. "I'm done, too. Joss, can you grab the cheese grater?"

"Hellooo," James calls. "Remember me? The kid you wanted to talk to? You're acting like you're nervous."

"I think we are a little," Dad says. "Here, maybe this will help." He hands James a box wrapped in blue paper.

"A present?" James loves presents.

"Yep."

Unwrapping the box, James pulls out a T-shirt and reads the front of it. If it's a joke, he doesn't get it. He reads it again. Wait a minute. He looks at his parents.

"I'm going to be a brother? You're having a baby?"

"We are," Mom says. "Are you happy?"

"Happy? *Happy?*" James cries. "This is the best news ever!" His parents smile and come to the table to hug him. "Hey, can I teach him Hebrew?"

"Hahaha," Mom laughs. "Sure. You can teach him—or her—all kinds of wonderful things, James."

## 13. Physical and Cognitive Development in Adolescence

### Today you will practice the following:

13.1 Evaluate the "storm and stress" perspective on adolescence in light of research evidence.

13.2 Summarize the physical changes that occur with puberty and the correlates of pubertal timing.

13.3 Discuss brain development during adolescence and its effect on behavior.

13.4 Identify ways in which thinking changes in adolescence and how these changes are reflected in adolescent decision-making and behavior.

13.5 Discuss moral development and influences on moral reasoning.

13.6 Describe the challenges that school transitions pose for adolescents and the role of parents in academic achievement.

James works his way through middle school in a revolving state of annoyance (pimples, cracking voice, and longer, skinnier legs), elation (Sally smiles at him most days between English and French), depression (some days Sally *doesn't* smile at him, and Hebrew isn't a foreign language option at his school), and excitement (he and his friends bring Words Can Hurt to the middle school as an official part of the health curriculum).

There are days he has no idea what to think. He eats the oatmeal his dad fixes for breakfast and tries to decide WWHD on those days. WWHD is What Would Heinz Do? It's a thing they learned in a class where you're supposed to decide if an old guy should steal a drug to cure his dying wife. James is still unsure if there's a right answer, but when he has thousand-mile-an-hour days, he likes to think about the situation. Some days, he thinks it's yes. Some days, he thinks it's no. One thing he knows for sure is that it's a hard question! Like, shouldn't the wife live if she can, even if helping her live means the guy goes to jail? But would she want to live while she's sick and old and stuff if he's in jail? James can't figure it out, but he hopes one day he will.

It's a lot easier with Words Can Hurt. It wasn't always. When he was a kid, he knows, he really wanted to punch everyone that bullied Zack or one of the girls on the playground or basically anyone else. It was hard not to. That's one of the challenges they face when they talk through their Words Can Hurt lessons. There's no "good" pushing, shoving, hitting, and stuff. There may be *necessary* violence sometimes (rarely, he thinks), but there's none that's good. When he was little, he really didn't get that, and he's glad he does now.

He and Zack still eat lunch together every day, although there's no chocolate babka anymore. James has to go to the Parks' house for that now. He and Zack both prefer pizza and fries most days, like today, when Zack sits down with his tray and says, "Hey, you going to ask Sally to the eighth grade formal?"

"What? Where did that come from?" he asks.

"From I heard that she turned down Trevor Martin because she's waiting for you to ask her."

James acknowledges this makes a difference. "That would be a yes then, my very good *yedida*."

## 14. Socioemotional Development in Adolescence

### Today you will practice the following:

*14.1 Summarize the processes by which self-concept, self-esteem, and identity change during adolescence.*

*14.2 Discuss the nature of parent–child relationships in adolescence.*

*14.3 Examine the developmental progression of peer relations in adolescence.*

*14.4 Analyze patterns of adolescent sexual activity, including sexual orientation.*

*14.5 Identify common psychological and behavioral problems in adolescence.*

James has a significant problem. He wants to have sex, but he doesn't want to have sex. Taking his parents at their word that he can talk to them about anything, he asks his dad if they can go for a drive. He decides this is good cover because they're already driving a lot together in preparation for James getting his driver's license in a couple months. Dad says sure, and they strap themselves into the family sedan.

Once on the open road, James is so glad he's the one driving. He knows his dad will look at him, and he's spared looking back by having to keep his eyes facing forward. His dad also can't see James's hands shaking, because he gets to hold tightly to the steering wheel. Yes, this is a good idea.

"Dad?"

"Want some music, son?"

"No, thanks. I, uh—," James clears his throat. "I actually wanted to talk to you about something."

"Oh?" James hears his dad shifting a little in the seat beside him.

"Yeah. Do you mind?"

"Of course not. What's up?"

Pretend casualness. Good. Good, James thinks, that'll help. He hopes his dad keeps it up.

"So, I hoped we could talk a little about sex." Pausing, he rushes on before his dad can speak. "Maybe. I mean, if that's okay, but if it's not, that's okay, too."

"No, it's fine. It's perfectly fine," Dad tells him, and by the soft, even tone of his voice, James knows his dad is trying hard not to freak out. "I do thank you for not bringing this up in front of your sister."

"Dad, she's five." James gives his father a long-suffering sigh. "Okay, so, I haven't gotten anyone pregnant, and I don't have an STD."

"James!"

"I thought that might relieve some worry." They both laugh, and his dad agrees he actually feels a little better knowing that. "But I do have a problem."

"That's fine, James. I'm happy to try to help."

"Yeah, okay, right. Thanks, Dad. I guess I'll just say it. God, this is so embarrassing."

"Don't be embarrassed."

"If I'm not, you'll be embarrassed for me when I finish, but here goes. I'm sure it's not unusual for guys my age to think about having sex or even to *be* having sex, and I'm pleased to say that I am fairly normal in that regard." Realizing what Dad must be thinking, he clarifies, "That I'm thinking about it a lot, not that I'm doing it all the time."

"Okay, also good to know."

"I should tell you that I would—have sex—except that, okay, this is where it's weird. I know girls like me. I've had opportunities to . . . you know."

"Yes, James, I know." His dad coughs.

"Right, well, I could have a lot of times. Most of those times, I even thought about it way before I knew I could. Like maybe I made a date with a girl thinking I could have sex with her later, and then later she indicated that was a definite possibility. But between the beginning of the date and her indication that we could engage in . . . sex, I realized I didn't want to." James grips the steering wheel. "What's wrong with me?"

Dad cracks his knuckles beside him and sits quietly for a minute. "Nothing, James. There's nothing wrong with you."

"Then why does that happen?"

"Do you know when you stop wanting to have sex with someone? Is it after you kiss her, before? Maybe during a conversation?"

"I do," he whispers, thinking about it. "I really do!"

"So? When is it?"

James takes a breath, feeling a little better. "I like talking. Somehow, on dates, we always end up talking about things we like, what our dreams are, that sort of stuff."

Dad says, "Perfectly normal. Adults do that, too."

"Good." James smiles. "But that's it. That when I always want to end a date. I can listen all night to a girl talking about making it big on Broadway or being the next Frida Kahlo, but as soon as I say something about drawing a building or designing a window, she wants to go back to making out. It's a total turnoff."

"And that," his dad says, "is what's called maturity. Son, you don't have to have sex until you want to have sex, and you certainly don't want to have sex just to say you've done it. It's hackneyed but true; you'll know when the time is right."

"So, I'm not weird?" James asks, relieved.

"Oh, God, no. You're very weird but not about that."

"Thanks, Dad."

"You bet. Anytime."

## 15. Physical and Cognitive Development in Emerging/Early Adulthood

> Today you will practice the following:
>
> 15.1 Describe the features and characteristics of emerging and early adulthood.
>
> 15.2 Summarize the physical developments of emerging and early adulthood.
>
> 15.3 Analyze physical and sexual health issues in emerging and early adulthood.
>
> 15.4 Compare postformal reasoning, pragmatic thought, and cognitive-affective complexity.
>
> 15.5 Explain how attending college influences young adults' development, and identify challenges faced by first-generation and nontraditional students.
>
> 15.6 Discuss vocational choice and the transition to work.

James's parents look at the boxes stacked in the foyer. His mom shakes her head. "I just don't understand," she says for the one hundredth time.

"What *I* don't understand," James counters, "is why you aren't grateful it's only this much."

He has four medium-sized packing boxes, a lamp, and three small boxes of books. It will easily fit in his trunk. Even though he doesn't need their help to move into his dorm two hours away, he knows they need to move him in. They'll follow him up there with his ten-year-old sister, Shelby, and help him get settled; then they can have a dinner together before they head home. It'll be nice, and then he'll start his trip into adulthood.

The dorm room is tiny but functional. He doesn't know his roommate, but that's okay. James is easygoing, and Zack's only an hour away. He can do this. After the ten minutes it takes to unpack and make his bed, they decide on oysters and wings. Dad saw a place on the way in, and they head over together. Over dinner, Dad says, "I'm proud of you, James. I know you can change your mind a dozen times about your major—"

"I won't," James says.

"I was going to say, but I suspect you won't. What you're choosing to study and why is really—" Unable to finish, his dad nods his head and smiles.

"Thanks, Dad." James thinks about his choices. He's double majoring in architectural engineering and religious studies and minoring in Hebrew. He's going to work with nonprofit agencies to repair, or rebuild when necessary, houses of worship of all faiths when they've been damaged. He knows that will sometimes be due to catastrophic weather events, but he knows it will more often be due to human violence. "You know," he tells his parents, "I wish I could go back to preschool and tell that kid Keith thank you. If he hadn't bullied Zack that day, I probably wouldn't be doing what I'm doing."

## 16. Socioemotional Development in Emerging/Early Adulthood

### Today you will practice the following:

16.1 Summarize psychosocial development in emerging and early adulthood.

16.2 Discuss influences on friendship and mate selection and interactions in emerging and early adulthood.

16.3 Analyze the diverse romantic situations that may characterize emerging and early adulthood, including singlehood, cohabitation, marriage, and divorce.

16.4 Compare the experiences of young adults as stepparents, never-married parents, and same-sex parents.

James maps out his educational plan. It's going to take him five years to get the dual degree plus his minor. That's if he doesn't make any missteps, particularly missteps that come in the guise of Julie Johnson. Geez, she's beautiful. He'll think about her later, he tells himself, as he works on the homework due in their Comparative Religion class. Later really means now, and just a minute ago, and the minute coming up.

He groans. This is not going to work in his favor. Unless . . . unless he takes her on a date and gets her out of his system. That always works. Resolving to ask her the next lecture period, he's able to put thoughts of her away and work on the reading for their class. He calls Zack at school to get his opinion, and his best friend agrees: get her out of his system.

His parents were right, James admits more than once each week when they talk by telephone. He is insanely busy. He has no idea why he thought he was up to the challenge of two majors plus a minor plus trying to have any sort of life. "You can do it," Mom always tells him. After she says that, he knows he'll have a care package coming in the mail in a few days: homemade chocolate chip cookies, some movie tickets, maybe a book or some Chef Boyardee. He never got to eat that growing up, but she sends it now that he's away. She tucks little letters in there, too—nothing life-altering but sweet and encouraging. Sometimes, it's Dad who sends the boxes. James knows even before he gets to the letter because there's a box of condoms every time.

Every phone conversation, every care package helps. Week by week, he gets closer to his goal. Hanging out with Zack does, too. Zack's the only person he knows who doesn't think he's odd for wanting to build temples and mosques when he's not Jewish or Islamic. He knows he's going to offend some people. He hopes the work eventually speaks for itself. The best months of his college career are definitely June and July after his junior year. He, Zack, Julie (because he was finally in love), and Zack's fiancée Rachel spend the summer in Israel. James wants so much to visit Palestine, but he can only arrange for an escort one afternoon. He leaves the others behind, not wanting to endanger them, and takes in as much as he can. Flying home a few days later, James wonders if architecture can end wars and then chides himself for his hubris.

Julie graduates before James does. Almost all his friends do. Once Julie finishes, they move into a small house off campus so James can finish his coursework and she can get her first "big girl" job as she calls it. They live on the cheap, which they learn how to do listening to James's parents talk about the months when Rosslyn was pregnant with James and Joss had lost his job. As James prepares to graduate the following year, three amazing things happen in the same week. Julie agrees to marry him. He's asked to work for a prominent revitalization non-governmental organization doing architectural engineering—and Julie tells him they're going to have a baby. Maybe not the perfect order, but it's perfect for James, he thinks, as he, his bride, Zack and his wife, James's sister, and their parents stand in a little wood-paneled room in city hall for the wedding ceremony of a lifetime—his lifetime anyway.

## 17. Physical and Cognitive Development in Middle Adulthood

### Today you will practice the following:

*17.1  Summarize age-related physical changes during middle adulthood.*

*17.2  Discuss common health conditions and illnesses and the roles of stress and hardiness on health during middle adulthood.*

*17.3  Contrast the findings of cross-sectional and longitudinal studies of crystallized and fluid intelligence over adulthood.*

*17.4  Analyze changes in cognitive capacities during middle adulthood, including attention, memory, processing speed, and expertise.*

Julie, an insurance actuary, delivers three children in the first ten years of their marriage. James thinks this is different from the ten-year age gap between Shelby and himself. The children are all close, however, and he delights in playing the same dad role that his own father did. There is no "Mom is the nurturer and Dad is the breadwinner" division in their house. It works well, as their two girls and one little boy demonstrate in their own egalitarian lifestyles. It amuses him to see the difference in his parenting and Zack's. He figures it's probably both his parents' influences, but Zack and his wife Rachel raise their children with much more traditional gender expectations, which makes for interesting family get-togethers. James doesn't care. Zack's his brother, and he'd love him if he decided he wanted to *be* a woman.

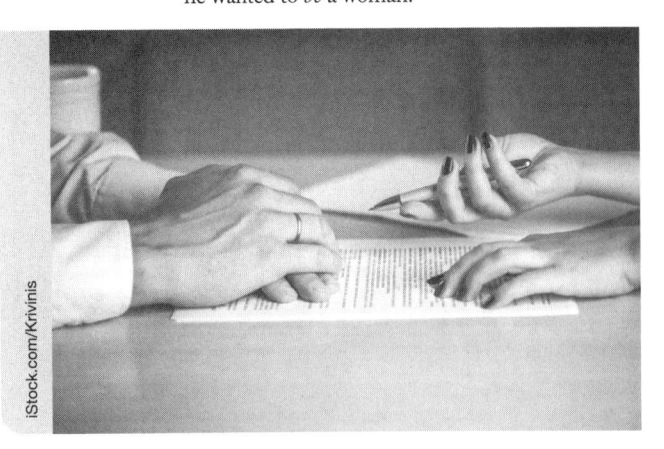

As the children grow, James and Julie begin serious discussions based on an offer James receives from an old employer. Erica Knox wants to launch a new nongovernmental organization specifically geared toward postviolence reconstruction projects. She wants the focus on houses of worship but will accept project proposals from all areas of need. Will James join her? She needs someone with his education and experience. No one else is an expert in this area like he is. After much discussion, he and Julie decide he should go for it. It's a big leap, but it's one he's been ready to make half his life.

## 18. Socioemotional Development in Middle Adulthood

### Today you will practice the following:

*18.1  Summarize the theories and research on psychosocial development during middle adulthood.*

*18.2  Describe the changes that occur in self-concept, identity, and personality during middle adulthood.*

*18.3  Analyze relationships in middle adulthood, including friend, spousal, parent–child, and grandparent relationships.*

*18.4  Discuss influences on job satisfaction and retirement planning during middle adulthood.*

"James." Julie pours a glass of wine and sits at the kitchen table. The lights are off other than the dim one over the stove. The kids are in bed. "James, we have to talk."

It's not the sentence anyone wants to hear, but James had warning. Julie called him at work earlier and asked if they could sit down quietly after the dinner madness and once the kids had gone to bed. Since they met all those years ago, he'd never been able to tell her no about anything. So, he knew this was coming.

He sits with his own beer and nods. "That's what you said earlier. Tell me what's wrong."

She looks at him like he should know, and for the first time in his adult life he wonders what he missed. They make every decision together, parenting the kids and business and houses, all of it.

"I'm really happy with my job," she begins.

"That's great! If you weren't, we really would have to talk."

She ignores his interruption and goes on. "The kids are happy at school with their friends and the other things they have going on. Jim's basketball and Anna's flute lessons. Mary's starting chess lessons next week."

"Babe, I know all of this. What's the problem?"

"The problem is" —she sighs— "that you're here for less and less of it all, and I can't be a single parent to three kids at three different schools and grow my career for the weeks that you run off to Charlottesville or Indianapolis or Atlanta or wherever you are that month."

Sitting very still, James thinks about her words. "You never said," he finally tells her.

"No, I didn't because I love you and I want you to love your career, but it's really hard now that they're getting bigger."

"I can see that."

"We just can't pack up and go with you anymore."

"No. No, I get that."

"I'm not asking you to do something different."

"Okay. Then what are you asking me?"

Julie drinks the last of her wine. Setting the glass carefully on the table, she looks at him and says, "I think we should consider a separation, James."

"What?" He's stunned. Never in his wildest imagination would he have expected that to be her answer. "I don't understand."

"Mom's already said she'll come and help with the kids until I figure things out."

"You've talked to your *mom* about this? Before you talked to me?"

She looks guilty, and he gets to his feet. "Can I at least have a night to think things through?"

"Of course."

James sleeps—lies awake without sleeping—on the couch and considers his options. He can leave the business, find someone else to step into his shoes and work with Erica Knox, his partner. He can do that, get a local job doing design or reconstruction or something he's qualified for and make his wife happy. He wonders for a minute if she's told the kids, but surely she hasn't. They would've acted strangely at dinner, and they hadn't.

But can he? He's still young with a lot of years left to work. Can he leave the thing he loves and that makes him who he is?

Anna tiptoes into the den and sits at the end of the couch where his feet hang over the armrest. He makes room for her and whispers, "Hey, doodlebug. Can't sleep?"

She doesn't ask why he's on the couch for the first time in her 13 years.

"No." Playing with the belt on her robe, she asks, "Can I come with you? Wherever you are? I know I have to finish out the year here, but next year I'm a freshman, and the high school has this long-distance option. I could do that, take my classes online, if you'll let me."

He's touched and desperately wants to say yes. "Why do you want to do that, Anna?" he asks instead. "And why do you think I'm going anywhere?"

"Because I heard Mom talking to Grandma and because I love the weeks we spend with you on location. I love what you do and watching you do it. I love being with you. Think of the education I'll get . . ." she finishes with a devious grin.

"What about Mom and your brother and sister? What about the flute?"

"Are you telling me I can't play the flute anywhere but here? Pah! Besides, Jim's going to college in a couple years, and I bet you a hundred bucks Mary'll want to live with you when she can, too. Of course, I'll probably be in college then, too," she says, wrinkling her brow as she does the math. "Please, Dad?"

"You sound like you're sure I'll go instead of staying here."

"Oh, God. Seriously? Look, I know you love Mom, and Mary's going to pitch a fit, but come on. Who's going to do what you do if you don't? People need you, Dad, and you need to do the work."

"You guys need me, too."

"I don't think you're going to poof out of our lives. I just think you'll stay somewhere else on the weeks between jobs. We'll adjust."

"You are a wise and pragmatic child, Anna Albert."

"Then that's a yes?"

"That's a yes."

## 19. Physical and Cognitive Development in Late Adulthood

### Today you will practice the following:

*19.1 Discuss age-related changes in brain and body systems in late adulthood, and identify ways that older adults may compensate for changes.*

*19.2 Identify risk and protective factors for health in late adulthood.*

*19.3 Summarize common dementias, including characteristics, risk and protective factors, and treatment.*

*19.4 Analyze patterns of cognitive change in late adulthood.*

When James is in his 50s, his dad suffers a single, fatal heart attack. Two years later, his mom has a series of small strokes that leave her bedridden until she, too, passes away. Although active due to his work and still fit for his age, as enters his later years, James becomes increasingly concerned about his own cardiovascular health. He begins having an annual checkup with a general practitioner and for the first time in his life takes up jogging. He jogs a mile each morning and, if not particularly graceful or enthusiastic, feels like he's doing his part to keep himself heart healthy. He doesn't eat fried food and steers clear of as much sugar as he can. He does have a fondness for cake.

Anna, his darling girl, has married and given him grandchildren who are doting. One grandson runs with him a time or two a week whenever he's not on location, and this pleases James particularly. Zack joins him most days when he's in town, too. They're both concerned with growing older. Jim and Mary are also married with children, although Mary has divorced and is raising her two girls by herself. Both live farther away than he'd like, but he sees them enough to remember their faces even if he is getting old, and he is definitely getting old. All the years of drawing fine lines and angles, tiny numbers, and labeling letters on graph paper have caught up with him. He wears glasses he's pretty well blind without. He doesn't complain much because without the bifocals he can't work his daily crossword puzzle. He's convinced the crossword keeps him mentally sharp, and his doctor tells him it probably does.

# 20. Socioemotional Development in Late Adulthood

## Today you will practice the following:

20.1 Examine the contributions of self-concept, personality, and religiosity to older adults' well-being.

20.2 Identify social contexts in which older adults live and their influence on development.

20.3 Summarize features of older adults' relationships with friends, spouses, children, and grandchildren, and identify how these relationships affect older adults' functioning.

20.4 Discuss influences on the timing of retirement and adaptation to retirement.

"Dad?"

"Hmm?" James looks up from his crossword puzzle. "Seven-letter word for 'arrogant walk.' Ends with *r*."

"*Swagger*," Anna says.

"That's it! Thanks, love."

"You're welcome. Now put your pencil down. You've got a letter."

"Eh? From whom?" She lays the letter on top of his newspaper, and he eyes the return address. The Albert Schweitzer Foundation. "What's this?"

"Dad! Open it!"

His daughter—fifty years old and sounds like she's fifteen, he thinks, laughing. "Okay, okay." Using the pencil as a letter opener, he slits the flap and pulls out a sheet of paper. He peers through the glasses slipping down his nose and reads. "I don't understand. This says I'm getting a prize. A medal?"

"I knew it!" She grabs the letter and reads it more quickly than he did. "Dad! You're getting the Gold Medal for Humanitarianism. It's one of the biggest awards in the world, like a Nobel or a Pulitzer."

"Well, what'dya know?" James stands and moves to the counter. "Tomato sandwich, Anna?"

"Oh, Dad. We're going out to celebrate. Champagne and caviar and—"

"I don't like caviar."

She laughs. "Champagne and cheeseburgers then." She comes over and hugs him. "You're too thin, Dad. I am so proud of you."

"Now? It takes a medal for you to be proud of me?"

"No. Of course not. It's all the things that led to the medal. Come on, let's go." She takes him to lunch at the Grand Lux, and while they sip the promised champagne, she asks, "Will you retire now?"

"Oh, I don't think so. What would I do with the time?"

"I don't know. Write a book? Design a cathedral? *Relax*."

James waves an absent hand at her. "I do all those when I'm on location, and the sex is better."

"Dad!" she says, laughing hysterically.

"What? I'm not even 80 yet."

## 21. Experience With Death and Dying

> Today you will practice the following:
>
> *21.1 Identify ways in which death has been defined and end-of-life issues that may arise.*
>
> *21.2 Contrast children's, adolescents', and adults' understanding of death.*
>
> *21.3 Discuss the physical and emotional process of dying as it is experienced over the lifespan.*
>
> *21.4 Summarize typical grief reactions to the loss of loved ones and the influence of development on bereavement.*

James is under contract with an Episcopalian congregation to design a new cathedral in their community. Their old church has nothing wrong with it, but they recently arranged to donate all their facilities to a small, nondenominational congregation largely composed of Latino immigrants meeting in a warehouse. The Episcopalian priest assures everyone involved that the Latino congregation can meet in the fellowship hall until the new church is built, and there's room for everyone. James has rarely been so touched and begins work on the design as soon as he gets the contract.

The priest provides James with a tiny apartment above the rectory for as long as he's on location. It's a comfortable space even if he does feel every stair in his knees at the end of the day. Small price to pay, he thinks, when he starts work each day. This is the culmination of every dream he's ever had for his work, and he takes all lines, angles, stones, and windows as seriously as he did his children—and Julie, he admits to himself with a twinge of sadness and guilt. When he finishes the initial sketches and shares them with the priest, he feels exceptionally good about the work, and the priest is thrilled.

Before work begins on the foundation, James takes one of the initial sketches of the cathedral, a 40° angle of the front and right side, and has the sketch professionally framed and shipped to Anna with a little note taped to the string holding the paper wrap over the frame. Having finished that, he spends a few hours each day watching the construction on the church to cap his career. When the windows are fitted into the gray stone walls, he buys himself a beer and goes to sleep happy and fulfilled. He has regrets, like Julie, who remarried and let another man help finish raising Jim and Mary, although Anna had been right. Mary spent the last two years of high school traveling with him. Anna had also been right about his weeks at home. He kept a small place, and the kids spent every day with him there and all their summers with him wherever he was. Other than the painful death of his marriage, much of his life remained the same. He feels good now and realizes Julie had been right.

He knows the priest will call on the telephone. So, he tidies his things in his room and leaves a small note with the words "Thank you, James" lying on his nightstand. He figures he might not die tonight, but it's coming soon. Age gets us all, he says to himself, and it does. James dies a week before the opening of the cathedral, and the priest calls Anna as he requested some days before. As his note on the framed sketch demanded, Anna waited until the call came before opening the wrap. Through the tears of her loss, she snips the string and pulls off the paper.

"Oh, Dad," she says, sniffing.

She examines the cathedral, the position beneath an ancient oak tree, the sun glinting off the stained-glass windows. Then she stares harder at the windows. Moving down the row of them, she recognizes the faces of her family in each biblical figure: her mom, Uncle Zack, Jim, Mary, herself. Clever Dad. It was so beautiful. She knows exactly where to hang it, but first, she has to call Uncle Zack, her brother, and her sister. This will be the hardest day of her life.

# CASE DISCUSSION QUESTIONS

1. During his mother Rosslyn's pregnancy with him, James's father, Joss, loses his job, which also provides the family's health insurance. They tighten their belts for a while, and shortly after James is born, Joss finds new employment. How might James's early life have been affected across any or all domains (biological, cognitive, and socioemotional) both positively and negatively if Joss had more difficulty finding a new job?

2. In early childhood, James makes a friend named Zack, and they will be friends for life. Because of Zack, James develops a strong distaste for bullies (and later terrorists). He also learns Hebrew and begins a fascination with world religions, houses of worship, and the people who populate them. This directly influences James's career path. How might James's life have been different if he hadn't met Zack?

3. In middle adulthood, Julie, James's wife Julie asks for a divorce. She raises logical complaints about their home life (e.g., James's travel makes it impossible for him to help with chauffeuring children every day). However, the very nature of her complaints strikes at the heart of who James is. How might James have salvaged his marriage? Was it doomed at this point?

4. James's entire life occurs over many decades that are, loosely, contemporary. Cars, telephones, televisions, and so on exist, but era-specific technology isn't presented (e.g., cell phones, space shuttles, or artificial intelligence). Would James's life have been different if he were born in a specific period, earlier or later? If so, how? Be specific.

# 4 Riley Everett

## Introduction

Welcome to your case study!

Congratulations! You will follow the lifespan of baby girl Riley Everett. Try to use your best judgment, textbook, classmates, instructor, and supplementary resources to make the best decisions to help her grow.

This semester you will observe Riley as she grows from infant to child to teen to adult. Who will she become in your care? Will you understand and agree with all decisions available within her circumstances? How will you feel about the tough decisions that forever shape her path in life?

## Meet Riley Everett

Riley is the first daughter of Kari Simmons and Mason Everett. Kari is 29 years old and is not involved in Riley's life. Mason is 32 years old. He has a high school diploma and works regularly but not full-time as a construction worker. To make ends meet, he has a second job working the counter in an auto parts store some evenings and weekends. Despite both jobs, Mason's income puts him just below the federal poverty line when accounting for Riley. He lives in a two-bedroom trailer that he makes payments on but is located on several acres of land owned by his parents.

Through this case study and your lifespan course, you will be asked to consider decisions regarding Riley's physical, emotional, and cognitive growth and development from several perspectives: her father Mason's and her grandparents' as well as those of her spouse, her potential children, other potential family members, friends, teachers, doctors,' and supervisors.

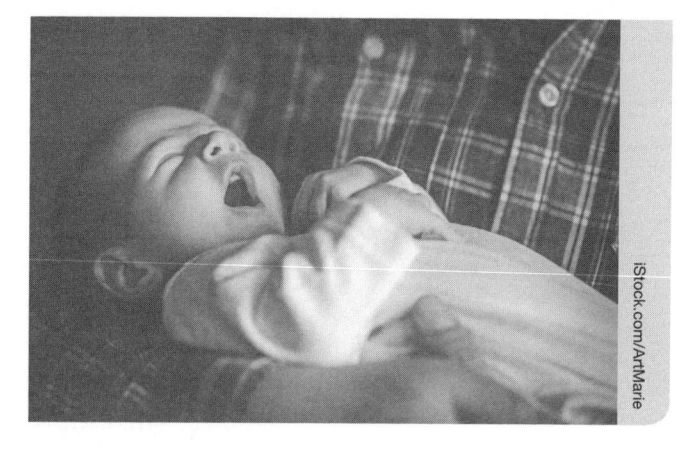

Now let's get started.

## 1. Development and Its Influences

### Today you will practice the following:

1.1 Outline five principles of the lifespan developmental perspective.

1.2 Explain three theoretical controversies about human development.

1.3 Summarize five theoretical perspectives on human development.

1.4 Describe the methods and research designs used to study human development.

Kari and Mason don't know one another well when Riley is conceived. They've been seeing each other casually for a couple of months, and the relationship, such as it is, could go either way, but Kari is arrested for trafficking methamphetamines. This isn't Kari's first drug offense, and she is sentenced to 18 months in prison. During her early weeks of incarceration, she realizes she's pregnant and reaches out to Mason. Early prenatal questioning leads to evidence that the baby might be impaired due to Kari's drug use. Kari wants Mason to pay money while she's in prison or give the baby away to a family that will pay or some support other solution she can't think of just now, but Mason petitions the family court to grant him sole custody with no visitation for Kari. The judge agrees and grants Riley's custody to Mason.

## 2. Biological and Environmental Foundations

### Today you will practice the following:

2.1  Discuss the genetic foundations of development.

2.2  Identify examples of genetic disorders and chromosomal abnormalities.

2.3  Discuss the choices available to prospective parents in having healthy children.

2.4  Describe the interaction of heredity and environment, including behavioral genetics and the epigenetic framework.

Prenatal examination and history taking uncover that Kari may have used meth for as many as nine weeks during her pregnancy before her arrest. This would've allowed for her drug use to affect her growing baby. During the 12th week of her pregnancy, decreased utero-placental blood flow and increased fetal blood pressure are detected. Kari's physical health is quite poor but stabilized by the prison doctors. Riley, named for Mason's beloved grandmother whose maiden name was Riley, enters the world five weeks early, small, and highly reactive. She's removed from Kari's immediate care as soon as she can be and taken to the prison nursery, where she's watched over by pediatric nursing specialists. It's difficult to know in the early days what may or may not be developmentally compromised in her due to Kari's drug use, but externally, she looks good. They say that she's a fighter, a little dragon. The doctors tell Mason the rest is a waiting game and give him some educational material on meth use during pregnancy as well as information on support groups local to his area. Mason takes her home once the doctors tell him she's able to be cared for outside the prison hospital.

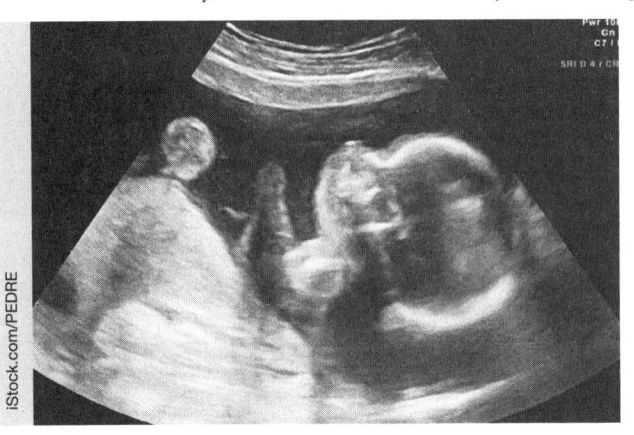

## 3. Prenatal Development, Birth, and Newborn Experience

### Today you will practice the following:

3.1  Describe the three periods of prenatal development that begin with conception.

3.2  Identify how exposure to teratogens can influence the prenatal environment.

3.3  Explain the process of childbirth.

3.4  Discuss the neonate's physical capacities, including development in low-birth-weight infants.

Riley is a lovely baby. She isn't round and fat like so many babies Mason's seen. Okay, most of those are on television shows, so he probably doesn't know much about babies at all, but Riley's different. She's long and kind of skinny. The pediatrician at the county health center says that might be genetic (Mason's sort of thin himself, and so is Kari, but she's a meth addict, so who knows about her), or it might be a result of Kari's drug use. It might be a combination of both, and they may never know. It doesn't seem to be impacting her health, he's reassured. All of her is long, though—her neck, her legs, her arms, her toes, and her fingers.

"Musician's fingers," his mother tells him while she rocks Riley after dinner one night. "Mark my words."

Mason grunts at his mother. "You're just mad that I quit piano in fifth grade."

"You played so well."

"I played 'Mary Had a Little Lamb,' Mom. Let's not exaggerate."

She laughs. "Okay. So maybe you weren't Mozart." Riley burps, and his mother shifts her to her shoulder. "What a good girl. Give Granny another one like that." She looks at Mason. "You have to go back to work soon."

"I know." He sighs. "I don't want to. I don't think she's ready to be left with a stranger. She still gets so upset all the time. How do I tell a babysitter or whoever to keep the lights dim because Riley's sensitive to rooms that are too bright or to play music when she's cranky because that seems to soothe her?"

"Why would you want to?"

"I just said I didn't!"

His mother cradles Riley again. "Remember that party we had last month?"

"What? Your retirement party?"

She smiles. "One and the same. Look, your dad keeps the blinds closed all day 'cause of his glaucoma, and you can't just play any music for this girl. She has taste, Mason. Leave her with me. Save yourself the money and the worry. Riley and her granny'll have a grand ol' time while Daddy's at work, won't we, sweetheart?"

Relieved to know his daughter will be safe, loved, and understood, he admits that he's sure they will.

## 4. Physical Development in Infancy and Toddlerhood

### Today you will practice the following:

4.1  *Discuss growth and the role of nutrition in development during infancy and toddlerhood.*

4.2  *Summarize brain development during infancy and toddlerhood.*

4.3  *Compare infants' early learning capacities for habituation, classical conditioning, operant conditioning, and imitation.*

4.4  *Describe infants' developing sensory abilities.*

4.5  *Analyze the roles of maturation and contextual factors in infant and toddler motor development.*

Unlike Riley's mother Kari, Mason never used any drugs of any type. He never smoked. He did drink with fair regularity but not after he brings Riley home. He has to put any spare pennies he has toward her care, and even if he didn't, he figures she deserves a substance-free upbringing given how her little life started out. If someone offers him a beer at dinner, he accepts, but he doesn't buy it anymore, and he's completely done with the bar scene.

The clarity of winning custody of his baby and keeping her life as pure and innocent as it can be pays off. He tells himself it does anyway. The pediatrician keeps telling him how great his baby dragon's doing at every checkup. She's growing and eating well, and she meets all the important milestones the doctor asks about. She sits up and crawls on time; she walks and runs. She doesn't like sleeping alone, and many nights Mason lets her sleep with him. He has a lot of talks with the pediatrician about co-sleeping. She tells him there's some evidence that co-sleeping increases the risk of sudden infant death syndrome (SIDS), although there's other evidence to the contrary. She explains, too, that the norms around co-sleeping are culturally bound and that Western culture tends to gravitate away from co-sleeping. If he thinks having Riley in bed with him is best, she says, "Use only a sheet and make sure you're on a firm mattress." Mason nods, "I do, but I also usually sit up and let her sleep on my chest." The doctor says that probably means he's not sleeping well.

Mason doesn't care. He says he'll sleep when she goes to Kindergarten.

The most amazing thing has been Riley's temperament. She remains sensitive to light and to overstimulation, but his mom notices her reaction to music early on. She's easily calmed by music as long as it's the right music. She likes classical, particularly sonatas for piano and violin. Those seem to be at just the right pitch to soothe her irritability. Now Mason and his mom play games to figure out which are her favorites. Bach? Wagner? No, not Wagner. Haydn? Brahms. It's definitely Brahms most days, but she likes Haydn, too.

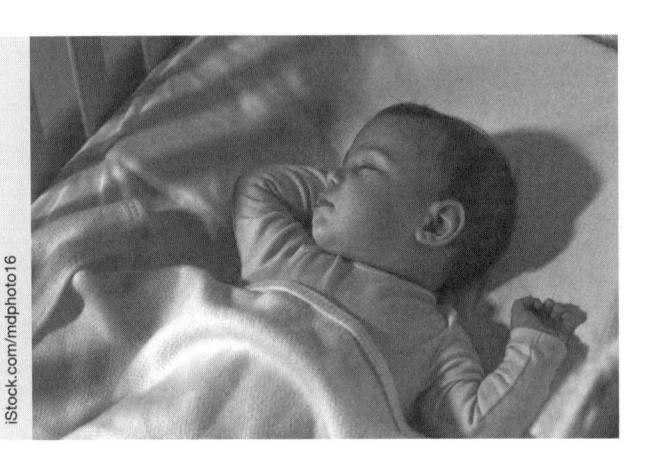

## 5. Cognitive Development in Infancy and Toddlerhood

### Today you will practice the following:

5.1 *Discuss the cognitive-developmental perspective on infant reasoning.*

5.2 *Describe the information processing system in infants.*

5.3 *Discuss individual differences in infant intelligence.*

5.4 *Summarize the patterns of language development during infancy and toddlerhood.*

It seems to Mason that every day when he gets to Mom's to pick up Riley, she's learned ten new words. He knows she hasn't, of course, but it seems like it. Just a couple months ago, she could say *dada* and *more* and *no*, and pretty much he was the only one who knew what she was saying. Now, it's like she knows the whole dictionary, or at least she babbles like she does, and sometimes he can pick out lots of real words. He has no idea how it happened. She talks to him all the time—not so much to anyone else other than his mom and dad. It's okay that she's a little anxious around strangers. He's just amazed at the words.

Until he buys the keyboard.

One day, they're in Walmart shopping for diapers. He knows he has to start toilet training her, but he doesn't want to. He's so happy with her being little. So, they're buying diapers, and he there's an endcap with these little electric keyboards on sale for $20. Mason never spends extra money, but she loves music so much. What the heck. He sticks the keyboard in the shopping cart and watches her eyes as she struggles to turn around and look at the packaging. Once they get home, he opens the box and curses at himself for forgetting batteries. He steals them from the remote. When does he watch TV anymore anyway? A minute later, Riley is happily plucking a note here and there. Ten minutes later, she has her long neck turned to the side and her head bent at an angle as she picks out bars of tunes he knows she's heard before. He'll look back in later years and remember that this was the night she stopped incessantly babbling and began incessantly playing the piano.

He had one thought that night. *Mom's going to be happy.*

## 6. Socioemotional Development in Infancy and Toddlerhood

### Today you will practice the following:

6.1 Summarize the psychosocial tasks of infancy and toddlerhood.

6.2 Describe emotional development in infancy, and identify contextual and cultural influences on emotional development in infants and toddlers.

6.3 Identify the styles and stability of temperament, including the role of goodness of fit in infant development.

6.4 Describe how attachment develops in infancy and toddlerhood.

6.5 Differentiate the roles of self-concept, self-recognition, and self-control in infant development.

Some days, it amazes Mason how one little step can make all the others so simple. He stopped all drinking and carrying on with his friends when Riley was born. After that, he's able to rearrange his work schedules just enough that he can start taking a couple of classes at the local community college. It's a bear—the time commitment between two jobs, two classes, and a newborn. Mom helps, and he figures this is the time, when Riley's so tiny that he can love on her when he gets home, but she doesn't even count time like big people do. As exhausted as he is most days of the week and most months of the year, he makes it work. By the time she's walking, he has three classes left to take to earn his associate's degree in electrical engineering, and his boss promised him full-time, full-benefits work when he completes it. That's the goal, he keeps telling himself.

Mom's still looking after Riley, for which he's so glad. His beautiful girl gets so anxious that it scares him sometimes. She's such an affectionate child with her family, openly loving and giving without any reservations. She'll smile at strangers when she's out with him or his parents, but otherwise, she doesn't show any interest in them and seems to ignore them if they show interest in her. He hopes she'll become more comfortable with other people in the future. She'll have to go to preschool eventually—Kindergarten, high school one day. He makes a mental note to talk to the pediatrician about it at her next checkup.

## 7. Physical and Cognitive Development in Early Childhood

### Today you will practice the following:

7.1 *Discuss physical development in early childhood.*

7.2 *Compare Piaget's cognitive-developmental and Vygotsky's sociocultural perspectives on cognitive development in early childhood.*

7.3 *Describe information-processing abilities during early childhood.*

7.4 *Summarize young children's advances in language development.*

7.5 *Contrast social learning and cognitive-developmental perspectives on moral development in early childhood.*

7.6 *Identify and explain approaches to early childhood education.*

It's Sunday, and Riley sits in her closet crying. She's trying to be quiet so Daddy won't hear her. She's pretty good at being quiet, but her nose is running. If she sniffs *or* blows, he'll hear her. She'll just let it run. She can hear him walking around their house and calling for her. Maybe he'll get tired of looking.

"*Riley! Come out!* This is silly."

Maybe not—she pulls her knees to her chest and holds her breath. It's really hard with all the snot in her nose. She hears him stop in her doorway and lets out the breath. Reaching toward the door to her closet, she knocks lightly. His steps come closer, and he speaks to her through the door.

"Hey."

"Hey, Daddy."

"Wanna talk about it?"

"No."

"Let's start this over." He coughs. "Hey."

"Hey, Daddy."

"Let's talk about this."

"Okay, Daddy."

"You're worried about tomorrow?"

"Yeah."

"I'm going to be with you the whole time, baby dragon. If anything goes wrong, what'll we do?"

Riley gets to her knees and pushes open the door so she can look up at him. "Breathe fire on 'em. Take no prisoners!"

"You got it. Now, come on out. Let's figure out the trouble."

She crawls out from the closet and onto Daddy's lap when he sits at the end of her bed. He hugs her close. That makes her feel better. Then he sticks the end of his sleeve in her face. She uses it to wipe her nose.

"Thanks."

"Anytime. We call this neo-chivalry." He plucks at her knee. "Cool pajamas."

She looks at the red pants with dragons flying all over them. They make her feel strong and powerful.

"Me, too. They were a birthday present." This is a game they play.

"Yeah? From anyone I know?"

Riley giggles and hugs him. "From you, Daddy!"

"That's right, baby dragon. Now, tell me why you were crying. And hiding! Because that's new."

"I'm scared," she whispers into his neck.

"Scared? Of what?"

"Tomorrow. I *told you*."

Daddy pats her back. "Are you afraid of the school or the people in the school?"

"Both," she admits, thinking about the new preschool she's supposed to start the next week. She doesn't want to go to school with a lot of kids she doesn't know!

"Want me to tell you a secret?"

"Okay."

"They have a piano, and Tuesdays are music days."

Well, maybe she can at least *try* it and see how things go.

As it happens, it goes very well. Riley likes preschool a lot. Her teacher tells her dad that she's doing well with reading, writing, and the math games they play. She also tells Daddy that Riley is a little quiet and doesn't play with the other children much. This is true, Riley thinks, listening. They're loud, and they run around all the time. The noise and movement make her wish she were a turtle with a shell she could climb into for protection instead of a girl with pretty brown braids her daddy puts in her hair every morning. No, she reckons, she really doesn't play much with the other children.

# 8. Socioemotional Development in Early Childhood

## Today you will practice the following:

8.1  Discuss young children's emerging sense of initiative, self-concept, and self-esteem.

8.2  Summarize the development of emotional understanding, regulation, and behavior in early childhood.

8.3  Identify four parenting styles and their associations with child outcomes.

8.4  Compare biological, cognitive, and contextual theoretical explanations of gender role development.

8.5  Explain the function of play and the form it takes during early childhood.

At a late-year parent–teacher conference with Riley's dad, her teacher tells him that Riley's doing better with her friends. She takes a long time to "open up," her teacher says. Riley doesn't know what that means, and she's not sure if it's good or bad. She'll ask Daddy later. Her teacher also says that Riley is a "very loyal friend." That sounds pretty good. She does have a friend. Her name is Holly, and she has two mothers. Riley has no mothers. Sometimes, if people ask, she says her mom is dead. She doesn't have a reason for saying it except that she doesn't really know where her mom is or why she doesn't have one. It's also easier. Holly has two moms because her grandma adopted her when her mama had her when she was "very young." The whole thing sounds weird to Riley, but she also thinks she's pretty weird without a mom.

She likes Holly and tries to teach her some piano when they get to visit the music room, but Holly doesn't understand. None of the other kids do, and Riley really doesn't know why that is at all. Her dad says it's like the monkey bars. All the other kids fly across them, but Riley can barely hang on one for a few seconds. She can play Bach after listening to a sonata once, but they can't play a scale. She gets that okay, she thinks, but it still seems a little funny to her. The only bad part about preschool is that it's going to end soon, and then she'll have to start Kindergarten with a bunch of new children she doesn't know. That makes her want to go back to the closet and hide again.

The best part about preschool happens on two days in May. The first is when Granny and Grandpa take her to Daddy's school. She gets to watch him graduate. He wears a silly black dress and a pointy hat, and they take lots of pictures together. She doesn't like pictures. She doesn't like the flashes, but it's over soon. After that, Daddy's home a lot more at night, and he doesn't work at the auto store anymore. He buys her a tiny yellow hard hat to match his big one and takes her to visit the construction site where he's working all the time now while she's in school. The noise is scary, but he reminds her that she's a fierce baby dragon, and no hammer can stand up to her fire. She rides on his shoulders and shakes hands with all the people he knows. It's the best day of her life, and she loves her daddy more than anyone in the whole world.

## 9. Physical and Cognitive Development in Middle Childhood

### Today you will practice the following:

9.1  Identify patterns of physical and motor development during middle childhood and common health issues facing school-age children.

9.2  Discuss school-age children's capacities for reasoning and processing information.

9.3  Summarize views of intelligence including the uses, correlates, and criticisms of intelligence tests.

9.4  Examine patterns of moral development during middle childhood.

9.5  Summarize language development during middle childhood.

9.6  Discuss children's learning at school.

Riley works her way through elementary school feeling like she's in a cocoon sometimes. It's not a bad feeling. If she doesn't mentally separate herself, she feels like everything around her—the other kids, the teachers yelling, the bright lights in the halls and classrooms, just everything—is too much. She gets anxious and nauseous and wants to go home. She closes herself off just enough to feel warm and safe. Dad is her biggest fan, she knows this, and he talks to the principal and to her teachers every year to make sure they understand there's not something wrong with her; she's just shy and a little sensitive to light and noise. Every year, they're nice about it and don't treat her like a freak (except third grade, but Daddy took care of that and fast), and he always hands her off the first day of school with a hug and a "Go get 'em, baby dragon." With so much support, she manages to make good, if not perfect, grades and plow through these early years quietly but successfully.

## 10. Socioemotional Development in Middle Childhood

### Today you will practice the following:

10.1  Describe school-age children's self-conceptions and motivation.

10.2  Examine the roles of friendship, peer acceptance, and peer victimization in school-age children's adjustment.

10.3  Discuss family relationships in middle childhood and the influence of family structure on adjustment.

10.4  Analyze the role of resilience in promoting adjustment to adversity, including characteristics of children and contexts that promote resilience.

Jasmine is Riley's BFF. Literally, Riley tells Daddy with emphasis: *best friend forever*. Mason says he understands and agrees to let Jasmine spend the night on an upcoming Friday. He's thrilled for Riley, who has been so shy all her life with everyone but family, but he's also worried. He and Riley have just moved for the first time in her life out of the two-bedroom trailer he had on his parents' land into a small three-bedroom cottage he built with his own two hands on an acre and a half of land he bought from them with cash he saved before starting the construction. He's never been so proud of anything in his life as he is of that house with the exception of Riley. But he's got boxes everywhere, a couple rooms that still need painting, and one that needs furniture. It doesn't look like the sort of place a parent would let a child sleep over.

"Please, Daddy, please!"

Riley would never consent to sleeping anywhere else yet, and even having someone else to their house is a big step for her. Mason caves.

"You bet, baby dragon. Just get me a phone number so I can talk to one of her parents."

"Thank you, Daddy!"

After speaking a couple times with Jasmine's mother, Philippa, it's decided that Mason will pick up both little girls from school on Friday, and Philippa will collect Jasmine from his house on Saturday sometime after lunch. It's a solid plan, and Mason prepares by buying hotdogs and potato chips and a half-gallon of the ice cream that Riley tells him on Thursday is Jasmine's favorite.

"Where's your coat," he asks as he makes the shopping list.

"I lost it," she says and points at the list. "Coke, too, please."

"This is all junk food. You know how I feel about junk food."

"You buy carrots. We might eat them."

He laughs and figures they'll talk about the coat later.

When he picks them up on Friday, two giggly little girls climb into the backseat of his late-model sedan. He smiles and says hello to Jasmine, who is an adorable eight-year-old Native American child. Turning back to the wheel, he spots another girl running to a school bus with a backpack bouncing off her shoulders with each step. She's wearing an unusual brown swing coat with white and pale blue dots the size of ping pong balls all over it.

"Riley?" he asks.

"Yes, Daddy?"

"Riley, is that your coat?"

She cranes her long neck to stare out the window. "Yes, Daddy."

"I thought you said you lost it."

"I did. Lydia asked for it, and I gave it to her. So, I lost it to Lydia."

"Hmm." Mason turns an evil eye on her. "Riley, that's not losing something."

"It's not?"

"No."

"Oh, it's okay, Mr. Everett. Riley gives people things all the time. If someone needs something and she has it, she just gives it to them. She's really nice that way."

Mason could think of a word other than *nice* but kept his mouth closed. Looks like he needs to buy his daughter a new coat—and have a talk with her about the ethics of sharing versus being taken advantage of.

# 11. Physical and Cognitive Development in Late Childhood

## Today you will practice the following:

*11.1* Describe school-age children's self-conceptions and motivation.

*11.2* Examine the roles of friendship, peer acceptance, and peer victimization in school-age children's adjustment.

*11.3* Discuss family relationships in middle childhood and the influence of family structure on adjustment.

*11.4* Analyze the role of resilience in promoting adjustment to adversity, including characteristics of children and contexts that promote resilience

In second grade, Riley's teacher arranges for her to spend time in the music room every morning before class starts, every day after lunch for a few minutes when the music teacher has her planning period, and every day during recess if Riley wants to skip going outside. It's the most wonderful gift anyone's ever given her. Playing before school starts lets her calm away any nervousness she has in the morning, and if she gets anxious during the day for any reason, she knows she's got two times to look forward to playing. She has no words to thank her teacher and the music teacher for what they've given her. Her dad is happy about it, too, when he sees her grades improve a little bit—she's not a *bad* student after all—and works with all her teachers until she finishes elementary school to allow her the same access.

# 12. Socioemotional Development in Late Childhood

## Today you will practice the following:

*12.1* Summarize the processes by which self-concept, self-esteem, and identity change during adolescence.

*12.2* Discuss the nature of parent–child relationships in adolescence.

*12.3* Examine the developmental progression of peer relations in adolescence.

*12.4* Analyze patterns of adolescent sexual activity including sexual orientation.

*12.5* Identify common psychological and behavioral problems in adolescence.

Riley doesn't talk to anyone at school about the music room and playing the piano. It's not that she's trying to hide anything. Really, she just doesn't know how to talk about what those minutes mean to her. Ms. Fleming, the music teacher, talks to her one day during her after-lunch time. She tells Riley how pretty her playing is and how much she likes to listen to her while she's lesson planning. This makes Riley a little shy but also happy. Ms. Fleming then asks her if she would like Ms. Fleming to give her some piano lessons. "Mostly theory," the teacher says, "because you already know how to play." Riley wants to say yes so much. She starts to and then stops. She knows they don't have the money for it and wouldn't dare ask her dad to pay for lessons when he just finished building their house and buying her a new coat. "Riley, we don't have to tell anyone here," Ms. Fleming says, "and it won't cost you anything. I just want to help."

Riley blows out a breath and smiles. "Oh, yes, please! Thank you!"

## 13. Physical and Cognitive Development in Adolescence

### Today you will practice the following:

13.1 Evaluate the "storm and stress" perspective on adolescence in light of research evidence.

13.2 Summarize the physical changes that occur with puberty and the correlates of pubertal timing.

13.3 Discuss brain development during adolescence and its effect on behavior.

13.4 Identify ways in which thinking changes in adolescence and how these changes are reflected in adolescent decision-making and behavior.

13.5 Discuss moral development and influences on moral reasoning.

13.6 Describe the challenges that school transitions pose for adolescents and the role of parents in academic achievement.

Riley's progress through elementary school teaches her two things. First, she's never going to be an athlete. Second, she can use music to help her learn better in her classes by connecting content from each class to certain types of music she studies with. Math is Haydn. English is instrumental soundtracks like *Star Wars* and *Last of the Mohicans*. Science is hard rock. Social Studies is indie and grunge. It works.

Of course, she has to study with headphones in the semi-dark in her room, but her dad says whatever helps is what she should do. Maybe what she does wouldn't work for Jasmine or someone else, but it works for her. She screws up her courage for middle school knowing she can fall back on her quirky strategies to keep herself successful.

At the checkup just before sixth grade starts, her doctor tells Dad that she's healthy and doesn't have to have meds for her anxiety and how stressed she gets when it's loud or too bright. She also says that it would be okay for her to have meds if she wants them. Dad leaves it up to her. She doesn't want them right now, but she'll keep the idea in reserve just in case. It's nice to know she has the safety net.

When she's alone with the doctor, she tells her that she's worried about her period. It hasn't started yet, but Jasmine's has and a lot of other girls that she knows. The doctor reassures her. She tells Riley that because Riley's thin and has coped with chronic stress since her birth due to an underactive behavioral inhibition system (this is a new term for Riley, and she makes a note of it), she might be a little later having her first period. She also says this is normal and nothing to be concerned about. Relieved, Riley leaves with a tetanus booster and her last HPV vaccine. That one always hurts, but her dad says it's important.

After the doctor, her dad drives her across town, away from their house.

"Dad? Where are we going?"

"Surprise, and before you say it, I know you don't like surprises. It won't be a real surprise. I promise. Just a tiny one. I want to show you a place, and you don't even have to get out of the car."

"Okay . . ." She remains skeptical but feels less uncertain. When they pull into a small parking lot behind a brick building at the branch campus of the state university that's near them, she looks at him and raises a brow. "You want me to go to college here in six years?"

"Nope. I hope you go somewhere better, although wherever you go is fine with me. Honey, that building over there with the white columns?"

"Yeah?"

"That's the music building, and they've got a piano instructor who's going to start giving you a lesson every week. I just wanted to bring you over and show you so that you could get your worrying out of the way ahead of time."

"What? Dad, how are we paying for this?" She doesn't know whether to be awed or terrified. Both, she figures as she thinks about meeting a new teacher the following week.

"'We' are cutting out your allowance and your Friday six-pack of Red Bull."

"Har-dee-har," she scoffs. "Please be serious."

"I've been saving, and your granny pitched in."

Riley knows she's hit the lotto jackpot of dads and has to swipe away a rogue tear that has the gumption to sneak out of her eye. "Thanks, Dad. You're the best." He really is, too.

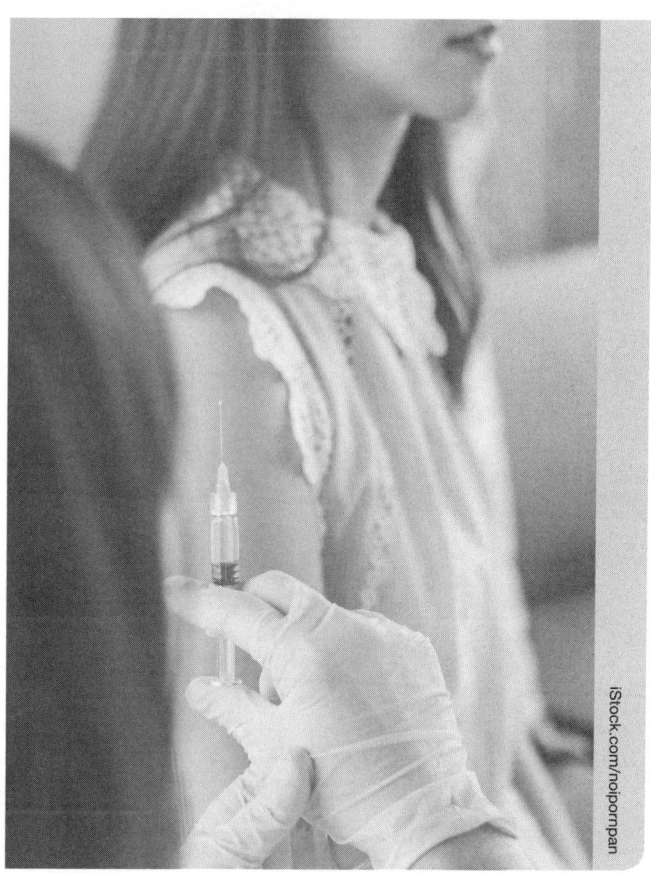

## 14. Socioemotional Development in Adolescence

### Today you will practice the following:

14.1  Summarize the processes by which self-concept, self-esteem, and identity change during adolescence.

14.2  Discuss the nature of parent–child relationships in adolescence.

14.3  Examine the developmental progression of peer relations in adolescence.

14.4  Analyze patterns of adolescent sexual activity including sexual orientation.

14.5  Identify common psychological and behavioral problems in adolescence.

Riley is dimly aware that she's supposed to be involved socially as she moves through middle school and high school. Her friends (and even her not-friends) go to weekend parties and football games. They do sleepovers and rafting trips. Jasmine still sleeps over a lot, and Riley stays with her sometimes, too. This usually happens when her dad—it's just too weird to be believed but also a little cool—stays over with Philippa, who he's been dating seriously for a couple of years now. But she doesn't do anything else. She and Jasmine go to the movies and to the varsity football games, where they see other classmates. Riley doesn't care about being a social butterfly. Boys notice her. She knows because they flirt with her. Sometimes, they're bold enough to ask her out. She's still shy, though, and prefers to spend every spare minute at the secondhand piano her granny and grandpa bought from the church when the congregation raised money for a new one. She doesn't think there's an expiration date on going out with boys, and she's too awkward about the whole process to think about it right now.

## 15. Physical and Cognitive Development in Emerging/Early Adulthood

### Today you will practice the following:

15.1  Describe the features and characteristics of emerging and early adulthood.

15.2  Summarize the physical developments of emerging and early adulthood.

15.3  Analyze physical and sexual health issues in emerging and early adulthood.

15.4  Compare postformal reasoning, pragmatic thought, and cognitive-affective complexity.

15.5  Explain how attending college influences young adults' development, and identify challenges faced by first-generation and nontraditional students.

15.6  Discuss vocational choice and the transition to work.

# CHAPTER 4  Riley Everett

Riley hears her dad park his truck behind the house. Any second, he'll walk into the kitchen and call out for her. It's the same every day and has been as long as she can remember.

"Hello!" he hollers. "Is there a hungry young dragon somewhere guarding my treasure?"

"Right here, Dad!" she calls back from her usual perch in the living room. She likes the corner of the sofa that faces the fireplace. Even when it's not cold enough for a fire, that whole wall just feels so homey to her.

"There she is," he says, coming to kiss the forehead she offers by tilting her face up to his. "But who guards my greatest treasure, this fierce dragon of mine?"

"Alas, it must be the angels."

"Only angels will do." He opens a Diet Coke and plops into his recliner, pushing the chair back so his feet lift a foot or so above the ground.

"Tough day?" she asks. Please don't let him ask, she prays to no one in particular.

"Nah. Just long. How about you?"

"It was good," she says.

"Hear from any colleges yet?"

Darn it. "It's still really early, you know."

"Not quite what I asked but probably near enough to an answer. Who got back to you, and what did they say?"

She sighs—no sense in putting it off really. Reaching across the space between them, she holds out the letter of acceptance from the flagship school in the state. She worked so hard in high school to keep the grades she needed to go to a school like this, and she never thought it would happen—not for her—a smaller campus, maybe; a lesser school farther away, maybe; but not the state's namesake university. She couldn't help being a little proud of herself.

"Riley! This is fantastic!" Dad whoops, pushing the chair back down so he can sit upright and read the letter a second time. "Honey, why didn't you tell me right away?"

She shrugs. "I don't know. It doesn't even seem real yet. Plus, there's the money."

He looks at her and shakes his head. "We'll make it work. You've got the maximum Pell grant award, remember? And you'll have the state scholarship for graduating with a 3.5 GPA." He gives her a wink. "Don't think I'm not aware of how much that took for you, Riley."

"But the grant and scholarship won't cover everything."

"No, you're right, but it'll cover a lot. I've been saving a little here and there, and if we have to take out some in loans, it's not the end of the world. You just have to finish in four years."

It's her turn to smile. "I promise."

"Riley, this is wonderful news. Dinner out to celebrate?"

Six months later, three months after her beloved grandpa passes away, Dad, Granny, and Philippa drive her and Jasmine to the state capital and their new dorm. It's not attractive. Riley's used to her lovely craftsman house with its beautiful personal details made by her dad's own two hands, like the lintel over her bedroom door of a snoring baby dragon asleep against her father's wing with tiny flames drifting out of her nose. This room is spartan and almost antiseptic.

Philippa looks around before pulling out a tape measure. She starts at the window but takes notes on every possible surface, vertical and horizontal, by the time Jasmine and Riley finish unpacking. They have matching bedding, cute office supplies, and new posters. Riley is nonetheless relieved when Philippa looks at Dad and declares, "Mason, we cannot go back tonight." She turns to Granny and asks, "Do you mind, Carolyn? No? Perfect. We have to outfit this room so the girls feel, well, if not at home, then at least posh enough to sleep at night." Dad doesn't even complain once. He asks if they can all eat dinner first.

Thanks to Philippa and not a little to Dad, Riley and Jasmine end up with a room so totally inspired by both parents that they manage to never leave it for another. They have to petition the housing office to keep the same room over the summers, but for four years, that one, ugly little freshman room is their home. They love it. They love even more spring break of their sophomore year when Riley's dad and Jasmine's mom get married (finally!). Not only is this wonderful for the newlyweds, but now the two girls are also the sisters they've felt like since grade school. Riley also surprises herself with the depth of her devotion to university study. She doesn't like every class, but she doesn't expect to. What she does like is every music class she takes to pursue her BFA in music performance, piano concentration, with a minor in theory. The classes she would rather not take? She thinks of them like the Brussels sprouts she has to eat to have the chocolate cake, and at university, there is *so much cake*.

## 16. Socioemotional Development in Emerging/Early Adulthood

### Today you will practice the following:

16.1 Summarize psychosocial development in emerging and early adulthood.

16.2 Discuss influences on friendship and mate selection and interactions in emerging and early adulthood.

16.3 Analyze the diverse romantic situations that may characterize emerging and early adulthood, including singlehood, cohabitation, marriage, and divorce.

16.4 Compare the experiences of young adults as stepparents, never-married parents, and same-sex parents.

In her junior year of college, Riley finds herself finished eating Brussels sprouts for courses. She has no classes left to take that aren't in the music department, and she's almost certain she's died and gone to heaven. Every now and again, she pinches herself to make sure she's not dreaming. Her performance classes are in a theater using a Steinway grand piano, and she's never heard anything so beautiful in her life. When her fingers move across the keys, nothing in the world is wrong or ever could be.

She's so focused on her studies that she doesn't have time (or even wants to find the time) for much socializing. Jasmine does what she's always done by dragging her to a movie now and again to blow off steam, but that's about it. She's 21 years old and hasn't been on a date. She hasn't been kissed. She hasn't done anything really. The truth is Riley isn't concerned at all. She knows she's at least of average attractiveness because she gets flirted with. Jasmine assures her she's attractive. She doesn't listen to her dad because it's his job to lie even if she looks like an anemic 65-year-old man with long brown hair. She just figures, as she always has, that she'll make time when something better than chocolate cake comes along.

Her favorite class third year is a composition class. She's working on a themes and variations piece centered on Clara Schuman. She wants to do a Riley Everett variation of a Brahms thematic interpretation of Schuman, who he almost certainly was in love with. If her idea is rejected by the instructor, with whose teaching assistant she's going to meet shortly, then she can go to her fallback, a variation for Rachmaninoff's *A Requiem for the Dead*. No one interprets that piece anymore.

She knocks on Mr. Andrews's door one minute before their scheduled meeting time, and a mumbled "Come in" greets her. Pushing the door open, she smiles at his hunched shoulders. He seems to be working on a score of his own. Once again, she's overcome with shyness and stuttering as if she never made it past Kindergarten. If she could only carry a piano around with her.

"I need an accordion hanging around my neck," she says, instantly mortified.

"Security blanket?" he asks without mocking her at all. He swivels in his chair and motions for her to sit in the room's only other chair, easily overlooked in the cramped space with towers of books and stacks of musical scores.

"Yes, actually. I'm terrible with people but good with the keys. It just occurred to me that I might fare better with the former if I always had the latter with me." Why is she babbling on to Mr. Andrews? And how old is he? Late 20s maybe. There's music, she thinks suddenly, and there's the thing people write music about. He is the why. She has no idea how that fact had gone unnoticed before.

"You are very good with the keys," he agrees. "I'd wager to say exceptional even. I also think you're much better than you think you are with people."

Riley blushes. She can feel the heat of it blooming under her skin. "Oh, no. Not at all." She thinks about explaining but decides against it. She always either talks too little or too much. She can feel herself wandering into "too much" territory now. If only he were marginally less attractive.

"Riley, I've seen you with classmates who're struggling. You teach as effectively as anyone paid to do it does, and you're poised and graceful when you do it."

Unable to stop herself, Riley stares at him. "Really, Mr. Andrews?"

"Call me Paul, please."

It suddenly feels very warm in the tiny office, and Riley remembers that Mr. Andrews is a graduate student in the same program she's pursuing. He's working on a doctorate and will do—what is it? She begs herself to pull it out of her memory—conducting.

"Paul."

"That's how I see you and others, too."

Oh, so not Mr. Andrews, just people in general. She doesn't know why she's disappointed; the compliment was high praise from anyone. She has no reason to be dissatisfied at all.

"That's so nice. Thank you, but I really didn't come here for flattery."

"No?" Mr. Andrews laughs. "I thought that's what all performers lived and breathed for."

"Not this one. Sorry. No, I came to talk about the themes and variations project. I have an idea, but it's complex. I didn't want to invest too much time if you thought Dr. Allen was going to say it doesn't meet the requirements."

He swipes a rogue wave of blonde hair from his forehead, and she balls her hand into a fist not to move it for him. These are the most unaccountable reactions. She almost stands and suggests another meeting time. Maybe Jasmine can help her figure out what's wrong with her.

Mr. Andrews interrupts her thoughts, replying about the project, "How about this plan? I'll take you to dinner at 519 West, and over a nice glass of whatever bottle you select, you can tell me your idea. I promise to give you my perfectly biased opinion when you're finished. Deal?"

"Biased?" she laughs.

"Riley Everett, I lost all ability to be unbiased about you the first time I heard you play. So, yes, biased. Now, dinner? Eight o'clock?"

She bends over his desk and grabs a pen and a sticky note. Without thinking twice, she scribbles the address to her dorm and hands it to him. "I'll meet you outside at eight, and be forewarned, I have a thing about punctuality."

His eyes twinkle—she had no idea eyes could actually twinkle—when he says, "Thanks for the tip. I really want to impress you, and any leverage you give me will be put to good use."

As she walks away from his office, she has the presence of mind to think *this is the beginning of the greatest love of my life. It may not last forever, but if it doesn't, there will never be another Paul Andrews to follow. Don't miss a minute thinking about yesterday or tomorrow.* She doesn't.

## 17. Physical and Cognitive Development in Middle Adulthood

### Today you will practice the following:

*17.1 Summarize age-related physical changes during middle adulthood.*

*17.2 Discuss common health conditions and illnesses and the roles of stress and hardiness on health during middle adulthood.*

*17.3 Contrast the findings of cross-sectional and longitudinal studies of crystallized and fluid intelligence over adulthood.*

*17.4 Analyze changes in cognitive capacities during middle adulthood, including attention, memory, processing speed, and expertise.*

After completing a Master of Fine Arts in music performance with a subspecialty in composition, Riley considers divergent offers from the Philadelphia Philharmonic Symphony and the Boston Symphony Orchestra. Head or heart? Riley's never followed her heart in her life. Heart it is then. She accepts the job in Philadelphia, where her career progresses at a steady, thrilling pace under the spotlights. She knows she deserves this. Part of her can even acknowledge her talent, but she doesn't see anything wrong with a bit of humility rather than hubris. Being humble keeps her real.

Riley is in her early 30s when she realizes one deliciously cold Saturday morning before rehearsal that she's pregnant. Paul is away for the week rehearsing at the Manhattan Symphonie, where he is now the lead conductor. She's so proud of him, but she's not certain what to do about a baby they've not planned for. As well, there's her own genetic background to consider. She knows how lucky she is to have not been born without an arm (God, the piano!) or hearing (God, Beethoven!), but she isn't unscathed from her mother's drug use. Riley doesn't think about her often, and when she does, it's in an unemotional sort of pondering—not today. She knows quite well that her aversion to lights—not spotlights, which is odd—her tendency to be overstimulated easily, and her obvious crankiness, too, if she's honest, are all hand-me-downs from that faceless ovum donor and the woman's meth use. She can't help but wonder about the fetus inside of her. Riley doesn't use drugs of any sort, and she drinks only the occasional glass of celebratory wine. That doesn't mean there isn't a terrible secret waiting to reveal itself inside the mitochondria of her unborn child—not from Paul, of course. Paul is godlike perfect. They've never talked about children before somehow, with them both so busy with work, and she can probably eliminate the question before he ever returns home—only she doesn't want to. What if her mother had done that in prison when she learned she was carrying Riley? She could have for sure, but she didn't. Riley wouldn't be here now. So...what? She'll talk to Paul at the end of the week when he's home for Manhattan's off week. If he wants a baby (that she maybe already loves a little), then they can consider genetic testing, or they'll take what they get and love it all the same, just like her dad did, once more demonstrating how all the best lessons in life come to us in adulthood but having been learned on childhood's knees.

## 18. Socioemotional Development in Middle Adulthood

### Today you will practice the following:

18.1  Summarize the theories and research on psychosocial development during middle adulthood.

18.2  Describe the changes that occur in self-concept, identity, and personality during middle adulthood.

18.3  Analyze relationships in middle adulthood, including friend, spousal, parent–child, and grandparent relationships.

18.4  Discuss influences on job satisfaction and retirement planning during middle adulthood.

"Honey, I'm home!"

Riley groans in good humor at the 1950s-inspired greeting from Paul as he comes through the door in the early hours Sunday morning. It's his off-week finally—not hers but that's okay. She'll go to New York when it is. She loves New York.

"Come here to me," she whispers as he brings the cold into their bedroom. "How was your day, dear?"

"Brilliant. Yours?"

"Brilliant." She pushes herself up on a mound of pillows. "Put on some coffee, would you please? I want to talk."

She watches his face fall and rushes to shake her head. "Not like that talk, just talk. Please make the coffee and some warm milk, too. Maybe a little chocolate sauce?"

"What is this? Paris?"

Riley lifts a shoulder. "Love?"

"Must be." He leaves, and she watches him shed layers as he moves through their tiny apartment in the historic district near Elfreth's Alley. Two tiny apartments in two expensive districts—they should give up one and one of them commute, but this is so much nicer, like they always have a mini-vacation to look forward to. "Heat milk or cream?" he calls from the kitchen.

"Milk is fine." Stretching her legs, she wonders how to talk to him. A baby would be enough news for anyone, but now she has to tell him about her mother. She's as nervous as she's ever been in her life. When he returns a little while later carrying a huge silver tray she unearthed one day at an antiques market for $10, she stays quiet and lets him fix her a mug of half steaming coffee, half milk with a big drop of chocolate syrup to finish it off. "Perfect, mocha man. Thank you."

Fixing his own, he leans over and kisses her. "My pleasure. Now, can I know what this talk is about?"

"Yes, but you have to let me tell you in my own way."

"Accordion conversation?" he asks, referring to the first day she came to his office and made that silly comment about needing to always have an accordion around her neck. It's their password for a difficult conversation, one that causes her a lot of stress.

"Accordion conversation," she confirms. "I've never talked much about my mother to you."

"Nope. Has something happened, or do you feel the need to tell me now? Either way is fine, you know."

"I know." Riley smooths the blankets over their legs and touches his knee. Staring at his hands—his fingers were like hers, long and thin, a musician's fingers—she finds the courage she needs. "Something has happened, and that means I have to tell you."

"Then whatever it is, I'm here for the worst."

"Good. So, let's start with the fact that I was born in a prison."

Over the next hour or so, she tells him about the woman called Kari Simmons and how Riley came to be Riley, flaws and all. She lets him baby her now and again because she knows it helps him cope with the things he's learning. She not only tries to keep it brief but also tries to cover all the essentials. At the end of everything, she realizes—not for the first time but maybe fully as she hasn't before—what an extraordinary hero her dad is.

"Your dad should be canonized," Paul says softly when she finishes.

"I know. He set a pretty high bar for other men to clear."

"No wonder you waited for me," he quips, flipping the longish hair into her face.

"Beast!" Riley laughs and gives him her mug. "More please."

He fixes her cup and hands it to her, saying, "I'm sorry and not sorry at all, if that makes any sense."

"Of course it does. I feel the same way, which is an odd thing to say about oneself." Sipping, she wishes she'd asked for whipped cream. "And now we get to the good part."

"Are you being sarcastic? I can't tell."

"I can't either." With a huge gulp of air, Riley expels the words "Paul, I'm pregnant" on the exhale.

He moves so quickly that all the spill-able items on the bed threaten to discharge their contents on the old quilt made by Granny. Halting in frustration, Paul takes her cup and his and places them on the tray; he then sets it on the floor for their St. Bernard to finish. Riley has the presence of mind to be glad the chocolate's finished but to wonder what the caffeine will do to him. Paul's definitely taking the monster for a walk next.

"Sweetheart, really?" he whispers, drawing her close.

"Really."

"And you're worried?"

"I would be foolish not to be."

"Well, it's your body. What do you want to do? There is any number of options."

"I thought about genetic testing. It's not like we can't afford it and maybe even afford fetal intervention if necessary. I really struggled as a kid. I still do a lot of times."

"I know."

"But my dad—"

"Loved you from the beginning not knowing what he'd get when his baby dragon hatched."

"Right. I feel like it's dishonoring him to care at all. Like, I get it for a couple who don't know if there are problems lurking or maybe who have silent problems to worry about like a family history of breast cancer or something. But this feels self-serving."

"Then the question comes down to whether or not you want children—or at least children we make together. There are lots of children out there who need good homes."

Riley laughed. "I thought about that and realized I'd always gravitate to the ones no one else wanted."

"So, this whole conversation was just enlightenment? We're having a baby?"

She hugged him close. "We're having a baby."

Riley continues to perform throughout her pregnancy. She isn't the first orchestral player to do so, although she is an exceptionally visible one. During the first of two off weeks that overlap for her and Paul, they fly Mason, Granny, Paul's parents, Jasmine and her husband, and their toddler Molly to New York for their city hall marriage, after which they eat pizza in their favorite Italian restaurant off Broadway. Paul's mother says she's never heard of it, and Paul reminds her that the best places aren't always well known. On the way back to Grand Central to take the train to their apartment, they're stopped by someone who recognizes Riley, and she signs an autograph and agrees to a quick picture with the fan. Paul stands to the side, enjoying her celebrity. "No one knows the conductor," he says with pride as he squeezes her shoulder a minute later, "but everyone knows my girl."

Their baby, a girl they name Haydn, is born on a beautiful autumnal Tuesday in Philadelphia. Although Paul is working that week, his pager is on constantly, and he's on standby. The drive is less than two hours, and Riley has almost ten hours left before she delivers Haydn by the time he arrives at the hospital. They both open the season a few weeks later but then take two months' maternity and paternity leave to be with the new love of their lives before returning to work mid-season. Haydn travels with Riley, but Paul joins them on all his off weeks, and Riley and Haydn join him on all of Riley's. It's a wonderful life until just after Haydn's third birthday, when Mason dies of a sudden heart attack. Long hours, chronic stress, and low social support have taken their toll. Riley wants to take time off to grieve indefinitely, but she feels like she may never come back from the loss if she does. She uses a month's bereavement, staying at home in her dad's house, her house, to pack up belongings and see to their storage just as her dad did when Granny died the year before. She arranges for the lintel above her childhood bedroom door to be removed and shipped to Philadelphia, where it's installed above Hayden's door. Then she returns to Philadelphia and establishes an endowed scholarship at the Curtis Institute of Music in her father's name. The Mason Everett Scholarship will pay the complete tuition and room and board charges for one exceptional student each year who would otherwise not be able to attend university to study music.

## 19. Physical and Cognitive Development in Late Adulthood

### Today you will practice the following:

*19.1 Discuss age-related changes in brain and body systems in late adulthood, and identify ways that older adults may compensate for changes.*

*19.2 Identify risk and protective factors for health in late adulthood.*

*19.3 Summarize common dementias including characteristics, risk and protective factors, and treatment.*

*19.4 Analyze patterns of cognitive change in late adulthood.*

When Haydn takes over the conductor's wand at the Manhattan Symphonie from Paul when she's 30 and has spent a couple rookie years at the Boston Pops, Paul and Riley decide to semi-retire. By choice, they open each season of the Philadelphia Philharmonic together—one show only—always her variation of Rachmaninoff. Riley's long hair is white now. She wears it classically styled in a low bun at her nape when she performs. At home with Paul, she braids it loosely and sits in his shirts and socks with a pair of pajama pants while working on a memoir. She's not sure her life is of any interest to anyone, but it's important for her to put the words to paper after so many years not speaking unless required.

At the end of the season-opening performance when Riley is 64, the audience applauds, and she watches Paul turn to bow. He extends an arm in her direction, and she rises to bend her head in acknowledgment of the audience's appreciation before sliding offstage. When Paul meets her in her dressing room, he looks concerned.

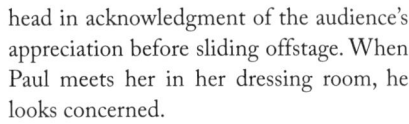

"What's wrong, sweetheart?"

"Why are so many people here? I don't like being around so many people, Paul. You know that. And why are the lights so bright?"

The look on his face changes from concern to something like sadness. He says, "I'm sorry. I must have gotten carried away and forgot. Cross my heart; it won't happen again."

Leaning in for a kiss, she touches his hair. "When did you get so gray?"

Riley's doctor confirms two days later that she has early onset Alzheimer's. She and Paul are devastated, and she begs him not to tell Haydn. At least not until Christmas, she compromises, and Paul agrees. They ask the doctor if it's possible that Riley's mother's drug use could have any part in her development of the disease, and he says that, yes, it's possible, either through direct influence or through Riley's lifelong battle with stress and increased levels of corticosteroids and chronic mobilization of her autonomic nervous system. Could this impair Haydn down the road, they ask? The doctor says it's impossible to tell, but it could happen. Riley feels guilty about Haydn and cheated for herself.

"I'm sorry," she tells Paul over lunch she later won't remember eating.

"I'm not. I love you, and I will love every minute with you no matter what."

She laughs but not with any real pleasure. "No, you won't, and you know you won't, but I love you for saying it."

He probably doesn't, she thinks from time to time, but she acknowledges that maybe she got the long end of the stick. She doesn't remember when she's awful. She doesn't remember what she doesn't remember either. It's ungodly sad to visit that black hole and not know the faces of people around her. She detests the looks of sadness on their faces when she doesn't know them because it's clear that she *should* and she's breaking their hearts when she doesn't, but really, what do they want from her? When she does remember, she apologizes, and Paul and Haydn are too sympathetic. Sometimes, she wishes they'd yell or curse at her, but they never do.

Paul helps her finish the memoir. Other than supporting her through the pregnancy with Haydn and the first year or two until they knew the baby was perfect (she would've been even if she hadn't been), this is the single most loving act he's done for her. She does remember the day she pens *el fin* under the final words. It's done. She gives Haydn executive power over the manuscript for the future day when she dies. Her daughter can decide what, if anything, to do with the words she finally found the ability to express.

## 20. Socioemotional Development in Late Adulthood

### Today you will practice the following:

20.1  Examine the contributions of self-concept, personality, and religiosity to older adults' well-being.

20.2  Identify social contexts in which older adults live and their influence on development.

20.3  Summarize features of older adults' relationships with friends, spouses, children, and grandchildren, and identify how these relationships affect older adults' functioning.

20.4  Discuss influences on the timing of retirement and adaptation to retirement.

In her mid- to late 60s, Riley is cared for by Paul in their Philadelphia apartment. Haydn asks them to move back to the New York apartment where she's living with her partner Madison. Jasmine asks her to move back home. Paul knows Riley can't remember any home other than the one she's in, and she wants to stay there. In the end, their child and even Riley's oldest friend find themselves unequal to the task of watching this central person in their lives disappear without going anywhere, and it's left for him to care for her. He does, lovingly and tenderly, remembering the day he first saw her walk into the theater for his class, remembering the day she first knocked on the door of his office, remembering all their firsts and all the other little days that make up a life.

Over the few years remaining, Paul hires a small orchestra to record a few of Riley's symphonies that have been performed over the years, and he plays them through the day every day. When she's lucid, she remarks on places where the orchestra has done particularly well. Some days, she remembers the works as her own. All days, he sits and reads to her: her favorite novels, the newspaper, her memoir. They walk in the park, and sometimes, they go to a show or to the mall. As the years move toward her 70th birthday, Riley wants to go fewer and fewer places, eventually holing up in their living room and bedroom completely.

## 21. Experience With Death and Dying

### Today you will practice the following:

20.1  *Identify ways in which death has been defined and end-of-life issues that may arise.*

20.2  *Contrast children's, adolescents', and adults' understanding of death.*

20.3  *Discuss the physical and emotional process of dying as it is experienced over the lifespan.*

20.4  *Summarize typical grief reactions to the loss of loved ones and the influence of development on bereavement.*

On the last day of the year when Riley is 71, she wakes up thinking about Haydn. Her daughter is a marvel, and she loves her more than is reasonable. Maybe not, maybe all mothers—all good mothers, she corrects herself—feel this way. She hopes she's just an ordinary mother when she loves her child a little too much. In a moment of feeling she can't wait anymore, she reaches for stationary in her bedside table to write a brief note. Paul can mail it later.

*My dearest Haydn:*

*You are the absolute light of my life, the one shining accomplishment of a long and happy life spent with your wonderful father. I have done two things worth mentioning in my seven* decades (so, why did I write 300 pp of memoir, eh?), and those two things are loving you and loving Paul. Listen to this, which is the only piece of wisdom I have to leave you: you will never go wrong loving.

Be happy, darling, as I have been. You are brilliant, and you have never been anything less than perfect.

Always,

Mom

P.S. Eat more chocolate, and don't cut your hair. Rescue a dog. Hang on to Madison.

She's been awake only a few minutes, but she tires so easily these days. Laying the pen on the table, she puts the note on the bed between her and Paul so she'll remember to ask him about mailing it when they get out of bed.

"I'll just close my eyes for a few more minutes," she whispers.

When Paul wakes later in the morning, Riley has passed gently away in her sleep. Holding her cooling hand, he reads the letter to Haydn and wonders if she somehow knew or if she didn't at all and just meant to send their daughter a little note. He places the letter on his bedside table and gathers Riley into his arms. Soon, he thinks, soon enough I'll call someone—just not yet.

## CASE DISCUSSION QUESTIONS

1. When her mother Kari was pregnant with her, Riley's father Mason petitions for sole custody of Riley and wins. He brings her home shortly after birth. How might her life's trajectory across any or all domains (biological, cognitive, and socioemotional) have been altered if he hadn't done this or if he'd lost? How does winning illustrate the concept of behavioral epigenetics when we look at Mason's subsequent behaviors?

2. In infancy, Riley's grandmother realizes that listening to classical music soothes Riley's irritability and sensory integration difficulties. This single discovery sets into motion a sequence of events that defines Riley's life across all domains (biological, cognitive, and socioemotional) for the entirety of her life. How might her life have been different in any or all of these domains if her grandmother hadn't made this realization? Be specific.

3. In late middle and early late adulthood, Riley is diagnosed with Alzheimer's disease. What do we know about early life experiences in Riley's past that might have contributed—likely did contribute—to her development of this form of dementia? Why would this be so?

4. Riley's entire life occurs over many decades that are, loosely, contemporary. Cars, telephones, televisions, and so on exist, but era-specific technology isn't presented (e.g., cell phones, space shuttles, or artificial intelligence). Would Riley's life have been different if she were born in a specific period, earlier or later? If so, how? Be specific.

# 5 Leonardo Ramirez

## Introduction

Welcome to your case study!

Congratulations! You will follow the lifespan of baby boy Leonardo Ramirez. Try to use your best judgment, textbook, classmates, instructor, and supplementary resources to make the best decisions to help him grow.

This semester you will observe Leonardo as he grows from infant to child to teen to adult. Who will he become in your care? Will you understand and agree with all decisions available within his circumstances? How will you feel about the tough decisions that forever shape his path in life?

## Meet Leonardo Ramirez

Leonardo is the first son of Alicia and Hector Ramirez. Alicia is 25 years old; Hector is 26. Both have high school diplomas, and they work as undocumented farm laborers in a fruit orchard. Although both Alicia and Hector work roughly full-time hours, due to their citizenship status, they are paid cash, and their earnings aren't tracked. This also means they have no health

iStock.com/debbiehelbing

insurance. Alicia, who doesn't qualify for any benefits such as WIC or Medicare, sees a doctor at a local women's clinic where she's able to pay on a sliding scale to get the prenatal care she needs. However, she has to be careful about scheduling appointments. If she misses work, she doesn't get paid, and they can't afford for her not to get paid. Hector and Alicia are considered the working poor, and they live in a low-income, rural neighborhood close to the farm that employs them. When Leonardo is born, he will be a U.S. citizen.

Through this case study and your lifespan course, you will be asked to consider decisions regarding Leonardo's physical, emotional, and cognitive growth and development from several perspectives: his parents' and potential younger siblings' as well as those of his spouse, his potential children, other potential family members, friends, teachers, doctors, and supervisors.

Now let's get started.

## 1. Development and Its Influences

### Today you will practice the following:

*1.1  Outline five principles of the lifespan developmental perspective.*

*1.2  Explain three theoretical controversies about human development.*

*1.3  Summarize five theoretical perspectives on human development.*

*1.4  Describe the methods and research designs used to study human development.*

During the 14th week of her pregnancy, Alicia contracts a case of rubella (German measles). She notices she has a rash on the first day, but because she works on a farm, she doesn't think much about it for another two or three days, when she begins to run a fever. Rashes are common, and it's easy not to worry until the fever appears. The hours of operation for the clinic where she receives her prenatal care conflict with her working schedule. If she doesn't go to work, she doesn't get paid. Of course, if she doesn't go to the clinic, both she and Leonardo are at high risk of medical complications as the pregnancy develops. Leonardo, in particular, faces health-related outcomes such as hearing loss and limb abnormalities. This seems like a no-win from Alicia's perspective. After speaking to a couple of women at her church who comment on the rash, Alicia decides to miss a couple of hours of work and have it checked out. She does her best to schedule the appointment close to her short lunch break to lose as little money as possible. Seeing the doctor allows her to be diagnosed and treated without further risk to herself or baby Leo. She's also able to make up the couple of hours of work she missed over the next couple of afternoons. Feeling more relaxed, Alicia coasts into the third trimester of her pregnancy feeling much better about her ability to make good choices without fear of negative repercussions.

## 2. Biological and Environmental Foundations

### Today you will practice the following:

2.1 Discuss the genetic foundations of development.

2.2 Identify examples of genetic disorders and chromosomal abnormalities.

2.3 Discuss the choices available to prospective parents in having healthy children.

2.4 Describe the interaction of heredity and environment, including behavioral genetics and the epigenetic framework.

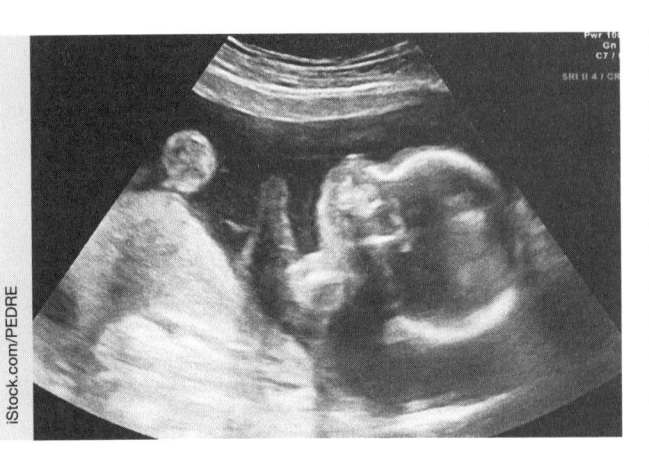

Hector watches Alicia as she works in the orchard. He's never had a baby before, and he doesn't know how to judge everything that's happening. He loves living in America, but his English is poor. Alicia learned English in high school and gets by in the community much better than he does. He has to trust that her growing belly and early evening fatigue are normal. She tells him they are. He's worried about two things in particular. He doesn't know if *la Rubéola* she had a few weeks ago has hurt the baby. Alicia seems fine, and she says the doctor told her the baby would be fine. Still, he'll feel better when he sees the baby for himself. He's also worried about the one thing he has zero control over and all the blame for. His *abuela*, his father's mother, would fall into the darkest valleys of despair when Hector was a boy. He remembers how he felt visiting, her still, silent body with its bony shoulders sitting on a hard chair. His mama told him such things could be passed on in the blood, and he worries he will have passed the darkness on to his own child even if he himself doesn't have those moments. Really, he just wants the baby to be born so he has more control over how his child is protected. Until then, he thinks with a smile, he'll watch Alicia and her growing belly with pride and excited anticipation.

## 3. Prenatal Development, Birth, and Newborn Experience

### Today you will practice the following:

3.1 Describe the three periods of prenatal development that begin with conception.

3.2 Identify how exposure to teratogens can influence the prenatal environment.

3.3 Explain the process of childbirth.

3.4 Discuss the neonate's physical capacities, including development in low-birth-weight infants.

Alicia calls the nurse midwife, who will deliver Leonardo, twice with Braxton-Hicks contractions, believing she's in labor. The midwife examines her and sends her home with assurances that many first-time mothers make the mistake of confusing Braxton-Hicks for labor. The third time, there's no confusion. The pain brings Alicia to her knees, and Hector helps her to the car before rushing her to the hospital.

After 15 long, loud, sweating hours of labor, Alicia pushes Leonardo into the world. His fat, round face is squished and squinting in the lights of the room, but he lets out a lusty cry that makes Alicia reach for him. Moments later, he's cradled at her breast, nursing happily while Hector looks on smiling at them both. The hospital sends an interpreter into the room to translate as Leonardo is weighed, measured, poked, and prodded. The Ramirezes are told he's absolutely perfect, and as long as he and Alicia are doing well, they can go home the following day.

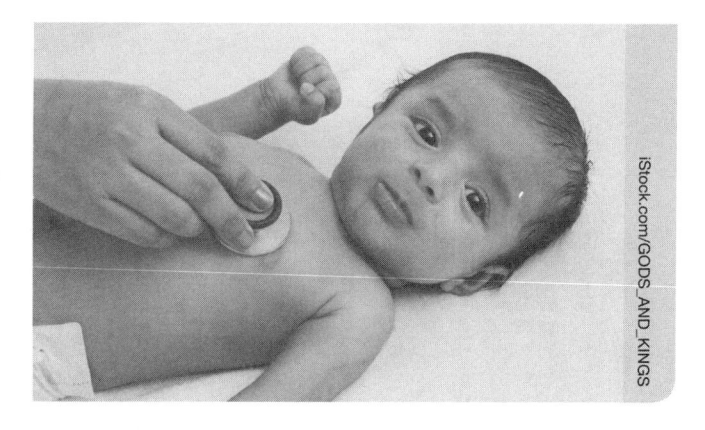

"Do you feel better now?" Alicia asks him later when the three of them are alone.

"What do you mean? How better?"

"Now that the baby is born and you see he's healthy?" she says, reminding him of his concerns about the measles.

"Oh, yes, that. I do feel better. I just worry about all the other things that might happen."

Alicia laughs. "Ah, Hector, don't. We live in the land of opportunity where anything is possible if you dream it and work hard, and our son is an American citizen. Relax and be happy."

He looks at both of them and nods. "You're right. You're right, Alicia." He knows she is, too, but he still worries.

## 4. Physical Development in Infancy and Toddlerhood

### Today you will practice the following:

*4.1 Discuss growth and the role of nutrition in development during infancy and toddlerhood.*

*4.2 Summarize brain development during infancy and toddlerhood.*

*4.3 Compare infants' early learning capacities for habituation, classical conditioning, operant conditioning, and imitation.*

*4.4 Describe infants' developing sensory abilities.*

*4.5 Analyze the roles of maturation and contextual factors in infant and toddler motor development.*

Alicia isn't able to take a proper maternity leave from work. She misses a few days, and when her postpartum lochia slows, she returns to the farm with baby Leonardo tucked securely against her in a cotton sling tied to her back. In this way, she can nurse him when he's hungry, pause when it's necessary to change him, and continue to work her normal hours. The farm owner who pays them isn't around often, but she doesn't worry about him often anyway. Other women have brought newborns with them from time to time, and she and Hector aren't quite able yet to pay the woman in their neighborhood who watches most of the babies. Alicia thinks that maybe when Leonardo wants to be crawling and becomes more difficult to keep off the ground while she works then it will be time to find another arrangement.

This transition occurs sooner than either she or Hector is ready for. Leo, who is a big boy with strong, sturdy legs and a sure gait from the moment he starts walking at 10 months, loves being beside both of them during the daytime, but it's quickly evident that he won't tolerate being confined to the sling any longer.

"Down!" he yowls, kicking against Alicia's sides. When she doesn't respond appropriately, he tries a different tactic. "¡Aba'o!" He can't quite say *abajo* yet, but he's gotten his point across before. Still, no response other than a laugh from *Mamá*. He continues the assaultive demonstrations until his foot lands a solid kick to her kidney.

Alicia takes their car and uses part of her lunch break to drive to the gas station a few miles away. The gas station has an old pay phone she uses to call her cousin Luci and ask her to come get Leo for the afternoon. Luci has papers, which is why she has a job with a regular paycheck. Alicia can only dream of such luxuries. But today is Tuesday, Luci's day off. *Gracias del Señor*.

"Heylo," Luci says when she answers. Her cousin's heavily accented English makes Alicia smile.

"*Hola, Luci. ¿Puedes venir por Leo por favor? No le gusta la honda hoy.*"

"*Sí, por supuesto. Necesito diez minutos.*"

"*Claro. Gracias, Luci.*"

Alicia hangs up before someone sees her talking and begins to sing to Leonardo. Sometimes this calms him, sometimes not. Today seems like a rowdy day. With Luci on the way to get Leonardo, though, things should ease. Her cousin would be there in ten minutes. She could endure anything for ten minutes, even the increasing ferocity of Leonardo's kicks into her hips and sides.

"Easy, baby," she soothes, but he wants to be down on the ground exploring. She can't blame him. If she were newly crawling and cruising and had the world, literally, at her feet, that's where she would want to be, too. A friend of her cousin's got work as a housekeeper in the rich neighborhood next to their own poor one. The friend is undocumented, too, but she says the lady she works for is nice. Luci's friend, Jasmin, doesn't get any more money than Alicia does, but she's allowed to take her daughter to work with her as long as nothing is broken. Alicia dreams about a job like that, one where she can help feed her family but where she doesn't have to worry about childcare or carrying a growing and heavy Leonardo on her back for the next four years until he starts school. She makes a reminder in her head to ask Luci about Jasmin's job and if there might be another one like it.

On her back, Leonardo is drooling onto her neck. She hears him babbling, but his lilting voice begins picking up speed and excitement while she works down the row of corn she's planting. "Loo-loo! Loo-loo!" he calls, and Alicia looks up. Luci is walking toward them. Alicia breathes out in relief even while Leonardo's kicking revs up into marathons of excitement. "Loo! Loo-loo!"

Arriving at Alicia's side, Luci laughs at Leonardo. "Leo! You're so adorable. Why does *Mamá* say you're bad, eh?"

"Not bad," Alicia corrects her, "just impossible to keep on my back."

"*Veo,*" Luci agrees. *I see.* "*Vaya* then, monster; come with me." She holds out her hands and wiggles her fingers, and Leonardo *hees* with excitement and comes close to jumping out of the sling altogether. Alicia quickly unknots the fabric and sets him on the ground.

"Thank you," she says. "He needs to be down, but I can't do that here."

"I know." Bending, Luci scoops Leonardo into her arms. "Is your car unlocked? I need the car seat."

"*Sí.* You know where we park, *¿nó?*"

"*Sí.*" She waves Leonard's hand. "Tell *Mamá 'adios,'* Leo."

"*I-o,*" he singsongs, making Alicia smile. She reaches to kiss his cheek before making shooing motions with her hands. "Now, go before I get into trouble!"

## 5. Cognitive Development in Infancy and Toddlerhood

### Today you will practice the following:

5.1   Discuss the cognitive-developmental perspective on infant reasoning.

5.2   Describe the information processing system in infants.

5.3   Discuss individual differences in infant intelligence.

5.4   Summarize the patterns of language development during infancy and toddlerhood.

Because the farm is staffed with a number of not only migrant workers like Hector and Alicia but also local citizens who speak only English, Leonardo is around English and Spanish speakers all day every day. It makes Hector laugh when Leonardo's first word is *mamá*, and he asks Alicia in Spanish, "What language do you think he's speaking in?" Alicia has no idea, but Hector loves his little boy's voice in whichever tongue he'll consider native. Sometime between 14 and 15 months, Hector notices that it isn't either–or with their son. There are words he uses that are clearly English and others that are just as clearly Spanish.

Leonardo's bilingual abilities astonish his parents. Neither knew it was possible to be born and just grow up knowing two languages. As Leonardo continues to learn new words in English and Spanish, Alicia and Hector have many long conversations about what's best for him. They live in America, and English is the language most people speak in the country. It's the language used most often internationally, too, Alicia says when she argues they should force Leonardo into speaking only English.

Hector argues that learning both doesn't seem to hurt their son's language development. Plus, if they force Leonardo to only speak English, how will Hector be able to communicate meaningfully with his son? Alicia, who doesn't speak fluent English, speaks enough to at least have a relationship with Leonardo no matter what they decide. Hector does not. They leave the conversation on the table for a year or two more, both wary of upsetting their other but also secretly pleased by Leonardo's abilities. Everywhere they go, he's able to learn new words or use the ones he already knows. Neither of them is quite willing to take that away from him yet, and Hector is loath to do so at all.

## 6. Socioemotional Development in Infancy and Toddlerhood

### Today you will practice the following:

6.1 *Summarize the psychosocial tasks of infancy and toddlerhood.*

6.2 *Describe emotional development in infancy and identify contextual and cultural influences on emotional development in infants and toddlers.*

6.3 *Identify the styles and stability of temperament, including the role of goodness of fit in infant development.*

6.4 *Describe how attachment develops in infancy and toddlerhood.*

6.5 *Differentiate the roles of self-concept, self-recognition, and self-control in infant development.*

Like many toddlers in their small community, Leonardo's world expands by degrees until most families on the street where they live consider him theirs. Everyone helps raise everyone else's kids, and this is a world where old prejudices die in the face of new and necessary alliances. Hector and Alicia's families are from Guadalajara in Jalisco, Mexico, but they live beside Juan and Lili from Juayúa, El Salvador. In another lifetime, neither family would've associated with the other, but now they're friends; they're family in this new world. So it is in the whole neighborhood where *Mexicano* and *Salvadoreño*, *Columbino* and *Boliviano*, where all their blended nationalities become *Latinx*. This is in part from necessity and in part because *los Americanos* call them so. Hector isn't sure he cares so long as they all trust each other and look after one another. Leonardo doesn't care either.

His favorite house after his own is Loo-loo's, *Mamá*'s cousin Luci's. Luci doesn't have any children for him to play with, but she always has *churros*. Leonardo loves *churros,* and *Mamá* doesn't feed him many. His next favorite house is *Tía Consuela's*. She's very, very old, and many people call her Granny. *Mamá* calls her *Tía*, though, and so does Leonardo. She doesn't walk, her hair is white, like snow, and all the other children in the neighborhood are there a lot because their *mamás y papás* come to take care of her. When Leonardo is at *Tía Consuela's* with his *mamá* or *papá*, he always has someone to play with, and someone has always brought *pupusas* or *tamales,* which are his favorite things to eat after *churros*. Sometimes he even gets to go back to his friends' houses because their *mamás y papas* say to his that he is *un ángel*.

*Tía Consuela's* is probably the best place to go other than home or Loo-loo's, but he wouldn't want to spend the night. He likes to sleep in his own bed after his own *mamá* sings him songs from her own home when she was little. When she turns out the light, he sticks his thumb in his mouth, closes his eyes, and wonders if he'll ever get to see Mexico for himself. It sounds beautiful.

## 7. Physical and Cognitive Development in Early Childhood

### Today you will practice the following:

7.1 *Discuss physical development in early childhood.*

7.2 *Compare Piaget's cognitive-developmental and Vygotsky's sociocultural perspectives on cognitive development in early childhood.*

7.3 *Describe information-processing abilities during early childhood.*

7.4 *Summarize young children's advances in language development.*

7.5 *Contrast social learning and cognitive-developmental perspectives on moral development in early childhood.*

7.6 *Identify and explain approaches to early childhood education.*

"*No tiene sentido para mí,*" Hector says, shaking his head.

Alicia looks at Leonardo's preschool teacher. He attends a program called Head start, and the teacher is nice. "My husband says what you say, it makes no sense to him. I'm sorry. He doesn't mean—"

"No, no," Mrs. Clifton says, waving her hand. "Please don't apologize. You're advocating for your child, you and your husband both, and this is great for Leonardo. Let me try explaining a different way."

"Thank you," Alicia tells her.

"The important thing to know is that Leonardo will do better in school—now and when he starts elementary school—if you and your husband continue to speak to him in Spanish at home. You can speak in English, too. That's okay. But research tells us that children who continue to learn their families' native languages do better at learning English than children who are forced to learn only English."

"Ah." Alicia turns to Hector around her growing belly and quickly translates. The smile that lights his face changes the atmosphere in the room. He gives Alicia an *I told you so* look, and she scowls at him but with love. "Okay."

"Okay?" Mrs. Clifton asks. "Good. Leonardo's English is good. So is his Spanish. He's a smart boy, and he's a sweet boy, too. He's looking forward to being a big brother."

Alicia puts a hand on her belly. "I hope so. He has to share his room, so I hope he loves the baby."

"No doubt he will." Mrs. Clifton closes Leonardo's folder and stands up. "Really, all I have to say right now is to keep doing what you're doing."

## 8. Socioemotional Development in Early Childhood

### Today you will practice the following:

*8.1* Discuss young children's emerging sense of initiative, self-concept, and self-esteem.

*8.2* Summarize the development of emotional understanding, regulation, and behavior in early childhood.

*8.3* Identify four parenting styles and their associations with child outcomes.

*8.4* Compare biological, cognitive, and contextual theoretical explanations of gender role development.

*8.5* Explain the function of play and the form it takes during early childhood.

Leonardo makes friends easily. When he transitions from preschool to elementary school, he has two groups of friends that slowly merge into one on the playground while they play soccer and tag. He has friends from his neighborhood, his *amigos*, and friends from preschool who want to be part of *los amigos*. Leonardo moves effortlessly between them until they form a tight bond of Latinx, white, and black kids who push, shove, and laugh and divvy up their lunches so no one eats what he brought and everyone eats what he wants most days of the week.

In his neighborhood, Leonardo watches some of the older boys. There seem to be two types: mean boys and boys who grow up to be like their fathers. Leonardo will be like his father. He doesn't want to be a mean boy and doesn't know why the fathers let the mean boys stay in the neighborhood where they have fights and break things and their *mamás* cry. *Papá* says it's because *Cuidamos a los que son nuestros*. We take care of our own, he says, but Leonardo isn't sure what that means other than the mean boys get to live near him and keep being mean. He'll never be a mean boy, he promises his *mamá*.

## 9. Physical and Cognitive Development in Middle Childhood

### Today you will practice the following:

9.1  *Identify patterns of physical and motor development during middle childhood and common health issues facing school-age children.*

9.2  *Discuss school-age children's capacities for reasoning and processing information.*

9.3  *Summarize views of intelligence including the uses, correlates, and criticisms of intelligence tests.*

9.4  *Examine patterns of moral development during middle childhood.*

9.5  *Summarize language development during middle childhood.*

9.6  *Discuss children's learning at school.*

Leonardo's years in elementary school fly past in a blur of rec league football, where he's a pretty good kicker, and school days, where he does well enough in his classes to cause his parents no worries even if he doesn't win any major achievement awards. Sometimes, when the parents of one of his neighborhood friends has to come to school for a meeting, he acts like an interpreter for them. Most of his friends don't speak Spanish or at least don't speak it fluently anymore. Their parents think it's better if they speak only English. Only Leonardo's parents and a few others in the neighborhood speak both Spanish and English at home. So, he helps teachers and parents communicate when he can, which helps his friends (usually, unless they've done something really bad, which is almost never). He likes doing this even when his friends get into trouble. He doesn't want any of them becoming like the rough kids in their neighborhood, and he likes that his *mamá* can talk to the schoolteachers without needing help. If he can help his friends and their parents, he wants to do that.

## 10. Socioemotional Development in Middle Childhood

### Today you will practice the following:

10.1  *Describe school-age children's self-conceptions and motivation.*

10.2  *Examine the roles of friendship, peer acceptance, and peer victimization in school-age children's adjustment.*

10.3 *Discuss family relationships in middle childhood and the influence of family structure on adjustment.*

10.4 *Analyze the role of resilience in promoting adjustment to adversity, including characteristics of children and contexts that promote resilience.*

"*Lo siento, m'hijo.*"

Leonardo shrugs off his father's apology. "*Está bien.*" It's okay.

*Papá* caught him looking at a set of LEGOS® while they shopped at the big discount store. They're buying things *Mamá* needs to help with *Señora* Valerio's daughter's *Quinceañera*. *Masa*, ingredients for *horchata, chiles anchos,* and several large chickens. Fortunately, these are dead. *Papá* tells him stories about killing chickens in the dooryard when he was growing up as a boy. The thought makes Leonardo shudder.

*Papá* doesn't drop the subject. "I know you don't get so many things as your friends get sometimes," he says in Spanish.

"It's not a big deal, *Papá*. I have what I need."

Leonardo decides this isn't the time to bring up working around the neighborhood in the summer. He's thinking about mowing lawns or walking dogs. He'll even walk the old people around the block so they get sun and exercise. They can talk about it later, though. *Papá* worries so much whether or not Leonardo frets about money. He doesn't want *Papá* to feel bad because he talks about working in the summer. It's hard to explain. Sometimes it's hard to understand even when he thinks about it. It would be nice to make a little money of his own, but he doesn't *need* anything, like he told *Papá*. Their family is happy, and he likes being at home with them. His *mamá* smiles and sings while she fixes dinner, and *Papá* dances with her around the kitchen, making her splash salsa on the walls. He has friends whose parents barely talk and who barely talk to their parents. Leonardo figures he might be poor, but he wouldn't take a silent, rich house over his quiet, poor one for all the money in the world.

## 11. Physical and Cognitive Development in Late Childhood

### Today you will practice the following:

11.1 *Describe school-age children's self-conceptions and motivation.*

11.2 *Examine the roles of friendship, peer acceptance, and peer victimization in school-age children's adjustment.*

11.3 *Discuss family relationships in middle childhood and the influence of family structure on adjustment.*

11.4 *Analyze the role of resilience in promoting adjustment to adversity, including characteristics of children and contexts that promote resilience*

In sixth grade, Leonardo writes an essay for a district contest. "The World Is Not Spanglish" by Leo Ramirez wins first place, and he gets to go to a special lunch with other contest winners. His *mamá y papá* go with him, while his little brother Ínigo stays at school doing whatever first-grade things he does. Leonardo doesn't remember much of first grade. The lunch is the fanciest he's ever eaten except the one at *Tía Consuela*'s house every Christmas. The whole neighborhood brings their best food for that celebration, but this one is good, too. He has a little teepee of asparagus and long green beans hiding a pile of mashed potatoes, and a path of gravy dots leads to a circle of steak he cuts with his fork and doesn't even need help with. The dessert is the best: half a pear cooked somehow and covered with hard chocolate. *Mamá* says she'll figure out how to make that. Finally, during dessert, the awards start. Leonardo is called last, and he tells the audience how his family, his neighborhood, is a world within a world and not two worlds mashed together. He explains how he walks in both and how he wishes everyone could, and he gives his brief speech twice, first in Spanish and then in English. He can see how proud *mamá y papá* are of what he's done, and a tiny flame of pride burns in his own belly. Somehow, he knows he's done something good.

## 12. Socioemotional Development in Late Childhood

### Today you will practice the following:

12.1  Summarize the processes by which self-concept, self-esteem, and identity change during adolescence.

12.2  Discuss the nature of parent–child relationships in adolescence.

12.3  Examine the developmental progression of peer relations in adolescence.

12.4  Analyze patterns of adolescent sexual activity including sexual orientation.

12.5  Identify common psychological and behavioral problems in adolescence.

At school, Leonardo's teachers alternatively ignore him or give him so much work that he hardly keeps up. He likes the latter better. The more he gets, the more he wants. He's not the smartest kid in the class, but he likes having the challenge of work to do, and he likes that teachers think he can do it. In fourth grade, his teachers assign him to a group called Frontier Peers. Once each week, he spends time in the library or on the playground with another fourth grader the teacher seems to think is somehow going to help Leonardo "stay involved" and "connected" with school. Leonard understands what the teacher means. He's poor, and his parents don't speak English well. *Papá* doesn't speak English at all. They don't have papers, like a lot of families in the neighborhood, and that makes Leonardo (and Ínigo) "at risk," even though he doesn't know what the risk is. The boy's name is Daryl, and he seems like an okay guy. Leonardo doesn't know if they have anything in common. Daryl's kind of skinny, and his mom is Chinese, which makes them have a little in common but not really. For the first time, maybe, Leonardo is mad at a teacher. Does she think that anyone who isn't white is automatically connected somehow?

"I'm not stupid," he tells Daryl to preempt any stereotypes and subsequent behaviors based on them.

"That's okay," Daryl says. "I'm not smart."

Leonardo laughs and slides into the library chair across from Daryl. This kid might be all right.

"Do you like *churros*? I brought some in my lunch today."

## 13. Physical and Cognitive Development in Adolescence

### Today you will practice the following:

*13.1  Evaluate the "storm and stress" perspective on adolescence in light of research evidence.*

*13.2  Summarize the physical changes that occur with puberty and the correlates of pubertal timing.*

*13.3  Discuss brain development during adolescence and its effect on behavior.*

*13.4  Identify ways in which thinking changes in adolescence and how these changes are reflected in adolescent decision-making and behavior.*

*13.5  Discuss moral development and influences on moral reasoning.*

*13.6  Describe the challenges that school transitions pose for adolescents and the role of parents in academic achievement.*

By middle school, Leo finds himself navigating the complex subculture of the *barrio* while trying to keep his head above water in his mostly white but fairly poor school. He hates to admit that his fourth-grade teacher was right, but Daryl turned out to be a good friend, probably his best friend outside the neighborhood, and he spends as much time at the Davises' house as Daryl spends at his. Daryl's mother is beautiful. She's young, and she came to America from China right after high school, just like Leo's *mamá* came from Mexico. Unlike *Mamá*, though, Mrs. Davis doesn't speak any English or only the same few halting words *Papá* speaks. Leo wishes he could translate for her at the school like he still does for so many of the Spanish families.

The kids in the neighborhood he used to think of as mean boys have all grown up and moved away, but more grew into their shoes. There always seems to be a supply of children from his world who don't make it through school, who get pregnant or get arrested, or who get kicked out of their houses and turn to the streets. Leo watches them with a wary, dawning comprehension. The line between success and defeat in their world is the bleeding edge of a razor. Even if he cuts himself, he wants to end up on the right side it. He starts watching *Papá* and the older men around them, and Daryl's dad, too, to figure out how to live the sort of life that would make them proud but would also lead him to be like them: good and strong, *un hombre de calidad*, a man of character. He'll never be a rocket scientist or an Olympic anything, but he can be something better. He can be a good person.

## 14. Social Development in Adolescence

### Today you will practice the following:

14.1   Summarize the processes by which self-concept, self-esteem, and identity change during adolescence.

14.2   Discuss the nature of parent–child relationships in adolescence.

14.3   Examine the developmental progression of peer relations in adolescence.

14.4   Analyze patterns of adolescent sexual activity including sexual orientation.

14.5   Identify common psychological and behavioral problems in adolescence.

Daryl points down the hallway as he and Leo walk toward their sixth-period French class. French—as if either of them needs to learn another language, Leo thinks. He looks where Daryl points. "Yes?"

"Laila Tracy," Daryl says, poking Leo in the ribs.

"Didn't you just break up with her?"

Daryl steers them into the *Mlle. Herbert's* class. "Technically she broke up with me, and we never dated anyway. We just hung out and decided it was a non-starter. I know she likes you, though."

The thought makes Leo hot and cold inside at the same time. Laila Tracy's easily the prettiest girl in their grade, maybe the prettiest girl in school. He spends many sleepless nights thinking about her, but he's sure plenty of other guys do, too.

"She'd never go out with me."

"Yes, she would. I'm telling you." Daryl turns to him as they sit down at their desks. "Would your parents care? You know, that she's not Mexican? My mom would probably care."

"That she's not Mexican?" Leo teases.

"Har."

"Probably, to be honest."

"You should go for it. YOLO, man, and it's Laila Tracy."

Daryl's right. You only live once, and someone else could swoop in and ask her out before he changes his mind. He'll call her after school.

## 15. Physical and Cognitive Development in Emerging/Early Adulthood

### Today you will practice the following:

*15.1 Describe the features and characteristics of emerging and early adulthood.*

*15.2 Summarize the physical developments of emerging and early adulthood.*

*15.3 Analyze physical and sexual health issues in emerging and early adulthood.*

*15.4 Compare postformal reasoning, pragmatic thought, and cognitive-affective complexity.*

*15.5 Explain how attending college influences young adults' development, and identify challenges faced by first-generation and nontraditional students.*

*15.6 Discuss vocational choice and the transition to work.*

When Leo and Daryl graduate from high school, their paths diverge. Daryl leaves town for college in a far corner of the state, while Leo stays at home. He's got a job restocking shelves at a discount home improvement store, and the money's pretty good. With it, he's able to help his family with their expenses so that *Papá*, who's aging quickly from the years on the farm, can work somewhat fewer hours. He also gets to keep an eye on Ínigo. His little brother is smarter than Leo ever was in school, and Leo wants him to go to college in a few years. Ínigo, on the other hand, likes to run with a fast crowd in *el barrio*. This troubles Leo. He wants to stay close to home for a while to see if he can keep Ínigo on the right path and take care of his parents a little, too.

After a few months saving up, he starts taking some education classes at the local community college, just a couple each semester, and he only takes one on campus. The other he takes online. He doesn't want to take more time than necessary away from home. He's not a whiz at much, no surprise there, but he likes the concentration he has to apply to the work. It makes him feel like he's using his brain unlike his brother who whizzes through everything. Leo even takes pleasure in the unrelated courses his advisor says all students have to take, something she mysteriously calls "the core." Whatever it all amounts to, in three years he has an associate's of arts in early childhood education. The diploma doesn't help with his stocking shelves, but eventually he gets a full-time job working for the same elementary school he and Ínigo attended. He's hired as a family liaison, which is principally an interpreter for Latinx families, but he'll also make house calls when needed and serve as a mentor to first-generation children. He takes *Mamá y Papá* and even Ínigo out to eat to celebrate when he accepts the offer.

## 16. Socioemotional Development in Emerging/Early Adulthood

### Today you will practice the following:

16.1  Summarize psychosocial development in emerging and early adulthood.

16.2  Discuss influences on friendship and mate selection and interactions in emerging and early adulthood.

16.3  Analyze the diverse romantic situations that may characterize emerging and early adulthood, including singlehood, cohabitation, marriage, and divorce.

16.4  Compare the experiences of young adults as stepparents, never-married parents, and same-sex parents.

Since middle school and his disastrous first attempts at "dating" with Laila Tracy, Leo's spent time with a number of girls. Days exist when he doesn't want to count the number of girls. He hopes no one ever asks—not that he's slept with all of them, no, not that. He's just thought a lot of things were love that ended up being something well short of it. Well, maybe a couple times were better than others, he thinks, as he looks at Regina Parredes in class one night. Regina lives in the same neighborhood he does, always has. Their mothers like to say they're crib buddies, but that makes Leo a little uncomfortable. Regina makes Leo uncomfortable, especially being in class with her since they broke up a few months ago.

After class, she catches up with him in the parking lot. He slows his walk to match hers, something he remembers without even realizing he remembers it.

"Hey," she says.

"Hey."

"Are you going to Luci's anniversary party?" she asks, referring to *Mamá*'s cousin's party to celebrate her tenth wedding anniversary. She's married a gringo no one liked at first but now everyone believes is Mexican adopted out at birth. Ricky's a good guy. "I'm making *Mamá's tamales*."

Señora Parredes's *tamales* are known throughout *el barrio* as probably the best in North America outside of Mexico. Leo stuffs himself on them whenever he gets a chance. The chance to see Regina and eat the Parredes *tamales* is a temptation too great for any man short of a saint.

"Then I'll be there."

"Leonardo?" she asks as they near his beatup old Chevy.

"Hmm?"

"Can you tell me why you decided to study education instead of something like computers or engineering?"

He smiles at her. "Can you tell me why you're so beautiful?"

Laughing, she half turns from him. "Charmer. That's easy. God made me that way."

"And there's the answer to your question."

"Oh, Leonardo."

"Why did we break up?"

"I cannot remember."

He opens his car door but waits a beat before getting inside. "Can I take you to the party? You'll need help carrying the *tamales*."

"If this is a date, yes," she teases.

"It is."

As she finishes turning, she yells over her shoulder, "Wear a tie!"

## 17. Physical and Cognitive Development in Middle Adulthood

### Today you will practice the following:

17.1 *Summarize age-related physical changes during middle adulthood.*

17.2 *Discuss common health conditions and illnesses and the roles of stress and hardiness on health during middle adulthood.*

17.3 *Contrast the findings of cross-sectional and longitudinal studies of crystallized and fluid intelligence over adulthood.*

17.4 *Analyze changes in cognitive capacities during middle adulthood, including attention, memory, processing speed, and expertise.*

Leo, having kept a close eye on Íñigo as his little brother grew up, is the loudest to cheer him across the stage when he graduates from college. The whole family's there: *Mamá y Papá*, Luci and her husband Ricky, and Regina, or Gina, to whom Leo is now engaged. After a celebratory dinner Leo's parents pay for, something he knows is a matter of pride for *Papá*, they disburse to various locations. Leo takes Gina on a walk around a nearby park before they make the long drive home. While they stroll away their dinner, Gina takes his hand. He squeezes hers, and when she clears her throat, he turns to look at her in curiosity.

"Yes?" he asks.

"I don't . . . Just . . . Leo, do you ever want to go back to school?"

"Do *you* want me to go back to school?"

She shakes her head with vigor. "Of course not. I want you to do or not do whatever makes you happy. I just wondered since we're here with Íñigo if you thought about it ever."

"Sometimes, I guess," he admits, "but when I sit down and think about what I would want to study and do, I realize I'm doing it already. If I find out sometime later that I'm wrong, I can always go then, right?"

"Right," she agrees.

"What about you?" he asks, aware that she's less than two years away from a bachelor's degree in elementary ed and a teaching license to go with it.

"Well . . ."

"Well?"

"Now that you mention it, I have thought it might be nice to finish. There's a campus close to home that has a program, and the tuition isn't much."

Putting his arm around her, he kisses her head. "Then we'll do it, get you enrolled for next semester."

Although Leonardo continues to work for the same elementary school well into his 30s, the same one where Gina now teaches, he picks up a couple contract jobs as an as-needed translator for monolingual Latinx parents at other area schools. The money helps him pay for the wedding and cushion his parents' retirement. Gina doesn't mind this last; when her parents get a little older, Leo suspects he and Gina will do the same for them. That's the way of their culture. As his parents become two of the community's elders, the family doctor warns Leo that he needs to take better care of his own health. He's gained a bit of weight in recent years—all those *tamales* he thinks—and he has high blood pressure. The doctor explains that Leo has several risk factors for coronary disease that he might not usually think of, things like growing up poor in a rough neighborhood. Leo feels pretty far removed from his childhood and wonders how he's supposed to change any of that now.

"You can't," the doctor confirms, "but you can reduce your already considerable risk by improving your diet, exercising more, maybe working a little less."

Leonardo makes some promises, but he really has no ability or even the will to keep them. Work less? How can he work less with so much to do and so many to support? The doctor doesn't understand at all. He goes home and tells Gina, who promptly proclaims that they're changing their household diet, eliciting groans from their three daughters.

"You can have *churros* every day, or you can have *Papí*," Gina tells them, putting an end to the complaining from everyone, Leonardo included.

## 18. Social Development in Middle Adulthood

### Today you will practice the following:

*18.1  Summarize the theories and research on psychosocial development during middle adulthood.*

*18.2  Describe the changes that occur in self-concept, identity, and personality during middle adulthood.*

*18.3  Analyze relationships in middle adulthood, including friend, spousal, parent–child, and grandparent relationships.*

*18.4  Discuss influences on job satisfaction and retirement planning during middle adulthood.*

Leo parks the car as Gina turns around in her seat to check the twins. "Which of you stinks?" she asks them, eliciting grins but no replies from the nine-month-old girls. Lisa, their three-year-old *princesa* holds her nose and points at the car seat closest to her. "Rosita?" Gina asks, and Lisa nods. "Not Yessica?" Leo would've sworn it was Yessi, but Lisa shakes her head.

Turning off the engine, he asks Gina, "Want me to take diaper duty and you can go inside with the other two, or you want me to take Yessi and Lisa inside while you change the stinkbug?"

"I'll change her," Gina offers. "Get me a Diet Coke when you get inside?"

"For you, I'll get a Diet Coke *and* a piece of the moon."

"Still a charmer." She laughs, shaking her head. "Love you, Leo."

"I love you more." Turning to the back seat, he points at Lisa. "Come along, *chica. Vamos lejos.*"

"*¡Sí, Papí! Vamos ahora.*"

She climbs out from the extended cab of his truck when he opens her door and then stands beside his door while he unfastens Yessi's buckles. So many safety contraptions. He hopes they actually work.

"*Bueno, cara,*" he whispers into her fuzzy head. "Let's go see *Tío* Daryl, okay?"

In answer, Yessi pulls his nose, and Lisa laughs at her. "Do you like that, *Papí*? I don't think I would like that."

"It's okay," he answers. Looking at Gina, he waves before setting off across the parking lot. This is their annual day of barbeque and family fun when Daryl brings his wife, Melanie, with their son, Mark, to a midpoint between their two houses, and the Ramirez family meets them there. This is the first time Daryl and Melanie have seen the twins, and Leo's unexpectedly proud to show them off. As soon as they enter, Lisa runs for Daryl, who has never made her feel like she is anything other than an actual princess, while their four-year-old Mark makes a beeline for Leo and Yessi. He bends to one knee so the boy can meet and touch the baby. After Lisa, Leo knows they're not particularly fragile, and he lets Mark poke her with fair thoroughness until he's distracted by the entrance of Gina with Rosita after which Mark repeats the process with Yessi's twin.

"Hey there, old man," Daryl calls as the women embrace.

"You're one to talk. Look at that gray."

Daryl straightens his thin shoulders. "Melanie says I'm distinguished."

"Full of it is more like it." Leo sits on a picnic bench and bounces Yessi on his lap. "Another couple years and the kids'll be wheeling us in here."

"For sure," his oldest friend agrees. "So, how's it going? You look happy. I was sorry to hear about your dad's passing last year."

"Yeah, thanks," he says, swallowing. "It's been hard, especially on *Mamá*, but we're managing. He lived the life he wanted and was content up to the end. If I die that happy, it'll have been a good life."

"I could say the same. Your dad set an admirable example for us."

"That he did."

"You, too, you know. What you do has to be fulfilling."

Leo nods again. "It really is, man. In some ways, nothing at all has changed since I started school. It's nice to feel I'm doing my part."

"And you do. The world is a better place with you in it."

Leo's flattered by Daryl's praise, but on a deeper level, his friend's validation answers a little question he asks periodically. *Am I making a difference?* He thinks he is. He has to believe he is.

## 19. Physical and Cognitive Development in Late Adulthood

### Today you will practice the following:

*19.1 Discuss age-related changes in brain and body systems in late adulthood, and identify ways that older adults may compensate for changes.*

*19.2 Identify risk and protective factors for health in late adulthood.*

*19.3 Summarize common dementias including characteristics, risk and protective factors, and treatment.*

*19.4 Analyze patterns of cognitive change in late adulthood.*

Leo knows not all things remain the same for all time. The world doesn't work that way, and thus, it's little surprise when the girls grow up, go to college like their brilliant mother, and move away. He and Gina stare at each other when Rosita—the last to fly the nest—drives away for the last time.

"Did you ever think they'd actually leave?" Gina asks him.

"Not really. No. Did you?"

"No." She walks back into the house and fixes coffee. "Do you remember how to live with me without the girls?"

"I remember how we got those girls, so . . . yes?"

"I had somewhat less vigorous activities in mind, but nothing's off the table," she says, negotiating.

"That's true. Nothing's been off the table before."

"Leonardo!" she yells, laughing. "Be serious please. I don't want us to have unrealistic expectations. Things . . . slow down," she said at last. "We get less energetic, you know."

"Do I know?" he asks her, a little confused.

"Well, if you don't, you should, and if you don't, you will soon enough!"

"As long as you don't develop dementia and forget who you're living with and making *tamales* for," he warns.

"I'll always remember, Leo. Promise me you will."

"I promise I'll always remember."

## 20. Socioemotional Development in Late Adulthood

### Today you will practice the following:

*20.1  Examine the contributions of self-concept, personality, and religiosity to older adults' well-being.*

*20.2  Identify social contexts in which older adults live and their influence on development.*

*20.3  Summarize features of older adults' relationships with friends, spouses, children, and grandchildren, and identify how these relationships affect older adults' functioning.*

*20.4  Discuss influences on the timing of retirement and adaptation to retirement.*

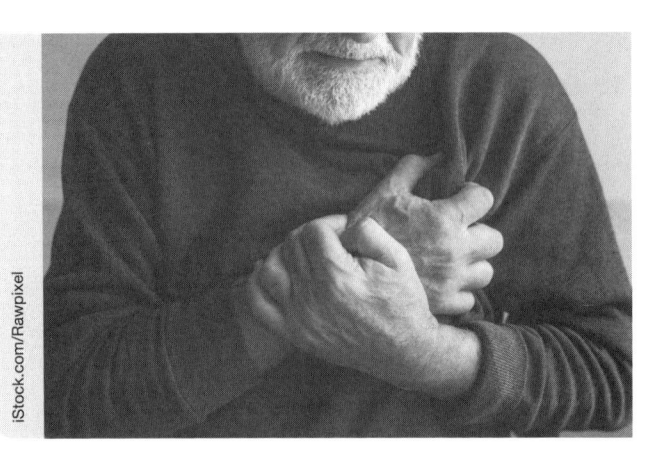

In his early 60s, Leonardo suffers a stroke. It's not fatal, and his coworkers are able to get an ambulance with first responders to the school where he's working at the time within five minutes. He's lucky. He suffers no permanent muscle or cognitive damage from the event, but his doctor reminds him of their many talks over the years. He tells Leonardo with Gina present that Leo must lose some weight, reduce his blood pressure, and get a little rest. He also suggests perhaps Leo should think about retirement. Gina promises to make sure those things happen.

A few months later, Leonardo and Gina welcome Rosita into their home to help care for Leonardo in his failing health. Their daughter promises Gina to help get *Papí* back in good health for Christmas and the living nativity at the church. With extreme diligence, Gina and Rosita manage to get Leonardo walking two miles each day even though they break the trek up into two one-mile walks. He also naps more regularly and eats better than he did previously. Gina accuses him of showing off for Rosita but secretly doesn't care what makes him do better so long as he's doing better.

## 21. Experience With Death and Dying

### Today you will practice the following:

*21.1  Identify ways in which death has been defined and end-of-life issues that may arise.*

*21.2  Contrast children's, adolescents', and adults' understanding of death.*

*21.3  Discuss the physical and emotional process of dying as it is experienced over the lifespan.*

*21.4  Summarize typical grief reactions to the loss of loved ones and the influence of development on bereavement.*

With a carefully restricted diet and rigid exercise regimen that Gina engages in with Leonardo, he lives until his mid-60s. At the birthday party for a second cousin 89 times removed (*joking!* he tells people), he begins feeling ill. By the time Gina gets him to the hospital, he's nearly incoherent. Leonard passes away from complications from the stroke two hours later while holding Gina's hand and waiting to have scans made.

Having not been prepared for Leo's sudden death, Gina's grief is sudden, deep, and lasts for a protracted time. She continues to live with Rosita until her own death at the age of 89, when she passes away from old age and complications arising from a recent bout of pneumonia.

## CASE DISCUSSION QUESTIONS

1. From toddlerhood, Leonardo is surrounded by both English and Spanish speakers, and he learns to speak both languages. This pleases his father Hector and, eventually, his preschool teacher. His mother Alicia, however, is annoyed. She wants Leonardo to speak only English and become more easily assimilated into American culture. For Hector, this poses a dilemma; Hector speaks only Spanish and doesn't want his relationship with Leonardo stunted. What do we know from Leonardo's preschool teacher and from attachment theory that would support Hector's position?

2. Throughout childhood, adolescence, and early adulthood, Leonardo has to navigate between a school system in which he doesn't fully excel, a street system he doesn't wish to join, and keeping his little brother off the streets. How do these competing tasks and the stress they cause impact Leonardo's life trajectory across any and all domains (biological, cognitive, and socioemotional)?

3. During her pregnancy with Leonardo, Alicia has to decide whether to visit a doctor for a rash or stay on the job. Why is this not as easy a decision as it would seem to be on the surface?

4. Why is Leonardo so concerned about Ínigo?

# 6 London Dennel

## Introduction

Welcome to your case study!

Congratulations! You will follow the lifespan of baby girl London Dennel. Try to use your best judgment, textbook, classmates, instructor, and supplementary resources to make the best decisions to help her grow.

This semester you will observe London as she grows from infant to child to teen to adult. Who will she become in your care? Will you understand and agree with all decisions available within her circumstances? How will you feel about the tough decisions that forever shape her path in life?

## Meet London Dennel

London is the third child of Laura Dennel and Douglas Dennel. Laura, who is 33, has a master's degree and works full-time, as does Doug, who is 32 and has a bachelor's degree, when they decide to have a third child. Because they both work full-time and live modestly

iStock.com/damircudic

CHAPTER 6  London Dennel

but comfortably in their suburban three-bedroom house, they can afford this child they want to complete their family. When London is born, she will join a four-year-old brother, Max, and a two-year-old sister, Chelsea.

Through this case study and your lifespan course, you will be asked to consider decisions regarding London's physical, emotional, and cognitive growth and development from several perspectives: her parents' Douglas and Laura, her grandparents' and siblings' as well as those of her spouse, her potential children, other potential family members, friends, teachers, doctors, and supervisors.

Now let's get started.

## 1. Development and Its Influences

### Today you will practice the following:

1.1  Outline five principles of the lifespan developmental perspective.

1.2  Explain three theoretical controversies about human development.

1.3  Summarize five theoretical perspectives on human development.

1.4  Describe the methods and research designs used to study human development.

During the 27th week of pregnancy, Laura phones Doug on a Thursday and asks him to collect Chelsea from daycare and Max from preschool. She wants to stop at the grocery store on her way home from work, and it's easier to shop without the kids wheedling extra goodies out of her on every aisle. After loading the bags from her speedy trip through the store into the trunk, Laura pulls onto the highway to head home. It's a short drive, barely enough time for a third of her Britney Spears *Circus* CD, the guilty pleasure she keeps hidden in the glove box. Halfway through "Womanizer," Laura pats her belly in time to the music and thinks about making pizza for dinner. There's probably enough time left for a quick homemade dough, and Max and

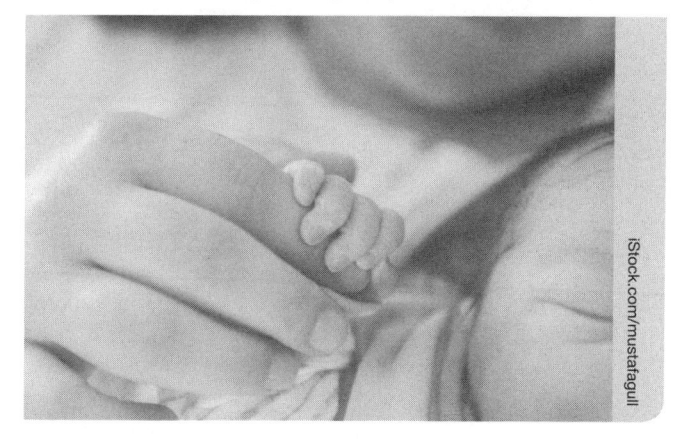

Chelsea love shaping their own pizzas into funny shapes. Deciding yes, pizza is good for dinner, she stretches her back the best she can just before the last chorus of the song, words she doesn't hear when her car is struck in the front passenger side door at 30 miles per hour, spinning her car 270° into oncoming traffic. Laura has no time to take any defensive measures; the accident begins and ends so quickly and with such violence the best thing for Laura is that she loses consciousness at the scene and doesn't feel the pain of the compound fracture in her right leg. However, losing consciousness also produces significant problems when Laura goes into preterm labor, an event that results in London's birth occurring 13 weeks early. Both mom and baby spend several weeks in their respective intensive care units before life takes any significant new directions.

## 2. Biological and Environmental Foundations

### Today you will practice the following:

2.1 *Discuss the genetic foundations of development.*

2.2 *Identify examples of genetic disorders and chromosomal abnormalities.*

2.3 *Discuss the choices available to prospective parents in having healthy children.*

2.4 *Describe the interaction of heredity and environment, including behavioral genetics and the epigenetic framework.*

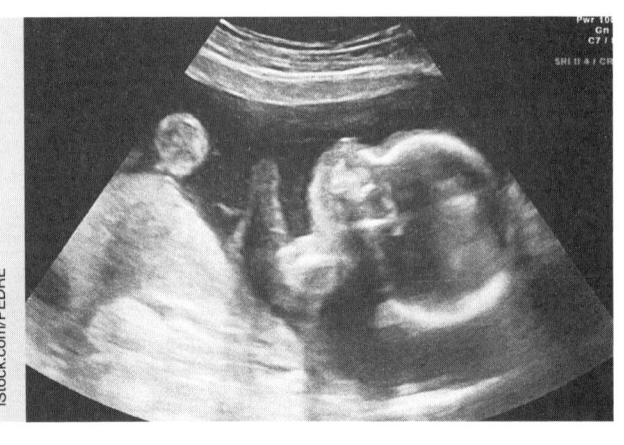

All of Laura's prenatal appointments show a perfectly healthy, normally developing baby. She and Doug are thrilled, as are London's brother- and sister-to-be. Max and Chelsea spend many hours helping their mom and dad redecorate Chelsea's room because the baby will share a room with her after he or she is born. Everyone agrees that it's a good idea to be surprised whether the baby is a boy or a girl, like the best birthday surprise, Max says, and Laura laughs, saying he's just right. Even though they don't find out the baby's sex, Laura and Doug are glad when prenatal testing confirms a healthy baby with no chromosomal abnormalities. They decide at that point not to screen for additional genetic problems even though they could do so. Their insurance will cover it, and Laura's graduate work in biogenetics informs their choices about the information they could gain from such testing. They know, however, they will love and raise their new baby regardless of any potential difficulties and decide the stress of knowing about looming problems would be bad for Laura's health and, subsequently, the baby's.

## 3. Prenatal Development, Birth, and Newborn Experience

### Today you will practice the following:

*3.1   Describe the three periods of prenatal development that begin with conception.*

*3.2   Identify how exposure to teratogens can influence the prenatal environment.*

*3.3   Explain the process of childbirth.*

*3.4   Discuss the neonate's physical capacities, including development in low-birth-weight infants.*

London is so small when the fetal surgeon delivers her. The emergency room team allows Doug to be in the room through the cesarean, but as soon as the baby is born, he's swept away and told to wait for London in the neonatal intensive care unit (NICU). Laura will be a while, he's told. It doesn't take long for the pediatric team to get to the NICU, and Doug is allowed to be right there while London is assessed. He's painfully aware of the difference in size between her and Max and Chelsea, both of whom went a couple days past their due dates.

"Fourteen and three-quarters inches long," the nurse says softly to a waiting assistant recording vital statistics. "Big for a 27-week baby. That's good. Hey, Dad, do we have a name yet?"

Doug sniffs. They said she was big. That's a good sign. "Uh, yeah. London. Her name is London."

"London. That's nice. London, you're a big girl to be so small. We like to see that." She turns to the assistant and says, "Two-point-two pounds."

"Wow!" A new face appears and looks impressed by the number that Doug can't compute other than to compare with Max's six-eight and Chelsea's seven-four. The newcomer holds out his hand, and Doug shakes it. "Mr. Dennel, I'm Dr. Sanchez, the NICU attending. I'm just popping in to take a look at—"

"London," the nurse supplies.

"London." He looks at the nurse. "What've we got?"

"Fourteen and three-quarters inches, two-point-two pounds, three and six APGARS. Good lung sounds, strong heart, and she's hungry. She's voided already. So, let's get her something to eat and see what happens."

Dr. Sanchez nods and smiles. "Good." Then he lifts London, who fits in a single hand like a kitten, and turns her this way and that, inspecting. "Dad, she's got good muscle tone, good color, and she's breathing well without help right now. I want to put her in an isolette with oxygen and a feeding tube. Let's see if we can keep her stable for a couple weeks and step up her feeding from there."

"Can I touch her?" Doug ventures, having been scared to ask before.

Dr. Sanchez looks at the nurse and assistant. "Dad hasn't held her yet?"

"We've been here all of five minutes but no."

Seconds later, London is cradled in his hands as the nurse explains how to do a thing she calls "kangaroo care," cuddling a naked London against his own bare chest.

"As much as she can tolerate as much as you can be here every day."

Gazing down at his daughter, Doug feels a swell of love and protection. "I think we can manage that." A nurse shows him to a rocking chair, and as he sits, he asks, "Can someone please check on my wife?"

"Of course," Dr. Sanchez assures him, "although I was informed on my way up that her surgery is going well."

Breathing in relief, Doug realizes how lucky they've all been that day.

## 4. Physical Development in Infancy and Toddlerhood

### Today you will practice the following:

4.1 *Discuss growth and the role of nutrition in development during infancy and toddlerhood.*

4.2 *Summarize brain development during infancy and toddlerhood.*

4.3 *Compare infants' early learning capacities for habituation, classical conditioning, operant conditioning, and imitation.*

4.4 *Describe infants' developing sensory abilities.*

4.5 *Analyze the roles of maturation and contextual factors in infant and toddler motor development.*

During the first weeks of London's life, Doug struggles to be everywhere at once. There's one of him and four locations he needs to be sometimes. London needs him, and so does Laura, who has a long and painful recovery ahead of her. Max needs taking to and from preschool, and Chelsea needs taking to and from daycare. He can't cope alone. Biting the bullet, he calls Laura's mother and asks her to come stay for a while. Both sets of grandparents had come initially, of course, when no one knew whether Laura or London would make it, but they left to allow things to quiet a few days later. Doug desperately needs someone now, and he knows that if he's able to take Laura home anytime soon, she will want her mom to be there helping her. So, with great reluctance, he calls Tammy and explains the situation. She tells him to breathe, to see to what he has to that morning, and she will be there by noon. He almost cries from relief.

With immediate concerns in Tammy's capable hands (Doug has no idea why he waited so long to call her—stereotypical mother-in-law reluctance probably, which is shameful), he passes many hours every day going between Laura's and London's hospital rooms. He holds London, doing the kangaroo care the nurse showed him when she was first brought to the NICU, and he talks to Laura and shows her photos and videos of all the children. He tries hard to be home for dinner every night. When Laura is able to sit in a wheelchair, he begins taking her to the NICU with him, and they take turns holding London, who seems to respond immediately to her mother's touch and voice. She's still tiny and frail, but the feeding tube has been removed, and Laura and Doug take turns feeding her with a syringe until she's ready for a bottle. Laura, saddened by her loss of breast-feeding what will surely be her last child, works through depression even while they watch London grow and put on weight underneath the translucent skin.

"I knew, of course," she tells Doug one day while he's got a naked London tucked inside his big flannel shirt. "I was just in bed too long, and I hadn't started producing milk yet anyway. I knew I wouldn't be able to nurse her, but it never really hit me until she was ready for the bottle."

"Try to think of our gains instead of our losses if you can," he says, reaching for her hand with his.

"I know."

She squeezes his hand, both of them grateful for so many things just then.

Over the next several months, London improves daily. They take her home when she's five weeks old. She's met the established goals of a whopping five pounds and a consistent eating and elimination schedule. She's also sleeping without any respiratory concerns, but Dr. Sanchez is sending her home with a breathing monitor she'll have to wear anytime they can't see her directly, like when they put her to bed or when she's in the car seat, to make sure she doesn't stop breathing for more than a second or two. They'll bring the monitor back weekly for several months to have the data in its memory read. Dr. Sanchez will be able to tell if London suffers from sleep apnea or other sleep and respiratory problems and, if not, will give their little wonder a clean bill of health.

At six months, this is precisely what she gets. Dr. Sanchez has a long conversation with Laura and Doug while London sits on his lap and chews his stethoscope.

"You know she looks great. She's looked great if I'm honest since the minute I saw her. A 27-week baby can come with a host of problems, but you had a good surgical team who got her out and up here fast, and Laura, you clearly took excellent care of yourself during the prenatal period before the accident. She had the best odds possible. So, let's talk about what you've seen and what you'll see moving forward."

Both Doug and Laura nod. "Please," Laura says. "She's so different from Max and Chelsea."

Dr. Sanchez chuckles. "Yes, she would be."

He spends a few minutes explaining the growth they've seen, both physically and also in terms of London's abilities. "Some of what you'll have seen you likely saw in her brother and sister and at the same times, particularly reflexive changes, social interactions—those sorts of things."

"Yes," Doug says, "but she's still small. She rolled over 'on time,' I guess you'd say, but she isn't sitting up yet or getting on her knees."

"Not to worry," Dr. Sanchez tells them. "You're right. She's small, but she's showing every sign she'll get to those soon. What you're seeing are typical preemie patterns. Some things she'll do at just about the proper age plus the extra 9 to 12 weeks she needed to gestate. That is, you'll hardly notice the difference between her and her siblings. Other things, she'll need to catch up with her peers in size before she'll catch up in skills."

"Will she?" Laura asks. "Catch up in size?"

"She should. There's no guarantee, but she should. Often preemies will by two or three, and then you'll begin to see that skill gap close. Your biggest concern will be respiratory problems—

asthma, flu, and the like. So, keep a good eye on her, make sure all five of you get flu shots every year, and don't delay going to the pediatrician if you're concerned about something. I'm not worried at all about her development."

Relieved on all fronts, the Dennels leave Dr. Sanchez's office a half hour later, after which they pick up Max and Chelsea and take everyone for an impromptu ice cream cone at Dairy Queen.

## 5. Cognitive Development in Infancy and Toddlerhood

### Today you will practice the following:

5.1 *Discuss the cognitive-developmental perspective on infant reasoning.*

5.2 *Describe the information processing system in infants.*

5.3 *Discuss individual differences in infant intelligence.*

5.4 *Summarize the patterns of language development during infancy and toddlerhood.*

Laura watches London's development like a hawk, always on the lookout for something to be wrong. The first thing she notices is that London doesn't speak like Max and Chelsea did. By her first birthday, she says *no* and *ma* and *dada* and *mah* for Max and *chessy* for Chelsea. She really doesn't say anything else. At her 12-month checkup, Laura raises the concern with the children's pediatrician.

Dr. Adams, in the middle of looking inside London's ears at the time, says, "Well, she's got a brain in here," which makes Laura laugh. "Seriously, Laura," the doctor tells her after she finishes the brief physical exam, "I understand your concerns, and we'll always keep a close eye on what might be considered delays of any sort with London."

"But . . . ?"

"But she doesn't have any other signs of developmental problems. My guess, if I had to hazard one, is that she isn't speaking because she either doesn't get a chance to or because she doesn't need to. There are four people in your house other than London, all of whom are used to filling the quiet. She also has two siblings who are each at an age where they're likely to speak *for* her. When London needs to speak or wants to speak, London will speak."

"You're sure?" Laura asks, hopeful but not convinced.

"One hundred percent? No, but pretty close. I'm not due to see her again until 18 months, but if you're still concerned in three months, make an appointment, and we'll see how she's doing."

Laura shakes Dr. Adams's hand. "Thank you. That makes me feel a lot better."

"Comes with the territory." She tousles London's sparse blond hair. "I'll see you soon, missy."

London waves backward. "Bye-bye."

"See?" Dr. Adams says on the way out the door. "No one's here taking up her airwaves. "Go home, Laura. She knows what she's doing, and soon you won't be able to shut her up."

## 6. Socioemotional Development in Infancy and Toddlerhood

### Today you will practice the following:

6.1 Summarize the psychosocial tasks of infancy and toddlerhood.

6.2 Describe emotional development in infancy, and identify contextual and cultural influences on emotional development in infants and toddlers.

6.3 Identify the styles and stability of temperament, including the role of goodness of fit in infant development.

6.4 Describe how attachment develops in infancy and toddlerhood.

6.5 Differentiate the roles of self-concept, self-recognition, and self-control in infant development.

As a toddler, London is a mercurial child. Her parents and her brother and sister doted on her when she came home from the hospital, and that never really stops. No one truly spoils her, but she's always aware that she's considered special. From time to time, that influences her mood and interactions with others. She is, overall, a sweet and loving child, but she can also be willful and demanding, behaviors that try Laura's patience and make her wonder what's going to happen when she starts school.

"I think it's time for something more structured than daycare," she tells Doug one night.

"Princess exerting her royal will again?" he asks.

"Yes, and even though Chelsea and Max are good about it, this won't serve London well either with her brother and sister or with friends, teachers . . . *the world*," she finishes.

"Agreed. Do you want me to help you look for a place? Military school maybe?"

Laura laughs. "I think Sunrise will probably be fine," she tells him, referring to the preschool both Chelsea and Max attended from age three until they started Kindergarten.

"Probably," he admits, "although I can call the Joint Chiefs and keep her on backup."

"You do that, but call Sunrise while you're at it. We're paid up at daycare through the end of the month. With any luck, they can start her next month. If not, find out how long the waiting list is?"

"Of course, my love. I'll do it tomorrow."

Laura sighs and sits down with a glass of wine. "Thank you. Now I can decide what color to paint the old naughty chair. We can't expect preschool to do it all."

"In that case, I'll go rummage in the attic for the chair while you ponder."

## 7. Physical and Cognitive Development in Early Childhood

### Today you will practice the following:

*7.1* Discuss physical development in early childhood.

*7.2* Compare Piaget's cognitive-developmental and Vygotsky's sociocultural perspectives on cognitive development in early childhood.

*7.3* Describe information-processing abilities during early childhood.

*7.4* Summarize young children's advances in language development.

*7.5* Contrast social learning and cognitive-developmental perspectives on moral development in early childhood.

*7.6* Identify and explain approaches to early childhood education.

"Doug and Laura, hi." Miranda Thompson, London's preschool teacher at Sunrise, shakes their hands in turn. They're on a first-name basis since Chelsea had been in her class only two years before and had just moved on to Kindergarten that year. "Have a seat."

"Thanks," Laura says, pulling one of the tiny chairs away from the moon-shaped table in the center of the room. "This is exciting, London's first parent–teacher meeting!"

Doug holds up a hand. "Before we get started, please tell me she behaves while she's here."

Ms. Thompson laughs a little. "Well . . ." she hedges. Laura groans, and the teacher hurries to reassure them. "Oh, it's not as bad as all that. London is outgoing and eager to please. I'm sure you know this about her. She's also doing well with numbers and anything technological I put in her hands."

"That's awesome!" Doug says. "What's the catch then?"

"I have a little trouble getting her to focus during story time," the teacher admits, "and she seems to have a tendency toward clumsiness on the playground. I have to watch her carefully when she climbs the ladder for the big slide or when she's on the monkey bars. Again, I'm sure you know this about her."

Laura agrees. "But I hoped being around other children might help with that," she says.

The teacher smiles gently. "She's around other children at home, too, and Max and Chelsea are probably a little more invested in London's success than her peers here are. I'm sure you're right, Laura, and being around other kids her age will help her achieve some growth. I just want to reinforce that she's a little behind. Nothing to be overly worried about, but we do want to work on these areas."

"We will," they assure her quickly. "We definitely will."

## 8. Socioemotional Development in Early Childhood

### Today you will practice the following:

*8.1* Discuss young children's emerging sense of initiative, self-concept, and self-esteem.

*8.2* Summarize the development of emotional understanding, regulation, and behavior in early childhood.

*8.3* Identify four parenting styles and their associations with child outcomes.

*8.4* Compare biological, cognitive, and contextual theoretical explanations of gender role development.

*8.5* Explain the function of play and the form it takes during early childhood.

Finishing her first year of preschool, London evidences big social gains. She doesn't bully her sister and brother much anymore (or her parents), and she's frequently helpful at home, doing tasks such as taking silverware to the table while Max and Chelsea lay plates for mealtimes or putting a fresh bag in the trashcan after one of her parents takes the trash outside to the big can in the garage. She likes helping. Her mom especially makes her feel good for the things she does by smiling and hugging her. Helping is fun.

Probably the best times she has at home are playing with Max and Chelsea. Max is seven now, and he has friends on their street who come over sometimes. Then he doesn't play with either London or Chelsea, but when they all play together it's the best. They teach each other everything, One day, London tells Max that a friend of hers at preschool said London was weird for liking computers because she's a girl. Max tells her that's stupid, that girls and boys can do all the same things—except peeing. Girls can't do that standing up like boys can, but she shouldn't care because it's kind of hard anyway.

## 9. Physical and Cognitive Development in Middle Childhood

### Today you will practice the following:

*9.1* *Identify patterns of physical and motor development during middle childhood and common health issues facing school-age children.*

*9.2* *Discuss school-age children's capacities for reasoning and processing information.*

*9.3* *Summarize views of intelligence including the uses, correlates, and criticisms of intelligence tests.*

*9.4* *Examine patterns of moral development during middle childhood.*

*9.5* *Summarize language development during middle childhood.*

*9.6* *Discuss children's learning at school.*

London likes elementary school a lot better than preschool. Kindergarten was scary, but every other grade is fun. She's good at lots of subjects, like math and science, and she isn't bad at anything. Well, she's not very good at physical education (PE), but no one conquers everything. At least that's what her dad tells her. In second grade, they have to run a mile in PE, and London gets a couple minutes into the job when she starts to feel like her chest is on fire. It's hard to breathe, and her eyes water until she can't see. She stops running even though Coach Parker yells at her. Mom has to pick her up at school that day, and London sees the doctor. The doctor listens to London breathe and then says, "Asthma," but London doesn't know what that means. She also says this isn't unexpected because London was "born so early." She gives Mom a bunch of papers for medicine and gives London a paper that says she doesn't have to run a mile for a while. That's not terrible, even though she doesn't want to be "the sick kid" either. After a few weeks of figuring out how to use the new inhaler the doctor gives her and learning to trust the sense she has of when it's okay to run and when it's not, she finally finishes the mile, and Coach Parker gives her a secret cookie for congratulations. Finishing feels like the biggest accomplishment London's ever managed.

In fourth grade, the elementary school wins something called "a grant," and even though London isn't sure what that is, she knows what it means. Every kid gets a brand-new tablet computer for the rest of the time they're in the elementary school. London is stoked! There are so many papers she and her parents have to sign, but she doesn't care. As soon as the tablet is in her hands, she figures out how to download a developer app and starts creating programs of her own. She starts small, building a world traveling app based on live cams all across the globe. Want to visit sub-Saharan Africa? Choose the Africam. That one is no more than a collection of cams sitting behind a frame with a menu. She builds an adjunct app that allows a person to control the frame like a television with a "remote" app for a smartphone. She thinks it's a cute package even if it isn't terribly sophisticated. By the time fifth grade starts, London has a small cottage industry going, and her parents help her set up an online payment system. Charging less than a dollar an app, she starts saving for long-term dreams like a car and college or maybe funding a scientist's cure for asthma. So far, she's made $11.88.

## 10. Socioemotional Development in Middle Childhood

### Today you will practice the following:

10.1  Describe school-age children's self-conceptions and motivation.

10.2  Examine the roles of friendship, peer acceptance, and peer victimization in school-age children's adjustment.

10.3  Discuss family relationships in middle childhood and the influence of family structure on adjustment.

10.4  Analyze the role of resilience in promoting adjustment to adversity, including characteristics of children and contexts that promote resilience.

"Mo-om!"

Max calls for Laura, and London gives him an evil look daring him to tattle. When she hears their mother's footsteps nearing the stairs, she leans against the doorway to Max's room and puts a hand over her chest, pretending to cough through an oncoming asthma attack. Max rolls his eyes.

"Oh, come on," he complains. "How dumb do you think she is?"

"Oh, come on," Mom says as her head appears at the top of the stairs. "How dumb do you think I am?"

London stands up straight and points at Max. "He started it!"

"Did not!"

"Yes. You. Did." London looks at Mom. "All I did was ask to use his laptop to write some SQL code, and Mr. High-and-Mighty has to birth a baby cow all over the—"

"Enough, London," Mom says, interrupting.

"But—"

"No *but*s." She looks at Max and smiles. "We'll figure this out. Your laptop is safe." To London, she says, "Come along downstairs, and let's have a talk about personal property and maybe creativity in trying to dupe your mother. Fake asthma? Really?"

"I just wanted to borrow it for a few minutes."

"Right," Mom agrees as they enter the kitchen. She hands London her own laptop from work. "The keyword in all of that was 'borrow.' It's his laptop, and if he says 'no' that's okay. Life isn't going to be a string of yeses, London."

"Well, that's dumber than fake asthma," she says, meaning this entirely. Mom laughs again, and London can't help smiling a little. "Imagine how happy everyone would be if everyone else always said yes."

Mom looks at her like she's a little green alien and then says, "I think the world was like that under the reign of Caligula."

"Who was that?"

"A Roman emperor, but you'll want to wait awhile before asking your teachers to tell you that bit of history."

## 11. Physical and Cognitive Development in Late Childhood

### Today you will practice the following:

*11.1* Describe school-age children's self-conceptions and motivation.

*11.2* Examine the roles of friendship, peer acceptance, and peer victimization in school-age children's adjustment.

*11.3* Discuss family relationships in middle childhood and the influence of family structure on adjustment.

*11.4* Analyze the role of resilience in promoting adjustment to adversity, including characteristics of children and contexts that promote resilience.

When it comes to computer coding, it's all systems go. London wants to be the best, but it's hard. She knows she's good, but whenever she finds a teacher who could help her be better, it seems like the teacher's more interested in helping her boy classmates. London has to eavesdrop on the extra lessons they get or to find out what books they're told to read. Every year, she comes in second place in the school science fair, and she knows she could win if she just had a little help. It's so frustrating, the idea that being a girl has anything to do with computers.

## 12. Socioemotional Development in Late Childhood

### Today you will practice the following:

*12.1* Summarize the processes by which self-concept, self-esteem, and identity change during adolescence.

*12.2* Discuss the nature of parent–child relationships in adolescence.

*12.3* Examine the developmental progression of peer relations in adolescence.

*12.4* Analyze patterns of adolescent sexual activity including sexual orientation.

*12.5* Identify common psychological and behavioral problems in adolescence.

London knows kids at school who compete with each other for best attendance awards or spelling bee contests. London codes. Her competition is always boys, which annoys her sometimes. She tries to get some of her female friends to get involved in computers with her, but most aren't interested. A couple have been from time to time, but then they become competition for London, too. That's weird. Like, she wants to be friends with them, but she's not going to dumb her work down just to keep them as friends.

## 13. Physical and Cognitive Development in Adolescence

### Today you will practice the following:

*13.1  Evaluate the "storm and stress" perspective on adolescence in light of research evidence.*

*13.2  Summarize the physical changes that occur with puberty and the correlates of pubertal timing.*

*13.3  Discuss brain development during adolescence and its effect on behavior.*

*13.4  Identify ways in which thinking changes in adolescence and how these changes are reflected in adolescent decision-making and behavior.*

*13.5  Discuss moral development and influences on moral reasoning.*

*13.6  Describe the challenges that school transitions pose for adolescents and the role of parents in academic achievement.*

Although Dr. Sanchez, the attending pediatric doctor in the NICU when London was born, as well as London's childhood pediatrician told her parents that she would mostly likely catch up with her peers in size in the first few years of life, she remains wiry through adolescence. Her height, slightly above average, is similar to her brother and sister, but her narrow frame gives her an androgynous appearance. This is emphasized by the short, blond pixie haircut she wears.

She still takes asthma medicine in the mornings and keeps a rescue inhaler in her book bag. Endurance activities will never be part of her repertoire. Instead, she focuses on strength, working out with free weights at the local YMCA with Max when she's not doing the bare minimum on her homework to make time for writing computer programs. She's taught herself basic programming languages and a couple advanced languages as well. Her most enjoyable hours now are creating novel human–machine interactions. She finally won a science fair (ninth grade) by engineering a robot that was more than the typical DC battery–powered one most kids brought to school. Hers, while not humanoid (why does everyone do that, she wants to know), interacts with its human in a way that includes ever-increasing sophistication based on prior interactions. She should've won a contract with NASA, but the science fair was a good start.

## 14. Socioemotional Development in Adolescence

### Today you will practice the following:

*14.1 Summarize the processes by which self-concept, self-esteem, and identity change during adolescence.*

*14.2 Discuss the nature of parent–child relationships in adolescence.*

*14.3 Examine the developmental progression of peer relations in adolescence.*

*14.4 Analyze patterns of adolescent sexual activity including sexual orientation.*

*14.5 Identify common psychological and behavioral problems in adolescence.*

Much to Laura and Doug's dismay, London begins "dating" in middle school, coming home many days with a new "boyfriend" to talk about. They can barely keep up. Chelsea helps, because she knows many of the boys London goes on about and is often friends with their older siblings. To their relief, no one seems to hold her attention for long. Rather, no one seems to successfully compete with a computer for London's attention.

In 10th grade, London attends her first homecoming dance with a date. Laura takes her shopping for a dress, all of which London rejects either on the hanger or without exiting the dressing room. She sends a text to her best friend Maggie Summerfield after she and her mom leave the third department store.

"I just want to wear pants," she types.

Maggie responds almost instantly as London knows she will. "Like jeans or something nice?"

"Nice. Like a suit or a tux or something."

"Wear that. Isn't that the point? If you like it . . ."

London turns to her mom. "Can we look at tuxes maybe?"

"London," Mom starts with a deep sigh, "could you not have decided this earlier? Max has a beautiful tuxedo at home. I will never understand why you children make life so difficult on me."

"No offense, Mom, but I'd kinda like to look for my own things. Like we were just looking for dresses."

"Good point," Mom says and takes her arm.

London attends the homecoming dance with a group of friends including the boyfriend of the week. She and Charles dance and drink a weird ginger ale punch and try to pretend that his parents aren't chaperones. Everyone has a great time. The DJ plays some oldies song that are all angsty and slow, and she and Charles slow dance without getting very close. She spies Maggie across the way dancing with their friend Ben and rolls her eyes. Maggie returns the look, and they both smile. Maggie looks great, London thinks. She's wearing a dress London tried on and hated, but it's perfect on her closest friend.

After the song, she disentangles herself from Charles's clutches. "I need to go to the bathroom," she tells him and is happy to see Maggie touching up her lipstick when she gets there.

"Tux is the bomb," Maggie says. "I'm so glad you wore it."

Grinning, London fixes her hair in the mirror. "Me, too. Thanks for helping me decide."

Maggie turns and puts a hip on the old porcelain sink beside her. "Of course. I always want you to do what makes you happy."

"I know."

Before London can thank her again, Maggie takes a step forward and kisses her.

"Like that," Maggie says.

"But I—"

"And I."

"Can I do that again?" London asks her.

"I'm kind of hoping you do."

## 15. Physical and Cognitive Development in Emerging/Early Adulthood

### Today you will practice the following:

*15.1  Describe the features and characteristics of emerging and early adulthood.*

*15.2  Summarize the physical developments of emerging and early adulthood.*

*15.3  Analyze physical and sexual health issues in emerging and early adulthood.*

*15.4  Compare postformal reasoning, pragmatic thought, and cognitive-affective complexity.*

*15.5  Explain how attending college influences young adults' development, and identify challenges faced by first-generation and nontraditional students.*

*15.6  Discuss vocational choice and the transition to work.*

"London?"

London looks up from notes she's making on a pad of paper. She's trying to combine work and pleasure by writing a new program as part of her AP physics project. A couple sticking points bug her, and the distraction is welcome.

"Dad?"

Dad sits across from her at the kitchen table and taps his fingers on the sticky top. Max hadn't cleaned it well after breakfast; she knows it was his turn because it's always his turn. When he moved back in after finishing college, Mom and Dad gave him extra chores. One of them is cleaning the table after every meal.

"Dad?" she repeats. "What's bothering you?"

He smiles and stills his hand. "Nothing, London. Nothing's 'bothering' me. Your mom and I wanted to make sure we had a few words with you now that you're off to college soon. Could you possibly give me your attention?"

"Sure." Pushing her work to the center of the table, she looks at him. "Is this the fiscal, academic, or sexual responsibility talk?"

Dad looks shocked, and she laughs.

"More of the latter, sort of," he says, laughing, too. "We can keep this lighthearted, but I want you to understand the seriousness of what I'm saying to you."

"All ears, Dad." She pauses and reaches across the table to poke at him. "If it's sex, why are you talking to me instead of Mom?"

Looking offended, he says, "Hey! This is an equal opportunity household! I'm the one available, and we're on the same page, Mom and I."

"Fair enough."

"We have zero real concerns about your ability to go to school and do well academically. I hope we've taught you to be careful with money. We've just finished paying off the medical bills from Mom's surgeries and—"

"I know all of this. No credit cards, no extra loans, low-key job on campus, and spend as little as I can."

"Right."

"So?" she asks, mildly curious. "The sex? If this is about safe sex, Mom covered that ages ago."

"I know. Look, London, this isn't easy for me, and there's a reason I'm talking to you instead of Mom. You're right about that. We're both a little concerned that once you're gone you'll remember things like safe sex and forget that you still have to be concerned about boys."

London sits quietly for a minute thinking about her dad's words. "But . . ." She looks at him and half grins. The whole thing is ludicrous. "But I date girls, Dad."

"That's exactly the point." He sighs. "London, you may not be interested in boys, but that doesn't mean you're not going to be *interesting to* boys."

"And . . . ?"

"And more than a quarter of young women are sexually assaulted while they're in college, sweetheart. You have to be aware, and Mom and I are worried you won't be because boys aren't on your radar."

She frowns and can feel her face making an unhappy shape while she thinks about her dad's words. Her parents are right; she hasn't thought about the possibility at all. Her high school is small, and everyone knows her. She's never had a second of trouble with anyone, boy or girl.

"I haven't thought about that, Dad," she admits.

"We don't want to scare you. We just want you to be aware."

"I will be. Now." They smile at each other, and she reaches for her homework. "While I've got you, can I bounce some ideas off you? I'm a little stuck."

## 16. Socioemotional Development in Emerging/Early Adulthood

### Today you will practice the following:

*16.1* Summarize psychosocial development in emerging and early adulthood.

*16.2* Discuss influences on friendship and mate selection and interactions in emerging and early adulthood.

*16.3* Analyze the diverse romantic situations that may characterize emerging and early adulthood, including singlehood, cohabitation, marriage, and divorce.

*16.4* Compare the experiences of young adults as stepparents, never-married parents, and same-sex parents.

In London's senior year of college, she wins a coveted study-abroad position in Ethiopia. She wants to work on a project to allow a group of women to improve the quality of life in a village called Timbala by providing them with tablets, rudimentary coding training, and satellite Internet access. She's convinced the women will do the rest, like figure out water irrigation and local primary education. The study abroad will last the entire fall semester, and she'll finish college five months after she gets back to the States.

She's never been as uncomfortable, hot, and dirty as she is in Timbala. There's nothing like doing without the luxuries of first world living to realize they aren't necessities, she thinks. She's also never felt more alive and engaged in purposeful activity. She leaves a girlfriend behind in the United States, and she misses her, but when she returns all she can think about is getting back to Africa after she graduates. When graduation day approaches, she searches for a fellowship that will send her back to Africa in the summer, and when she's offered one, she asks her girlfriend to go with her. A lot of back-and-forth negotiations go on before she finally leaves alone with her parents' support and a suitcase of donated tablets. The saddest part, she realizes, is that she's okay leaving alone.

## 17. Physical and Cognitive Development in Middle Adulthood

### Today you will practice the following:

*17.1* Summarize age-related physical changes during middle adulthood.

*17.2* Discuss common health conditions and illnesses and the roles of stress and hardiness on health during middle adulthood.

*17.3* Contrast the findings of cross-sectional and longitudinal studies of crystallized and fluid intelligence over adulthood.

*17.4* Analyze changes in cognitive capacities during middle adulthood, including attention, memory, processing speed, and expertise.

London's fellowship ends a couple months before she turns 26. Returning to the States, she finds her old room ready for her. Max, at 33, is living in a nearby town with his wife and infant son. Chelsea has moved to California to pursue an acting career, which means she's waiting tables and flashing smiles at anyone who looks remotely important. Mom and Dad seem happy to have her back. Or maybe they're just relieved she made it back from the wilds again. She wishes they could see how beautiful where she lives is.

"What now?" Mom asks over lasagna that first night.

London shakes her head. "I don't know. I really don't. Graduate school holds zero appeal for me, but neither does selling dresses at Macy's. What am I good for?"

"Plenty," Dad says, "but give yourself a day or two to settle in. I think Mom's just glad to know it's not going to be bonbons and *Gilmore Girls* binging."

"Heh. No. Not that."

In fact, London finds a job more quickly than she expects to. Idleness has never been her friend, and she starts looking as soon as the jet lag wears off. When she finds the listing, she doesn't hope she'll be considered, but she calls and tells Max about it anyway.

"It's in global development technologies at the Gates Foundation," she tells him. "Developing programming. Not coding but—"

"I know what you mean." Max laughs. "Go for it. You'll absolutely not get it if you don't apply. I'll help you with your résumé," he offers. She's glad of this better he's the marketing guru in the family.

"Thanks, Max."

To her surprise and excitement, she is hired for the job after a phone interview, Skype interview, and West Coast in-person interview. The foundation feels like the perfect fit.

The day after her birthday, she boards a plane for Seattle, where if nothing else she'll be on the same coast as Chelsea. This feels like a fitting next step. Chelsea is waiting for her when the plane lands and, taking London's arm, says, "Champagne to celebrate and then shopping for some IKEA things to get you started."

London takes a deep breath. Life Part II has begun.

## 18. Socioemotional Development in Middle Adulthood

### Today you will practice the following:

*18.1 Summarize the theories and research on psychosocial development during middle adulthood.*

*18.2 Describe the changes that occur in self-concept, identity, and personality during middle adulthood.*

*18.3 Analyze relationships in middle adulthood, including friend, spousal, parent–child, and grandparent relationships.*

*18.4 Discuss influences on job satisfaction and retirement planning during middle adulthood.*

On a wet and blustery Thursday, London turns the light off at her work station and grabs her coat—quitting time. Actually, it's well past, but she doesn't mind. Work is even better than she thought it might be, than she hoped it could be. It never occurred to her that she could be so happy inside an office after three years in the African mountains.

On the elevator, she smiles when the doors open on the floor below hers to catch Harriett Neal, also on her way home by the looks of things. Harriett has her coat draped over one arm and her briefcase in the opposite hand. She works in legal and has been in a few meetings with London.

"Hi."

"Hi."

They laugh at the simultaneous greetings.

"Headed home?" London asks for lack of anything better to say.

Harriett tilts her head to the side and appears to be considering her options. "I should," she confesses, hefting the briefcase. "Catching up from a long weekend off last weekend. It was my brother's wedding."

"Congratulations!"

"Thanks." She dimples. London drops her eyes to hide a smile. She likes dimples. "I should go home and catch up, but the rain's stopping, and the evening's so nice. I thought I might stop for a drink on the way home."

London thinks how long it's been since she went out for a drink—probably since Chelsea was last up a few weeks before. "That sounds nice."

The elevator doors open, and as Harriett steps into the lobby, she says, "It would be nicer if you joined me."

Looking up, London sees the dimples again, but this time she smiles back. "I would like that."

## 19. Physical and Cognitive Development in Late Adulthood

### Today you will practice the following:

*19.1  Discuss age-related changes in brain and body systems in late adulthood, and identify ways that older adults may compensate for changes.*

*19.2  Identify risk and protective factors for health in late adulthood.*

*19.3  Summarize common dementias including characteristics, risk and protective factors, and treatment.*

*19.4  Analyze patterns of cognitive change in late adulthood.*

"I'm sorry, London," Dr. Oliver tells her at the end of their annual appointment.

Beside London, Harriett asks, "Isn't there anything that can be done?"

"I doubt it. We'll send you on to a specialist, of course. We always do. But you've taxed your eyes most of your life with close computer screen work. It was almost inevitable that your eyesight would be the first thing to fail and that you would notice significant declination rapidly." Dr. Oliver pauses and sighs. "I'm sorry again."

"I know," London says, attempting to comfort the doctor. "And the rest?"

"Everything is well within normal range. I'd like to see a bit more lung capacity, but you've struggled with that your whole life. If you and Harriett can maybe get outside and walk a bit more or maybe a stationary bike at the gym?"

Harriett shifts beside her. "Of course. Whatever she needs."

"*She* is sitting right here," London complains.

Dr. Oliver stands. "Indeed you are, and there's generally nothing wrong with you that a hot meal and a good nap won't fix. I'll have my nurse call with the appointment for the eye doctor."

"Thank you," she and Harriett murmur at the same time. Harriett takes her elbow as they stand and make their way toward the door. She swallows the urge to say she can make her own way. She really can't, and besides, it makes Harriett feel good to help. Whatever makes Harriett feel good makes her feel good.

"Let's go home," Harriett says in the elevator. "You can fix me lunch, and I'll read the news to you."

"You're not worried I'll slice off a finger or use sugar instead of salt?" she grumbles.

"Pfft," Harriet admonishes. "You're getting old, not senile. Yet."

They both laugh, and London is reminded that life is always what you make it. She thinks about her years in Africa when running water didn't exist and electricity was a memory. Yes, life is still nearly perfect.

## 20. Socioemotional Development in Late Adulthood

### Today you will practice the following:

20.1  Examine the contributions of self-concept, personality, and religiosity to older adults' well-being.

20.2  Identify social contexts in which older adults live and their influence on development.

20.3  Summarize features of older adults' relationships with friends, spouses, children, and grandchildren, and identify how these relationships affect older adults' functioning.

20.4  Discuss influences on the timing of retirement and adaptation to retirement.

"Happy birthday, dear London, Happy birthday to you!"

London tears at the sounds of family and friends. More friends than family, but she isn't complaining. It's her 80th birthday, and 80 years ago no one in her life would've believed this day would ever come. She's glad it has even though she's lived through her parents passing 20 years before and the love of her life Harriett just six months ago.

She lives in Los Angeles now with Chelsea, her sister who never married or had children and who wanted her there with her. Max would've taken her in, but it would've felt like just that no matter how hard he tried, she knew. It would've felt like *being taken in*. With Chelsea, it's more living in a new home that's still partly hers, and Chelsea doesn't coddle her because of her blindness. Thank God.

London tries to be cheery. Today's easy. The people here love her, and she's eating a delicious cake with champagne in a delicate flute just near her fingertips. She's not the social butterfly her two-time Oscar-winning sister still is at 82, but she is known for her work within her small world, and she is loved. She is loved greatly, and she has loved greatly. That, she thinks as Chelsea hands her a gift, is more than most and much more than enough.

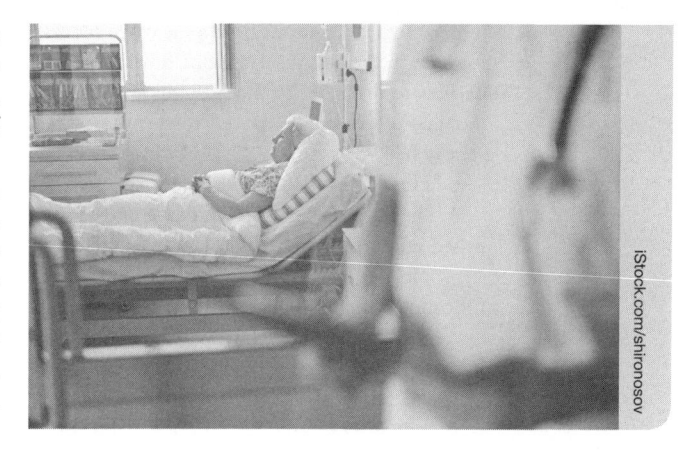

## 21. Experience With Death and Dying

### Today you will practice the following:

21.1 Identify ways in which death has been defined and end-of-life issues that may arise.

21.2 Contrast children's, adolescents', and adults' understanding of death.

21.3 Discuss the physical and emotional process of dying as it is experienced over the lifespan.

21.4 Summarize typical grief reactions to the loss of loved ones and the influence of development on bereavement.

"Ms. London?" the home health worker asks when she first arrives in the morning. "How are you today?"

London spends overnights by herself, but she has a caretaker during the day from brunch through early dinner. The woman helps her bath and tidies the house as well as cooks and takes care of the mail. Heidi, she's called, and London likes her well enough. She'd rather have Chelsea, but her sister died two years before at 84.

"I'm fine, Heidi. How are you?"

"Just fine. My daughter has some croupy something. She's home with my mama today, but it's all fine."

"I'm sorry to hear that. I hope she's better soon."

"Me, too. She doesn't sleep well when she's sick, and that means I don't sleep well when she's sick."

They both laugh at this truism of parenting even though London has no experience herself. Heidi sets a cup of coffee in front of London and starts a pan of sausage. This is probably London's favorite part of the day.

"Ms. London, how are you feeling?" Heidi asks two days later. On the day between, London had been tired and spent much of the day on the sofa listening to a radio play. This morning, she shrugs.

"I think I have a cold or possibly the flu. My chest is a bit tight," she admits.

Knowing London's health history, of course, Heidi makes an appointment with the doctor for later in the day, but London's breathing deteriorates rapidly before the appointment. Heidi decides to drive her to the hospital late in the morning, where London is admitted for pneumonia and eventually moved to the ICU. The doctor tells Heidi London is quite ill, which shocks her.

"How is that possible? She was fine two days ago."

The doctor asks, "Has she come into contact without anyone ill? Ms. Dennel has a compromised immunes system and lifelong respiratory difficulties."

"No. I—" Heidi pauses. "My daughter has a cold. London hasn't seen her, but I was near her. Of course I use sanitizer and all manner of cleaners . . ."

"Relax," the doctor says, patting Heidi's shoulder. "That may have nothing at all to do with it, but if she has family, I would call them."

That sounds so ominous, Heidi blanches. "I will," she says and turns away to telephone Max, who is 89 himself. What does anyone expect him to do?

As it turns out, Max's children fly with him to be with London, who slips quietly into a semi-coma and never fully wakes again. Heidi returns home to make arrangements for her own family before coming to the hospital to assist the Dennels in London's final hours. She passes three days after entering the hospital from complications due to pneumonia. Her brother, sister-in-law, and two nephews are at her side.

## CASE DISCUSSION QUESTIONS

1. When London is born prematurely, her father, Doug, spends many hours each day holding her naked against his bare chest in kangaroo care fashion, hoping this will help her breathe better and gain weight faster as the nurse says it will. He thinks she'll also feel less pain if he holds her like this. However, London's mother, Laura, is also ill at this time. How might London's future development have been altered across any and all domains (biological, cognitive, and socioemotional) if Doug had spent most of his time with his wife instead of his daughter during these early weeks?

2. In middle and late childhood, London discovers a love of computer coding. She also discovers the difficulty of gender norms when she tries to get teachers to help her learn more about computers and coding when they would rather help her boy classmates. How might London's life have been different both positively and negatively across her lifespan if these norms didn't exist (or if she'd been a boy)? Be specific.

3. In adolescence, London embraces her homosexuality, and she comes out to her mom casually. Laura just as casually expresses her support of London's sexuality. In what ways are London's future developmental gains across any and all domains (biological, cognitive, and socioemotional) enhanced by this early and low-key support?

4. Early in her life, London seems to have difficulty with boundaries, particularly those around the personal property of others. What might have been the outcome for London if her parents hadn't developed strategies to intervene and redirect her behavior?

# 7 Edward Archer

## Introduction

Welcome to your case study!

Congratulations! You will follow the lifespan of baby boy Edward Archer. Try to use your best judgment, textbook, classmates, instructor, and supplementary resources to make the best decisions to help him grow.

This semester you will observe Edward as he grows from infant to child to teen to adult. Who will he become in your care? Will you understand and agree with all decisions available within his circumstances? How will you feel about the tough decisions that forever shape his path in life?

## Meet Edward Archer

Edward is the first child of Brendon and Jared Archer, a Caucasian couple who've been married for several years. The Archers are upper-middle income. Jared is 32 years old and holds a bachelor's degree. He works a full-time job in advertising. Brendon is 41 years old, holds a master's

iStock.com/ArtisticCaptures

**CHAPTER 7** Edward Archer  143

degree, and is a full-time high school counselor. The couple owns their home in a middle-class, suburban neighborhood, and Jared's state-sponsored health insurance covers the family. A couple years ago, Brendon and Jared decided they wanted to adopt a child they could love and raise. From this process, they become the parents of Edward.

Through this case study and your lifespan course you will be asked to consider decisions regarding Edward's physical, emotional, and cognitive growth and development from several perspectives: his fathers' Brendon and Jared, and his grandparents' as well as those of his potential siblings, spouse, children, other family members, friends, teachers, doctors, and supervisors.'

Now let's get started.

## 1. Development and Its Influences

### Today you will practice the following:

1.1  *Outline five principles of the lifespan developmental perspective.*

1.2  *Explain three theoretical controversies about human development.*

1.3  *Summarize five theoretical perspectives on human development.*

1.4  *Describe the methods and research designs used to study human development.*

Brendon and Jared decide well before they're married that they want children. They also decide they prefer to adopt than search for a surrogate, decide which of them gets to donate sperm, and all the other complications that come with gay couples having "their own" children. They know any children they adopt will be as much their own as any they might possibly create. They start the process five years or so into the marriage, assuming it'll take more time than they want to get a baby. If they were heterosexual, their application would have many advantages, but they're not and so it doesn't.

Brendon lobbies for an older child, and Jared agrees that they'll probably at least foster an older child eventually. But they have a plan: a baby is what they want if they can get one. When the adoption agency calls and offers them a possibility, they jump at it. They will be able to adopt an as-yet-unborn child, but the baby's records will be sealed. They're told the mother is healthy and is not nor has ever been a drug user. They know she's white and young—no information on the father and nothing on extended family. They can go with this child about whom they know next to nothing, or they can wait on another child. They want this one.

## 2. Biological and Environmental Foundations

### Today you will practice the following:

2.1 *Discuss the genetic foundations of development.*

2.2 *Identify examples of genetic disorders and chromosomal abnormalities.*

2.3 *Discuss the choices available to prospective parents in having healthy children.*

2.4 *Describe the interaction of heredity and environment, including behavioral genetics and the epigenetic framework.*

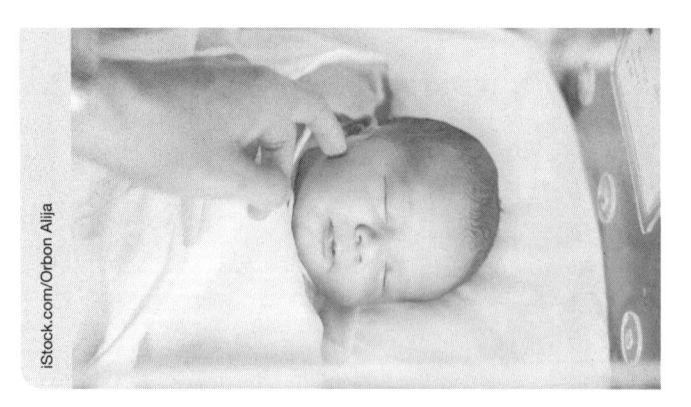

Edward's adoption records will be sealed, and if Brendon and Jared ever meet his mother, it will only be briefly when their baby is born. They know nothing about their baby's development other than what the adoption agency has told them: Mom doesn't smoke, drink, or use any drugs; she's healthy; and no negative results have come of any prenatal testing. If anything arises, they'll be informed.

## 3. Prenatal Development, Birth, and Newborn Experience

### Today you will practice the following:

3.1 *Describe the three periods of prenatal development that begin with conception.*

3.2 *Identify how exposure to teratogens can influence the prenatal environment.*

3.3 *Explain the process of childbirth.*

3.4 *Discuss the neonate's physical capacities, including development in low-birth-weight infants.*

Edward's prenatal development, to the best of Jared's and Brendon's knowledge, is both normal and well supported medically. Mom has proper prenatal care and remains healthy throughout the pregnancy. Sometime several months into waiting for their baby, they receive separate calls on their phones: the baby is going to be born, would they like to come to the hospital?

They would.

The soon-to-be-fathers wait in nervous anticipation in the hospital waiting room until a nurse and a social worker approach in the early hours of the morning. The nurse looks at Brendon, while the social worker looks at Jared.

"Dad?" they both say at the same time. Everyone laughs, nervousness causing tremors in both men's voices.

The nurse touches each of their elbows. "Would you care to come to the nursery and meet your son?"

Following both women down the hallway, Brendon asks a litany of questions. Is the mother all right? Did the labor and delivery go well? How were the baby's APGARS? Is he . . . ? No one wanted to say "normal," but biological parents typically get to see firsthand and have that reassurance without asking.

The nurse pauses in walking and looks at them both. "It was a long delivery, but both of them were fine. The mother did well, and you can see her soon if you'd like. Baby's APGARs were excellent, 8 and 10, and he's absolutely perfect."

He is, too, as the new fathers can see when they take turns holding him in the hospital nursery only a minute or so later. He's long and has a crop of dark curls. When he begins to fuss, Brendon hums a lullaby to him, and he quietens. Their family, full of love before, is complete now.

## 4. Physical Development in Infancy and Toddlerhood

### Today you will practice the following:

4.1 *Discuss growth and the role of nutrition in development during infancy and toddlerhood.*

4.2 *Summarize brain development during infancy and toddlerhood.*

4.3 *Compare infants' early learning capacities for habituation, classical conditioning, operant conditioning, and imitation.*

4.4 *Describe infants' developing sensory abilities.*

4.5 *Analyze the roles of maturation and contextual factors in infant and toddler motor development.*

Edward, a chubby and affectionate baby, loses much of his dark hair shortly after birth. This is replaced with fine, brown curls. His eyes, the dark blue of most infants when they're born, are now a rich chocolate, and his fair skin has a mole or two on his back. His fathers think he's perfect, and the pediatrician assures them he is.

If Edward has any troubles at all, it's only that he doesn't like to sleep alone in his nursery. At school, Jared asks all the teachers who are parents—mostly mothers—if they've ever had this trouble and listens to their advice, from "let him cry it out" (which sounds demonic) to "just tuck him in bed with you and Brendon" (which sounds like a recipe for infanticide). Batting it back and forth and losing sleep in the meantime, he and Brendon decide to move Edward's crib into their room for a while. Like magic, their baby becomes somnolent at 8 p.m. every night and doesn't wake until seven in the morning.

Even when they oversleep, one of Edward's dads takes time to cuddle him while he takes his morning bottle. They know parents—Jared's sister is one of them—who change the diaper and sit the baby in the car seat with a bottle propped on a pillow so they can multitask in the mornings before work. Jared and Brendon want Edward to feel loved and wanted from the beginning, and so they hold him. He eats almost constantly, but they become adept at multitasking *while* holding him, a feat of which they are both quite proud. Within a few months, Edward sits on the bathroom counter in front of Brendon playing patty cake with himself in the mirror while Brendon brushes his hair and fixes his tie.

"Bay-beeee," he drools, pointing at his own reflection.

Brendon wipes Edward's chin with a washcloth and scoops him into his arms, passing him to Jared as he walks into the closet for his shoes.

"Baby," Jared croons. "Such a smart boy."

Edward squeals, and both dads laugh with him.

Sliding his jacket on, Brendon holds out his arms. "Ready," he says. "It's my day. You'll remember to pick him up?"

Jared rolls his eyes. "Like I'd forget."

They kiss quickly among a flurry of I love yous, and Brendon rushes from the house with Edward clapping and drooling on his freshly dry-cleaned blazer.

"It's a good thing you're cute," he mutters as he opens the back door on his Volkswagen and bends to tuck the baby into his car seat.

## 5. Cognitive Development in Infancy and Toddlerhood

### Today you will practice the following:

5.1 Discuss the cognitive-developmental perspective on infant reasoning.

5.2 Describe the information processing system in infants.

5.3 Discuss individual differences in infant intelligence.

5.4 Summarize the patterns of language development during infancy and toddlerhood.

Edward's crib is returned to the nursery when he's eight months old, and he makes no fuss over the transition. Brendon and Jared take turns reading his bedtime stories—classics and modern favorites both—before tucking him in together. He's such a good-natured boy that it's hard to leave him, which they do like clockwork at 7:50 p.m. nightly.

When Edward is ten months old, Jared notices that he's babbling along with his dads when they read to him. His rhythm and cadence are the same as theirs even if the words are unintelligible. Jared praises his son and begins to spend time pointing to basic objects in the stories. "What's that, Edward?" he asks, and often Edward responds with a sound that nearly resembles the picture in question.

Although he isn't yet walking without holding on to furniture (or his dads' pants legs), Edward does his best to keep up with his cousins when they visit family. At his grandma and grandpa's house, he has two cousins who are not much older than he is, and at Granny Sue's house, he has three cousins, but Greg is five and isn't interested in babies. Edward and his cousins "play" near each other in happy harmony for long stretches of time even if they don't interact much. When he's at home after visiting, Edward uses spoons, bananas, and sometimes a shoe to pretend he's talking to his cousins or his grandparents. "Lo! 'Lo!" he yells and laughs when one of his dads pretends to talk back. Soon, this becomes his favorite game at home.

## 6. Socioemotional Development in Infancy and Toddlerhood

### Today you will practice the following:

6.1 *Summarize the psychosocial tasks of infancy and toddlerhood.*

6.2 *Describe emotional development in infancy, and identify contextual and cultural influences on emotional development in infants and toddlers.*

6.3 *Identify the styles and stability of temperament, including the role of goodness of fit in infant development.*

6.4 *Describe how attachment develops in infancy and toddlerhood.*

6.5 *Differentiate the roles of self-concept, self-recognition, and self-control in infant development.*

At 13 months, Edward's favorite game is peekaboo. He plays with anyone who will sit with him long enough. His conversational skills are improving, and he appears to understand the rudiments of dialogue: I say something, and then you respond. Much of the time, Jared and Brendon have no idea what he says, but Edward clearly infuses his babbling with tone and inflection and a great deal of enthusiasm. Dinnertime conversation is everyone's favorite time of the day.

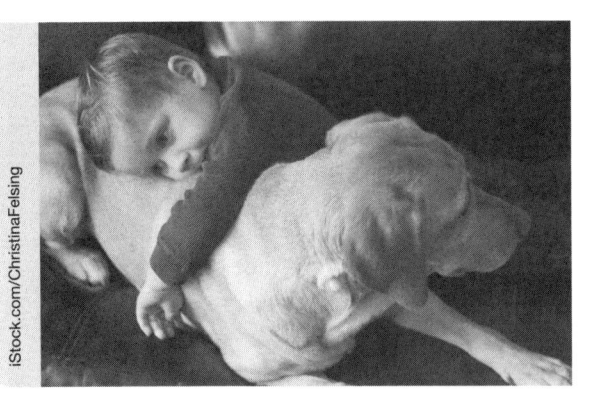

Edward clearly loves his dads. He is openly affectionate and behaves as any normal, securely attached child does when left at or collected from daycare. That is, he fusses for a few minutes when he's left and is delighted when he's picked up. His best friend, however, is the family's English Mastiff, who was brought into the family as a puppy only a few months after Edward's arrival. The rate of Duke's growth has quickly outpaced Edward's, but he's gentle with the toddler. Downtime often finds Edward lying on the floor with his head resting on Duke's side. For his part, Duke is a reserved but formidable guard dog, standing between Edward and anything new to their lives, including trash that blows in their direction in the park. Once satisfied a new person is harmless, Duke relaxes and licks Edward's head as if to say, "Mine. Be careful with him," and he lies down to observe once more. Brendon hopes Edward never gets it in his head to try to ride the poor beast.

## 7. Physical and Cognitive Development in Early Childhood

### Today you will practice the following:

7.1 Discuss physical development in early childhood.

7.2 Compare Piaget's cognitive-developmental and Vygotsky's sociocultural perspectives on cognitive development in early childhood.

7.3 Describe information-processing abilities during early childhood.

7.4 Summarize young children's advances in language development.

7.5 Contrast social learning and cognitive-developmental perspectives on moral development in early childhood.

7.6 Identify and explain approaches to early childhood education.

Edward, who at his five-year checkup is in the 60th percentile for height and 65th for weight, appears completely normal, average, and without any discerning or concerning characteristics. Brendon and Jared are relieved. Over the past five years, they've talked about the possibility of genetic testing for Edward. It's expensive, but they can afford it. Such testing would tell them what sort of potential illnesses loom in Edward's future. After the checkup, they put away the idea for good. He's a healthy, normal kid, and anything that might happen now could happen to any parent. They'll take what comes, which they would've done anyway.

One thing they do is begin a process they've both dreaded and anticipated for all of their time with Edward. After the birthday party and all the gifts, after a couple days of routine, Brendon calls Edward to the table on a Saturday morning and sits him down. Jared joins them with two mugs of coffee and a tall glass of chocolate milk. Edward eyes the chocolate milk with suspicion. This is a treat.

"Dad and I want to talk to you," Jared begins, and Edward's eyes flick and back and forth between them.

"Did I do something wrong?"

"No, Son, nothing like that."

"Is someone sick? Granny Sue?" he asks, his tone elevating in pitch. Brendon's mother had been sick over the winter but was, as far as Edward knew, improving.

"Granny Sue's fine. Everyone's fine," Brendon says, patting his hand. "Nothing's wrong, bud. We just want to tell you a couple things. We waited until you were a big boy, and now you are."

Edward nods at that. He *is* a big boy, five years old. He'll go to Kindergarten in September. "What do you want to tell me, Daddy?"

"Do you remember when you had your birthday party and your cousins and friends came to help you celebrate?" Jared asks.

"Uh-huh," Edward answers, paying more attention to his chocolate milk than the question.

"Did you notice anything different about the parents of the other children than your parents?"

Edward scrunches his eyes to think. Maybe there was one difference. "Ben's daddy was without anyone else. Ben doesn't have another daddy *or* a mommy."

Jared sighs while Brendon chuckles. Edward recognizes mommies then and doesn't count them any differently than second daddies. Brendon doesn't know if that makes things easier or harder.

"Well, that's true," Jared agrees.

"Is that what you mean?"

"Not exactly." Jared points to Brendon. "One daddy." Then he points to himself. "Two daddies."

"I got two daddies. So?"

"But most of your friends have only one daddy," Jared ventures.

"Right, but they have a mommy so that's okay."

"That's also true," Jared tells him. "I wanted to ask you about the mommies. Do you ever wonder why you have two daddies instead of a daddy and a mommy or maybe why you don't have a mommy?"

Edward shrugs. "No," he whispers, and both dads know he isn't telling the truth.

"Edward?" Brendon prompts.

"Sometimes I wonder why I don't have a mommy, but I know I'm super special because I have two daddies."

"Bud, you are on point today," Jared says and raises his hand for a high five. Edward stretches upward until their palms touch before pulling his glass back to his mouth. "That's what we wanted to talk about . . . your mommy, not having two dads."

"Okay." Edward looks at both of them. "Do I have a mommy?"

Jared nods, and so does Brendon. "You do. She grew you in her tummy just like other mommies, and then she gave birth to you on your birthday."

"Where is she? What's her name?"

Jared and Brendon were prepared for these questions. Brendon ruffles Edward's hair and starts talking while Jared warms their coffee.

"I don't know her whole name, but I do know that her first name is Ginni."

"That's a pretty name," Edward says.

"I think so, too."

"Where is she?" Edward asks again.

"I don't know," Brendon tells him. "See, Son, when you were born, you were adopted."

"I was a dopted what?"

He and Jared look at each other, momentarily confused. When they figure out Edward's misunderstanding, they smile, careful not to laugh and make him feel silly.

"Oh, no, Edward. Dad and I *adopted* you. You weren't a thing called 'dopted.'"

"What does that mean? 'Dopted."

"It means that your mommy loved you so much that she wanted you to come live with me and Dad so you could have the best life you could have."

"My mommy didn't want to live here, too?"

"I don't know, Edward, but I think she probably couldn't for some reason. The most important thing for her was making sure you had a good home with good parents."

"Like you and Dad!" he shouts, holding his hands above his head Superman style.

"Like me and Dad."

Jared sits at the table again and catches Edward's eye. "Do you have any questions about your mommy right now?"

"No. I don't think so. Maybe. Is she pretty?" he asks, giggling.

"Well," Jared says, a low and serious tone in his voice, "I think she must be for sure since you are such a handsome guy."

Edward giggles again. "I think she's pretty, too."

"Anything else?" Jared asks.

"No. Can I play with Duke now?"

"Yes, you may. If you decide you want to talk about your mommy again, that's always okay with both me and Daddy."

"Okay." Edward slides from his chair and runs to the doorway, calling after the dog. As they hear the thumps of large, heavy feet, he turns and runs back to the table. "Sorry! Forgot!" He kisses both dads so quickly they don't register much more than air and then bolts from the room to find his dog.

Jared looks at Brendon and blows out a short burst of air. "Not bad at all."

"Nah," Brendon says. "We've got this."

CHAPTER 7   Edward Archer

# 8. Socioemotional Development in Early Childhood

## Today you will practice the following:

8.1 Discuss young children's emerging sense of initiative, self-concept, and self-esteem.

8.2 Summarize the development of emotional understanding, regulation, and behavior in early childhood.

8.3 Identify four parenting styles and their associations with child outcomes.

8.4 Compare biological, cognitive, and contextual theoretical explanations of gender role development.

8.5 Explain the function of play and the form it takes during early childhood.

Jared's sister Beth babysits for the two dads routinely so they can have a biweekly date night. They return the favor on off weeks. One Saturday night, Jared runs inside to collect a drowsy and heavy Edward, and Beth stops him at the door as he leaves.

"Jay, did you know Edward's favorite toy is a stuffed pink pig?"

Jared, who knows where this is headed, looks at her and whispers over Edward's ear, "Pigs are pink."

Narrowing her eyes, Beth says, "You know what I mean."

"I do, and I'm torn between amusement and annoyance. Do you think his pink pig is going to make him gay?"

"No but—"

"What? The pink pig plus being raised by gay dads might?"

She lifts her shoulders. "Well?"

Jared fights to keep the irritation out of his voice. "I could remind you that his favorite pastime is wrestling with a 150-pound dog."

"Mine might've been, too, if I'd had Duke as a child!"

"What's good for the goose isn't good for the gander." Jared paused. "I love you, and I know you're only thinking of what's best for Edward. So, I'm going easy on you here, but I'd like you to consider something."

Beth crossed her arms over her chest and clenched her jaw. "What?"

"Do you think kids of straight parents—kids like yours—are less likely to be gay than they are to be straight because they're born to straight parents? Like that's the only way to identify themselves?"

Beth waved him away as if he were being ridiculous. "Of course not. If Matthew were gay, he'd just be gay, and I suspect my being straight wouldn't have anything to do with it."

"Then tell me why it should be any different for Edward." She opened her mouth, but Jared didn't wait. "It's cold. I want to get him home. Thanks for watching him tonight."

PART I  The Cases

## 9. Physical and Cognitive Development in Middle Childhood

Today you will practice the following:

9.1  Identify patterns of physical and motor development during middle childhood and common health issues facing school-age children.

9.2  Discuss school-age children's capacities for reasoning and processing information.

9.3  Summarize views of intelligence including the uses, correlates, and criticisms of intelligence tests.

9.4  Examine patterns of moral development during middle childhood.

9.5  Summarize language development during middle childhood.

9.6  Discuss children's learning at school.

In elementary school, Edward applies himself diligently to all his subjects even though he doesn't particularly love any of them. He's aware that his dad works at the high school a couple miles away and all the teachers at all the schools know each other. He works hard because there's no other way to be the kid of a school staff member.

In fifth grade, his math class does a unit on statistics, which dismays both his dads. "Statistics? Really?"—this from the father who spends his daytime hours predicting who will buy what and why.

"It's not that different from advertising, Dad," he tells him. "Want me to show you?"

"God, no. Just keep making As, and we're good."

The teacher has assigned a monthlong stock market project, and Edward spends hours after school, with Duke covering his bed, mapping out strategy, buying his imaginary stocks, and building a portfolio. He makes and loses a year's worth of the family's income before finally beating his other classmates for most diversified portfolio, best profit–loss ratio, and most earned. Finally, he thinks, there's something he's good at: making money. If only it were real.

## 10. Socioemotional Development in Middle Childhood

Today you will practice the following:

10.1  Describe school-age children's self-conceptions and motivation.

10.2  Examine the roles of friendship, peer acceptance, and peer victimization in school-age children's adjustment.

10.3  Discuss family relationships in middle childhood and the influence of family structure on adjustment.

10.4  Analyze the role of resilience in promoting adjustment to adversity, including characteristics of children and contexts that promote resilience.

Elementary school brings a dawning awareness for Edward that his family is different from the norm. He has two parents, which he hears is a good thing, but he has two fathers, which he learns makes him odd if not exactly a social pariah. He has cousins at the school, and they help stick up for him when kids on the playground push him around or make fun. He tries hard not to push back. He likes his family, and although he's happy to defend it, he'd rather people just not care one way or the other.

In sixth grade, a boy named John loses his dad in a car accident. It's terrible. No one else in the grade has had a parent die before. Edward doesn't know how that would feel, but when he tries to imagine it, he gets cold and sad inside. John is one of the boys who made fun of Edward for having two dads, but he figures that doesn't matter when your mom dies. Edward asks his dad to drive him to John's house after the funeral, and he goes to the door and asks for John. They talk for only a few minutes. Edward tells him how sorry he is about the accident, and John asks him if he wants to come inside and have some potato casserole. Waving his dad off, Edward goes inside with John, and they spend a few hours playing video games and talking about school. Every now and then, John sneaks downstairs and gets some cookies or something else for them to eat. At the end of the day, Edward's dad comes back for him. He and John share a fist bump, and Edward figures he can ride his bike back over the next day. Just to check on him.

## 11. Physical and Cognitive Development in Late Childhood

### Today you will practice the following:

*11.1* Describe school-age children's self-conceptions and motivation.

*11.2* Examine the roles of friendship, peer acceptance, and peer victimization in school-age children's adjustment.

*11.3* Discuss family relationships in middle childhood and the influence of family structure on adjustment.

*11.4* Analyze the role of resilience in promoting adjustment to adversity, including characteristics of children and contexts that promote resilience

The worst thing happens to Edward in sixth grade. He finds out he needs glasses. This, of course, is a legacy of his unknown genetics.

"Can't I have laser surgery?" he begs his dads. "Contacts?"

"No, not yet, not either," they both tell him.

"But *why*? Glasses are the kiss of death!"

"You better not be having any kisses," his dads tell him.

Edward stares at himself in the mirror. "I don't think you have to worry about that now."

## 12. Socioemotional Development in Late Childhood

### Today you will practice the following:

12.1 Summarize the processes by which self-concept, self-esteem, and identity change during adolescence.

12.2 Discuss the nature of parent–child relationships in adolescence.

12.3 Examine the developmental progression of peer relations in adolescence.

12.4 Analyze patterns of adolescent sexual activity including sexual orientation.

12.5 Identify common psychological and behavioral problems in adolescence.

Edward tosses Duke's lead onto the washing machine when he comes in the back door. It's cold outside! In the kitchen, he puts hot chocolate in the microwave just as the phone starts to ring. Looking at caller ID, he sees *Bridgewood Adoption Agency* scrolling across the screen. His dad—man, high school makes you gray fast—rushes into the room in his socks, and Edward hands him the receiver.

"Something you want to tell me?" he asks.

Dad shakes his head. "Not yet. Maybe. Hopefully." He presses the talk button. "Hello? This is Jared North."

Edward grabs his hot chocolate when the microwave dings and wanders into the den with Duke. "Hear that, buddy? We're going to get a brother or sister."

## 13. Physical and Cognitive Development in Adolescence

### Today you will practice the following:

13.1 Evaluate the "storm and stress" perspective on adolescence in light of research evidence.

13.2 Summarize the physical changes that occur with puberty and the correlates of pubertal timing.

13.3 Discuss brain development during adolescence and its effect on behavior.

13.4 Identify ways in which thinking changes in adolescence and how these changes are reflected in adolescent decision-making and behavior.

13.5 Discuss moral development and influences on moral reasoning.

13.6 Describe the challenges that school transitions pose for adolescents and the role of parents in academic achievement.

"Dude, let me hold her. It's my turn!"

"Shh," Edward admonishes, but he hands over the tightly swaddled bundle of baby sister to John. "Damn, she's cute, huh?"

"Yeah." John bounces Valerie up and down slowly in his arms as he wanders around the den, Duke at his heels protecting the family's newest charge. "Is she, like, all loud and stuff?"

Edward shrugs. "Sometimes but not much. She sleeps in my dads' room right now, and they pretty much take care of everything she needs. She just sleeps and smiles when I have her unless she needs a clean diaper. I'm pretty good at that."

John looks at her face, sleepy and content since Edward gave her a bottle a few minutes ago. "I don't know . . . Coach Denver acts like seeing a newborn is all the birth control we need, but she kinda makes me feel funny, like—"

"*I know,*" Edward agrees. "My dad says it's because we're 'in puberty,' and our biology says it's time to make babies."

"Can we fast-forward until we're on the other side of it? Because all I'm getting from 'puberty,'" John says with emphasis on the word, "is acne and a voice that cracks whenever I try to talk to Sarah Jane Williams."

"I'll look for the Tardis," Edward promised. "Meanwhile, maybe I'll take that one back so you can set up the PlayStation?"

## 14. Socioemotional Development in Adolescence

### Today you will practice the following:

14.1 Summarize the processes by which self-concept, self-esteem, and identity change during adolescence.

14.2 Discuss the nature of parent–child relationships in adolescence.

14.3 Examine the developmental progression of peer relations in adolescence.

14.4 Analyze patterns of adolescent sexual activity including sexual orientation.

14.5 Identify common psychological and behavioral problems in adolescence.

Edward spends his spare time play-re-creating the work he did for the stock market assignment in elementary school. He tracks a number of individual stocks and creates his own imaginary portfolio. His friends love it. They call it Edward's Fantasy Finance. What they don't know is that he's been saving birthday and Christmas money since sixth grade until he has enough to create a real portfolio, which he does as soon as he has enough to meet the minimum threshold. His dads sign for him to open the account as he's underage.

He tells his best friend John, who borrows $100 from his dad and gives it to Edward to invest. John tells a couple other friends, who give him another $100. In a couple months, Edward doubles their money, and John returns his dad's original $100 while leaving the rest invested with Edward. Edward's dads call him Alex P. Keaton, which he doesn't understand at all but makes them both laugh when they say it. He'd try to figure it out, but he's too busy making money and trying to get a girl (*any girl*) to notice him.

## 15. Physical and Cognitive Development in Emerging/Early Adulthood

### Today you will practice the following:

15.1 *Describe the features and characteristics of emerging and early adulthood.*

15.2 *Summarize the physical developments of emerging and early adulthood.*

15.3 *Analyze physical and sexual health issues in emerging and early adulthood.*

15.4 *Compare postformal reasoning, pragmatic thought, and cognitive-affective complexity.*

15.5 *Explain how attending college influences young adults' development, and identify challenges faced by first-generation and nontraditional students.*

15.6 *Discuss vocational choice and the transition to work.*

"You're sure?" Brendon asks Edward on the eve of his 18th birthday.

"Of course. I wouldn't ask if I weren't." He looks from one dad to the other. "Were you looking forward to the empty nest? It's not like Valerie's off to college already. You've got her another nine years."

Brendon frowns at him and shakes his head. "What are you talking about, the empty nest? You're welcome to stay or go as long as you need. I just want to make sure you're happy with this choice. Living on campus is a big part of college."

Edward shrugs. "Yeah, but those are things I don't care about. Course, if you want to spend more money . . ."

Both dads laugh. They know how seriously this soon-to-be economics major takes money.

Jared throws up his hands. "Fine. You can stay here, but if your grades fall—"

"They won't. I promise."

Edward pursues his college degree for three and a half years, finishing a semester early despite John and other friends' best efforts to drag him to Friday night football and after parties. He loves his friends, but he has dreams, too. The spring semester after graduation, he and his girlfriend visit the three campuses where he's been accepted to business school. Jennifer will finish in May with the rest of their classmates, and he has plans for them, but first he has to decide among Harvard, Duke, and the University of South Carolina. They like all three campuses, and all three offer Edward good packages. The only school he truly falls in love with is South Carolina, and with Jennifer's unqualified support, he accepts their offer.

Back at home, Jennifer's parents, his dads, Valerie, and John take him out to celebrate. Every step he's wanted to take, he's made happen. Looking at his dads' faces around the table, he knows these are the people who made it possible.

## 16. Socioemotional Development in Emerging/Early Adulthood

### Today you will practice the following:

*16.1  Summarize psychosocial development in emerging and early adulthood.*

*16.2  Discuss influences on friendship and mate selection and interactions in emerging and early adulthood.*

*16.3  Analyze the diverse romantic situations that may characterize early and emerging adulthood, including singlehood, cohabitation, marriage, and divorce.*

*16.4  Compare the experiences of young adults as stepparents, never-married parents, and same-sex parents.*

Jennifer sits on Edward's bed while he sorts through his closet. He has 18 years' worth of mostly junk to get rid of as he prepares for his move to Columbia, South Carolina. A few months remain before he goes, but 18 years probably get the better of mere months, he thinks. On his bed, Jennifer flips through a box of old photographs that cover *Edward: The Awkward Years.* She laughs when she comes upon a picture of him with shaggy hair, braces, and a pimple that needed its own zip code. He keeps sorting, half holding his breath as she works her way to the bottom of the box. He knows when she gets there, because she grows quiet, eventually asking, "Ed, what's this?"

He pokes his head from the closet and says, "What's what?" although he knows.

"This," she replies, holding a small box.

"Oh, that? Nothing much. You can look if you want." He returns to the closet.

He counts the seconds. *One . . . two . . . three . . . four . . .*

"Edward?"

He joins her on the bed. "Jennifer." Kissing her cheek, he makes his appeal. "I'm pretty sure I can't do much without you anymore, and I'm very sure that whatever I do, I don't do well unless your hand is in it. Don't make me go to Columbia alone. Marry me."

She laughs and takes the ring from the box. "I have to marry you, don't I? Who's going to explain advanced calculus to you so you can finish your MBA? Besides, who'll cook for me when you're gone?" she asks, referring to Edward's hobby of amateur gourmet cooking.

"Good point," Edward agrees. "Whatever it takes for you to say yes, I'll take it."

"Yes," Jennifer whispers, kissing him.

## 17. Physical and Cognitive Development in Middle Adulthood

### Today you will practice the following:

17.1 *Summarize age-related physical changes during middle adulthood.*

17.2 *Discuss common health conditions and illnesses and the roles of stress and hardiness on health during middle adulthood.*

17.3 *Contrast the findings of cross-sectional and longitudinal studies of crystallized and fluid intelligence over adulthood.*

17.4 *Analyze changes in cognitive capacities during middle adulthood, including attention, memory, processing speed, and expertise.*

Jared suffers a heart attack during Valerie's junior year of college. Cardiologists find significant blockage in one artery and perform an angioplasty. Jared is warned off a long list of his favorite foods and put on a diet regimen. Brendon tries to help, but tensions run high in the household due to Brendon's and Valerie's attempts to become healthier for Jared's and Jared's irritation at the required changes to his lifestyle. Valerie complains to Edward and Jennifer, who now have a toddler of their own.

Jared passes away the following year of a second heart attack despite everyone's attempts to make the necessary changes to keep him well. Edward, mourning deeply and watching the devastation run through his family, decides to pay for the genetic testing his dads never wanted for him. He's specific with the geneticist. They want to know only about his risk for cardiovascular disease, late-life killers like diabetes, and any diseases he might be a carrier for and have passed along to his son. The results are reassuring. He is remarkably unscathed genetically. If he suffers any major ailments as he ages, it will be because he makes poor lifestyle choices.

## 18. Socioemotional Development in Middle Adulthood

### Today you will practice the following:

18.1 *Summarize the theories and research on psychosocial development during middle adulthood.*

18.2 *Describe the changes that occur in self-concept, identity, and personality during middle adulthood.*

18.3 *Analyze relationships in middle adulthood, including friend, spousal, parent–child, and grandparent relationships.*

18.4 *Discuss influences on job satisfaction and retirement planning during middle adulthood.*

When Edward returns home from work a night shortly before their oldest child, Eddie, leaves for college, Jennifer waits for him at the kitchen table. She has a glass of water and a half-eaten chocolate bar in front of her as well as an opened envelope. He has no idea what he's done wrong, but it's clearly something.

"Babe," he says, laying a kiss on her cheek as he drops his briefcase in a chair. "How was your day?"

"Good. Jim," she says, indicating a junior lawyer at the firm where she's a partner now, "got a new client that's pretty interesting. Nothing else really except this." She waves the letter.

"What is that?"

"It's from Harrington," their bank, she means. "Why didn't you tell me you were divesting your retirement account? That seems like the sort of decision husbands and wives make together."

"We didn't talk about it?" he asks, knowing they didn't. He meant to, but ultimately, he thought the money was his and so he should be able to reinvest it as he saw fit. Looking at her now, he realizes the tax penalty isn't the only penalty he's going to pay.

"We did not."

"I made a 28 percent return on that money within seven months, Jen."

"It was a huge gamble, and you should've told me."

Edward knows he has no choice but to capitulate. She's probably right. "You're right," he says and tries to keep the placating tone out of his voice.

"Do you mean that?"

"I do." Taking her hand, he gives her his most sincere smile and says, "I should've made certain we were together on this. I just wanted to make sure we had enough when the nest was empty and we decided it was time to do all the things we keep talking about doing . . . Alaskan cruises, Mexican summers, taking our honeymoon again . . ."

She smiles at that. "Okay, but, Ed, this was a huge gamble. Please let's talk before doing something so risky next time."

"I promise."

## 19. Physical and Cognitive Development in Late Adulthood

### Today you will practice the following:

*19.1* Discuss age-related changes in brain and body systems in late adulthood, and identify ways that older adults may compensate for changes.

*19.2* Identify risk and protective factors for health in late adulthood.

*19.3* Summarize common dementias including characteristics, risk and protective factors, and treatment.

*19.4* Analyze patterns of cognitive change in late adulthood.

Brendon, who has lived in a small condo near Edward and Jennifer for nearly 20 years, passes away in relatively good health but of advanced age when Edward is 60. The loss rocks him, and he finds the ensuing depression unexpected and difficult to work through. Jennifer suggests he seek the advice of his physician, which he does, and the doctor recommends a low dosage of an antidepressant. The medicine seems to help. Although Edward's mourning process lasts a considerable amount of time, he faces it squarely. At the doctor's suggestion, he begins taking a short jog in the mornings, and after a few weeks, Jennifer joins him. He doesn't know if the antidepressants or the jogging will help him live as long as his dad did, but he's not ready to leave his family. He'll do whatever he can to continue living a healthy life with them, which he's able to do for many more years.

## 20. Socioemotional Development in Late Adulthood

### Today you will practice the following:

*20.1* Examine the contributions of self-concept, personality, and religiosity to older adults' well-being.

*20.2* Identify social contexts in which older adults live and their influence on development.

> 20.3 Summarize features of older adults' relationships with friends, spouses, children, and grandchildren, and identify how these relationships affect older adults' functioning.
>
> 20.4 Discuss influences on the timing of retirement and adaptation to retirement.

On Edward's 75th birthday, he receives a telephone call. His youngest daughter, Mary, brings the phone to him with a brief shake of her head; she doesn't know who the caller is. Taking the phone, Edward puts it to his ear, expecting maybe to hear one of John's children. His best friend of more than 50 years died two years before, leaving a gaping hole in his own life. He's wrong, though; the voice is female and unknown.

"Mr. Archer?"

"Yes. This is Edward Archer. Who's this?"

"This is Elena Brantley, Mr. North. I understand it's your birthday. Felicitations."

"Thank you. Do I know you, Ms. Brantley?" Edward, innately suspicious, wonders who the woman is and how she knows it's his birthday. He's certain he knows no Elena Brantley.

"No, you don't, but I'd like for us to know one another. That's why I've called. I hoped I could come see you one day this week. I'll be close to where you live and thought maybe you would enjoy a visit. Brantley is my married name. My maiden name is Ellis."

Edward shakes his head to himself. "I'm sorry. I don't know any Ellises. Should I?"

"Maybe not," she says. "My mother was Ginni Ellis. *Our* mother was Ginni Ellis. I'm your sister, Edward."

Edward sits quietly without speaking for a moment. He has a sister. Valerie is his sister. Does he want another? Perhaps not. He might not even like this woman, this Elena Brantley. However, she might have information he would like to know about his biological mother. He's never been curious enough about her to go in search of her himself, and she is almost certainly dead now. Elena Brantley can possibly give him something that would ... what? Fill a need? Not that—satisfy some curiosity maybe.

"I see," he says at last. "This is a shock."

"I'm sure it is. If I've upset you—"

"Not at all. When would you like to get together?"

"Wednesday or Thursday maybe? I'll be passing through Johnsonville on my way to visit my children. I believe that's quite close to you."

"It is," Edward confirms. "There's a barbeque place just off the highway at exit 94. We could meet there Thursday at 12:30 p.m. if that's convenient."

"Sure. I'll look forward to it."

Edward and Jennifer meet Elena Brantley, a warm and generous 60-something who resembles Edward in coloring and stature but not much else. They like her, but Edward feels no immediate affinity or sibling bond.

Elena shows Edward the small cache of information she's put together on their mother Ginni. Adopted when she was days old, Elena never knew Ginni either, but she sought her out as a teenager. It took her parents several thousand dollars and more than a year, but they found her finally. Elena approached Ginni alone, and Ginni wasn't pleased to meet her daughter.

"Was she a prostitute?" Edward asks.

"I never knew for sure," Elena confides, "but it certainly seems possible."

Jennifer turns the photographs around and looks at them closely. "She was lovely," she says and smiles.

"Yes, she was." A wistful tone enters Elena's voice. "Days come and go when I wish she'd cared more, but then I remind myself she cared enough to let us go."

The statement made Edward think. "Do you think there are more of us? Brothers and sisters?"

"No." Elena shook her head. "I've checked hospital records and birth records. It's just the two of us."

"You'll have to come for the holidays then. If you want to," he adds. "I have another sister. Her name is Valerie. My dads adopted her when she was an infant, too, and I'm sure she'd love to meet you."

They make a plan for December, after which Jennifer and Edward say good-bye to Elena and see her off to her children. Edward hadn't known what to expect or what he wanted from this meeting, but he goes home feeling satisfied and somehow lighter. Jennifer rides the whole way with her hand in his.

## 21. Experience With Death and Dying

### Today you will practice the following:

21.1  *Identify ways in which death has been defined and end-of-life issues that may arise.*

21.2  *Contrast children's, adolescents', and adults' understanding of death.*

21.3  *Discuss the physical and emotional process of dying as it is experienced over the lifespan.*

21.4  *Summarize typical grief reactions to the loss of loved ones and the influence of development on bereavement.*

Edward declares his intent to live forever. He works diligently at the task. As his 70s progress, reality slowly overcomes will, and he finds himself unable to jog like he used to. Many days, he has difficulty with a short walk to the end of the street and back. He gets confused easily, asking Jennifer or Mary if the volatile Microsoft stock is up or down. Each time, Mary gently reminds him that Microsoft is a blue chip and Mom died three years before. He tries to remember, but his mind feels like Swiss cheese. He doesn't know how he can still make money when he doesn't even know what the stocks are anymore, but he does.

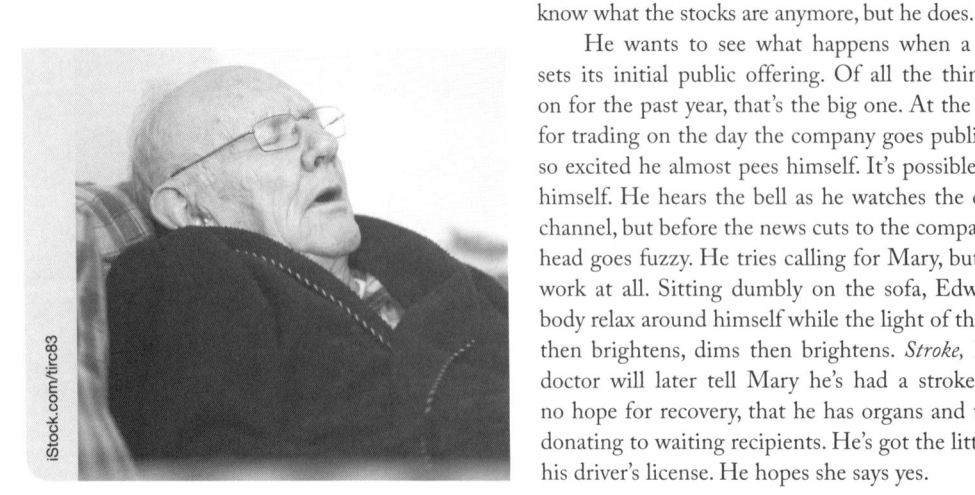

He wants to see what happens when a new retailer sets its initial public offering. Of all the things he's held on for the past year, that's the big one. At the opening bell for trading on the day the company goes public, Edward is so excited he almost pees himself. It's possible he does pee himself. He hears the bell as he watches the cable trading channel, but before the news cuts to the company CEO, his head goes fuzzy. He tries calling for Mary, but that doesn't work at all. Sitting dumbly on the sofa, Edward feels his body relax around himself while the light of the world dims then brightens, dims then brightens. *Stroke*, he thinks. A doctor will later tell Mary he's had a stroke, that there's no hope for recovery, that he has organs and tissues worth donating to waiting recipients. He's got the little symbol on his driver's license. He hopes she says yes.

## CASE DISCUSSION QUESTIONS

1. In early childhood, Edward's fathers Jared and Brendon have a talk with him to begin what will be lifelong conversations about his adoption. In doing so, they introduce the concept of Edward having two dads. This forthright form of communication is a hallmark of Edward's life. How might his continued development across any and all domains (biological, cognitive, and socioemotional) have been different if Jared and Brendon ignored the adoption and same-sex parents issues? Why?

2. In late adulthood, Edward receives a call from what he'll learn is his half-sister; they share a biological mother. This relationship enriches his remaining years. What is important about this relationship to Edward beyond the superficial, and how does it change his life for the better?

3. What are the moral and practical implications of Edward's mother giving him up for adoption without his birth father knowing he exists?

4. What are the positive outcomes that result from Edward's experience with depression?

# 8  Aiza Morris

## Introduction

Welcome to your case study!

Congratulations! You will follow the lifespan of baby girl Aiza Morris. Try to use your best judgment, textbook, classmates, instructor, and supplementary resources to make the best decisions to help her grow.

This semester you will observe Aiza as she grows from infant to child to teen to adult. Who will she become in your care? Will you understand and agree with all decisions available within her circumstances? How will you feel about the tough decisions that forever shape her path in life?

## Meet Aiza Morris

Aiza is the first daughter and second child of Kristy and Trina Morris. Kristy is a 36-year-old white woman, and Trina is a 35-year-old African American woman. Both are professional women. Kristy is a physician and works at a local hospital in the emergency room as a trauma specialist. Trina, a lawyer, has her own practice specializing in women's legal aid. The couple has a two-year-old son Devon, who is the biological child of Trina and an anonymous Caucasian

iStock.com/Wavebreakmedia

sperm donor. Aiza will also be Trina's biological child, conceived with the assistance of an anonymous Caucasian donor.

Through this case study and your lifespan course, you will be asked to consider decisions regarding Aiza's physical, emotional, and cognitive growth and development from several perspectives: her mothers' and her grandparents' as well as those of her spouse, her potential children, other potential family members, friends, teachers, doctors, and supervisors.

Now let's get started.

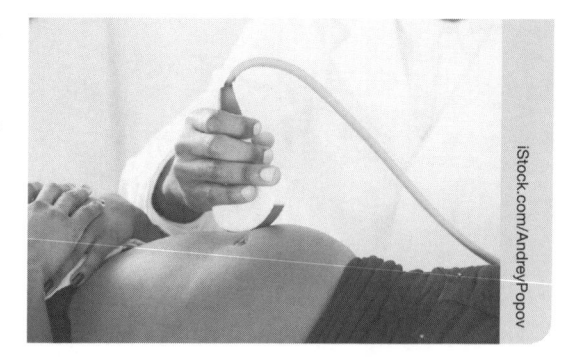

## 1. Development and Its Influences

### Today you will practice the following:

1.1 *Outline five principles of the lifespan developmental perspective.*

1.2 *Explain three theoretical controversies about human development.*

1.3 *Summarize five theoretical perspectives on human development.*

1.4 *Describe the methods and research designs used to study human development.*

As upper-income professionals, the Morrises live in an affluent, urban neighborhood. Trina gets the best prenatal care from the head of obstetrics at the hospital where Kristy works, and Aiza is born at 38 weeks' gestation with Kristy and Devon beside Trina the entire time.

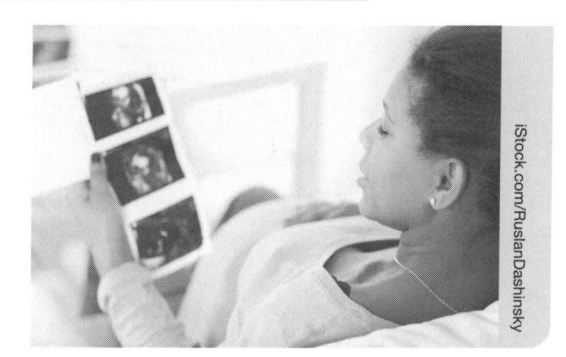

## 2. Biological and Environmental Foundations

### Today you will practice the following:

2.1 *Discuss the genetic foundations of development.*

2.2 *Identify examples of genetic disorders and chromosomal abnormalities.*

2.3 *Discuss the choices available to prospective parents in having healthy children.*

2.4 *Describe the interaction of heredity and environment, including behavioral genetics and the epigenetic framework.*

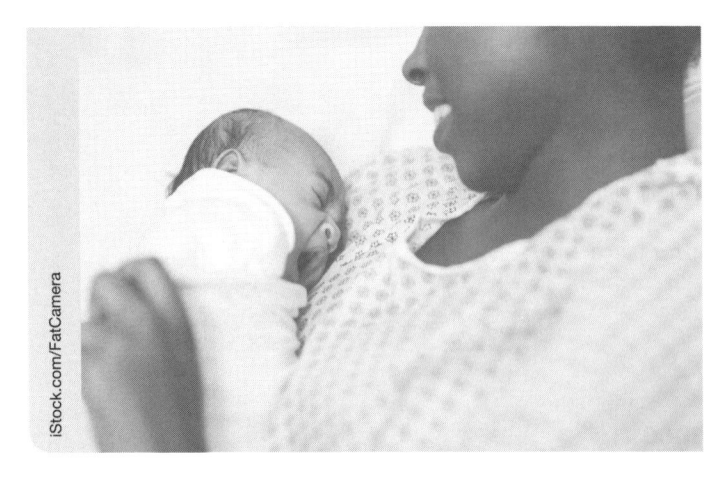

Trina, who is 35 when Aiza is conceived, has few prenatal issues. She's fit and healthy and has all the advantages financial resources can offer. However, she is also technically of advanced maternal age, and her OB-GYN keeps close tabs on her for any negative effects she and Aiza may experience because of this. Aiza's moms, on the other hand, believe that 40 is the new 30 and aren't surprised when Trina's prenatal lab work always comes back within normal limits. Although Trina requires in vitro fertilization (IVF) for conception, because she and Kristy rely on sperm donation, they opt for only minimal preimplantation testing on the embryo. Their IVF isn't an opportunity to create a perfect baby but, rather, the opportunity to create a baby. The rest they leave up to Trina's diet, exercise, and the care of her capable doctor.

## 3. Aiza's Prenatal Development, Birth, and Newborn Experience

### Today you will practice the following:

3.1 Describe the three periods of prenatal development that begin with conception.

3.2 Identify how exposure to teratogens can influence the prenatal environment.

3.3 Explain the process of childbirth.

3.4 Discuss the neonate's physical capacities, including development in low-birth-weight infants.

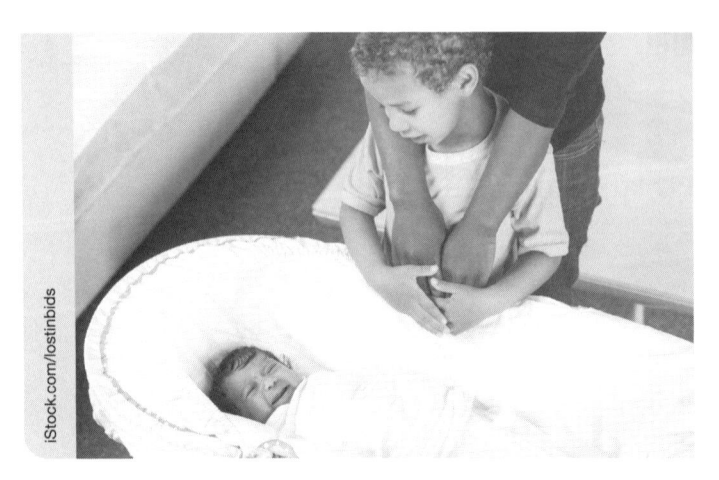

Trina delivers Aiza with Kristy by her side and Devon jumping up and down at the head of the hospital bed. As Aiza crowns, Devon peeks where the obstetrician sits on her stool, prepared to catch the baby, and he makes a face of extreme disgust, causing all in the room to laugh. Afterward, he stays near Trina's head but bounces in anticipation until they hear Aiza's first lusty cries.

"There she is!" Kristy says with a completely unnecessary announcement. "Look at our girl."

Already crying from the abrupt drop in hormones, Trina holds out her arms. "Let me have her." Kristy cuts the cord and quickly wraps their new daughter in a swath of hospital blanket before handing her to Trina, who tucks Aiza close to her body and stares at her. "Ah, you are a beauty, aren't you?"

Devon disagrees.

"She's dirty, and she's bleeding."

Kristy laughs. "Oh, no. Sweetie, she's not bleeding. She's just got a little blood on her from being born. The nurses will get her all cleaned up in a just a few minutes."

"I can hold her?" he asks, still working on grammatical structure in his tender toddler years.

"Yes, baby," Trina tells him. "Let Mommy sit you on the bed, and you can hold your baby sister."

## 4. Physical Development in Infancy and Toddlerhood

### Today you will practice the following:

4.1 Discuss growth and the role of nutrition in development during infancy and toddlerhood.

4.2 Summarize brain development during infancy and toddlerhood.

4.3 Compare infants' early learning capacities for habituation, classical conditioning, operant conditioning, and imitation.

4.4 Describe infants' developing sensory abilities.

4.5 Analyze the roles of maturation and contextual factors in infant and toddler motor development.

"Dis li'uhl piggy went 'oo market, dis li'uhl piggy went 'ome . . ."

Devon holds his baby sister on his lap and sings to her. He has to reach a long way to touch the tips of her toes, and she wiggles as he sings.

His mom hands him a bottle and asks, "Do you want feed Aiza, Devon?"

"Me do it!" he yells. Mommy bends down and helps him start feeding his baby sister. When everything is okay, she stands and starts working on dinner. "See's eating." He giggles, so happy he can help.

"She is," Mommy says. "You're a big helper, Devon."

"Me like helping."

Aiza spends the first two years of her life at a distinctly low-level physical position. Devon holds her on the floor in the room where his moms happen to be whenever they let him, and their moms get down to their children's level for a couple hours every evening after dinner. They're climbed over, kissed, slobbered on, and ridden like ponies before reading bedtime stories. Kristy and Trina rotate bedtime routines: Kristy with Devon one night while Trina takes care of Aiza and swapping the next night. Theirs is a busy family. On weekends, Kristy and Trina take Devon to the local museum and story time at the library and, whenever they're in town, to traveling musicians' shows or other cultural events. Because they don't want to leave Aiza behind, they tote her along in a stroller or baby backpack. Devon likes the dinosaur museum, but Aiza likes the jazz shows and any events that allow her to interact with exhibits. The children's mothers find it harder to keep up with their toddler than with their preschooler some days.

## 5. Cognitive Development in Infancy and Toddlerhood

### Today you will practice the following:

*5.1  Discuss the cognitive-developmental perspective on infant reasoning.*

*5.2  Describe the information processing system in infants.*

*5.3  Discuss individual differences in infant intelligence.*

*5.4  Summarize the patterns of language development during infancy and toddlerhood.*

Aiza lies on her back and grabs her toes. Rolling back and forth, she sings to herself. Although her moms don't understand her gibberish, Devon tells them she's singing real words. They believe him. Thus far, they know she can say *mama* and *ma* to refer to the two of them, *Deh* for Devon, the obligatory *no*, *hi* and *bye-bye*, *more*, *Aye-ee* to refer to herself, *Lalock* to refer to Sherlock their cat, and a half-dozen other common words. The singing? Well, they figure that's Devon's domain. Their son seems confused by their confusion, but they enjoy watching him lay his head beside his sister's before bedtime while he teaches her new songs. Aiza seems particularly fond of "The Itsy Bitsy 'Pider."

## 6. Socioemotional Development in Infancy and Toddlerhood

### Today you will practice the following:

*6.1  Summarize the psychosocial tasks of infancy and toddlerhood.*

*6.2  Describe emotional development in infancy, and identify contextual and cultural influences on emotional development in infants and toddlers.*

*6.3  Identify the styles and stability of temperament, including the role of goodness of fit in infant development.*

*6.4  Describe how attachment develops in infancy and toddlerhood.*

*6.5  Differentiate the roles of self-concept, self-recognition, and self-control in infant development.*

When Aiza turns a year old, Trina decides she's ready to return to full-time legal practice. After the first three months, she started corresponding with the office electronically and by cell phone, consulting on low-profile cases and providing needed information on cases that hadn't closed when she left to have Aiza. Occasionally she and Aiza travel together to the office for an hour or two. Now, she's ready for full-time practice again. Devon, in preschool and without the need for full-time care, is less a concern than their Aiza. After much conversation, Kristy and Trina decide the best answer is to hire a nanny three days each week. Trina will take Fridays off unless she has to be in court, which is unlikely. Kristy will continue to take her normal Wednesdays off. With a nanny the rest of the week, Aiza will be cared for all day, and someone will be there to collect Devon at the end of his preschool day at St. Andrews.

The moms spend a few weeks interviewing candidates they've secured through word of mouth from friends and coworkers. They also have Devon spend some time in each interview, along with Aiza, so they can get a feel for how the prospective nannies get along with their children. By the deadline Trina's given herself for returning to work, América Elizondo has joined the family three days a week, and Devon is eating out of her hand. Secure in the children's well-being, Trina dresses in a smart suit, kisses her wife and baby, and snaps her fingers at Devon. "Come along, babe. Time to go."

## 7. Physical and Cognitive Development in Early Childhood

### Today you will practice the following:

7.1 *Discuss physical development in early childhood.*

7.2 *Compare Piaget's cognitive-developmental and Vygotsky's sociocultural perspectives on cognitive development in early childhood.*

7.3 *Describe information-processing abilities during early childhood.*

7.4 *Summarize young children's advances in language development.*

7.5 *Contrast social learning and cognitive-developmental perspectives on moral development in early childhood.*

7.6 *Identify and explain approaches to early childhood education.*

It's not until second grade at St. Andrews that Aiza realizes she's different from her classmates. On the playground, a new girl called Amanda asks her, "What *are* you?" and the question catches the attention of several other classmates.

Stung, Aiza stares at her. "What do you mean 'what am I?' I'm a girl, just like you."

"No," Amanda says, shaking her head. "Not that. I mean, you're not white like me, and you're not brown like Tiana. You're kind of *light brown*, but I don't see anyone else that color. So, what are you?"

"I'm brown and white," Aiza tells her. She's offended, but she doesn't know why. "I guess I am light brown."

"What's brown *and* white?"

Aiza decides she doesn't like Amanda, and she mostly likes everyone.

"I have a brown mommy, and my father was white. I'm brown, but I'm also white." This seems obvious to her. Looking at her other friends, it seems pretty obvious to them, too. Reassured, she continues. "Why do you care?"

"I've never seen a brown person with green eyes before," Amanda taunts.

"Now you have."

"And you don't braid your hair like all the other brown people I know."

Yes, Aiza definitely dislikes Amanda.

"I like to wear it like this. I have curly hair. Who cares about that?"

Close to Aiza's right elbow, her friend Susanna Webster says, "I wish my hair was curly like yours."

Aiza gives Amanda a smile that says she's unconcerned with the new girl's opinion and intertwines her fingers with Susanna's. "Jump rope?"

## 8. Socioemotional Development in Early Childhood

### Today you will practice the following:

8.1 *Discuss young children's emerging sense of initiative, self-concept, and self-esteem.*

8.2 *Summarize the development of emotional understanding, regulation, and behavior in early childhood.*

8.3 *Identify four parenting styles and their associations with child outcomes.*

8.4 *Compare biological, cognitive, and contextual theoretical explanations of gender role development.*

8.5 *Explain the function of play and the form it takes during early childhood.*

Weekday evenings are predictable in the Morris household. Trina and Kristy work together fixing dinner. Neither is an outstanding cook, but they both prepare passable meals. No one's died yet anyway, they joke a few times a week. Monday and Tuesday, Devon helps while Aiza takes care of other household tasks like taking out the trash and cleaning the litterbox. On Thursday and Friday, the children switch. The moms are intent on allowing both Devon and Aiza to find their own paths, particularly whether they want traditional or atypical gender identities and the roles that go with them. However, they're also determined to make sure both can do all chores around a house and don't expect any division of labor based on body parts. The family doesn't talk about it unless one of the kids brings it up, but it's important for Trina and Kristy.

The only chore Aiza pushes back on is the litterbox. "It's so gross!" she complains. To be fair, her brother does, too.

When Aiza exerts her will, Kristy (the bad cop) approaches the situation with loving firmness. Aiza learns there are boundaries, that if a chore is on her list, it's pretty much nonnegotiable, but she also learns that her mom is ready and willing to listen to her concerns. When Aiza says she doesn't like "dirty" chores, Kristy points out that she doesn't mind taking out the trash. Faced with her own inconsistency, Aiza agrees that maybe the litterbox isn't *so bad* a couple days each week. She also admits that she doesn't like doing it after Devon because her brother doesn't do such a good job. *That,* Kristy tells her, is a legitimate complaint, and she will have a talk with Devon to correct that problem right away.

## 9. Physical and Cognitive Development in Middle Childhood

### Today you will practice the following:

9.1 *Identify patterns of physical and motor development during middle childhood and common health issues facing school-age children.*

9.2 *Discuss school-age children's capacities for reasoning and processing information.*

9.3 *Summarize views of intelligence including the uses, correlates, and criticisms of intelligence tests.*

9.4 *Examine patterns of moral development during middle childhood.*

9.5 *Summarize language development during middle childhood.*

9.6 *Discuss children's learning at school.*

Aiza spends the last two years of elementary school in a strange sort of space that's devoid of Devon's presence since he moved on to the upper school at St. Andrews. It's weird. Their school is so small that she's used to seeing him all the time or being in classes where the teachers have had him pretty recently. Now, it's just Aiza, and she kind of likes it. It's not that she and her brother aren't close. They are. It's just nice to see what it's like to be out of his shadow. Everyone loves Devon Morris.

All her teachers expect her to be great at everything. She knows because she's heard them talking to her moms about it. Probably it's because they're both so educated and have such great jobs. Aiza's not sure why that automatically means she has to be good

**PART I**  The Cases

at everything. She's not even sure she's good at anything yet. She likes a lot of different things she studies but not any one class over all the others. Mostly she *likes* a unit here or there in all of them. She makes good grades, but she also knows that at St. Andrews everyone makes good grades. You don't get to stay if you don't.

## 10. Socioemotional Development in Middle Childhood

### Today you will prefer the following:

10.1  Describe school-age children's self-conceptions and motivation.

10.2  Examine the roles of friendship, peer acceptance, and peer victimization in school-age children's adjustment.

10.3  Discuss family relationships in middle childhood and the influence of family structure on adjustment.

10.4  Analyze the role of resilience in promoting adjustment to adversity, including characteristics of children and contexts that promote resilience.

Aiza still doesn't like Amanda Tate. It's been four years, and she's tried. Well, she's tried twice, but she did try. Amanda is what's more commonly known as a mean girl. The label is honestly come by, as her mama would say. Aiza isn't a mean girl. She's not a saint, much to the dismay of the head, but she's not a mean girl. Each of them has her faction, too. Amanda's is white, which makes Aiza feel like a traitor to Mom, but the truth is what it is. Aiza's friends are more like a rainbow. She worries sometimes that she collects the St. Andrews misfits and then dismisses the thoughts. Who cares? Everyone needs a home.

## 11. Physical and Cognitive Development in Late Childhood

### Today you will practice the following:

11.1  Describe school-age children's self-conceptions and motivation.

11.2  Examine the roles of friendship, peer acceptance, and peer victimization in school-age children's adjustment.

11.3  Discuss family relationships in middle childhood and the influence of family structure on adjustment.

11.4  Analyze the role of resilience in promoting adjustment to adversity, including characteristics of children and contexts that promote resilience

In sixth grade, Aiza's social sciences teacher invites a guest lecturer to their classroom for a week. His name is Dr. Lambert, and he's a geologist. He tells the class he studies rocks and explains where he goes to find them and exactly what he does with them. Aiza is interested in this—rocks a little but more the other stuff Dr. Lambert talks about. He explains about one type of geologist, a geophysicist he calls it, who studies the geomagnetic forces in and around the Earth, and that sounds so cool to Aiza that she can't stop thinking about it. She asks her moms for all sorts of magnetic kits for Christmas that year and begs them to take their family vacation in Washington, D.C. the next year so she can visit the Smithsonian and NASA. Devon, who's off playing junior varsity football and writing poetry (poetry, ha!), agrees with reluctance to the Washington trip; he can visit Folger Library and the Library of Congress, he says. In the meanwhile, Aiza talks América, their nanny, into teaching her how to make magnetic slime after school. There are some false starts, but she gets the hang of it and gives all her friends containers of the black goo for Christmas.

## 12. Socioemotional Development in Late Childhood

### Today you will practice the following:

12.1  Summarize the processes by which self-concept, self-esteem, and identity change during adolescence.

12.2  Discuss the nature of parent–child relationships in adolescence.

12.3  Examine the developmental progression of peer relations in adolescence.

12.4  Analyze patterns of adolescent sexual activity including sexual orientation.

12.5  Identify common psychological and behavioral problems in adolescence.

Amanda sneaks up behind Aiza at the upper school open house for rising seventh graders. Aiza's moms are talking to Ms. Eddleman, who will be her homeroom teacher in a few months—and Amanda's.

"Morris," Amanda whispers.

"Tate." Aiza turns around and faces Amanda. "What do you want?"

"Why don't you like me? Or white people?"

Aiza laughs. "White people? *I'm* white. My mom's white. Get over yourself, Amanda."

She sees Devon coming toward her in the hallway and waves. She's not scared of

Amanda, but it's always nice to have her brother around. When Devon joins them, he looks at the door.

"Ms. Eddleman? Sorry, Aiza."

"I'll live."

He looks at Amanda. "Slumming, Amanda?"

Aiza watches as Amanda loses her capacity for quick comebacks. It's so painful any comedy in the situation falls flat. Amanda tries to shoot her an evil look but fails. Before the situation can deteriorate further, Aiza's moms return and wave at her and her brother. As Aiza walks away, she glances back at Amanda.

"See you Monday." In the car, she glares at Devon. "What *was* that? Is Amanda in love with you or something?"

Devon shrugs and grins at her. "Or something."

## 13. Physical and Cognitive Development in Adolescence

### Today you will practice the following:

13.1 Evaluate the "storm and stress" perspective on adolescence in light of research evidence.

13.2 Summarize the physical changes that occur with puberty and the correlates of pubertal timing.

13.3 Discuss brain development during adolescence and its effect on behavior.

13.4 Identify ways in which thinking changes in adolescence and how these changes are reflected in adolescent decision-making and behavior.

13.5 Discuss moral development and influences on moral reasoning.

13.6 Describe the challenges that school transitions pose for adolescents and the role of parents in academic achievement.

When she's 14, Aiza sits alone with her doctor. Their moms have taken her and Devon to the pediatrician for their normal checkups, and that means five or ten minutes of private time for questions and answers of an intimate nature. She swings her legs over the side of the examining table and waits. The silence makes her feel awkward.

"We talked about a lot of things with your moms, Aiza. I want to double-check a few of those."

She shrugs. "Okay."

"No drugs?"

"No drugs," she confirms. If this is what the doctor wants to know, she'll be done fast. Devon was.

"No alcohol?"

"Only on New Year's when Mom gives me and Devon a glass of champagne."

"Good." Dr. Bennett looks at her with narrowed eyes. "And sex?"

Aiza laughs. "*No sex,*" she assures her.

"Good again." Dr. Bennett nods. "Aiza, can I help you with anything you didn't want to say in front of your parents?"

She thinks about it. Is there? "I don't think so. Only . . . What if there is one day?"

"Then you'll call and tell the receptionist you have a question."

Aiza realizes that Dr. Bennett's answer makes her feel a lot better even though she can't say why. "Thank you, Dr. Bennett," she says. "That helps a lot."

"That's what I'm here for."

At 15, they repeat the process—and at 16 but with an exception. Near the end of the conversation, Aiza asks, "How much 'doctor–patient confidentiality' do I enjoy here?"

"Fairly complete," Dr. Bennett assures her. Holding up first, then two, then three fingers, she runs back through their topics. "Drugs, alcohol, sex?"

"Door number three."

"Complete confidentiality unless you have HIV."

"I don't."

"Then you're safe telling or asking me anything."

"Whew." Aiza blows out a breath. "I'm not," she rushes to say. "I'm not having sex. I'm not even thinking about it. But I might soon. I was thinking about . . ."

"Options?" Dr. Bennett supplies.

"Yeah."

They agree that—condoms aside, because they're critical for other preventions—Aiza should try the ring. Dr. Bennett hands her a paper prescription that she folds and slips into the pocket of her jeans.

"Thank you."

"Of course. It's good you're being forward-minded, although I encourage you to continue waiting."

Aiza gives her a half smile. "We'll see."

## 14. Socioemotional Development in Adolescence

### Today you will practice the following:

14.1 Summarize the processes by which self-concept, self-esteem, and identity change during adolescence.

14.2 Discuss the nature of parent–child relationships in adolescence.

14.3 Examine the developmental progression of peer relations in adolescence.

14.4 Analyze patterns of adolescent sexual activity including sexual orientation.

14.5 Identify common psychological and behavioral problems in adolescence.

In the upper school at St. Andrews, Aiza navigates a complex social maze. She's in school with what are predominantly wealthy white kids, and she knows she's one of them. She's also a wealthy brown kid, as Amanda Tate goes to great lengths to remind her as often as possible. Susanna Webster—thank God for Susanna—remains a good friend and keeps her steady when she might lose her head over Amanda's stupid antics. She has other friends and spends time with them, at football games when she goes to see Devon play and at after parties when her moms let her go. The parties are nearly as bad as school. Devon's always there, and he either ignores her (kid sister kills the football-star vibe) or kills her fun when she starts to get lucky with a guy who doesn't yet know she's Devon Morris's little sister. It's always the same.

"Hey, Devon!" and he answers her with a look of such condescension that she slinks into the background like a wallflower, *or* she'll hear "Do we have a class together?" or something equally stupid from a guy she doesn't know and who knows he doesn't know her.

"I don't think so. I'm sure I'd remember."

A smile, a flirtatious leaning in with one shoulder—Aiza smiles back.

"Me, too. I'm [fill in the guy of the night's name], and you are . . . ?"

"Aiza." She never gives a last name. They'll find out soon enough. When she's super unlucky, they find out just about . . .

"Hey, Aiza! You get that text from Mom?"

There is no text from Mom.

"No, Devon," she says to her brother, who's standing full on between them by now. "Don't you have someplace to be?"

"I do," he answers. "Right here."

Thus ends every party she attends with her brother. Although she isn't boyfriendless, dateless, or even worried about first kisses (check), second base (check), or even finding someone she might want to do more with, Devon sure does get in the way, which is funny because she knows he's had sex before.

In 10th grade, she meets Dale Linwood when Devon brings him home one day after football practice. Dale is everything Devon is not: tall and wiry, all American with blond hair and blue eyes, quiet and gentle. Devon treats her like the kid sister she is, but although he shuts his door in her face, she manages to speak to Dale without tripping over her tongue when they run into each other in the kitchen a little while later. Much to Devon's dismay, Aiza and Dale start dating soon after that, and he takes her to his senior prom in the spring.

Trina helps her shop for a dress. After hours in fitting rooms at all the stores all the girls she knows are shopping at—God, they even run into Amanda Tate—Mom suggests they try a smaller boutique in town. Exhausted but determined, Aiza says okay, but this is the last one. When they arrive, Aiza looks around the shop and shakes her head.

"You weren't kidding. It's not much bigger than Mama's closet in here."

"Well," Mom says, laughing, "Kristy always did like her clothes. Remodeling the guest room into a dressing room was a good investment."

Aiza laughs with her in amusement as a dapper man in his 30s approaches them. She senses Mom opening her mouth and turns to her, finger in the air.

"No. Absolutely not. No one needs your gaydar to know how this guy's not straight, Mom. Not everything is 'part of the community.' Some things just are." Mom purses her lips, but her eyes are twinkling. "Thank you."

Approaching, the man—his tag reads *Prescott*—holds a hand on the air. He speaks before reaching them. "Prom?" Aiza nods. "What a charming face and that hair! Makes me wish I were a hairdresser." He turns and motions for them to follow, speaking to Aiza over his shoulder. "Of course, with those eyes, there's really only one dress in the store you can wear."

"But I haven't looked at anything yet."

"That's how I earn my keep." They arrive at the center of the boutique where a half-dozen other mothers and daughters (and one father–daughter pair) stand and sit in various configurations. A handful of mothers are alone, and Aiza hears girls calling from inside fitting rooms, too.

"*Maman,*" Prescott says to Mom in French, "you'll sit here with this."

Mom sits in the plush white chair and accepts the champagne flute. Aiza raises a brow. Mom lifts a shoulder as if to say, "If I have to do the shopping and the paying, at least I can have Cristal while I'm so put upon."

"You," Prescott says, waving a hand up and down in front of Aiza, "will follow me."

Inside a fitting room, Aiza strips to her underwear and a bra bought just for the day's shopping. Prescott knocks on the door after an absence of several minutes, which she opens wide enough to take the perfectly sensible heels from him before reaching for the dress. He'd said there was only one, and she finds that hard to believe with all she's tried on throughout the day. Dutifully, she works herself into the long gray gown with embroidered overskirt in all the colors of a summer garden. She never would've picked it for herself to try on, but staring at herself in the mirror, she's forced to admit Prescott's eye. It's perfect, as her mother agrees five minutes later.

When she and Dale shop for his tux, he asks her what color tie and cummerbund to get, and she shakes her head at him. "Wear what you want to. No matter what it is, you're going to look great."

"But I don't want you to think I clash with your dress," he says.

Aiza smiles at him, thinking of her dress with its rainbow of colors. "I don't think that's going to happen. It's your prom. Wear whatever makes you happy."

## 15. Physical and Cognitive Development in Emerging/Early Adulthood

### Today you will practice the following:

15.1  *Describe the features and characteristics of emerging and early adulthood.*

15.2  *Summarize the physical developments of emerging and early adulthood.*

15.3  *Analyze physical and sexual health issues in emerging and early adulthood.*

15.4  *Compare postformal reasoning, pragmatic thought, and cognitive-affective complexity.*

15.5  *Explain how attending college influences young adults' development, and identify challenges faced by first-generation and nontraditional students.*

15.6  *Discuss vocational choice and the transition to work.*

"Hi, Mama."

Aiza kisses her mom on the cheek on a Wednesday afternoon—once again Kristy's day off at the hospital—and tosses her book bag on the kitchen table. It's a *good* day. She got an A back on an essay she worked hard on, and the assignment in her human geography class is so cool she almost wet herself when Dr. Morales okayed it. She can't wait to tell her mom. This is definitely one of the perks of living at home while she goes to college. Devon texts her all the time about the latest party he's been to at his school, and he seems clueless whenever she asks about classes. That, she figures, is another perk; she's never going to fall behind because she's not using college for anything other than education—even if Dr. Morales *is* young, hot, and single.

"How was your day, sweetheart?"

"So good. Remember that paper you helped me edit?"

"I do."

"I got an A."

"Hey, that's great! I know how hard you worked on that."

"Yeah. I would've been disappointed if I'd failed. An A or B would've been okay, but a C would've been the worst."

Mama looks at her with that *time for another life lesson* face. "Have I taught you nothing? Has Mom taught you nothing? Sit down, please."

Aiza sits. She points at Mama's beer on the little paper coaster from their trip to the Grand Canyon the year before. "Can I have one of those?"

"You're 20. No, you may not." Aiza rolls her eyes, but Mama ignores her. "What have we always told you and your brother?"

"To do our best, and if we do our very best then outside validation doesn't matter."

"That's part of it. Do you believe that?"

Aiza hitches a shoulder. Mostly she does, but the world turns on different forms of validation, and she believes that, too.

"I believe my own sense of worth or evaluation of a product doesn't come from someone else's," she says carefully, "but I also believe that someone else's is important for how I make my way in the world."

Mama eyes her. "That's true enough," she concedes. "What else?"

"The world lives in the Land of C."

"And . . ."

Aiza sighs. "*And* C is average, not failing."

"A C hard earned," Mama adds, "is nothing to fear or be ashamed of. The word *average* exists for a reason, Aiza."

Aiza fights rolling her eyes not out of respect but because she knows Mama's right. She just hates admitting it.

"I know."

"You're a smart girl, Aiza. Don't let the world dumb you down. Now, what else? You seem more chipper than an A on an essay warrants."

"Oh, I am," she tells Mama. "We're doing an assignment in our human geography class that's something like a third of our grade. I don't know, but it's a lot. Anyway, we get to choose our topic as long as Dr. Morales approves it, and today he gave me back my proposal with a thumbs-up."

"That's great, Aiza. What do you want to do?"

"I want to write a paper that theoretically explores the use of GPS technology and long-range, low-emission MRI to track the populations of undocumented immigrants and transients in America. They're the hardest to count in the census. We learned that in class. I think the technology isn't there yet to do what I'm thinking, but hey, if you can dream it, you can do it, right?"

Mama nods her head. "Yes, you can."

Aiza hops up from the table. "Well, if I can't join you in a beer, I'm going to my room to get started." She drops a kiss on her mom's head and grabs her book bag. She's so excited!

## 16. Socioemotional Development in Emerging/Early Adulthood

### Today you will practice the following:

16.1  Summarize psychosocial development in emerging and early adulthood.

16.2  Discuss influences on friendship and mate selection and interactions in emerging and early adulthood.

16.3  Analyze the diverse romantic situations that may characterize emerging and early adulthood, including singlehood, cohabitation, marriage, and divorce.

16.4  Compare the experiences of young adults as stepparents, never-married parents, and same-sex parents.

Aiza kicks off her heels and puts her feet in Susanna's lap. They're at her favorite place, one of those Europeanesque coffee houses with crappy little iron tables on the sidewalk and real—*real*—hot chocolate poured from little pots of steamed milk and hot chocolate sauce. Every time she comes here, she makes herself go to the gym after in penance. It's worth it.

Today, she and Susanna are sharing—*sharing*, it's sacrilegious—a chocolate croissant. Aiza has a "little coffee," which is what she's called an espresso since she was a child and didn't know the difference. Susanna has her customary mug of black, no sugar—like a trucker, Aiza kids. They haven't seen each other in months. Susanna goes to university in New York at Pratt. Aiza misses her terribly, but whenever Susanna sends a postcard hand sketched or delicately watercolored, Aiza knows this is the best thing for her friend.

The weekend football game, a playoff game to see who gets a bowl bid, plays on a screen inside the bar next door, and Aiza can see the scores flashing along the bottom even if she doesn't watch the action. Devon's on the defensive line for the team opposing the one for whom Dale is the star quarterback. Poetry in motion, she thinks and laughs. Following her eye, Susanna whistles.

"You've still got a thing for Dale Linwood? I thought that ended when he left for college."

"It did. Doesn't mean I can't appreciate the athlete. He and Devon both graduate this year. I wonder what he'll do."

"No draft for either of them, you don't think?"

"I don't think Dale was ever interested. He just wanted to go to college." She shrugs. "I don't know about Devon. If he could play, maybe he would. It's one in a 100,000, though, you know? I think Mama wants him to come home and leave the concussions for someone else."

"I don't blame her." Susanna picks at the crumbs on their shared plate. "Do you know what Dale majored in?"

"Something stupid like philosophy."

"Damn. He always was a brainiac. Why stupid?"

"What's he going to do with *that*?" She leans back in her seat and wiggles her feet. On cue, Susanna starts to rub one. "You ever see an ad for a philosopher?"

"My guess is the man's going to graduate school then. He can be a professor like your oh-so-fine Dr. Morales."

"Huh."

Aiza hasn't thought of that possibility. She squints through the bar's windows in time to see Dale pass the ball off to a teammate who runs for the game-winning touchdown. Probably she should feel bad for Devon. Her brother probably has no plan other than the NFL. She can't help smiling. Dale won. The camera shows the players taking the field hugging and slapping each other's butts. She doesn't understand that. Moments later, her phone rings.

"Aiza!"

"Congratulations, Dale. That was a great last play."

"You saw?"

"Yeah. Susanna and I are watching from Café Noisette through the window at Patty's."

"That's a bowl game!"

"I know. Congrats."

"So, listen, I gotta go. The team's celebrating, but I wanted to see if we could maybe, I don't know, get together or something when I come back next weekend. It's my parents' anniversary, and they're having a big party. Maybe you could come to that with me if you wanted."

Aiza winks at Susanna. "Maybe. Yeah, sure, we can do something. Your parents' thing sounds nice, Dale. Let me know when you get in what you want to do."

When she hangs up, she makes a face at Susanna that's half hopeful and half chagrined. "Am I just fishing in the past because the present's dry, or is this really about Dale?"

"Aiza, you've dated every eligible bachelor in the tristate area. I think it's safe to say this is about Dale. Finish your coffee so we can shop for new shoes. You always feel better when you buy new shoes."

"True that," she agrees, lifting her cup. She salutes Susanna with it. "To best friends and old loves."

## 17. Physical and Cognitive Development in Middle Adulthood

### Today you will practice the following:

*17.1  Summarize age-related physical changes during middle adulthood.*

*17.2  Discuss common health conditions and illnesses and the roles of stress and hardiness on health during middle adulthood.*

*17.3 Contrast the findings of cross-sectional and longitudinal studies of crystallized and fluid intelligence over adulthood.*

*17.4 Analyze changes in cognitive capacities during middle adulthood, including attention, memory, processing speed, and expertise.*

Aiza spends a good portion of her 20s working her way up the research and development ladder at a tech innovation firm in Chicago. She's not wild about the wind, but she loves the work. By the time she finishes her bachelor's degree in geophysics, Dale's completed his master's in philosophy and has started a PhD program in North Carolina at Duke. This is, she points out, the epitome of a long-distance romance. It is also, he points out, one with a finite timeline, after which they'll be able to be together. They both know that's not necessarily true. Dale will have to find work in Chicago, or Aiza will have to move.

She decides to worry about that when it's time to worry about that and focuses on her career.

Now and again, she's able to hire Susanna to render a concept for a patent filing. She loves the technical drawing Susanna produces. She's so clean and precise with her work that it's almost impossible to believe the renderings are done by a human hand. Through it all, she reminds herself of her motto: if you can dream it, you can do it. Through many out-there projects, the thought keeps her going.

When Dale finally arrives, assistant professorship at the University of Chicago secured, she feels the weight of stress lifting from her shoulders. The work hasn't changed. Her apartment hasn't changed. Nothing has changed but the distance between them, and that alone allows her to be more daring, more productive, and less prone to insomnia and minor illnesses. As she enters her 30s, she looks forward to a long and vital career making the incredible come to life.

## 18. Socioemotional Development in Middle Adulthood

## Today you will practice the following:

*18.1 Summarize the theories and research on psychosocial development during middle adulthood.*

*18.2 Describe the changes that occur in self-concept, identity, and personality during middle adulthood.*

*18.3 Analyze relationships in middle adulthood, including friend, spousal, parent–child, and grandparent relationships.*

*18.4 Discuss influences on job satisfaction and retirement planning during middle adulthood.*

Dale and Aiza travel back home for her moms' 35th wedding anniversary. After champagne toasts and cake and a sweet dance Kristy and Trina do alone to "Unforgettable," the first song played at their wedding, Dale puts his arm around Aiza's waist.

"Do you remember the first time we met at your house?"

"I remember Devon slamming his door in my face."

He laughs. "Me, too."

"I thought you were so cute."

"I was!" he agrees, and she laughs.

Pointing to her moms, Dale asks, "Do you remember the first date we had when we got back together?"

"Your parents' anniversary party."

"Yep. Fitting, isn't it?"

Turning in his arm, she smiles up at him. "What's that, Dr. Linwood?"

He puts his mouth near her ear and whispers, "I don't want to steal their party for us, so let me be quiet about it. I don't want to wait another day to ask you to become Mrs. Linwood. Will you, Aiza? Will you marry me?"

Moving her head a fraction, she kisses his cheek. Then she turns again to look at her parents. "Are you going to stop helping with chores and grocery shopping after we're married?"

"What?"

"I'm serious, Dale. Will we stay a pretty equal household?"

"On my honor."

"Then yes. I will marry you."

"Whew." He squeezes her waist. "If you want, we can slip outside for a minute. I've got a ring and everything. The proposal just sort of slipped out without any real thought or preparation."

She laughs and shakes her head. "There's time. Let's have cake first. After they've had their night we can have ours."

Aiza finds she needs to delay their nuptials twice. She loves Dale, and she wants to marry him and no one else. She also wants to make sure she's going to be everything he needs her to be. When she's 34, they finally meet in the same little white church that his parents married in 40 years before and agree to love, honor, and cherish. Aiza is glad the word *obey* no longer appears in the ceremony.

They discuss children. She's older already. He's older still. Devon's had two by this time, and Aiza loves holding them and being the favorite auntie. She never has the big tug toward motherhood, though, and Dale doesn't feel strongly either way. After a year or two, they decide children aren't in their immediate future. Dale has a vasectomy with the agreement that, should they change their minds, they'll travel to the Middle East and adopt a child there.

## 19. Physical and Cognitive Development in Late Adulthood

### Today you will practice the following:

19.1 *Discuss age-related changes in brain and body systems in late adulthood, and identify ways that older adults may compensate for changes.*

19.2 *Identify risk and protective factors for health in late adulthood.*

19.3 *Summarize common dementias including characteristics, risk and protective factors, and treatment.*

19.4 *Analyze patterns of cognitive change in late adulthood.*

Aiza makes three concessions to aging. She refuses to make more. When required, she begins wearing a pair of reading glasses for up-close work, particularly for work on the computer. Her hair, always a mane at least halfway down her back, has become too much to manage, and she chops it off (herself) in the bathroom one morning. She allows it to curl naturally as she always has but concedes the shorter length is easier to maintain as she ages. She also slows down her innovation and begins a project of curation.

"To see what I've actually brought to life and what I've only incubated," she explains to Dale. "I'd like a tangible legacy of both, but mostly I'd like to leave behind a record of what's left to do."

"I understand. Let me help you."

Together, they buy the patents available for purchase from those projects whose terms have expired, and they negotiate permissions for the product development under Aiza's direction for which the company still holds the patents. Aiza collates Susanna's renderings, and they begin a process of looking to the future by looking to her past.

"There's still so much left to do," she says as they finish assembling the opus.

"You don't have to stop yet," he tells her.

"No, but I will soon."

## 20. Socioemotional Development in Late Adulthood

### Today you will practice the following:

20.1  Examine the contributions of self-concept, personality, and religiosity to older adults' well-being.

20.2  Identify social contexts in which older adults live and their influence on development.

20.3  Summarize features of older adults' relationships with friends, spouses, children, and grandchildren, and identify how these relationships affect older adults' functioning.

20.4  Discuss influences on the timing of retirement and adaptation to retirement.

As Aiza approaches her late 50s, Trina's health begins to deteriorate. She's been working in the high-pressure legal field for 40-plus years, and she underwent two painful and stressful rounds of IVF to have Devon and Aiza. Kristy notices the little signs first: Trina's shortness of breath and fatigue and finally her easy flushing that seemed to indicate high blood pressure. Although Kristy got her to a cardiologist for a relatively early diagnosis of cardiovascular disease, Trina passes away in her late 70s. Kristy, still fit and active and in excellent physical health, grieves extensively. Devon, who lives closer to her, makes frequent weekend trips with the kids to keep her occupied and in touch with the here and now, but he confides to Aiza that he's worried about Mama and whether or not she'll ever get over her broken heart.

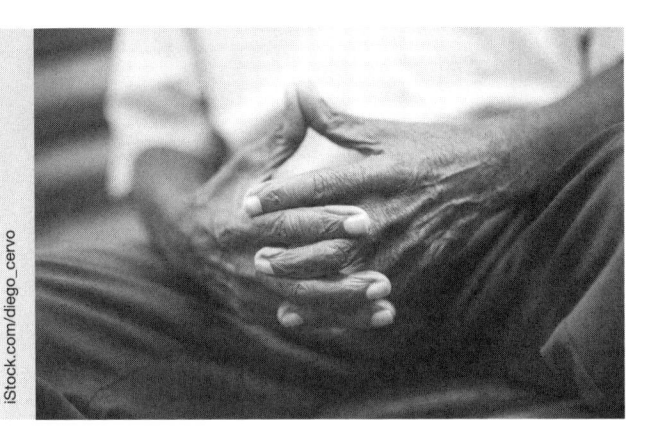

Dale and Aiza travel every four or five months to visit Kristy. It's not enough, Aiza knows, as she sees her mom wasted away a little more each time she arrives. Kristy passes away of natural causes in her early 80s, and Aiza knows it's really a broken heart that's taken Mama from them. As she and Dale take walks around the block and see the occasional show in Chicago, she watches him and selfishly hopes she goes first. She doesn't want to be left with a broken heart like Mama.

## 21. Experience With Death and Dying

### Today you will practice the following:

*21.1 Identify ways in which death has been defined and end-of-life issues that may arise.*

*21.2 Contrast children's, adolescents', and adults' understanding of death.*

*21.3 Discuss the physical and emotional process of dying as it is experienced over the lifespan.*

*21.4 Summarize typical grief reactions to the loss of loved ones and the influence of development on bereavement.*

Aiza is 84 years old when her wish is fulfilled. Despite Dale's threatening type II diabetes and determination to exercise as little as humanly possible, she passes away before he does from complications suffered after a routine surgery. No one is at fault, and none of the doctors could've foreseen what happened. She throws a blood clot that travels to her lung—a pulmonary embolism—and is gone before the emergency medical technicians can arrive at the house. They find a distraught Dale trying valiantly to perform CPR and begging her not to die.

In the weeks after her death, Dale touches all the belongings she left behind, including the curated work they put together as a team some years before. With a sad smile, he lifts the bound pages and sits in his recliner to rifle through them. Tucked between the second and third pages, he finds a note written in her tidy hand.

*My darling Dale,*

*Remember how we so loved Rumi that we would read him in bed together on Saturday and Sunday mornings? I remember. So it, my love, that if you're reading this I'm no longer there with you. (Oh dear, that's rather cliché, isn't it?) If I'm no longer with you, then remember that Rumi said also, "Don't grieve. Anything you lose comes around in another form." You are never without me, and I am never without you.*

*Always,*

*Aiza*

His fingertips tap the note as he cries. Don't grieve, she says. May as well tell the stars not to die before their light reaches us.

## CASE DISCUSSION QUESTIONS

1. In early childhood, Aiza has an antagonistic relationship with a classmate named Amanda, who pokes fun at Aiza for being biracial. Aiza defends her heritage and herself strongly. This relationship with Amanda will persist throughout their school years. How does Aiza's biracial background make her an easy social target? How does it create occasional confusion in Aiza?

2. Although she often feels burdened by her brother Devin's academic and athletic success and her mothers' career successes, Aiza looks forward to college. In early adulthood, she has a conversation with her mom about an idea for combining emergent technology with sociological theory to track and count immigrants and transient populations. Considering Aiza's background of privilege, what experiences and values in her childhood explain her choice of project and ultimate career direction?

3. One of the reasons Aiza opts to remain childless is that she and Dale marry when she's 34. She doesn't want the concerns associated with advanced maternal age with which her own mother contended. What impact will this decision make both positively and negatively on the second half of Aiza's life trajectory across any and all domains (biological, cognitive, and socioemotional)? Be specific.

4. Aiza's entire life occurs over many decades that are, loosely, contemporary. Cars, telephones, televisions, and so on exist, but era-specific technology isn't presented (e.g., cell phones, space shuttles, and artificial intelligence). Would Aiza's life have been different if she were born in a specific period, earlier or later? If so, how? Be specific.

# 9 Zack Park

## Introduction

Welcome to your case study!

Congratulations! You will follow the lifespan of baby boy Zack Park. Try to use your best judgment, textbook, classmates, instructor, and supplementary resources to make the best decisions to help him grow.

This semester you will observe Zack as he grows from infant to child to teen to adult. Who will he become in your care? Will you understand and agree with all decisions available within his circumstances? How will you feel about the tough decisions that forever shape his path in life?

## Meet Zack Park

Zack is the first son of Rebecca Alpern-Park and Joseph Park. The couple has been married for two years. Rebecca is 30 years old, has a master's degree, and is Caucasian and Jewish. Although she is practicing, she doesn't keep kosher. Joseph is 34, holds an MD, and is a third-generation

iStock.com/AlenaZamotaeva

Korean American. His elderly grandmother, who speaks little English, lives with him and Rebecca. Rebecca is an aspiring writer, while Joseph is working to establish his medical practice. The Parks are upper income and live in a wealthy, historic district in their town. Joseph's health insurance is excellent, and Rebecca takes good care of herself during her pregnancy.

Through this case study and your lifespan course you will be asked to consider decisions regarding Zack's physical, emotional, and cognitive growth and development from several perspectives: his mother Rebecca's, his father Joseph's, and his grandmother's as well as those of his potential siblings, his spouse, his children, other family members, friends, teachers, doctors, and supervisors.

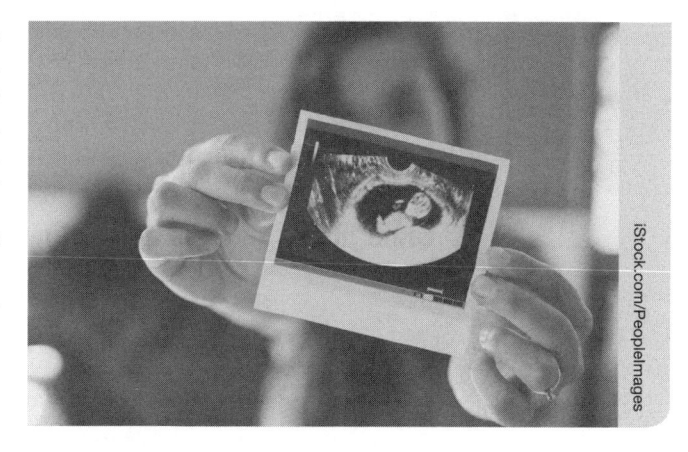

Now let's get started.

## 1. Development and Its Influences

> ### Today you will practice the following:
>
> 1.1  Outline five principles of the lifespan developmental perspective.
> 1.2  Explain three theoretical controversies about human development.
> 1.3  Summarize five theoretical perspectives on human development.
> 1.4  Describe the methods and research designs used to study human development.

Rebecca and Joseph are excited to learn Zack is on the way. They've wanted to get pregnant for a few months, and although neither was nervous that they hadn't managed it so far, they're both relieved to see the little blue + in the window of the home pregnancy test. It's the perfect time in their lives, and Joseph in particular is eager for their child to know his grandmother while she's still alive. They have only one concern. Rebecca has suffered from obsessive-compulsive disorder (OCD) to greater or lesser degrees since her adolescence. For the past few years, she's been successfully treated using a serotonin reuptake inhibitor (SSRI), which the obstetrician recommends she discontinue for the baby's health as long as her psychiatrist is in agreement with the recommendation. The psychiatrist agrees but leaves the final decision up to Rebecca. She's nervous about her ability to control her OCD without the SSRI, but she's also nervous about the potential for harm to her baby if she doesn't stop taking the meds. She and Joseph have several long conversations about the options.

## 2. Biological and Environmental Foundations

> ### Today you will practice the following:
>
> 2.1  *Discuss the genetic foundations of development.*
>
> 2.2  *Identify examples of genetic disorders and chromosomal abnormalities.*
>
> 2.3  *Discuss the choices available to prospective parents in having healthy children.*
>
> 2.4  *Describe the interaction of heredity and environment, including behavioral genetics and the epigenetic framework.*

Rebecca and Joseph meet with Rebecca's psychiatrist together. Although they agree their choice is the best one for their growing family, they also know Rebecca will need everyone on the same page supporting her through the next several months. In the waiting room, Joseph flips through an issue of *GQ* while she tries to remember the keys to Chopin. She hasn't played piano since seventh grade, but trying to remember is soothing. She moves her fingers on her knees and hopes Joseph doesn't think she's crazy.

"You're not crazy."

"I'm a little crazy," she whispers.

"Okay, maybe a little, but life would get boring without a little crazy."

"Mrs. Park?"

The receptionist has appeared without Rebecca noticing. Score one for Joseph. Score all of them for Joseph. She loves him.

They enter Dr. Wen's office and sit on the sofa across the room from his desk. It's just homier, Rebecca thinks every time she comes here. The desk is so . . . *clinical.* Dr. Wen joins them and shakes her hand and then Joseph's.

"Rebecca! You look great. Pregnancy agrees with you."

"Thank you." She taps her knees again. "You've spoken with my OB, I think?"

"Yep." Dr. Wen nods. "Dr. Lucas and I conferred about your case. You know, this isn't all that uncommon, women needing to decide what to do about an SSRI or other psychotropic meds during pregnancy."

"It's not?"

"Not at all. Now, unlike some, you've got a little higher dosage of Paxil, and you've been on Paxil for a lot longer than many."

"Yeah."

Joseph clears his throat to ask, "What exactly does that mean?"

"It means that Rebecca really accustomed to coping with her illness without medication. She'll also feel the lack of Paxil pretty acutely. It's not addictive, so I don't mean that. She's coping well right now, and that's due in large part to her Paxil. With the higher dose, we'll have to wean her more quickly to get her off altogether, and she'll definitely feel that. She'll also just miss it. She's dealing with significant debilitation without treatment."

"That's why I'm here," Rebecca says, reminding both men that she, the patient, is in the room. "If I'm going to do this, and Joseph and I agree it's the right thing to do, then I need help getting through the next seven months."

Dr. Wen nods. "Yes, you do. After speaking with Dr. Lucas, we decided on the following schedule to get you off the Paxil." He hands her a card with a rough calendar handwritten on it. If she follows it, she'll be off the Paxil in two weeks. A little jolt of fear shoots through her at the thought; she's been taking it so long. Seeing her face, Dr. Wen smiles. "There's more. Here's the contact information for a psychotherapist in the area. She's great with patients who have OCD. I think you and I slacked off on psychotherapy—and I didn't push it—because you responded so well to Paxil. We need new methods now. And here's the information for a support group for people with OCD. Some are in therapy, some are on meds, some do both, and some do neither. The group is open seven days a week, kind of like Alcoholics Anonymous, but not everyone goes every day. I would encourage you to go as often as you need to. This is where you'll find your greatest support."

Rebecca looks at all three cards and tries to process the information. "Thank you," she says even as she's still thinking.

"Of course. Look, Rebecca, I think your first step should be calling this psychotherapist. The tools she can give you right away will help replace the Paxil in profound ways. Then get yourself to the support group where you can commiserate without other—"

"Crazies?" she asks, smiling.

"You know it."

He asks if they have other questions. Joseph asks one or two, and Dr. Wen gives him a resource on loving someone with OCD. They leave soon after, both determined to get through the next seven months and to enjoy as much of it as they can. Rebecca grits her teeth. She wants to enjoy it. She really does. Maybe it can all work out.

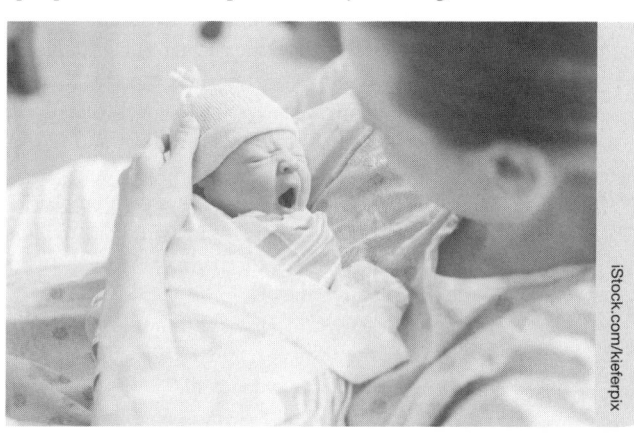

## 3. Prenatal Development, Birth, and Newborn Experience

### Today you will practice the following:

3.1 *Describe the three periods of prenatal development that begin with conception.*

3.2 *Identify how exposure to teratogens can influence the prenatal environment.*

3.3 *Explain the process of childbirth.*

3.4 *Discuss the neonate's physical capacities, including development in low-birth-weight infants.*

Joseph continues to work throughout Rebecca's pregnancy. With a small but bustling medical practice he's attempting to grow, it's important he be in the office as much as possible. It's also important for the practice he wants to grow because he's practicing community-based general care. His clients are often uninsured or underinsured, and to assist with drains on healthcare systems like emergency room visits, he likes to be as accessible as possible. This leaves Rebecca alone much of the day and, often, at night, too.

Thanks to the suggestions of her obstetrician Dr. Lucas and psychiatrist Dr. Wen, she's begun seeing a psychotherapist twice a month. Ms. Ivers has a master's in counseling and a postgraduate certificate in applied behavioral analysis. She's highly regarded in the therapeutic community, and she has room in her client list to begin seeing Rebecca right away. From the start, the two hit it off. Ms. Ivers agrees with Dr. Lucas and Dr. Wen about her decision to stop taking Paxil, to get some therapeutic help to learn coping strategies, and to join the support group. Coordinated care, Joseph calls it, and Rebecca knows how important he thinks it is.

In their third session, Rebecca rolls her eyes at herself and half laughs. "I feel like an alcoholic in the group meetings," she tells Ms. Ivers.

"Why is that?"

"Because we all agree to take our illness 'one day at a time' like addicts do in AA. 'Just for today I will not wash my hands with bleach,' or 'Just for today I'll leave the house without triple-checking to make sure the curling iron is unplugged.'"

Ms. Ivers nods. "It's a good strategy, both in AA and in cognitive behavioral therapy."

"Is it?" Rebecca asks, unconvinced.

"Yes. Let's take the curling iron example since I know that's not you."

Rebecca touches her short boy cut. "Okay."

"Suppose I always triple-check that I've unplugged everything, and the only way I can make it through the day is to know that I've triple-checked, right?"

"Yeah."

"So, *just for today*," she says with emphasis, "I double-check instead of triple-check. I play out the scenario instead of imagining it. You know the one I mean?"

"I do," Rebecca admits. "What's the worst thing that could happen if I don't fill in the blank or if I do fill in the blank?"

"Exactly. Of course, with the curling iron, I could burn down the house and kill the family pets. If I live in an apartment, maybe I burn down the whole building because it has substandard wiring, and a little old lady dies and—"

"Oh my God!" Rebecca says, horrified.

Ms. Ivers laughs. "Okay. Admittedly, that went a little far, but that really is sort of worst-case scenario. So, today, I play it out, but of course, I *have* unplugged the curling iron. I know that. Nothing bad happens. The goal? Maybe I go a week double-checking instead of triple-checking and try hard to note that the world isn't ending every day. I also try hard not to let the obsessions that started the whole routine overtake my world. I've learned to not only talk to myself but trust myself as well."

Rebecca finishes for her. "And next week I try just one day of only checking once before I leave."

"That's the idea, and really, who shouldn't check once? That's only the smart thing. Once we get to this point, then we attack those obsessive thoughts. What was your just for today today, Rebecca?"

She takes a deep breath. On the exhale, she says, "Just for today I won't look for patterns of three or tap on my knees to make myself less anxious."

"Ah," Ms. Ivers says, "the old three rears its head."

"So I'm not only crazy, but I'm cliché, too?"

They laugh together, and Ms. Ivers nods. "Afraid so. Good goals, though. The concern, of course, as Dr. Wen will have explained to you, is that with your elevated anxiety and the cessation of Paxil, you'll experience sustained or exaggerated periods of serotonin flooding. Stress hormones, too, like corticosteroids, but really we're most concerned about your serotonin levels and how that can affect your baby's development, specifically cerebral development."

"I know."

"Our goal is to keep you as even-keeled as possible for as much of your pregnancy as possible. We can do this. I like the one-day-at-a-time plan. I'd also like to see you keeping a daily log of your activities and how you feel throughout the day. If you'll start that tomorrow, tonight even, then when you return, we can have a talk about it. Just be sure to bring the log with you."

"Good. Okay." Rebecca breathes deeply again. "Good. I think we can do this. Thank you."

"I think we can, too, Rebecca. Keep the faith, and call me whenever you need to."

Rebecca uses the rest of her pregnancy and the log Ms. Ivers asks her to keep as the springboard for a memoir. As a writer, she likes the idea of sudden memoir—autobiography written as it's happening—and the log forms the backbone of that for her. She wonders why women don't talk about mental illness and pregnancy and wonders if doing so might help others. She hopes so anyway.

Just as she finishes a draft of the section on the second trimester, left behind weeks ago now, she feels a wave of complete exhaustion. Her back aches, and she wishes Joseph were home to give her a massage. Texting him, she says only *Tired and cranky. Come home soon please.*

He does, but when he gets there, he takes a careful inventory of her pale face and constant stretching of her back then asks her a series of questions. Deciding she's in labor, he gathers her overnight bag for the hospital and calls Dr. Lucas, who meets them there.

As expected, it's a long labor, nearly 12 hours. Most first labors are, Joseph reassures her as she breathes and crunches ice chips. She transitions in the 13th hour and within 30 minutes of pushing delivers their beautiful son Zachary. Holding him, touching him, and seeing his perfect little face—such a politic combination of both their genes—Rebecca knows the hard work of being without the Paxil was worth it. Joseph takes a hundred pictures of them in the first hour, and she's never been happier in her life.

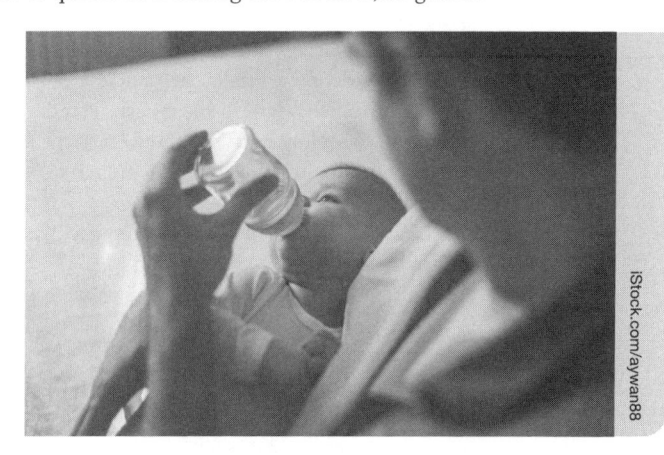

## 4. Physical Development in Infancy and Toddlerhood

### Today you will practice the following:

*4.1 Discuss growth and the role of nutrition in development during infancy and toddlerhood.*

*4.2 Summarize brain development during infancy and toddlerhood.*

*4.3 Compare infants' early learning capacities for habituation, classical conditioning, operant conditioning, and imitation.*

*4.4 Describe infants' developing sensory abilities.*

*4.5 Analyze the roles of maturation and contextual factors in infant and toddler motor development.*

Just as they did with the decision to discontinue her Paxil during the pregnancy, Rebecca and Joseph have discussed what to do once their baby is born. Rebecca feels like the frequent group meetings and the psychotherapy with Ms. Ivers helped her make it through the pregnancy unmedicated and mostly sane. (No one's perfect.) She also feels like she's done the best she can for as long as she can. Joseph agrees. More than that, they've taken to heart the words of Rebecca's obstetrician, who gives them information about newborns, their temperaments, and how temperament can change some if Mom is high strung or even the opposite. Joseph and Rebecca both know that she's more than "high strung," and they worry that she might affect the baby's early temperament, which is already likely to be more than a little reactive. For these reasons, as well as Rebecca's own mental health, they've made the decision that she'll begin her meds again as soon as the baby is born, and Zack will be formula fed.

Joseph worries that Rebecca will feel guilty that she isn't breast-feeding Zack, but nothing could be further from the truth. When Zack wakes at 2:45 in the morning—*every morning*—Rebecca pats Joseph's butt and says, "Give him his bottle, won't you?" And there are as many nights that he gets home and she's feeding him a bottle while cooking dinner as there are nights that she hands him the spatula and rocks Zack in the old rocker in the kitchen while Joseph cooks. Of course, Joseph's *halmeoni*, his grandmother, gets her share of baby feeding, too, and that's maybe the biggest perk aside from Rebecca's meds to Zack being a bottle-fed baby.

Joseph returns from his practice late on a Thursday, afraid he's missed dinner. Coming through the door, he smells the delicious scent of his wife's meatball soup and hears Zack babbling. Moments later he sees them standing in the doorway, Zack tugging on Rebecca's earlobe and drooling onto her shoulder. Rebecca laughs at her messy predicament and raises her eyebrows at Joseph. Raising a finger to her lips to keep him quiet, she points to the kitchen.

"*Halmeoni*," she whispers. "I found her like that when I brought Zack down after his nap. Joe, she's a wonderful treasure in our lives."

Curious, he peeks over Rebecca's shoulder, earning himself a swipe from Zack's sloppy fist in the process. His grandmother sits at the kitchen table polishing Rebecca's silver candlesticks to be lit before the Shabbat meal the next day. The family has brass candlesticks that need less upkeep, but *Halmeoni* knows Rebecca loves these. Even though she isn't Jewish, Joseph's grandmother appreciates the culture and traditions Rebecca embraces and wants their son to grow into in his home.

"Joe, I love our family."

"Of course you do." He squeezes her shoulder and kisses Zack's head. "We are the perfect family." Moving away from her, he steps into the kitchen and speaks to *Halmeoni*. "*Insa, halmeoni. oneul halu eo ttaes-eo?* Did you have a good day?"

She smiles and nods. "*Dang-yeonhaji jagiya. hwanjaneun eottaess ni? sesang-eul dasi gu haessni?* Of course, darling. How were your patients? Did you save the world again?"

Rebecca joins them, smiling like Joseph's grandmother. "Save the world? *Halmeoni*, Joe is the world. Our world. Right, Zackie?"

## 5. Cognitive Development in Infancy and Toddlerhood

> Today you will practice the following:
>
> *5.1* Discuss the cognitive-developmental perspective on infant reasoning.
>
> *5.2* Describe the information processing system in infants.
>
> *5.3* Discuss individual differences in infant intelligence.
>
> *5.4* Summarize the patterns of language development during infancy and toddlerhood.

At 15 months, Zack is a slender, dark-headed, quiet boy. *Halmeoni* is his favorite person, but she may be edged out in his affections by Felix, the family cat. Felix, in repeated shows of extraordinary patience, allows Zack to pull his tail (and his whiskers), poke in his ears, and on occasion eat a pellet or two of his food.

No longer taking a bottle, Zack spends a good portion of each evening on the kitchen floor with Felix while one of his parents or his grandmother makes dinner. When Mommy and Daddy talk and *Halmeoni* cooks, Zack cruises around the table between his parents and waits for his grandmother to pass him a treat from the cooking food. Accomplishing these tasks, he starts to count his steps: one, *hana*, two, *du*, three, *se*, four, *ne* . . .

"Zack?" Daddy calls to him.

"Mmm . . ." He blows bubbles, looking at his father.

"Did you just count in Korean and English? *Hangug-eolo mid-eul su iss-eoyo, jagi?*"

"Mmm . . ." He blows more bubbles and nods his head.

"That's good!" Daddy says.

"Is good boy, Zack," *Halmeoni* says.

Zack reaches for more food, and she gives him a piece of cucumber.

"*Hana, du, se, ne* . . ."

"Good boy!" they clap, and Zack claps, too.

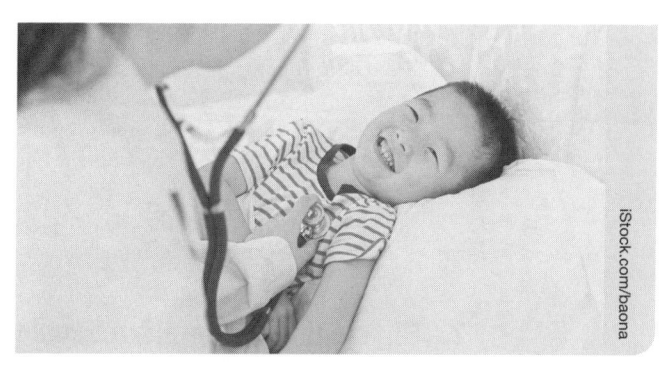

## 6. Socioemotional Development in Infancy and Toddlerhood

> Today you will practice the following:
>
> *6.1* Summarize the psychosocial tasks of infancy and toddlerhood.
>
> *6.2* Describe emotional development in infancy, and identify contextual and cultural influences on emotional development in infants and toddlers.
>
> *6.3* Identify the styles and stability of temperament, including the role of goodness of fit in infant development.
>
> *6.4* Describe how attachment develops in infancy and toddlerhood.
>
> *6.5* Differentiate the roles of self-concept, self-recognition, and self-control in infant development.

As Zack approaches his second birthday, Rebecca carries him to the pediatrician for a checkup. The vaccinations worry her—what about autism? She doesn't care what the pediatrician says about "research" or at least she doesn't care much—but she dutifully submits to each and every one. She understands her fears are irrational, and look how healthy this beautiful child of hers is!

"He really is," Dr. Greysmith agrees when Rebecca comments. "How's his temperament?"

"Lovely," Rebecca tells her. "He quite literally could not be a better baby."

"Wonderful. Well, I think he's doing great. Good weight-to-height ratio. He's in the 65th percentile for both. He's meeting all developmental milestones as expected. He's engaging," she finishes with a huge smile as Zack laughs and claps to show off.

"I love coming here," Rebecca confides, "if only so you can remind me that he's perfect."

"Well, consider yourself reminded. Now, any questions for me?"

"Only one. He's speaking, of course. Pretty much what the books say to expect. But he's speaking almost everything in both English and Korean."

"Both are spoken in the home if I remember correctly?"

"Right, but will that confuse him?"

Dr. Greysmith shakes her head. "Shouldn't. Do you plan to introduce Hebrew?"

"I do unless you tell me that's just too much."

"I shouldn't think so. I'll be interested to see how our little guy progresses. Keep me posted, will you?"

Rebecca nods. "I will. Thank you. It's so nice to have validation now and then."

"Don't I know it. My adolescent has me questioning every moment of medical school right now."

They share a laugh before Rebecca rises to leave. One more moment of reassurance. She wishes Zack's checkup weren't an entire year away.

## 7. Physical and Cognitive Development in Early Childhood

### Today you will practice the following:

7.1 *Discuss physical development in early childhood.*

7.2 *Compare Piaget's cognitive-developmental and Vygotsky's sociocultural perspectives on cognitive development in early childhood.*

7.3 *Describe information-processing abilities during early childhood.*

7.4 *Summarize young children's advances in language development.*

7.5 *Contrast social learning and cognitive-developmental perspectives on moral development in early childhood.*

7.6 *Identify and explain approaches to early childhood education.*

Zack's used to other kids looking at him funny in school. He wears a kippah, and not many Jewish boys do anymore. If that's not bad enough, he's clearly Asian-American and wearing a kippah. It's like his parents want to see just how much a target they can make him for teasing. No one actually bullies him, though. There seems to be an unwritten rule about bullying anyone about religion—except the Muslim kids. All bets are off with them.

"Hey."

It's the same every morning in line for their pancake on a stick or Pop-Tart. Zack's best friend James turns up, says hi, and thumps his kippah. James isn't Jewish, but he also doesn't care that Zack is.

"Hey."

"What are you making for the science fair?" James asks.

"I don't know. My dad wants me to do Mount Vesuvius. You know, with baking soda and vinegar." He lifts his shoulders and dares to tell his friend the truth. "It just seems boring to me. What about you?"

"No idea. At. All."

"So, a volcano, too?"

James laughs, and they take their Pop-Tarts and orange juice.

"Probably," James admits.

"What about PE? You going to do the fund-raiser?"

"Sure! If there's one thing I actually can do, it's throw a basketball."

Now, Zack laughs. "Yeah, if no one's running toward you. I don't like basketball, so my dad's going to write a check. It feels like cheating, but I don't care. My dad says that discretion is the better part of valor. He also says that's the wrong saying, but it makes sense for the situation. Whatever, man, I'm not throwing *any* balls and giving people more reasons to make fun of me."

## 8. Socioemotional Development in Early Childhood

### Today you will practice the following:

8.1  Discuss young children's emerging sense of initiative, self-concept, and self-esteem.

8.2  Summarize the development of emotional understanding, regulation, and behavior in early childhood.

8.3  Identify four parenting styles and their associations with child outcomes.

8.4  Compare biological, cognitive, and contextual theoretical explanations of gender role development.

8.5  Explain the function of play and the form it takes during early childhood.

"Is it time?" Zack asks Mom.

She nods and touches his head. "It's time, sweetheart."

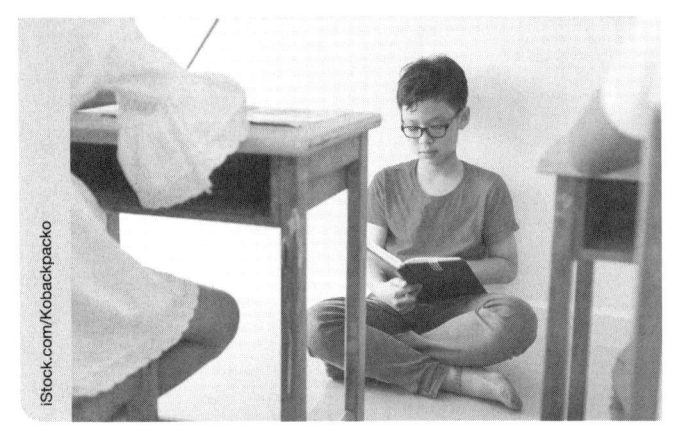

She looks at him like this is a good thing. The icy lump in Zack's stomach tells him something else altogether. He looks at her and tries hard not to cry.

"Does it *have* to be time?"

"Oh, baby." Mom gets on her knees at straightens his kippah. "Zack, honey, it's just Grandma and Grandpa Alpern. There's nothing to be scared of."

"Mom, I've never been in charge of lighting the menorah candles before. Not ever. Now you want me to do it in front of people who will care if I get it wrong? Thanks."

"Zack, it's going to be fine. I promise. Your grandparents love you. All of them." She sighs and pulls him into a hug. "Would you feel better if we did it together? You and I?"

A world of terror melts away at the words, and he nods into her shoulder. "Would you?"

"I would be honored." Standing, she holds her hand out to him. "Will you escort me to the table then, Zack?"

He smiles and nods. Then he takes her hand and skips a step. "Let's get this show on the road!"

## 9. Physical and Cognitive Development in Middle Childhood

### Today you will practice the following:

9.1 *Identify patterns of physical and motor development during middle childhood and common health issues facing school-age children.*

9.2 *Discuss school-age children's capacities for reasoning and processing information.*

9.3 *Summarize views of intelligence including the uses, correlates, and criticisms of intelligence tests.*

9.4 *Examine patterns of moral development during middle childhood.*

9.5 *Summarize language development during middle childhood.*

9.6 *Discuss children's learning at school.*

Zack is nearing the end of elementary school. He can speak, read, and write in English, Korean, and Hebrew now, and his best friend James is interested in Hebrew. Zack teaches him a little bit here and there when he can, but for Zack, this is his people's language and where his whole culture comes from. His teaches try to talk to him about his language "fluidity," they call it, and his parents are called to school all the time about testing him. They always say no, and Zack always ignores what his teachers say about him being special. His family is special, he thinks, but he isn't. He's just lucky to be part of that family. Mostly, he wishes everyone paid him just a little less attention.

Except at home, of course. He loves spending time with *Halmeoni*, and he loves having James sleep over. Sometimes he thinks *Halmeoni* isn't completely happy unless both he and James are at the house. James loves her cooking, and she spends lots of time in the kitchen whenever they have sleepovers. Sometimes, James comes to temple with him, too. Zack likes those days because afterward he and James lie around in the living room while the adults have big adult meals and he and James solve all the religious problems in the world. Zack doesn't understand why things seem so hard for the adults in the world to fix. They seem pretty easy to him and James.

One day, he's going to grow up and change the way people think about other people who are different than they are.

## 10. Socioemotional Development in Middle Childhood

### Today you will practice the following:

10.1  *Describe school-age children's self-conceptions and motivation.*

10.2  *Examine the roles of friendship, peer acceptance, and peer victimization in school-age children's adjustment.*

10.3  *Discuss family relationships in middle childhood and the influence of family structure on adjustment.*

10.4  *Analyze the role of resilience in promoting adjustment to adversity, including characteristics of children and contexts that promote resilience.*

Two days every week after school, Zack rides a bus downtown to his dad's office. This lets his mom take care of things like shopping and taking *Halmeoni* to her own doctor's appointments or meeting with people about the books she writes. His dad is a doctor. Zack thinks that's pretty cool. When the bus drops him off, Dad makes him do his homework before he does anything else. In between seeing patients and making notes about seeing patients—Dad calls this his own "homework"—Dad quizzes Zack on his weekly spelling words and, sometimes, his math. Zack likes doing schoolwork with his Dad. Even more, he likes it when he's all finished because then his dad lets him play in one of the spare exam rooms. Sometimes Dad even pulls out his old, old Resuscitation Annie, a fake woman in a weird blue exercise outfit Zack gets to practice examining.

Dad takes him home those two days every week, and Mom and *Halmeoni* call out to them when the door opens, "Do we hear our two handsome men coming home?"

Zack and Dad always call back, "Yes, you do! Do we hear our beautiful women calling to us?"

They meet in the kitchen, where the delicious smells of *Halmeoni*'s authentic Korean dishes (on Mondays) and Mom's not-quite-kosher foods (on Thursdays) make their mouths water. Mom always covers Zack's face with kisses, and *Halmeoni* always slips him some before-dinner treat he knows he shouldn't have. While Dad has a beer and sits at the table to talk to Mom about his day, Zack does his chores. He takes the trash outside to the trash can and, on Mondays, the cans to the street. The trash is collected on Tuesdays. Then he washes his hands and joins his family for dinner. After they eat, Zack walks the dog to the corner and back on his leash while Mom and *Halmeoni* clean the dishes. Before bedtime, he sits at the table with Mom, and she teaches him some of the prayers from the Talmud or from the tiny prayer book she's kept for him since he was born.

"How was your group today?" she always asks when they're finished. She means the no-bullying group he and his friends started.

"Good." Zack asks for a cookie, and she hands him two from the plate in the middle of the table. "Lots of kids come, so I think they like it."

"I'm sure they do," she says, brushing hair off his face. "And your test tomorrow? Not worried?"

"Nope!" Zack smiles. Mom worries about a lot of things, he knows, but he never does. "Can I take my shower now? I got a new book at the liberry today and want to read some before I go to sleep."

"Li*brary*," Mom corrects, "and yes, you may."

"Thanks!" He jumps up from the table and dashes through the living room, where Dad and *Halmeoni* are watching TV. " 'Night!" he yells.

"Good night," they say, waving.

## 11. Physical and Cognitive Development in Late Childhood

### Today you will practice the following:

*11.1* Describe school-age children's self-conceptions and motivation.

*11.2* Examine the roles of friendship, peer acceptance, and peer victimization in school-age children's adjustment.

*11.3* Discuss family relationships in middle childhood and the influence of family structure on adjustment.

*11.4* Analyze the role of resilience in promoting adjustment to adversity, including characteristics of children and contexts that promote resilience

Zack is in his father's medical office one day when he's finally allowed to play with the coveted model brain. He loves the brain, but his dad says it's too expensive for Zack to maybe break it. Now, his dad says he can look at it and take it apart as long as he sits at the big desk in the office. Once he had the pieces spread before him, he starts trying to name them and see if he can remember their functions. He isn't very good, but he knows some.

"Dad?"

His dad stops filing the day's medical charts and looks at him. "Can I help?"

"Yeah. I forget what this one is," he says, holding up a blue piece for Dad to see.

"That's the thalamus." Dad turns away and started filing again, but Zack wants to know more.

"What does the thalamus do? Is it important?"

Dad nods. Zack thinks he even looks a little bit sad. "It's very important, and it does a lot of things."

"Oh yeah? Like what?" Zack asks.

"Well," Dad says, laying down his files, "it's complicated, and it's not the thalamus alone, but that's one of the key parts of the brain that makes your mom worry so much."

Zack turns the little blue plastic piece over in his hands, staring at it. Then he turns back to Dad. "And me sometimes?"

Dad nods. "And you."

After a second, Zack smiles and fits the piece back into place in the center of the brain. "That's cool! It's like knowing where a bone is broken so you know where to put on a cast!"

Dad's face told him that might not be perfectly correct, but it was close enough.

## 12. Socioemotional Development in Late Childhood

### Today you will practice the following:

*12.1  Summarize the processes by which self-concept, self-esteem, and identity change during adolescence.*

*12.2  Discuss the nature of parent–child relationships in adolescence.*

*12.3  Examine the developmental progression of peer relations in adolescence.*

*12.4  Analyze patterns of adolescent sexual activity including sexual orientation.*

*12.5  Identify common psychological and behavioral problems in adolescence.*

In fifth grade art class, Zack's teacher has students work the whole year on a family project. They can use any materials they want as long as they complete a "this is my family" composition by the time the annual school art walk comes around in April. Zack chooses clay, and he's excited! For months and months, he works on each individual member of his family. For Dad and *Halmeoni* and himself, he uses a toothpick to carefully pull the eyes into just the right slant, rounded on top and kind of flat on the bottom. Each time he works on the project, he thinks about Kindergarten, when kids uses to bully him for looking different. It's why he and his friend James started their club to stop bullying. He doesn't feel different now; he feels like everyone is different in some way even if not all of those ways can be seen.

It's March when the art teacher takes Zack's finished sculpture to the local pottery studio to be fired. Zack thinks that a funny word for finishing his family project. When he gets it back, it's shiny and white. The teacher says that's what porcelain looks like when it's all finished. He loves it, and so does his family when they see it. Mom touches the tiny *kippah* he added to his own head, and *Halmeoni* touches everyone's faces gently with one fingertip. There are so many nice projects, Zack doesn't want to say that his is the best, but in his heart he knows that his parents think it is. That's all that matters.

## 13. Physical and Cognitive Development in Adolescence

### Today you will practice the following:

*13.1 Evaluate the "storm and stress" perspective on adolescence in light of research evidence.*

*13.2 Summarize the physical changes that occur with puberty and the correlates of pubertal timing.*

*13.3 Discuss brain development during adolescence and its effect on behavior.*

*13.4 Identify ways in which thinking changes in adolescence and how these changes are reflected in adolescent decision-making and behavior.*

*13.5 Discuss moral development and influences on moral reasoning.*

*13.6 Describe the challenges that school transitions pose for adolescents and the role of parents in academic achievement.*

Zack's 13 when his dear *Halmeoni* passes away. Nothing's wrong with her; she's just old, and she dies. Dad gets sad for a long time. Zack is sad, too, but he doesn't want to talk to his dad about it. That feels unfair. He doesn't say anything and tries to focus on his schoolwork. It's his last year of middle school, and he's taking algebra with his friend James. It's a high school class, and they have to do well, or they'll start high school with bad marks on their report cards. Fortunately, Zack has all the reason in the world to bury himself in work. He likes math, and no one at home seems to think anything's weird about him studying all the time.

He's started walking to his dad's office on Mondays and Thursdays after school. The bus is no longer a fun or particularly safe place to be, but he still loves hanging out with his dad and playing with Resuscitation Annie. Sometimes, he and Dad sit in the exam room Zack plays in, and his dad asks him questions about symptoms to see if Zack can correctly guess a diagnosis or if Zack knows there are follow-up questions he's supposed to ask. He has a little divider in his head; on one side is the part that knows his dad is trying to groom him to become a doctor, and on the other is the side that has decided not to think about being a doctor or anything else for a while. It's bad enough being the weird Korean Jewish kid everywhere. Most people know he's Dr. Park's son, too. For just a little while more, he wants to be Zack as much as he can.

"What would you do if a woman came in complaining of pain in her upper back and unusual fatigue?" Dad asks one day while Zack's poking around at Resuscitation Annie.

Zack doesn't look up but answers, "Send her for an echo and labs to check for heart attack."

"*Hmph,*" Dad says, but Zack knows he's pleased. That was a hard one, and he got it right. He doesn't always.

He's still not ready to declare his intentions yet.

## 14. Socioemotional Development in Adolescence

### Today you will practice the following:

14.1  *Summarize the processes by which self-concept, self-esteem, and identity change during adolescence.*

14.2  *Discuss the nature of parent–child relationships in adolescence.*

14.3  *Examine the developmental progression of peer relations in adolescence.*

14.4  *Analyze patterns of adolescent sexual activity including sexual orientation.*

14.5  *Identify common psychological and behavioral problems in adolescence.*

"Big day," Dad says, standing in Zack's bedroom doorway.

"Mmm-hmm," Zack agrees, feigning nonchalance. He's so nervous; he feels like Mom with all her little rituals to keep her anxiety under control—not that he'd tell his dad that.

"Need some help with your tie?"

Zack shakes his head. "No, thanks. I'll be down in a minute," he says, hoping to nudge his father politely from the room. It seems to work, and he has a few minutes to himself before both parents call him downstairs.

"Zack, it's time to leave!"

"Coming," he whispers, then repeats himself more loudly, "coming!"

It's Shabbat following his 13th birthday, and although Zack relaxed his math studies a bit to prepare for his bar mitzvah, he's still terrified. Actually, he's only afraid of misspeaking in the synagogue. Studying for the 12 readings was pleasurable for him. He asked his mom so many questions that she finally said, "No more. Ask the rabbi," and he did. Rabbi Stein seemed pleased, as if Zack's interest were novel, although he couldn't understand why. Bruce Tennenbaum had his own bar mitzvah just the month before.

Mom says having the ceremony on Shabbat is nice. Other members of the temple can come and see him become a man. Zack laughs at that. He's 13 and feels more like a baby than a man, but he loves his religion and its customs. He sees, too, the wisdom in Mom's preferences. He likes being wrapped in the blessings of his synagogue—even if he is scared witless.

He completes the first reading in the Torah and sees that Rabbi Stein is pleased. Moving on, he says, "We are fortunate. Our life comes from God, and that life is a gift. Gods gives us even more than that. How empty our lives would be without the wisdom to live them properly. This is like the gift of an advanced technology—or better still a small child—without any information on how to use it or care for it. You would be frustrated, yes? Our lives could be like that. So frustrating and seemingly pointless. But we have the Torah, which is like an instruction manual for our lives. Through its teachings, we have the keys to unlock the full richness of God's gift."

When he finishes, he glances first at the rabbi and then at his mom, who is beaming with pride. He knows this ceremony is the event that signifies his becoming a man and not the study that has made him a man, but with nearly everyone in the synagogue watching him, it feels awful and terrifying anyway. For the next while, he closes his eyes now and again as he reads, trying to forget all the people and just remember who he is and what he's doing. It seems to work, as he realizes he's doing fine because he's been preparing for this with his mom's help his whole life.

Afterward, his parents throw him a posh party at the country club. The menu is kosher because so many of their friends from the synagogue will come by, but Mom made sure to include some of his favorites. There's a cool bagel station, with all different kinds of bagels on sticks standing up on the table, and a candy station with his name on all the candy wrappers, macaroni and cheese with different veggie toppings, and a cool burger station, too. Mom and Dad compromised on the party. She got "elegant" decorations, and he got "fun." Zack didn't care as long as some of his friends came, which they do.

"I don't get the whole 'I'm a man now' thing," his friend Marybeth from school says during a break between dances.

"Me either," James admits, even though he and James have talked about it more than once.

"I'm not really. A man," Zack says. "Not like you're thinking. I'm still just like you. It's more like a rite of passage. More like I'm not a little boy anymore."

Marybeth chews on a burger with hot ketchup and onions. "That makes more sense," she says around a mouthful.

James looks at her and laughs. "You're gross, you know that?"

"That's why you're both secretly in love with me."

James looks at her like she might've just lost the last remaining part of her mind. "Is that it?"

"That's it," she confirms. After licking her fingers, she points to a boy across the room. "Who's that, Zack?"

"Eric. He's from my synagogue."

"Introduce me?"

"Sure, if you get Hannah Roni to go to the movies with me." Hannah is Marybeth's best friend and even then is dancing with little old Mr. Mandel not 15 feet away.

Marybeth looks at him like she's disappointed in the level of challenge. "Done."

## 15. Physical and Cognitive Development in Emerging/Early Adulthood

### Today you will practice the following:

15.1 *Describe the features and characteristics of emerging and early adulthood.*

15.2 *Summarize the physical developments of emerging and early adulthood.*

15.3 *Analyze physical and sexual health issues in emerging and early adulthood.*

15.4 *Compare postformal reasoning, pragmatic thought, and cognitive-affective complexity.*

15.5 *Explain how attending college influences young adults' development, and identify challenges faced by first-generation and nontraditional students.*

15.6 *Discuss vocational choice and the transition to work.*

Zack's mom hugs him for the 100th time. When she draws away, he hears her soft *hmph* as his dad says, "Rebecca, are you ready?"

"Of course, I'm not ready. How can I be ready to leave him so far from home?"

"Mom," Zack reminds her with a smile, "I'm an hour and a half away. You can't even get through *La Bohème* in the time it takes to get to me."

"When you put it that way . . ."

"What other way to put it is there? I'll be home in three weeks for the fall parade. Think of all the mischief you can get into and store up to tell me about when I'm home."

She *hmphed* again, but her lips twitched this time. "I'll miss you, you know."

"I do know, and I'll miss you."

Dad slips him 50 bucks "just because," and his parents turn toward the waiting elevator. Zack's a little sad—maybe more nostalgic about childhood—at their leaving. That feeling dissipates when his mother turns to him halfway down the hall and calls back, "Don't forget, son—always wear a condom!"

He closes the door and shakes his head. "Really, Mom?"

"Hey, can I come out now?"

"Rachel, God, I forgot you were in there for just a minute. Of course. I'm sorry!" he says to the girl he met at an orientation event a couple nights before.

She slips from his bathroom, a cute smile on her face when she asks, "You do have the condoms, don't you?"

## 16. Socioemotional Development in Emerging/Early Adulthood

### Today you will practice the following:

*16.1 Summarize psychosocial development in emerging and early adulthood.*

*16.2 Discuss influences on friendship and mate selection and interactions in emerging and early adulthood.*

*16.3 Analyze the diverse romantic situations that may characterize emerging and early adulthood, including singlehood, cohabitation, marriage, and divorce.*

*16.4 Compare the experiences of young adults as stepparents, never-married parents, and same-sex parents.*

Zack thinks for some weeks about how best to have the conversations he needs to have. There are three, but they're mostly the same conversations. His dad, never really a go-between for him, will be the least likely to complain. Because of this, Zack decides to have one conversation instead of many. He can talk to everyone at once, rip the Band-Aid off quickly, and let everyone come at him with all their complaints.

He has them over to his apartment just off campus before final exams in December. It's an inconvenience for his parents, who'll be seeing him in a few days anyway. He admits to a certain amount of cowardliness with Amy, his current girlfriend, too. She'll be leaving to visit her own parents after exams, sparing him from long, heart-to-hearts.

His mother hands him her coat when she gets there, and he takes it along with his dad's. He doesn't have a coat closet. He barely has a closet. The coats are thrown across his bed along with Amy's. She's been there helping him with dinner, and he's done a pretty good job of not letting on that there's anything to let on about.

"Mom." He hugs her tight. "Dad." They shake hands and hug.

"Dr. and Mrs. Park, it's so nice to see you again," Amy tells them as they come into the tiny living room. "Can I get you something to drink? Zack has red and white wine and, if I'm not mistaken, a couple beers in the fridge. I don't think there's any liquor, but I know there's green tea and maybe even some jasmine."

Mom shoots him a look to say that she understands Amy's nervousness but that she should be calmer anyway. Zack gives her a tight smile. His mother's anxiety is legendary, and he's not going to admonish Amy—not tonight anyway.

"White wine would be lovely, Amy. Thank you," Mom tells her. "Joseph?"

Dad says he'll get a beer but for Amy not to wait on him. Everyone starts to relax slowly, and Zack opens his own beer at last when the roast beef is on the table, and he calls everyone to sit down from the eight feet or so away where they sit on the sofa chatting. He waits until dessert, a plum pudding he made from *Halmeoni's* recipe and strong black coffee, to drop his bombshell.

"You might've guessed I've brought you all here for a reason." When Amy looks at him with big eyes, he realizes too late that the reason she's guessed is very much the opposite of his real reason. Nothing to do now but pull the Band-Aid for both of them, although he feels doubly bad for her. "I have some news, and since it affects each of you, I thought maybe I could share it like this instead of one by one."

"Good news, I hope," Mom says lightly as she eats another bite of her dessert.

"Well," Zack says, "I think so. I hope everyone else will, too."

Amy sits up straight in her chair. "You got into medical school!" she shouts.

"You applied to medical school?" his parents ask at the same time.

Looking first at Amy and then at his parents, he says, "Yes and yes."

Everyone reacts well, but he expected that at this point.

"That's great!"

"Wonderful!"

"I had no idea . . . so proud."

Zack waits for them to realize he's not talking. Mom turns to him first. "What is it?"

"It's not close. In fact, it's quite far away."

Mom goes white, but Amy frowns and looks at him. "I thought you were applying to State."

"I did, and I got in. I got into both med schools in the state."

"Then I don't understand," she says, and the color of her face tells Zack she's not sad; she's angry.

"I want to go to the other school. It has a better reputation. I'll get a better education, and my chances of getting a better internship when I'm finished are ten times better."

Dad nods and finally speaks. "Sounds like you've thought a lot about this."

"I have actually."

"What do you want to do when you're finished?"

"Come home. Practice with you."

"I don't understand why you have to go so far away to be able to do that," Mom says. She was always going to be the hard one, Zack knows.

"I don't, Mom. I want to." Across from Mom, Amy sits, lips pressed together, eyes dark. He's not going to fight with her. They had a talk last week about her postgraduation plans, and she wants to go just as far in the opposite direction to study business. He supports that decision of hers. They have to support each other, he thinks, or they don't work. "Please try to understand," he says, taking his mom's hand.

"I'm proud of you," she replies.

"I figured that." Risking a glance across the table, he asks, "Amy?"

She shrugs. "We already planned to be five hours apart. What's a few more when you're talking about an airplane?"

Zack has no illusions. Mom likes Amy well enough now, but she doesn't see her as daughter-in-law material. Amy hasn't ever mentioned marriage either. Thinking about continuing a long-long distance relationship signifies a greater commitment to him, though, and he knows they'll have to talk about where they're headed before spring rolls around. For now, he's happy to have won the somewhat grudging support of these important people in his life.

"Thank you. All of you. This is really important for me."

## 17. Physical and Cognitive Development in Middle Adulthood

### Today you will practice the following:

17.1 *Summarize age-related physical changes during middle adulthood.*

17.2 *Discuss common health conditions and illnesses and the roles of stress and hardiness on health during middle adulthood.*

17.3 *Contrast the findings of cross-sectional and longitudinal studies of crystallized and fluid intelligence over adulthood.*

17.4 *Analyze changes in cognitive capacities during middle adulthood, including attention, memory, processing speed, and expertise.*

Zack didn't appreciate—didn't know how to appreciate—the work his dad did before he started the work he does every day, not until he starts his own medical school education. He both loves and hates the long hours, the grueling coursework, and somewhat less-than-uplifting motivation of the professors. His internship is ridiculously arcane. Then he finishes, and he's ready to join his father's practice, which becomes Park and Park. Everything has been worth it.

Although it alternately amuses and dismays his mother, Zack refuses to settle down. Mom asks, "Didn't your father and I show you a good marriage?"

"No," he tells her, "you showed me a wonderful marriage. Think of it this way, Mom. I just haven't found a woman as perfect as you."

Until he does—Rachel Siegel brings her two-year-old daughter Dalia into the practice for a sore throat. Rachel is new in town, having moved into a small house on Main Street after her divorce from Dalia's father. Zack sees her as she checks out after seeing his father, eyes meeting across a not-so-crowded lobby. He falls—hard. Suddenly the slight belly his long hours and fried-food habit create embarrass him. Although his dad has warned him—as if he doesn't know already—of the dangers of trans fats and a sedentary lifestyle, Zack loves bad food and working long hours. Each year, his cholesterol climbs a bit, and his body mass index creeps toward the unhealthy range. He knows that, as one of the only two community physicians in their town, his stress levels are high, increasing his allostatic load and creating a vector for later ill health. The least he can do is stop eating poorly.

His dad watches Zack watching Rachel Siegel when she brings little Dalia in for a follow-up appointment. They haven't had a date yet, but Zack talks about her at least once each day. His dad doesn't care one way or the other if Zack ever gets married—unlike Rebecca—but if Rachel gives Zack some impetus for eating better? Well, there's nothing wrong with that, Joseph thinks.

# 18. Socioemotional Development in Middle Adulthood

## Today you will practice the following:

*18.1  Summarize the theories and research on psychosocial development during middle adulthood.*

*18.2  Describe the changes that occur in self-concept, identity, and personality during middle adulthood.*

*18.3  Analyze relationships in middle adulthood, including friend, spousal, parent–child, and grandparent relationships.*

*18.4  Discuss influences on job satisfaction and retirement planning during middle adulthood.*

"Is it always about food with your family?"

Zack laughs at Rachel but nods at the same time. "Yes. Always."

They share a second bowl of spiced rice pudding at the kitchen table, their position just right to see Dalia sitting on his mom's lap for a Bible story. Zack's dad is outside trimming the lawn he mowed before dinner. He can't believe how domestic their quiet little life has become since getting married. Rachel works at the local television station as an advertising rep, selling what they call "major accounts," while Dalia goes to daycare Tuesdays, Wednesdays, and Thursdays. Zack spends Tuesdays through Fridays at the practice, spending Monday at home with Dalia and taking care of household chores. Dad spends Mondays through Thursdays at the practice, using Fridays for the same thing.

Although both women are strong in their Jewish faith, Rachel is different from Zack's mom. Rachel is business suits and high heels, bold lipstick, and garage bands. Rebecca uncustomarily doesn't judge. She adores her daughter-in-law and her new granddaughter, who calls her Nonna, and would spend every minute with her if she could.

"Do you think," Rachel asks, "that your mom's disappointed she doesn't yet have grandchildren of her own?"

"Well, no." Zack licks his spoon and puts it on the table. "She does. Have a grandchild of her own, that is."

Raising a brow, Rachel looks at him archly. "Oh? Since you're an only child, is there something you wish to tell me?"

He nods at Mom and Dalia. "Blood is blood, and love is love. Sometimes the two intersect but not always. That's okay. Why? Do you worry she's not happy with Dalia?"

"Not at all," Rachel rushes to say. "It's only, I worry Dalia would be—I don't know—downgraded if we had another baby."

"Honestly, I've never seen Mom like this with anyone. I'm sure she'd love any baby you gave her, but, Rachel, Dalia need never worry about Mom's affections. You don't either."

She exhales and on the sigh says, "Good." The word makes Zack look at her. "What?"

"What what? What was that for?" he asks.

"Nothing." She holds a hand on the air boy scout style. "Nothing at all. Yet. Ask me in another seven months, Dr. Park."

"Really?" Heart thumping, he reaches to kiss her.

"Really." She sighs again. "I think we're probably a bit too old for this, but what the hell, right? Dalia'll have someone to boss around, and maybe I can get you to eat a little better."

He laughs. "Maybe."

## 19. Physical and Cognitive Development in Late Adulthood

### Today you will practice the following:

19.1  Discuss age-related changes in brain and body systems in late adulthood, and identify ways that older adults may compensate for changes.

19.2  Identify risk and protective factors for health in late adulthood.

19.3  Summarize common dementias including characteristics, risk and protective factors, and treatment.

19.4  Analyze patterns of cognitive change in late adulthood.

Zack often wonders what it is about Jewish women that makes them so much heartier than their counterparts. The synagogue is filled with little old ladies but far fewer little old men. Asian men, on the other hand, seem to hold their own. His parents live well past an age when he expected to lose them, for which he's grateful, entering his own early-late adulthood before losing his mother to a series of small strokes in her late 80s before his father from a clearly broken heart the year after. Although he misses them dearly, he finds it difficult to mourn the courageous, productive lives of the people who raised him.

Rachel hounds him daily about his eating habits, which have only grown poorer with age. He likes foods his health doesn't like. It's a terrible combination as he ages, and in his 60s he finds himself on beta blockers and cholesterol-lowering drugs, both of which annoy his wife but do little to deter his twice-weekly trips to the burger joint around the corner from the practice that's now Park and Stiegel as Dalia has finished medical school and joined him.

Zack reacted more negatively to Dalia's plans than he wanted to. He's a modern man, or likes to think he is, and he should support his daughter's career choice whatever that might be. It bothered him as much as it did her and Rachel when he wanted her to do something slightly more feminine. Both Rachel and

Dalia pointed out that Rachel's career wasn't precisely girly. After prayer and soul-searching, Zack has realized both how honorable the choice was and how honored he should be by Dalia's choice. Now he works beside his lovely daughter every day of the week and couldn't be happier—living proof, he thinks, that old dogs can learn new tricks.

## 20. Socioemotional Development in Late Adulthood

### Today you will practice the following:

20.1 *Examine the contributions of self-concept, personality, and religiosity to older adults' well-being.*

20.2 *Identify social contexts in which older adults live and their influence on development.*

20.3 *Summarize features of older adults' relationships with friends, spouses, children, and grandchildren, and identify how these relationships affect older adults' functioning.*

20.4 *Discuss influences on the timing of retirement and adaptation to retirement.*

"Dad?"

Zack looks at his son, Joe, a lawyer in the state capital 40 minutes away. For Joe to come in the middle of the week, the news is bad. When the kids' mother died the year before, Joe spent more than a month with him even though Dalia lives a couple blocks away. Since then, they see him once or twice a month. Joe's caseload is heavy.

"Hi, son. What brings you here on a Tuesday afternoon?"

Going into and returning from the kitchen, Joe hands him a diet Coke and sits down across from him. "I've got bad news, Dad. I'm so sorry, but James Albert passed away."

Zack thinks for a minute. Joe has to mean someone Zack doesn't know very well. He can't mean his old friend from the Kindergarten playground who he kept in touch with all throughout college and even later when they could—not that James Albert surely.

"Dad?"

"Huh? I don't . . . not my friend James the engineer?"

"Yes, Dad. I'm sorry. I know this is unexpected."

Zack thought about that. "It is. It's very unexpected. We're both so young!"

That makes Joe smile. He always likes making the kids smile. "Dad."

"I don't know what to feel. James. Damn, it always seemed like he'd live forever." Like he always feels he'll live forever himself. "Are there arrangements?"

"I'm not sure. His daughter Anna called me earlier. She said she'll let me know."

"Good. That's good. You'll let me know?"

"Yes, Dad. Of course." He reaches and pats Zack's knee. "I'm really sorry, Dad."

Zack feels himself nodding. Me, too, he thinks.

## 21. Experience With Death and Dying

> Today you will practice the following:
>
> 21.1 Identify ways in which death has been defined and end-of-life issues that may arise.
>
> 21.2 Contrast children's, adolescents', and adults' understanding of death.
>
> 21.3 Discuss the physical and emotional process of dying as it is experienced over the lifespan.
>
> 21.4 Summarize typical grief reactions to the loss of loved ones and the influence of development on bereavement.

Zack pens letters to both his children. Funeral details have existed in his will since his was 35, and he sees no need to change those now. These are different sorts of letters. He wants Dalia to know how much he's loved her from the very beginning and how much practicing with her for nearly 20 years has meant to him. He tells her to retire early, sell the practice, and live. Travel, enjoy her husband, and do all the things she's put off for however long it's been. Inside the envelope, he tucks the diamond engagement ring he gave Rachel before they were married. Some things don't need to wait for probate, he thinks. He wants Joe to know how proud he is that he struck off on his own course, that he didn't follow blindly in his dad's and grandfather's footsteps, and that he loves his career and his place in it. He tells him it's okay to retire, too, and to live a little along the way. He reminds his son that he, too, found love later in life and that when it's meant to be, he'll find the perfect man and not to worry about it so much. He tells Joe not to settle, to live the life he wants, and to be true to himself. Inside Joe's envelope, he tucks the plain platinum wedding band he gave Rachel the day they wed. Now his children have some portion of their mother that was a demonstration of their father's love for her. He's not sure what that means, only that he wants to do it.

He doesn't feel well. He hasn't felt well in a number of weeks. High blood pressure, he's sure—probably artery blockage. It's his own fault—no reason to drain the health care system. He's old, and he's ready to go. He misses Rachel and doesn't want to be mortal without her any longer. The children will understand. He's sure of it. Leaving the letters and a copy of his will on the kitchen table, he takes some time off work to read and be quiet with himself before the heart attack he knows is coming. He's made a point of checking in with Dalia every morning. So, when he doesn't, she sends a nurse from the practice to check on him. He hasn't been gone long, long enough that when the ambulance arrives, they telephone Dalia immediately to ask her to come to the hospital, but they arrive without lights and sirens.

Zack is buried in the family plot near the synagogue. His children and grandchildren (Dalia's children) are in attendance as well as many members of the synagogue and the community who knew him through the practice or through his worship. He was 77 when he died.

# CASE DISCUSSION QUESTIONS

1. During her pregnancy with Zack, his mother Rebecca chooses to discontinue use of Paxil for OCD and consistently attends therapy and a support group. What impacts both positive and negative might Rebecca's choice in this case have on Zack's life's trajectory across any and all domains (biological, cognitive, and socioemotional)?

2. In early and middle childhood, Zack is a biracial, Jewish classmate often bullied by peers who don't understand why he wears a *kippah* or has a funny hat on his head every day. How do Zack's early negative experiences explain certain outcomes we see from him, such as forming an antibullying group with his friends and teaching his best friend to speak Hebrew?

3. In childhood and adolescence, Zack is close friends with James, a classmate who helped him form the antibullying group. How does their friendship offer us insight into the socioemotional growth of adolescents from differing backgrounds?

4. Zack's entire life occurs over many decades that are, loosely, contemporary. Cars, telephones, televisions, and so on exist, but era-specific technology isn't presented (e.g., cell phones, space shuttles, and artificial intelligence). Would Zack's life have been different if he were born in a specific period, earlier or later? If so, how? Be specific.

# 10 Bliss McCallen

## Introduction

Welcome to your case study!

Congratulations! You will follow the lifespan of baby girl Bliss McCallen. Try to use your best judgment, textbook, classmates, instructor, and supplementary resources to make the best decisions to help her grow.

This semester you will observe Bliss as she grows from infant to child to teen to adult. Who will she become in your care? Will you understand and agree with all decisions available within her circumstances? How will you feel about the tough decisions that forever shape her path in life?

## Meet Bliss McCallen

Bliss is the first daughter of Misty McCallen and Cody Mackey, a pair of Caucasian teenagers. Misty, 16 and the only child of a single mother, is in high school when she meets

iStock.com/romrodinka

Cody. Misty works at the local Dairy Queen, and Cody drives to the drive-through window one day while she's taking orders and handing out food. She and her mother, Mary Jo, live in subsidized housing that her mother qualifies for due to her low income from working as a waitress for many years. Cody, 19 and a high school dropout, spends nights rotating between friends' spare rooms and couches since his mother Shirley kicked him out in his senior year of high school. Misty qualifies for Medicare as a poor, pregnant woman, and Bliss will continue to qualify once she's born.

Through this case study and your lifespan course, you will be asked to consider decisions regarding Bliss's physical, emotional, and cognitive growth and development from several perspectives: her mother Bliss's, her father Cody's, and her grandmothers' as well as those of her potential spouse and children, other family members, friends, teachers, doctors, and supervisors.

Now let's get started.

## 1. Development and Its Influences

### Today you will practice the following:

1.1 Outline five principles of the lifespan developmental perspective.

1.2 Explain three theoretical controversies about human development.

1.3 Summarize five theoretical perspectives on human development.

1.4 Describe the methods and research designs used to study human development.

Misty is terrified when she learns she's pregnant. She isn't dating the baby's father, Cody. She's not even sure she remembers his last name. Macky? McKay? Mackey, she thinks. That doesn't help her much. She has no idea where he lives, and the one piece of information she does have—his phone number—is useless. When she tries to call it, it's no longer a valid number. Just when she begins to convince herself it's no big deal—her mom's done all the work with her, and no one knows where her dad is—she runs into Cody at a gas station where they're both putting gas into their battered cars. She's visibly pregnant at this point, and when she tells Cody he's going to be a father, he loudly and meanly says he couldn't be the baby's father. They only slept together one time, which is true, and she barely knew him when they did, which is also true. If she'll sleep with a stranger that easily, who knows how many men she slept with around then? No, he doesn't believe it's his baby, even though Misty knows it is, and even if she's telling the truth, he doesn't want anything to do with it—or her.

## 2. Biological and Environmental Foundations

### Today you will practice the following:

2.1 Discuss the genetic foundations of development.

2.2 Identify examples of genetic disorders and chromosomal abnormalities.

2.3 Discuss the choices available to prospective parents in having healthy children.

2.4 Describe the interaction of heredity and environment, including behavioral genetics and the epigenetic framework.

Misty, who used to use her paychecks to buy clothes and gas for her car, now saves as much as she can for baby things. Her mother isn't thrilled to have a new baby arriving, but she's at least supportive emotionally, which is what Misty needs. Despite the stares and gossip, she manages to finish her junior year of high school as her belly grows, and just after summer break starts, Misty spends a Saturday when she's not at Dairy Queen decorating a corner of her bedroom for the baby. She's having a girl, and even though she knows it shouldn't matter, she's kind of glad. She puts up a white crib she bought for $10 at Goodwill and covers the mattress she spent $27 to buy new at Walmart with sheets a girlfriend gave her at a small baby shower engineered by the Spanish club. The sheets are white with little pink and blue sheep jumping over fences all over. She likes them.

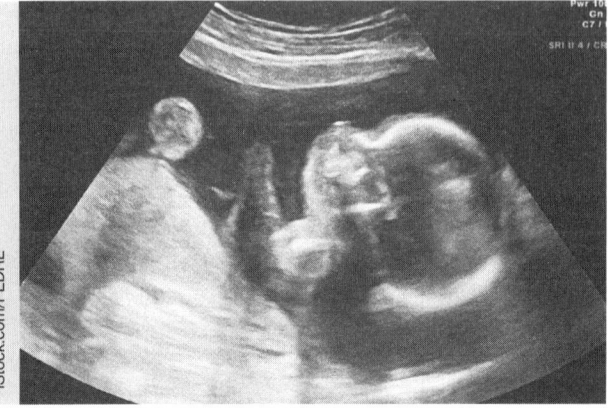

There isn't room for other furniture, like a changing table or a dresser. Misty cleans out two drawers in her own secondhand dresser to make room for the baby's clothes. Her mom bought a two-high white cubby thing Misty puts together and sticks at the end of the crib. She puts diapers and wipes in the cubbies and, as weird as it seems, a fancy mirrored tray like rich ladies might use on top. She bought that at Goodwill when she got the crib, and she uses it to hold all the stuff for keeping up with her baby's necessaries: baby powder, diaper cream, baby lotion, and sunscreen—silly, she knows, but it seems nice to give her baby something fancy to start off life with.

## 3. Prenatal Development, Birth, and Newborn Experience

### Today you will practice the following:

3.1 Describe the three periods of prenatal development that begin with conception.

3.2 Identify how exposure to teratogens can influence the prenatal environment.

3.3 Explain the process of childbirth.

3.4 Discuss the neonate's physical capacities, including development in low-birth-weight infants.

Bliss is born in the predawn of a late June morning. Misty labors for six hours, not very long she thinks, although it feels like forever, before her obstetrician suggests that a cesarean section seems more appropriate than continuing the way they've been going. Misty, who is slim and isn't progressing in her labor despite being fully dilated and effaced, wants to keep trying, but her mom overrules her. Twenty minutes later, Bliss is in her arms, tiny and perfect. The doctor tells Misty that Bliss's presentation during all of Misty's pushing was transverse with her shoulder coming out first instead of her head.

"I probably couldn't have delivered her vaginally no matter what?" Misty asks.

"Probably not, and I know you're disappointed," Dr. King tells her.

"No, it's all right. I'm just glad she's okay."

"She's much more than okay. You did great. So did she. Now get some rest."

"Thanks, Dr. King," Misty tells her.

"Yes, thank you," Mary Jo echoes.

Dr. King smiles and leaves, saying she'll be back in a little while to check in again.

An hour later, a county social worker arrives. She has a number of papers with her, some leaflets, and a couple of books. After saying nice things about the baby, she pulls up a chair and tells Misty she's there to talk about "resources" Misty has at her disposal to help being a young, single mother a little bit easier. Misty, although young and not very well educated yet, knows she needs help. Shifting the baby a little in her arms so she can see everything the social worker—Mrs. Mina Lowell—had to show her, she nods.

"Thank you. I appreciate this so much."

## 4. Physical Development in Infancy and Toddlerhood

### Today you will practice the following:

*4.1 Discuss growth and the role of nutrition in development during infancy and toddlerhood.*

*4.2 Summarize brain development during infancy and toddlerhood.*

*4.3 Compare infants' early learning capacities for habituation, classical conditioning, operant conditioning, and imitation.*

*4.4 Describe infants' developing sensory abilities.*

*4.5 Analyze the roles of maturation and contextual factors in infant and toddler motor development.*

Over the summer, Bliss bonds with Misty, who continues to work at Dairy Queen after she heals from her surgery. The weeks after the surgery are pretty nice, Misty thinks, even though her recovery feels like it's taking forever. Her mom and other neighbors in their housing unit help out with so much that all she has to do is sit around and take care of Bliss. She's not quite a live baby doll, especially during those overnight feedings or really messy diapers, but Bliss knows all the way down to her toes that of all the options available to her when she got pregnant, she chose the right one for herself.

Going back to school is another matter altogether.

"Are you sure this is the best way?" Misty asks her mom. "I can do my senior year online and still finish."

"Misty," her mom says, "you can do what you want to, but I think this is the right choice. You've got some daycare assistance for a little while. You should use it."

"But I don't like feeling like a mooch," she complains.

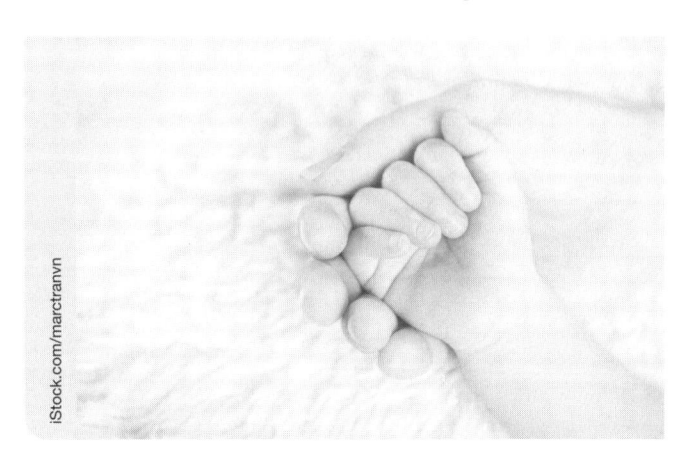

"You're not. You do know why this money is available, right? Mrs. Lowell explained it to you. It's all sliding scale based on your own income. As you finish levels of schooling, you pay more. As you make more money, you pay more. The whole system is designed so that you get more school and make more money."

"I guess . . ." Misty allows.

"No guessing. Hon, you can't sit at home until she goes to Kindergarten and then go back to high school. This is the thing that makes girls *not* go back to school. Now, put on your shoes, and get to school. I'll get the baby to daycare, and you can pick her up after school. Just think: nine months and you'll be done."

"Like carrying her," Misty says, leaning over to kiss Bliss.

"Go!"

"I'm going."

## 5. Cognitive Development in Infancy and Toddlerhood

### Today you will practice the following:

*5.1* Discuss the cognitive-developmental perspective on infant reasoning.

*5.2* Describe the information processing system in infants.

*5.3* Discuss individual differences in infant intelligence.

*5.4* Summarize the patterns of language development during infancy and toddlerhood.

Misty has a love–hate relationship with Bliss's daycare—not the daycare itself but the existence of it. She loves that it exists and she has an affordable place to take Bliss before school and that she feels safe leaving her daughter for a few hours every day. She absolutely hates all the firsts that she misses during Bliss's first year of life. She misses Bliss's first word (*mama*), her first time counting to three on her pudgy little fingers (she counts backward starting at her pinky), and her first attempt to "read" (holding the book upside down like so many kids). There are others, too. It's true that she sees a lot of Bliss's firsts, like the first time she rolls over and her first steps, but so much of what becomes her little mind the daycare teacher sees before she does. It makes her sad. One thing Misty does like is seeing Bliss's face when she picks her up because Bliss is always happy to see her, and just as Misty is close to graduating from high school, Bliss starts holding her arms open and saying, "Mama!" when she arrives. It may not make up for missing all the firsts, but it is heartwarming all the same.

## 6. Socioemotional Development in Infancy and Toddlerhood

### Today you will practice the following:

*6.1* Summarize the psychosocial tasks of infancy and toddlerhood.

*6.2* Describe emotional development in infancy, and identify contextual and cultural influences on emotional development in infants and toddlers.

*6.3* Identify the styles and stability of temperament, including the role of goodness of fit in infant development.

*6.4* Describe how attachment develops in infancy and toddlerhood.

*6.5* Differentiate the roles of self-concept, self-recognition, and self-control in infant development.

Misty thinks about Cody only now and then. Bliss keeps her so busy (*so busy*), and she has to finish high school and keep her schedule at Dairy Queen. When he happens to cross her mind, she usually thinks, "How am I supposed to think about *you*, too?" She's not even upset that he isn't around, although she realizes that she will one day be upset for Bliss that he hasn't been. They meet with Mrs. Lowell, the social worker, once each quarter, and Mrs. Lowell reminds her that she's supposed to be pursuing child support from Cody to receive any benefits from the state or county. Misty reminds Mrs. Lowell that she's given her all the information on Cody that she has. If Mrs. Lowell wants to pursue child support for Bliss, Misty will happily take it (even though she's not sure that's true; she doesn't want Cody showing up on her doorstep demanding all sorts of rights).

Bliss, right now, is a happy, affectionate little girl even, although their family is just the three of them: Bliss, Misty, and Mary Jo. Sometimes, Misty gets impatient with her, usually when she's trying to get ready for work or if she's doing homework. Mary Jo didn't finish high school after Misty was born, and Misty understands better now why that was. She tries not to yell, and she never touches Bliss in anger, but it's hard not to be annoyed when she doesn't need much more time to finish something or she has to get out the door to work. They can't afford for her to lose her job or fail a class.

"Bliss!" she snaps one day, trying to get her uniform for work out of the dryer. "Stop! I have to get dressed."

Bliss, 18 months old, lifts her arms and begins to cry, fat tears falling down her face. She repeats, "Mama, mama, mama, mama . . ." over and over, but Misty doesn't pick her up. When Misty walks past her to get to the bathroom, Bliss's volume grows louder, and Misty feels guilty. Half-dressed for work, she goes back to Bliss and picks her up.

"I'm sorry. Mama's sorry. I didn't mean to yell, baby, but I'm in a hurry. Want to sit in the bathroom and play with your dolly while I put on my makeup?" Bliss nods, and together they pass a few minutes while Misty finishes getting ready for work.

Most days are easier, but every now and then, they repeat the scene. Bliss wants attention when Misty needs to study for a test or take a shower. Forget dating. Everything is baby, school, work, baby, lather, rinse, repeat. In the back of Misty's head is her mom's voice, "I told you so." Mary Jo hardly needs to say it aloud. Fortunately, Bliss seems to be remain happy most of the time. Misty tells herself that losing her temper every now and then is okay. Surely all parents do it.

## 7. Physical and Cognitive Development in Early Childhood

### Today you will practice the following:

7.1 *Discuss physical development in early childhood.*

7.2 *Compare Piaget's cognitive-developmental and Vygotsky's sociocultural perspectives on cognitive development in early childhood.*

7.3 *Describe information-processing abilities during early childhood.*

7.4 *Summarize young children's advances in language development.*

*7.5 Contrast social learning and cognitive-developmental perspectives on moral development in early childhood.*

*7.6 Identify and explain approaches to early childhood education.*

Just before preschool starts, Bliss sees the pediatrician for her four-year checkup. For a while, she's been on the Dr. Stoddard's radar due to slow growth, which she tells Misty isn't terribly uncommon in low-income children. Bliss is also somewhat irritable sometimes, and Misty comments that she's wondered if Bliss has attention deficit disorder or attention deficit hyperactivity disorder.

"I really don't think so," Dr. Stoddard tells her, "although that's a common default these days."

"What do you think it is then?"

As Dr. Stoddard continues to examine Bliss, eliciting occasional giggles from the girl, she tells Misty, "There's a complex of factors that cluster together in low-income kids. I think that's what we're seeing here."

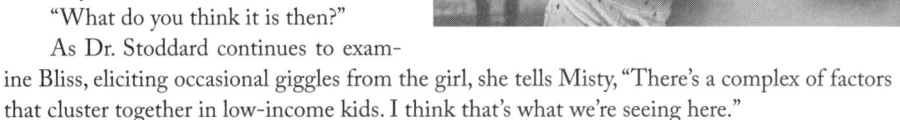

Misty isn't sure what "a complex of factors" means, but she says, "Okay," anyway. "What can I do? I can't poof us into the middle class."

Dr. Stoddard smiles. "No, unfortunately most people can't, but wouldn't it be wonderful if we could? For Bliss, what we're looking for are a couple tiny tweaks in her world. Read to her at night or whenever is convenient for you. Even if you're reading your own schoolwork aloud, make that a time when you sit together and read."

"She wouldn't understand my homework," Misty points out, a little confused.

"No, she wouldn't, but she'd like some of the funny words, and she'd love the time with you."

"Okay," Misty replies, unconvinced. "What else?"

"Mostly time. Give her little chores in the kitchen or have her help you out when you're doing something else. Make sure she knows that love is more important than the resources you may not have, that your job is to keep her healthy and safe."

"I don't understand how this changes her health."

"Neither do we, but it does. I promise."

Misty nods. "Then I promise to read college algebra and Brit Lit to her," she says seriously, referring to two of the courses she's taking at the local community college.

"Excellent!"

## 8. Socioemotional Development in Early Childhood

## Today you will practice the following:

*8.1 Discuss young children's emerging sense of initiative, self-concept, and self-esteem.*

*8.2 Summarize the development of emotional understanding, regulation, and behavior in early childhood.*

*8.3 Identify four parenting styles and their associations with child outcomes.*

8.4  Compare biological, cognitive, and contextual theoretical explanations of gender role development.

8.5  Explain the function of play and the form it takes during early childhood.

Bliss, who attends a Head Start program in her town, has three best friends. Sonia Herman has the prettiest pink hair bows in all her class, and Lila Lewis is the best speller in all the class. Jamal Jones plays hide and seek better than anyone else and is probably the best reader. The four of them play together on the playground almost every day, and Bliss makes them promise to be best friends forever. Lila has the same color hair and wears the same tennis shoes Bliss does, so she knows they'll be friends forever.

Sometimes, only Lila and Sonia play with her—not because Jamal doesn't like *her* but because he doesn't like to be the only boy in a group of girls. Bliss thinks this is stupid, but Sonia kind of agrees with him. Bliss doesn't have a daddy, and her mommy doesn't have a daddy either. They do all the girl things and all the boy things in their house. It seems funny to her that there are boy things and girl things at all. One day, she's going to put one of Sonia's hair bows in Jamal's afro. That'll teach him about girl things, she thinks.

## 9. Physical and Cognitive Development in Middle Childhood

### Today you will practice the following:

9.1  Identify patterns of physical and motor development during middle childhood and common health issues facing school-age children.

9.2  Discuss school-age children's capacities for reasoning and processing information.

9.3  Summarize views of intelligence including the uses, correlates, and criticisms of intelligence tests.

9.4  Examine patterns of moral development during middle childhood.

9.5  Summarize language development during middle childhood.

9.6  Discuss children's learning at school.

"Bliss, please sit down."

Mrs. Anderson stood over her with *that look*, the look that says she really, really likes you but she's running out of patience. Bliss considers whether or not she could push her further and decides no—that's probably not the best idea. Finding her desk, she sits and takes out her homework. Mrs. Anderson always checks homework first, and Bliss has been working so hard on her handwriting (which is awful). She hopes this will be the day her teacher praises her efforts. Last week, she missed two math problems that she actually worked correctly, but Mrs. Anderson couldn't read well enough to know that. Bliss is trying to be much more careful now.

"What did you get for number four in the reading homework?" Sonia asks, leaning over from her desk on the next row.

Bliss checks. "Red noses," she whispers back. When Sonia frowns at her own paper, Bliss giggles. She knows that's one she got right because Mama helped.

At the front of the room, Mrs. Anderson clears her throat and all the children get quiet. "I'm coming around now to check your homework. After that, we'll do math groups B and C and reading groups A and D in your circles. Once I check your homework, move quietly to where you're supposed to be, please."

Bliss claps under her desk. She's in reading group A, which means she's starting there today. She loves reading. Also, Sonia's in her reading group. She gets to do the thing she likes best in school with the friend she likes best. This is going to be a great day!

## 10. Socioemotional Development in Middle Childhood

### Today you will practice the following:

10.1 Describe school-age children's self-conceptions and motivation.

10.2 Examine the roles of friendship, peer acceptance, and peer victimization in school-age children's adjustment.

10.3 Discuss family relationships in middle childhood and the influence of family structure on adjustment.

10.4 Analyze the role of resilience in promoting adjustment to adversity, including characteristics of children and contexts that promote resilience.

After the break-in at her apartment building, Bliss has trouble sleeping for a few weeks. She tries to sleep with her mom or her grandma, but both of them tell her she has to be a big girl and stay in her own bed. Her mom sits with her some when she has bad dreams. That helps a little.

In school, she draws pictures of burglars in black masks climbing into her bedroom window while she sits up in bed with the covers pulled to her chin. Her face is frightened, and the burglar has a big smile. When the teacher sees her pictures, she asks Bliss about them, and Bliss tells her what happened. After that, Bliss talks to the school counselor and school nurse, who wants to make sure she's getting enough sleep. She isn't, but she tries to sound like she is.

On career day, when all the kids dress up as the sort of worker they want to be when they grow up, Bliss can't decide. Before the break-in, all she knew about were waitresses, fry cooks, and supermarket cashiers. When she picks out a costume, she ends up wearing a stethoscope with a badge and carrying a pad of paper. The teacher asks what she's supposed to be, and Bliss, smiling, says, "A nurse. *And* a policewoman. *And* a counselor. I haven't decided yet."

"I think those are all very good careers to think about, Bliss," her teacher says, "and you've got plenty of time to think."

## 11. Physical and Cognitive Development in Late Childhood

### Today you will practice the following:

11.1 *Describe school-age children's self-conceptions and motivation.*

11.2 *Examine the roles of friendship, peer acceptance, and peer victimization in school-age children's adjustment.*

11.3 *Discuss family relationships in middle childhood and the influence of family structure on adjustment.*

11.4 *Analyze the role of resilience in promoting adjustment to adversity, including characteristics of children and contexts that promote resilience*

Bliss gets off the bus after school and walks through the confined space of the housing complex to get to their apartment. It's a daily routine. In the building where she lives, Mrs. Van Andel watches her after school along with a few other kids. Mostly they do their homework in front of the Disney Channel and eat cookies with milk. It's not exciting, but by the time Bliss's mom gets there, she almost never has homework left to do. That's good.

The wind blows hard the day she finds police and police tape blocking her way. The bus drives away before she can get back on, and she isn't allowed to go forward. A nice policewoman in a big, puffy jacket asks her where she lives. Bliss tells the officer her address and that she stays with Mrs. Van Andel in the same building during the afternoons until her mom gets home. The woman drives her in a fancy police car to her building.

"What happened?" Bliss asks, referring to the taped-off parking lot and building.

The lady, whose name is Officer Bennett, says, "There was a robbery. We're sorting it out now."

"Did anyone get hurt?" Bliss wants to know. She's worried that she or her mom or grandma might get hurt. "Did you catch him? The bad guy?"

"No, not yet, but we're going to."

No one's hurt. That's good, she thinks. "How do you know you'll get him?"

"How do you know it's a him? Hmm?"

"Fair enough. Girls can rob people too, I guess."

"I guess they can, and I know because that's our job. We wouldn't be very good if we didn't get him . . . *or her*, now would we?"

Bliss thinks about that as the car pulls up in front of her building. "No, I guess not. How will you catch him . . . *or her*?" she asks, echoing the officer's inflection.

"The usual, I suspect. We'll ask around for witnesses, look for clues in the apartments, take descriptions of the stolen items to pawn shops, things like that."

Bliss admits this is pretty cool. "Thanks for driving me," she says, slipping from the car.

"It was my pleasure, Bliss." Officer Bennett turns the car off and locks it when she gets out. "I'll walk you inside to . . ."

"Mrs. Van Andel."

"Mrs. Van Andel's apartment."

"Thanks." Bliss looks back at the police car as they walk inside. She thinks she might have an answer the next time she's asked in school to write about what she wants to be when she grows up.

## 12. Socioemotional Development in Late Childhood

### Today you will practice the following:

*12.1 Summarize the processes by which self-concept, self-esteem, and identity change during adolescence.*

*12.2 Discuss the nature of parent–child relationships in adolescence.*

*12.3 Examine the developmental progression of peer relations in adolescence.*

*12.4 Analyze patterns of adolescent sexual activity including sexual orientation.*

*12.5 Identify common psychological and behavioral problems in adolescence.*

At the end of fifth grade, Bliss's mom and grandma come to the assembly to watch all the kids graduate. She's going to middle school at the end of summer, and she can't wait. She's also super excited that her family is there for graduation. Mom doesn't come to many things at her school. Bliss thinks it's because people look at her mom funny. Grandma says they "judge" her, but Bliss doesn't know what that means. "You will," Grandma always tells her, but it sounds awful, and Bliss hopes Grandma's wrong about that.

She's one of the lucky kids on graduation day. About half get to leave after the assembly. Their parents take them out of school early to do special celebration things. Mom signs her out, and the three of them go to the restaurant where Mom works to get burgers and fries. The waitress even brings Bliss a bowl of vanilla ice cream with chocolate sauce. She feels like a princess. Mom is smiling, and she seems proud of Bliss—Grandma, too. Bliss is happy to be going to middle school with her friends and to be away from all the elementary school babies. Getting ice cream to celebrate it? That's just a super-duper bonus.

## 13. Physical and Cognitive Development in Adolescence

### Today you will practice the following:

*13.1* *Evaluate the "storm and stress" perspective on adolescence in light of research evidence.*

*13.2* *Summarize the physical changes that occur with puberty and the correlates of pubertal timing.*

*13.3* *Discuss brain development during adolescence and its effect on behavior.*

*13.4* *Identify ways in which thinking changes in adolescence and how these changes are reflected in adolescent decision making and behavior.*

*13.5* *Discuss moral development and influences on moral reasoning.*

*13.6* *Describe the challenges that school transitions pose for adolescents and the role of parents in academic achievement.*

Across the street from the bus stop where Bliss lives, a billboard advertises a "gentlemen's club." Bliss knows what that is. The advertisement shows a girl in an outfit kind of like a bikini (*kind of,* Bliss always thinks) standing in a thing kind of like a woman-sized birdcage (*kind of,* she reminds herself, thinking of the metaphors). She can't tell if the girl looks older than her years because of her lifestyle or if she's meant to look younger than she is and just can't quite pull it off. Either way, Bliss thinks, is tragic.

"That's what happens to girls who aren't quite smart enough or pretty enough or anything enough to get out of places like this," Keisha Rayne says to her one day while they wait for the bus.

"What's what happens?" Bliss asks, not sure how literally to take the statement.

"Get trapped by circumstance," Keisha says, nodding toward the birdcage. "Sad but true."

Bliss doesn't want to get trapped, but she figures by the time a girl figures out it's happened, it's too late to avoid it.

"Stupid is as stupid does," she says to Keisha, "or something like that."

"Something like that," Keisha echoes as the bus pulls to a stop, cutting off their view to the billboard. "You and me, girl? We don't have the luxury of being stupid, not even for a minute."

## 14. Socioemotional Development in Adolescence

### Today you will practice the following:

*14.1 Summarize the processes by which self-concept, self-esteem, and identity change during adolescence.*

*14.2 Discuss the nature of parent–child relationships in adolescence.*

*14.3 Examine the developmental progression of peer relations in adolescence.*

*14.4 Analyze patterns of adolescent sexual activity including sexual orientation.*

*14.5 Identify common psychological and behavioral problems in adolescence.*

"Dad?" Bliss calls from her bedroom at Cody's house—*her* bedroom. She didn't have to share space in this apartment, luxury of luxuries.

"What is it, Bliss?"

"Can I go out with Hunter Lyon Saturday night?"

Dad scowls at her, darkly. He's made it clear he doesn't like her going on when he has her—not because he doesn't like her going out but because he doesn't have her often and feels like he has so much time to make up for, having first not known she was born and then not knowing how to find her since Mama didn't put his name on her birth certificate.

"Bliss . . ." he starts, but she holds up a hand.

"I know it's not what you prefer," she says, "but hear me out. First, it's Hunter, and you actually like Hunter. Second, it's not an all-evening date, which I know is kinda taboo. There's some barbeque tasting downtown that only goes from four to eight. We thought we might go right when the thing started and Hunter could drop me off early, like six or seven."

She watches him consider the request and finally nod. "I guess, but two hours tops. Promise?"

She crosses her heart with an index finger before going back to the phone. "Cross my heart," she tells him and means it. She'll only be gone for two hours, but she has no intention of going to the barbeque festival.

Hunter Lyon talked her out of her virginity six months before. It wasn't pretty or enjoyable in the back cab of his 4×4 Chevy, but she loves him and that's that. It's easier to find time to be together when she's at Mama's apartment than Dad's, but she still manages pretty well—well enough that Hunter keeps coming around anyway. That's good enough for her.

"Thanks, Dad," she says and drops a kiss on his cheek. Speaking into the phone, she says, "Yep, I can go. Four to six, you think? Perfect!"

## 15. Physical and Cognitive Development in Emerging/Early Adulthood

### Today you will practice the following:

*15.1 Describe the features and characteristics of emerging and early adulthood.*

*15.2 Summarize the physical developments of emerging and early adulthood.*

*15.3 Analyze physical and sexual health issues in emerging and early adulthood.*

*15.4 Compare postformal reasoning, pragmatic thought, and cognitive-affective complexity.*

*15.5 Explain how attending college influences young adults' development, and identify challenges faced by first-generation and nontraditional students.*

*15.6 Discuss vocational choice and the transition to work.*

Bliss graduates from high school with decent but not stellar grades and extracurricular achievements. Because of the local labor market, her high school counselor, and time, she decides to get her certified nursing assistant's license (CNA). Attending the same community college her mom didn't manage to finish, she takes the 12-week program and completes it in the top third of her class.

She takes a job in a local family practice clinic, where she's assigned to work with a small, perpetually happy Filipino man, Dr. Luis Vilar. Bliss likes Dr. Vilar so much; she respects his gentleness with patients and his firm guidance with them regarding their health. By working alongside Dr. Vilar, Bliss learns to be compassionately resolute, and because she interfaces with patients first and for longer periods than he does, it's Bliss who builds and maintains his patient list. They become a good team, and she figures out that it's self-nurturing to have a place and purpose in life. By the time she's 22,

Bliss earns more money than her mother does at 38, and she moves out of the family apartment into a studio of her own in a revitalized area downtown.

## 16. Socioemotional Development in Emerging/Early Adulthood

### Today you will practice the following:

*16.1* Summarize psychosocial development in early adulthood.

*16.2* Discuss influences on friendship and mate selection and interactions in early adulthood.

*16.3* Analyze the diverse romantic situations that may characterize early adulthood, including singlehood, cohabitation, marriage, and divorce.

*16.4* Compare the experiences of young adults as stepparents, never-married parents, and same-sex parents.

On a blustery Monday, not a special day at all, Bliss clears the trash from Dr. Vilar's three exam rooms near the end of the day. As she carries the trash bags to the chute used by the entire practice, she hears Dr. Vilar welcoming someone into his office with enthusiasm. Bliss pauses in his doorway on her way back to the coat closet as she prepares to go home.

"You have company?" she asks with some curiosity. They don't usually have visitors.

"I do!" Dr. Vilar tells her, joy animating his face. "Bliss, this is my son, Fábio. Fábio, this is our newest CNA and our best hire ever, Bliss McCallen."

Dr. Vilar's son reaches to shake her hand, saying, "It's a pleasure to meet you."

"Likewise," Bliss assures him and can't resist tweaking her boss and the son at the same time. "They really named you Fábio?" Not that the man wasn't bodice-ripper-cover worthy.

Both men laugh, and Fábio replies, "They really did. Fábio from *fabius*, originally Latin for *bean*. I'm told my parents called me 'little bean' for the duration of my mother's pregnancy. Thus . . ."

"Thus, Fábio," Bliss says, laughing. "That's a charming story."

"I agree, and there are at least a dinner's worth of others." His eyes smile, and he seems kind. "If you'd like to join me. I'm sure Dad will understand if I put him off a night."

Bliss feels awkward. Working as closely together as they do, Dr. Vilar knows a lot of her history, including her poverty, her lack of a father for the first half of it, her cycle of single mothers with crap jobs and no aspirations. She would never be an acceptable date for his son.

Dr. Vilar pats her shoulder. "I think you should go. Fábio, be sure to get her home at a reasonable hour. I need her sharp for our patients in the morning."

Our patients? Maybe he doesn't mind so much. She looks at Fábio.

"Okay, Little Bean, one dinner, but these stories better live up to their billing."

## 17. Physical and Cognitive Development in Middle Adulthood

### Today you will practice the following:

*17.1* Summarize age-related physical changes during middle adulthood.

*17.2* Discuss common health conditions and illnesses and the roles of stress and hardiness on health during middle adulthood.

*17.3* Contrast the findings of cross-sectional and longitudinal studies of crystallized and fluid intelligence over adulthood.

*17.4* Analyze changes in cognitive capacities during middle adulthood, including attention, memory, processing speed, and expertise.

---

Bliss continues to work for Dr. Vilar throughout her career. With his encouragement and support of alternate scheduling when necessary, she pursues a bachelor of science in nursing, the first in her family to receive a college degree. Her mom and grandmother are proud. Her dad is over the moon. Not wishing to detract from her success, Fábio waits until her birthday a month later to ask her to marry him, "Since you'll be the breadwinner now," he teases. She might be, they both agree, because Fábio's position as a construction foreman is in jeopardy due to the economic downturn. Jointly, they agree to worry about that when it happens. They're both penny pinchers. Everything will be okay, they believe. Besides, Cody's paying for the wedding as apology for the lost years and congratulations for Bliss's graduation.

The degree means a different set of duties at work, more hands-on time with patients, and more money. She loves the responsibility. She becomes the practice's go-to nurse for teenage girls contemplating sex and for teen moms in moments of crises. It feels cliché in the beginning but only long enough for her to realize how natural it actually is, which is about the time it takes her to see one patient. By the time she finds herself pregnant with her and Fábio's first child, Bliss feels like she's the poster child for how to do better than the last generation.

*And it was so close,* she thinks when the face of Hunter Lyon pops up in her mind.

## 18. Socioemotional Development in Middle Adulthood

### Today you will practice the following:

*18.1* Summarize the theories and research on psychosocial development during middle adulthood.

*18.2* Describe the changes that occur in self-concept, identity, and personality during middle adulthood.

**CHAPTER 10** Bliss McCallen

*18.3 Analyze relationships in middle adulthood, including friend, spousal, parent–child, and grandparent relationships.*

*18.4 Discuss influences on job satisfaction and retirement planning during middle adulthood.*

Bliss and Fábio have two children, both daughters. Sol and Leonora are born three years apart when Bliss is 30 and 33. Leonora arrives six months after the death of Mary Jo, Bliss's grandmother. Both girls are adored, spoiled, and taught rather traditional Latin values. Once, Bliss would've rebelled against such gender conformity, but she finds the easy way the family falls into their behavioral patterns comforting. Neither she nor Fábio would dream of restricting the girls' occupational or avocational choices. Within their home, she's embraced the more culturally normative expectations she's learned from the Vilars. Fábio assures her she's perfectly normal.

"Darling, you were raised in a world where one sex had no choice but to be both sexes. I suspect a traditional division of labor is, in fact, comforting to you. Don't worry, your secret is safe with me."

Bliss lifts a skeptical brow. "Promise?"

"Cross my heart. If I break my promise, I'll buy you a pair of earrings of your choice."

Laughing, Bliss stands on her toes to kiss him. "I'll settle for dinner and a movie."

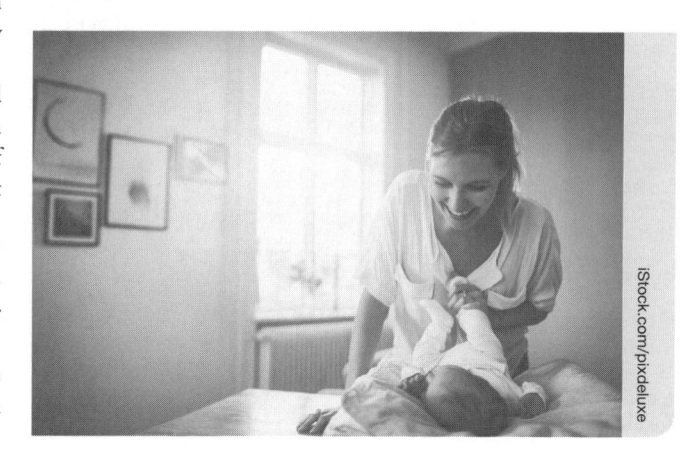

## 19. Physical and Cognitive Development in Late Adulthood

### Today you will practice the following:

*19.1 Discuss age-related changes in brain and body systems in late adulthood, and identify ways that older adults may compensate for changes.*

*19.2 Identify risk and protective factors for health in late adulthood.*

*19.3 Summarize common dementias including characteristics, risk and protective factors, and treatment.*

*19.4 Analyze patterns of cognitive change in late adulthood.*

Fábio and Bliss joke that his physical health as they age is better than hers just because he's more active on the job than she is. They joke about it, but it's also true. She spends all day every day indoors with long periods of relative inactivity seeing to the well-being of other people. The idea of going to a gym is nice, but somehow she never gets around to it with the girls and making dinner and just . . . life. Dr. Vilar, before retiring, made good use of the practice's small in-house gym, using the treadmill most days of the week even when he did nothing else, and he lived past 80. Bliss realizes she should do the same, but she never finds the motivation.

"I'm probably going to get Alzheimer's or heart disease or something terrible before you do," she tells Fábio all the time once the kids are grown and have families of their own. Her own mother recently passed away from complications due to ischemic heart disease; Bliss suspects that will likely be her lot as well.

"I did say 'in sickness and in health,' if you'll recall."

Bliss kisses him. "I'd rather it be in health."

"And we don't always get what we want. Bliss, you had a difficult childhood, and that's going to take a toll on you eventually. We'll do whatever we can to keep you healthy, and we'll face whatever gets thrown at us. Just don't be a fatalist about it."

"I'm trying," she says, and she is.

"Just think about what you would say to a patient in your own position."

Bliss laughs. "Ha! I'd tell her to cut out red meat, start jogging every day, and find a hobby she loves."

Fábio walks to the refrigerator and opens the door. Pulling out a package of ground beef and another with two rib eyes, he tosses the beef into the trash can over her shriek of objection. "No red meat. I know better than to suggest you jog, but haven't you been talking about joining a book club?"

"Actually, yes," she admits.

"Then do it!"

"Will you do it with me?"

"My name is Fábio," he reminds her. "Promise me no bodice rippers, and I'll consider it."

## 20. Socioemotional Development in Late Adulthood

### Today you will practice the following:

*20.1 Examine the contributions of self-concept, personality, and religiosity to older adults' well-being.*

*20.2 Identify social contexts in which older adults live and their influence on development.*

*20.3 Summarize features of older adults' relationships with friends, spouses, children, and grandchildren, and identify how these relationships affect older adults' functioning.*

*20.4 Discuss influences on the timing of retirement and adaptation to retirement.*

Bliss and Fábio have dinner with one girl or the other once each week. They want to see their grandchildren, and if making things easy on their daughters is the way to do it, then that's a small price to pay. Besides, seeing Sol and Leonora is always a pleasure, too—not so much the sons-in-law, but they've learned to live with them. One of the pleasures of full-family get-togethers is the cajoling both girls do with their parents: *Please sell the house and come live with us.* Then the other: *No, absolutely not. Come live with us. We have more room.* Then: *We're on one floor,* and on and on. It makes her and Fábio feel cherished.

When Fábio has a heart attack on the job one day—he's 72—these little pretend arguments become suddenly more real. Bliss puts off thinking about anything while she nurses Fábio back to health, but after the second heart attack the next year, the one from which he doesn't recover, she gives in. As her training tells her to do, she mourns his death for a year before making any decision. Then she carefully packs his clothes, his work boots, his hard hats (except the one she buried him with) into boxes for storage while letting the children help her pack her own things for moving. The house sells quickly, and she agrees to live with Sol during the fall and winter and Leonora during the spring and summer. She'll take little enough with her for the moves to be disruptive, and this way, when either is ready to pull her hair out over Bliss's presence, there won't be long to wait before her departure. She'll also be able to maximize her time with each of her grandchildren.

She just can't believe Fábio went first.

"It definitely shouldn't have been you," she says to his gravestone. "And I hope you know how angry I am that it was."

She's retired by now and spends part of each day at the nearby cemetery where a double plot waits for her body, and her gravestone needs only her death date. Sol thinks her morbid for ordering it when she ordered Fábio's. Leonora thinks she's practical. She just wanted to save them the bother.

"The girls and I have an arrangement for now," she tells him. "Six months with Sol, then six months with Leonora. Crazy, I know. They want to help, and it's easier to let them than it is to fight them." Leaving her daily flower on the gravestone, she says, "You are loved, and you are missed. Don't go anywhere without me, Little Bean."

Then she returns home to wait.

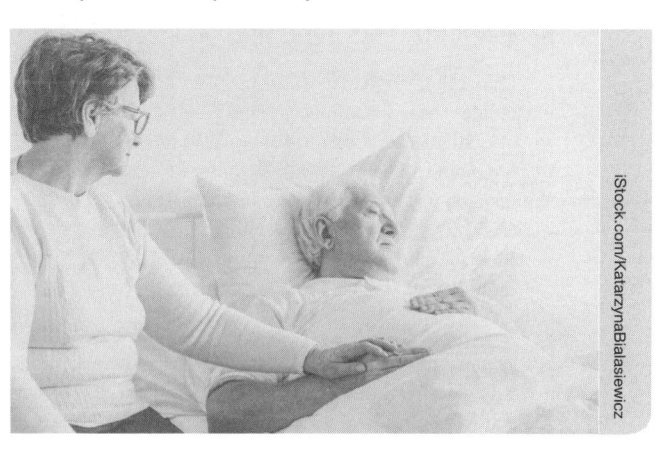

## 21. Experience With Death and Dying

### Today you will practice the following:

21.1  Identify ways in which death has been defined and end-of-life issues that may arise.

21.2  Contrast children's, adolescents', and adults' understanding of death.

21.3  Discuss the physical and emotional process of dying as it is experienced over the lifespan.

21.4  Summarize typical grief reactions to the loss of loved ones and the influence of development on bereavement.

Bliss continues to live and to remain healthy well into her 80s, well beyond the point she wants to if she were asked. Fortunately, she isn't asked. When her youngest grandson, Gabriel, marries his college sweetheart, Tatiana, Bliss writes a hefty check for their honeymoon in Portugal. She's happy to use some of her savings to help them celebrate the beginning of their life together in the same place she and Fábio spent their honeymoon. After the couple returns and she sees the beautiful photos they took, Bliss feels as if all the things she wanted to do or could have wanted to do have been done. There is just the waiting now.

That winter, at Leonora's house, Bliss develops a cold. The cold persists until she knows she's quite ill, and she asks Leonora to take her to the doctor. Diagnosed with pneumonia, she's hospitalized as a precaution, but she doesn't make it back home. Bliss passes away in the hospital surrounded by her daughters, sons-in-law, grandchildren, and two great-grandchildren. She's 85 years old.

## CASE DISCUSSION QUESTIONS

1. During her pregnancy, Bliss's mother Misty decides she will continue going to high school after Bliss is born. She has one year to finish, and her mom will help out with Bliss during school hours to make things easier. How important is Misty's decision to complete high school to Bliss's development across all domains (biological, cognitive, and socioemotional)? Why?

2. Bliss's mother Misty is also a daughter born to a teenage single mother (Mary Jo). Mary Jo and Misty both work in the food service industry, and Misty still lives at home, of course. What do we know about systemic poverty, education, and public health that both predict Bliss's birth and make this truly an optimal case outcome for her?

3. In early adulthood, Bliss takes a position as a CNA with Dr. Vilar. This choice leads to more than consistent and fulfilling employment. Dr. Vilar becomes a mentor, encouraging Bliss to pursue a bachelor's degree. He also becomes her father-in-law. Discuss the impact the relationship between Dr. Vilar and Bliss has on her future development across any and all domains (biological, cognitive, and socioemotional).

4. Bliss's entire life occurs over many decades that are, loosely, contemporary. Cars, telephones, televisions, and so on exist, but era-specific technology isn't presented (e.g., cell phones, space shuttles, and artificial intelligence). Would Bliss's life have been different if she were born in a specific period, earlier or later? If so, how? Be specific.

# 11 Poppy Bell

## Introduction

Welcome to your case study!

Congratulations! You will follow the lifespan of baby girl Poppy Bell. Try to use your best judgment, textbook, classmates, instructor, and supplementary resources to make the best decisions to help her grow.

This semester you will observe Poppy as she grows from infant to child to teen to adult. Who will she become in your care? Will you understand and agree with all decisions available within her circumstances? How will you feel about the tough decisions that forever shape her path in life?

## Meet Poppy Bell

Poppy is the second daughter and third child of Wendy and Brian Bell. Wendy is a Caucasian 36-year-old speech therapist; she has a master's degree and works in a hospital after graduate school and a school once Poppy's siblings are born and start preschool. Brian, 38 years old and also a master's degree holder, teaches math at the same school.

iStock.com/JNemchinova

CHAPTER 11  Poppy Bell      235

Through this case study and your lifespan course, you will be asked to consider decisions regarding Poppy's physical, emotional, and cognitive growth and development from several perspectives: her parents', her siblings', and her grandparents' as well as those of her spouse, her potential children, other potential family members, friends, teachers, doctors, and supervisors.

Now let's get started.

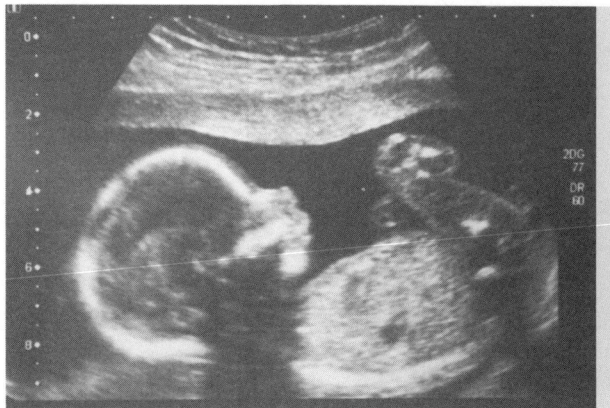

## 1. Development and Its Influences

> Today you will practice the following:
>
> *1.1  Outline five principles of the lifespan developmental perspective.*
>
> *1.2  Explain three theoretical controversies about human development.*
>
> *1.3  Summarize five theoretical perspectives on human development.*
>
> *1.4  Describe the methods and research designs used to study human development.*

Poppy is conceived as a result of Wendy's on-again-off-again affair with Brian's friend Sam. Sam Gunderson is 44 years old and, as someone with a bachelor's degree, works as a research scientist for the state department's Fish and Wildlife program. The affair, lasting approximately three years, has produced no other pregnancies, and when Wendy learns she's going to have Poppy, she decides not to tell Brian that Sam is the father. The truth outs when routine prenatal testing reveals that both of Poppy's biological parents are carriers of cystic fibrosis, but Wendy and Brian knew from their pregnancies with Poppy's brother Leaf (five years old) and sister Clover (seven years old) that only one parent was a carrier (Wendy).

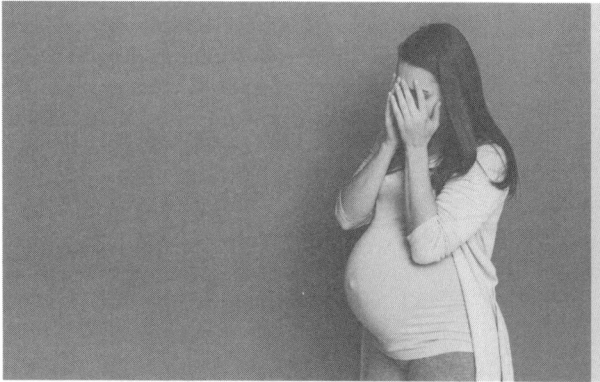

Wendy's admission that Poppy's biological father is Sam stuns both fathers. Brian isn't sure whether or not he wants to remain married to Wendy and spends days at a time away from the house, during which periods Wendy has to cope with both small children, her job, and her pregnancy. Leaf and Clover know there's trouble between their parents and intuit that Brian blames Wendy. They start to blame her, too, for offenses unspecified, making their care even more challenging. In deference to Wendy's efforts to save her marriage, Sam doesn't come around during the pregnancy. Neither father is present during the labor and delivery of Poppy, which is normal and uneventful after a healthy and relatively uneventful pregnancy.

When Wendy returns home after having Poppy, Brian has returned, this time for good, he promises, but there are several voice mails from Sam as well. All three adults know there is difficult terrain to navigate moving forward.

## 2. Biological and Environmental Foundations

### Today you will practice the following:

2.1  Discuss the genetic foundations of development.

2.2  Identify examples of genetic disorders and chromosomal abnormalities.

2.3  Discuss the choices available to prospective parents in having healthy children.

2.4  Describe the interaction of heredity and environment, including behavioral genetics and the epigenetic framework.

Poppy's parents are all well educated. Wendy has had two healthy, normal pregnancies before Poppy, and she's familiar with pregnancy dos, such as eating well and exercising, and with don'ts, such as drinking or being around people who smoke. The biggest challenge Wendy faces is stress—stress from not knowing when or if Brian will be at home, whether or not Sam will want anything to do with the baby, and when Clover and Leaf will act out in anger because they feel she's to blame for all the turmoil. She is, and her obstetrician warns her not to let stress get the better of her. She doesn't want Poppy's developing fetal brain bathed in serotonin or an excess of corticosteroids passing the blood-brain barrier. Wendy spends the first and last 15 minutes of each day in meditation hoping that will help, as her doctor assures her it will.

## 3. Prenatal Development, Birth, and Newborn Experience

### Today you will practice the following:

3.1  Describe the three periods of prenatal development that begin with conception.

3.2  Identify how exposure to teratogens can influence the prenatal environment.

3.3  Explain the process of childbirth.

3.4  Discuss the neonate's physical capacities, including development in low-birth-weight infants.

"She's squidgy," Leaf says, bending over his new baby sister.

"And wrinkly like an old man," Clover adds.

Wendy agrees somewhat. "She's both of those things a little, but she won't stay that way. Give her a couple days, and she'll look just like both of you did," she promised.

Clover gives her a funny look. "Why does Poppy have two daddies? I only have one daddy."

She says this as if Poppy is somehow better equipped in the father department. The question makes Wendy smile and want to cry simultaneously. She's grateful Brian isn't there when Clover asks it.

"Well, sweetie, because both your daddy and Uncle Sam are her daddies."

*Don't ask,* she prays.

"I know that, but *why?*"

"Because Mommy and Uncle Sam made a baby together last year, and that baby became Poppy."

"And you and Daddy made me and Leaf?" Clover looks like she might put the puzzle together all by herself. Wendy hopes not.

"Yes, we did." Answer what they ask but don't volunteer information.

"And you didn't want to make Poppy with Daddy?"

Wendy sighs. "It wasn't like that. I didn't decide not to make Poppy with Daddy or *to* make Poppy with Uncle Sam. She just got made."

Leaf leans over his baby sister again. "Will Uncle Sam be our daddy now, too? Will we have two daddies like Poppy?"

*Damn cystic fibrosis,* Wendy thinks. *There but for prenatal testing go I.*

"No, Leaf. You and Clover still have your daddy. Poppy may have two daddies, but she may not have Uncle Sam as her daddy, either. We'll just have to see."

Phrasing things is so complicated. She doesn't want to say "just one daddy" because that will make Clover and Leaf feel shortchanged. Every sentence is a possible minefield.

If nothing else, the children seem fascinated with their baby sister. That's something. Wendy has ten weeks off from work thanks to the well-timed spring break plus her maternity leave. For the moment, both fathers are being cautious, kind, and attentive to Poppy, who is adorable and healthy. When Wendy looks at her, she can't imagine life before Poppy, but she also can't imagine the life that led to her. She knows she'll never cheat on Brian again, but she also knows that may not be enough to save her marriage.

## 4. Physical Development in Infancy and Toddlerhood

> ## Today you will practice the following:
>
> *4.1 Discuss growth and the role of nutrition in development during infancy and toddlerhood.*
>
> *4.2 Summarize brain development during infancy and toddlerhood.*

4.3  Compare infants' early learning capacities for habituation, classical conditioning, operant conditioning, and imitation.

4.4  Describe infants' developing sensory abilities.

4.5  Analyze the roles of maturation and contextual factors in infant and toddler motor development.

In her infancy, Poppy is a quiet, sweet baby. She is doted on by her brother and sister, who take her everywhere. Clover and Leaf encourage many of her firsts, such as crawling and walking, and they spare Wendy the challenge of teaching Poppy to eat with a fork and spoon. When Poppy starts walking three weeks after she begins crawling, Wendy says it's because she can't stand to be left out of her brother and sister's fun.

Once she's walking, Poppy becomes a hider. Wendy often finds herself unable to find Poppy at the worst times, like when she's working the children like an assembly line through their baths or when Sam comes by for a visit or, worst of all, when she needs to leave for work. Hide-and-seek is a game, and although having Poppy play hide-and-seek at awful times would make Wendy mad, this isn't hide-and-seek. Poppy just hides. Wendy generally enlists Clover's help finding her sister; Clover seems to be the Poppy Whisperer.

"Clover?" Wendy calls one snowy morning on the way to the family SUV. She needs to drop Poppy at daycare before going on to the K–8 school where she and Brian both teach. He's gone on ahead of her.

"I know," the eight-year old says happily, "go find my sister."

"Please." Turning her attention to Leaf, Wendy points to the backseat. "All right, cowboy, into the saddle."

Clover finds Poppy standing in the bathtub she shares with her brother and sister. She's got the shower curtain closed, and with her winter coat and Wellies on, Poppy is so cute that Clover has to overcome the urge to turn on the shower.

"Poppy," she says, trying to sound stern but not hateful. She's not mad at all. "Why are you hiding in here? Mom's going to be mad."

"Shh," Poppy answers, holding a finger to her lips. "Duh walls're loud."

"The walls are loud?" Clover asks, making sure she understands.

"Yeth," Poppy says. "Bad wallth."

Clover nods. "Yes, bad, bad walls. You're right, Poppy. Bad walls to be loud, so let's go outside with Mom, and you won't have to hear the loud walls, okay?"

Poppy looks skeptical, and for all Clover knows maybe she should. Clover doesn't know exactly what Poppy means by the walls being loud. She'll try to figure that one out later after they escape Mom's wrath.

"Okay," Poppy agrees.

She holds out her hand, and Clover takes it to help her climb over the side of the bathtub. Together, they troop down the stairs and back outside where Mom is just getting Leaf buckled into his car seat.

Mom turns around and sees both of them, and her eyes get that relieved look Clover knows means she probably won't yell in the car—probably. Personally, she doesn't know why Mom has such a hard time finding Poppy when she hides. She only has maybe five or six places she goes. It's not that hard. Clover thinks Mom's maybe a little bit lazy even though Mom says she's just busy.

"Ready?" Mom asks when they're all in their seats.

"Ready," they all say, Poppy just a second behind Clover and Leaf.

Mom laughs and pulls out of the driveway. *Another day begins,* Clover thinks, wondering if her dad is giving a math test today. She can't remember.

## 5. Cognitive Development in Infancy and Toddlerhood

### Today you will practice the following:

5.1 Discuss the cognitive-developmental perspective on infant reasoning.

5.2 Describe the information processing system in infants.

5.3 Discuss individual differences in infant intelligence.

5.4 Summarize the patterns of language development during infancy and toddlerhood.

Sam knows that Wendy and Brian are struggling to make their marriage work. His portion of blame in that troubles him, but he knows he isn't solely responsible. He also finds himself unable to apologize for Poppy, the child he never thought he'd have and without whom his life would be incomplete. He couldn't have guessed how many holes in a heart a child could fill.

So far, they've all managed to avoid court dealings. Brian, Poppy's legal father, can't quite forgive Wendy and Sam for their affair (understandable, Sam thinks), but he also wants Poppy to know Sam as one of her fathers. Sam doesn't have come-and-go access to her, but he does have generous visitation even if it's informal. He also pays what they all agree is fair child support each month, also informal. His favorite outings with Poppy are when he takes her on nature hikes at some of the preserves where he does geological surveys for the Fish and Wildlife program for the state, his employer.

"Dat one?" she asks with almost each step.

"Long leaf pine," he replies each time she points to the same tree.

"Dat one?"

"Golden maple, Poppy."

"Dat one?"

"That's a Poppy."

She jumps up and down, clapping her hands in glee. "Pop-pee!"

"That's right. Poppy, just like you."

Sam makes a mental note to toss some poppy seeds around a couple parks where folks are unlikely to notice his subterfuge. His daughter won't always be so easy to please. He'll take advantage of her easy nature as long as he can.

## 6. Socioemotional Development in Infancy and Toddlerhood

### Today you will practice the following:

6.1  Summarize the psychosocial tasks of infancy and toddlerhood.

6.2  Describe emotional development in infancy, and identify contextual and cultural influences on emotional development in infants and toddlers.

6.3  Identify the styles and stability of temperament, including the role of goodness of fit in infant development.

6.4  Describe how attachment develops in infancy and toddlerhood.

6.5  Differentiate the roles of self-concept, self-recognition, and self-control in infant development.

Wendy keeps close watch on all three of her children. Although it's clear Clover and Leaf adore Poppy, it's equally clear they're growing increasingly jealous of the attention Sam gives her. She understands and wishes she could magically make everything better for everyone. The opportunity for Poppy to bond well with Sam will pass if they don't spend enough time together while she's small, and all of Poppy's parents want her to have a strong bond with him. At the same time, Clover and Leaf are very much aware that Poppy's getting special treatment right now, and they may already have figured out that she always will. So far, no one's taking anything out on her, except Brian occasionally when he ignores her in his adolescent temper tantrums, but Wendy worries Poppy will soon face trouble from all sides.

## 7. Physical and Cognitive Development in Early Childhood

### Today you will practice the following:

7.1  Discuss physical development in early childhood.

7.2  Compare Piaget's cognitive-developmental and Vygotsky's sociocultural perspectives on cognitive development in early childhood.

7.3  Describe information-processing abilities during early childhood.

7.4  Summarize young children's advances in language development.

7.5 *Contrast social learning and cognitive-developmental perspectives on moral development in early childhood.*

7.6 *Identify and explain approaches to early childhood education.*

On a balmy Wednesday evening in April, Sam, Wendy, and Brian sit on the Bells' deck with cold beers all around and some hors d'oeuvres. Wendy, who feels she knows both men well enough to navigate the conversation, speaks slowly, mindful of the outcome. They're talking about what's best for Poppy.

"I just don't understand the need," Sam's complaining. "Poppy's been in a pretty ordinary daycare all along. Why go to such an extreme opposite for preschool?"

Wendy mediates. "Clover and Leaf both attended The Goddard. It was perfect for them. I . . ." She paused and glanced at Brian. "*We* want Poppy to have the same opportunities her siblings had."

Brian jumps in with more than a bit of anger. "If it's about money, we're not asking you to pay any more each month."

"But it's not." Sam rolls the beer can between his hands. "I just don't know why it's necessary."

Wendy holds up a hand before Brian can point out that Sam isn't the parent who works in a school. "Why don't you go visit the school? Take a tour. Then visit a couple preschools. Either or both of us will go with you, or you can go by yourself. Whatever you're most comfortable with."

With obvious irritation, Sam admits the logic of Wendy's suggestion, and she smiles in relief. "I can do that."

Beside Wendy, Brian nods. "Fine. I'll go ahead and put the deposit down at The Goddard. That'll hold her place, and we can get it back if you feel that strongly she shouldn't go after you do your round-robin of preschools."

"Thank you for your patience," Sam says.

After Sam leaves, Wendy clears their mess from the deck, ignoring Brian as long as she can. She only wants what's best for Poppy, that's true, but thinking back, it was Brian who chose The Goddard for Clover and Leaf. Who's to say that is the right choice for Poppy? Who's to say that was the right choice for Clover and Leaf? Brian thinks it is; that's clear. Wendy wonders if maybe she should spend some time looking at other schools, too. She works in a public school. So does Brian! They should be open to possibilities other than the most expensive private preschool in the county.

She passes Brian between their bed and the master bathroom. Pausing midstep, she says, "I'm going to look at a few options, too. Not with Sam, just to make sure we really are making the best choice."

The look on his face tells her what he thinks of this idea, and he isn't happy. They don't speak again that night, and Brian sleeps in the den with a pillow and a blanket he pulls from the closet.

## 8. Socioemotional Development in Early Childhood

### Today you will practice the following:

8.1  *Discuss young children's emerging sense of initiative, self-concept, and self-esteem.*

8.2  *Summarize the development of emotional understanding, regulation, and behavior in early childhood.*

8.3  *Identify four parenting styles and their associations with child outcomes.*

8.4  *Compare biological, cognitive, and contextual theoretical explanations of gender role development.*

8.5  *Explain the function of play and the form it takes during early childhood.*

"Clover? Are you awake, Clover?" Poppy cracks the door to her sister's room and whispers, waiting for a response before she tries again. "Clover? It's Poppy."

Clover pulls the quilt over her head and groans. "I know who it is, Poppy. I'm 12, not stupid."

"Are you sleeping?"

"I *was*."

"Sorry." Poppy is sorry to wake Clover up, but now that she is awake, Poppy slips into the room and closes the door behind her. She climbs into the bed, ignoring Clover's attempts to kick her out. Snuggling under the quilt, she puts her head on the pillow beside Clover's. "Daddy's not here."

Clover turns away from her and says, "I wonder why."

"Do you know? Why? Why is Daddy gone again?" Clover breathes in and out a lot of times but doesn't answer her. After a minute, Poppy loses patience. "Clover? Why is he?"

"He and Mom are having trouble," she says, and her voice sounds a little funny, like maybe she's mad.

"Because of me," Poppy says, and she knows that's the reason even if Clover doesn't say it. "I'm sorry." She wishes just one time Clover would tell her she's wrong, but she never does. "I'm going to make a Pop-Tart. Do you want one?"

"No."

"Okay. I'll ask Leaf."

Clover makes an ugly laugh. "Don't bother. He definitely won't want one if Dad's gone again."

Poppy climbs from the bed and swipes at her cheeks, wet with tears. She doesn't want Clover to know she's crying. "Okay. I'll . . . I'll see you."

"See you," Clover says, but she doesn't turn around.

## 9. Physical and Cognitive Development in Middle Childhood

### Today you will practice the following:

9.1 *Identify patterns of physical and motor development during middle childhood and common health issues facing school-age children.*

9.2 *Discuss school-age children's capacities for reasoning and processing information.*

9.3 *Summarize views of intelligence including the uses, correlates, and criticisms of intelligence tests.*

9.4 *Examine patterns of moral development during middle childhood.*

9.5 *Summarize language development during middle childhood.*

9.6 *Discuss children's learning at school.*

In third grade, Poppy fails math, as much as a single subject can be failed in primary school. Miss Deering, her teacher, spends many hours with her in class, before class, after class, and meeting with her parents, but everyone is confused. Poppy's prior grades and scores on standardized math assessments indicate she should be completing work with flying colors, but she simply is not. It's Sam who voices the possibility no one's willing to contemplate.

The K–8 school at which both Wendy and Brian work is small, and in the upper elementary and middle grades, subject-specific teachers may cover an entire grade. Poppy's father Brian is the only math teacher for both the fourth and fifth grades. When Poppy leaves third grade, Brian will be her math teacher. Sam suggests that maybe she doesn't want to be in Brian's class. Offended, Brian reacts with hostile denial, but Wendy admits there may be merit to the idea. Brian has been out of the house more than in it lately, and she knows Clover and Leaf blame their sister for Brian's absence. The isolation at home hurts Poppy more than it might because she's always been so loved by both her brother and sister. She's not sure what the solution is. Transfer Brian to third grade for two years? Hardly. He isn't qualified cross-categorically, and he would divorce her if she suggested it.

"Poppy," she asks that night at bedtime, "how do you feel about homeschooling?"

Poppy looks at her as if she's just returned from Mars. "Homeschooling? Are you serious? That's the worst idea I've ever heard. I want to be at school with Clover and Leaf and all my friends."

"And having Dad next year for math?"

Wendy watches Poppy pale. Her narrow shoulders shrug under her nightgown. "I don't know," she says softly.

"You can't stay in school, Poppy," she exaggerates, "if you don't pass math, and you can't stay in school if you don't take math with Dad next year. So, you tell me what you want to do."

"I don't want to be in class with Dad. He hates me."

"Oh, Poppy." Wendy pulls her into her arms. "Dad doesn't hate you. He really doesn't."

"Do you promise?"

Wendy thinks back to her own childhood, when a parent's promise was all she needed to feel better. She nods. "I promise. Dad loves you very much, sweetie. Both of your dads do."

"Then why doesn't he ever sleep here anymore, and why does Clover blame me?"

"Those are harder questions, Poppy, and we will talk about them, but right now I need *your* promise that your math grades are going to look better in the future."

Poppy nods. "I promise."

## 10. Socioemotional Development in Middle Childhood

### Today you will practice the following:

10.1 Describe school-age children's self-conceptions and motivation.

10.2 Examine the roles of friendship, peer acceptance, and peer victimization in school-age children's adjustment.

10.3 Discuss family relationships in middle childhood and the influence of family structure on adjustment.

10.4 Analyze the role of resilience in promoting adjustment to adversity, including characteristics of children and contexts that promote resilience.

Wendy remembers when she thought of Clover as the Poppy Whisperer. Those days are gone. Clover is gone—along with Leaf and Brian. And Poppy wanders the house like a ghost. Although the divorce will be formal enough in a few months, custody isn't, at least not for now. All three parents manage to agree without much debate that the children should be able to choose their dwellings and change their minds and not worry about judges or guilt. For now, Clover and Leaf are living with Brian, but Wendy suspects this is as much because they want a break from Poppy as it is because they want to live with their dad. She misses them more than she can say, and when she thinks about it for more than seconds at a time, she can't help crying. The questions that follow are inevitable.

"Mom? Why are you crying?"

Wendy doesn't believe in lying to children so much as it's possible not to do so. "Just a little sad, Poppy. Nothing for you to worry about."

"Do you miss my brother and sister?"

"I do, yes." Wendy kneels and looks into Poppy's face at her level.

"Me, too."

They hug, and Wendy struggles for composure until Poppy releases her and wanders away to find some quiet activity to occupy her time. Wendy never really knows anymore. She probably should.

## 11. Physical and Cognitive Development in Late Childhood

### Today you will practice the following:

*11.1  Describe school-age children's self-conceptions and motivation.*

*11.2  Examine the roles of friendship, peer acceptance, and peer victimization in school-age children's adjustment.*

*11.3  Discuss family relationships in middle childhood and the influence of family structure on adjustment.*

*11.4  Analyze the role of resilience in promoting adjustment to adversity, including characteristics of children and contexts that promote resilience.*

Poppy, much to her own surprise, makes it through fourth and fifth grade math. Dad treats her like a regular student—thank God—when she's in class, but he also helps her on things she doesn't understand at home. She feels a lot better about things now. It's only when she's nearly ready for the middle grades at school that she begins having real problems.

She overhears her mom and dad arguing before dinner one night about how much Poppy looks like her father—Sam—and how much that bothers her dad—Brian—every time he looks at her. Clover walks by while they're fighting and gives Poppy an ugly look. She hates Poppy for being the bomb that blew up her happy pre-Poppy family. When Poppy wins the seventh grade science fair, demonstrating classical conditioning with a parakeet, a project she completes with her father—Sam's—help, she's so proud. She also senses the loosening of the last binds in her parents' marriage.

## 12. Socioemotional Development in Late Childhood

> **Today you will practice the following:**
>
> *12.1  Summarize the processes by which self-concept, self-esteem, and identity change during adolescence.*
>
> *12.2  Discuss the nature of parent–child relationships in adolescence.*
>
> *12.3  Examine the developmental progression of peer relations in adolescence.*
>
> *12.4  Analyze patterns of adolescent sexual activity including sexual orientation.*
>
> *12.5  Identify common psychological and behavioral problems in adolescence.*

Poppy is so excited. Her dads—both of them—and her brother *and* her sister—who is her favorite person in the world—are coming over for Thanksgiving dinner. She and Mom started cooking yesterday. They made a cake and two pies. Clover likes pumpkin pie, and Leaf likes apple. So does their dad, the one she shares with them. She likes cake best, and so does her other dad. Mom likes all sweets. They already boiled eggs they'll devil today; Mom says she needs to let Poppy touch them with her magic wand, and they'll be ready (haha). When she gets up Thanksgiving morning, Mom already has the turkey in the oven. Poppy puts a tiny apron on, and Mom hands her a bag of carrots and a vegetable peeler.

"Get to it."

"Okay!"

"You're chipper this morning."

"I love Thanksgiving," Poppy reminds her mom.

Mom laughs back. "I know. Now, let's get busy so we have food to eat when everyone gets here."

"Yes, ma'am."

They work together for hours. Mom tells her before lunch to go get a bath and put on something nicer than her Scooby Doo pajamas. Poppy wants to know who doesn't like Scooby Doo, but she's shooed from the kitchen and sent on her way. Once she's clean, she's allowed to set the table with the good china (she personally thinks they should use the good china every day) and put ice water in glasses all around the table. The doorbell rings at exactly two minutes before they're all supposed to arrive, and Poppy skids into the hallway to answer it, almost crashing into the windows beside the door when she can't stop.

"Clover!" she yells when she throws the door open.

Her sister glances in her direction for a second. "Hey."

Their dad and Leaf come in the house, and Clover pauses only long enough to not come in with Poppy's other dad. She goes straight to the stairs and heads for her room. Poppy decides to say hi to everyone and then go see Clover for a few minutes.

"Hi, Dad," she says, hugging Sam. "I'm really glad you came."

"I'm really glad you invited me, sweet pea."

Poppy stops in the hallway and looks up at him, hands on her hips. "Really? My real name is the name of a flower, and now my nickname will be the name of a flower? Puh-lease."

He laughs and hugs her again. "Fair enough. Let's go check on everyone else, shall we?"

"Will you? I want to go upstairs with Clover. I'll come right back."

"Okay. Run along then. I'll tell the others where you are."

"Thanks, Dad." Taking off down the hallway in her slick shoes, Poppy slides onto the bottom stair and runs headlong up them. At the top, she turns left and then right into Clover's room. She's glad Clover didn't close the door so she doesn't feel like she absolutely had to knock. Even so, she stops right inside the door and clears her throat the way she's seen grown-ups do. "Clover?"

"Go away, Poppy."

"You used to never tell me to go away," she whispers.

"Yeah, well, you used to *not* be the reason Mom and Dad got a divorce and I have to live with Dad."

Confused, Poppy says, "But you don't have to live with Dad! They said we could live where we wanted."

"Right," Clover says, sitting up and looking at her like she wanted to make her disappear with her eyes. "And where I want live is where you *don't* live. Got it?"

Poppy stares. "Got it," she whispers.

Poppy leaves Clover then. Walking to her own room, she thinks about her sister. Clover is graduating from high school in a few months and then going to college. She doesn't want her to leave home mad at her. Poppy doesn't know where Clover wants to live—with Mom or with Dad—but she's sure it isn't with Sam. If Poppy lives with Sam, then Clover can live wherever she wants to. Drying the tears she doesn't want any of her parents to notice, she walks downstairs slowly and asks to speak to her dad before talking to all of her parents. She hopes she doesn't break her mom's heart, but she has to fix Clover's if she can.

## 13. Physical and Cognitive Development in Adolescence

### Today you will practice the following:

13.1 Evaluate the "storm and stress" perspective on adolescence in light of research evidence.

13.2 Summarize the physical changes that occur with puberty and the correlates of pubertal timing.

13.3 Discuss brain development during adolescence and its effect on behavior.

13.4 Identify ways in which thinking changes in adolescence and how these changes are reflected in adolescent decision-making and behavior.

13.5 Discuss moral development and influences on moral reasoning.

13.6 Describe the challenges that school transitions pose for adolescents and the role of parents in academic achievement.

Poppy's ambivalence about living with Sam troubles her. She finds it painful that her dad is so understanding about her feelings, too. Her relationship with Clover is definitely better now that her sister lives with Mom again. Leaf still lives with their dad. He seems to view both Poppy and their mom as being at fault in his broken home and doesn't want much to do with either of them. Poppy misses them all. She misses her old life.

At the same time, she loves having her other dad so much of the time, and she's able to appreciate how much she missed not being with him more when she was little. He treats her like she matters and lets her go to either of her other houses anytime she asks for as long as she asks. She's pretty sure he's a saint walking around disguised as a man.

When she's 15 and staying with Mom for a few days (Clover visits Dad), she gets sick. In bed, vomiting, doesn't know what's up or down. Mom tries to get her to eat, but she can't. She pushes the food away.

"Take it out," she whispers. "Throw up."

"Okay, honey. I'm going." Mom leaves and returns. The smell of food is gone. "Can you tell me anything, Poppy? I'm really worried."

"Head," she whispers again. It's all she can manage.

After a pause, Mom says, "It's only 3:30. I think we should go to Dr. Lamb's. I know you think you can't get out of bed, but you can. Let's just get in the car and go. Come along, honey, I'll help you."

The walk downstairs, out into the sun, and the drive to the doctor's office are all excruciating. Once, Mom has to pause at a green light so Poppy can lean out her door and vomit. She's shivering and begging God to die by the time they get to Dr. Lamb's, the family's general practitioner. Fortunately for Poppy, it's late in the day, and Dr. Lamb doesn't have many patients waiting. The nurse takes her to a room where she can lie down to wait in the dark, and she doesn't even care how long it is that she waits. The room is cool, and there's no noise from anywhere until Dr. Lamb arrives with her mother. It takes less than a minute for the doctor to softly say, "Migraine," which Poppy's pretty sure she could've diagnosed herself.

She leaves and returns with the nurse. "Jamie will give you a shot, Poppy. It's going to hurt, but I think you probably won't even register the pain. In a few minutes, the migraine will start to wear off, but you might feel a little nauseous. If that's the case, ask, and Jamie will give you something for that. I'm giving your mom some prescriptions for the next time this happens."

Next time?

Everything Dr. Lamb says is true. The shot does hurt; she kind of knows that but finds she can't care. The shot is also magic, like ambrosia. In almost no time her shoulders become less tense as the pain ebbs. She keeps waiting for the headache to return, but it doesn't. Nausea takes its place.

"Throw up," she whispers to Mom, still in a roadkill state.

Mom leaves and returns with the nurse, who lifts her head and gives her a pill and a small paper cup of water. The pill doesn't work as fast as the shot, but it doesn't take long. Once she feels like she can open her eyes and speak without dying, Poppy asks for the doctor.

Dr. Lamb returns, nodding and smiling as she gives Poppy the once-over. "Looking better."

"Thanks," Poppy says softly, "to you."

"You had a question," Dr. Lamb said.

"You said 'next time' when you were in here before. Why do you think this will happen again? I haven't had a bad headache before."

Dr. Lamb sighs. "The best predictor of a migraine, Poppy, is a migraine. I hope you never do have another one, but after today don't you want to be prepared?"

She agrees that seems sensible and leaves with Mom soon after speaking to Dr. Lamb. On the ride home, Mom reaches across the seat of the car and touches her knee.

"You've got too much stress," she says.

Poppy looks out the window. "I don't have too much stress."

"You always take on too much. Like the divorce. Leaf. I know you blame yourself, but none of it is your fault. If you carry around all that guilt, it's going to start hurting you at some point."

Poppy, truly angry for maybe the first time, turns to look at Mom. "Not my fault? Those are just words, Mom. The same words you and Dad keep saying because you think somehow saying them makes me believe them? Everyone's actions—including the divorce but especially the isolation of my brother and sister—tell the true story. Say one thing; do another. My whole life is an ongoing remake of *Gaslight*."

"Poppy!"

"Just take me to Dad's. He can fill the prescriptions."

"If that's what you want."

She knows she hurt her mom's feelings, and part of her feels bad about that—not a big enough part. "It is."

## 14. Socioemotional Development in Adolescence

### Today you will practice the following:

*14.1 Summarize the processes by which self-concept, self-esteem, and identity change during adolescence.*

*14.2 Discuss the nature of parent–child relationships in adolescence.*

*14.3 Examine the developmental progression of peer relations in adolescence.*

*14.4 Analyze patterns of adolescent sexual activity including sexual orientation.*

*14.5 Identify common psychological and behavioral problems in adolescence.*

Poppy begins working a part-time job at the local supermarket and begins dating almost without the notice of her parents. Clover, 22, and Leaf, 20, are off at college, and her parents are all busy with their careers. No one really cares what she does with most of her time. Her bio-dad always wants to meet whatever new guy she's going out with, and her mom doesn't let any guy pick her up without coming to the door. Really, it's all pretty low key, though. She's pretty sure she could bring home her English teacher—Mr. Apple is so hot—and no one would notice—not that she'd actually date her English teacher because, ew, gross.

She starts dating Harry at the beginning of junior year. For Poppy, this means a reasonable amount of time to be asked to homecoming. She's not one of those girls who gets a new guy at the beginning of October and then feels like that's an auto-invite to the biggest event of the football season. You have to ease into that one. Harry—well, two and a half months is reasonable, respectable. There's one problem, though; she's definitely not going to have her first major event requiring pictures and all that entails if it involves the parental units—all three of them. If her mom had been successful in keeping Poppy's parentage from her dads, she would've been among the 1 to 3 percent of kids raised in the world by fathers who didn't sire them and didn't know they didn't. She'd checked. Does she really want to get into all that with Harry and, more importantly, Harry's parents? It bears thinking about.

"What's there to think about?" Harry asks her when she puts him off about homecoming. "You get a dress. I get a suit or something else *suit*able. You see what I did there?"

Poppy laughs. "Yes, I see."

"We become beautiful, take some pictures with everyone else down by the river, then eat a bunch of food, go the dance, and drink a bunch of bad not-spiked punch while we dance poorly, leave, eat some more, and then go home. Sounds simple to me."

"I wish it were that simple."

"What's not? Do you already have a date? Like a date you made back in February or something?" For a second he looks serious. "I'm not really serious, but tell me if you do."

"I don't," she assures him. "Can we just take pictures with your parents?"

Harry frowns. "That's most unexpected. You don't want yours there? Not even one of them? I know they don't live together, so maybe you don't want to make things awkward by having them together for pictures, but you don't want either of them there?"

No time like the present.

"I'm pretty sure I don't want *any* of them there," she corrects.

It's almost worth it just to see his face try to puzzle out her words.

"That's what I asked."

"No, it's almost what you asked. You asked don't I want either of my parents there when we take pictures, and 'either' implies two. I have three."

"Oh." She gives him another minute or so to work this out. "So, like you have two same-sex parents and a surrogate or something?"

"Or something, but it's a little more exotic than that." Poppy can't believe she's made it this far without being the complete gossip of her high school. Maybe it's true that everyone has their own problems and isn't concerned with anyone else's. Dang. Teenagers really are a selfish bunch. "I have parents, a mom and dad, who were married when Mom got pregnant with me. I was baby number three, if it matters."

"Okay . . ." Harry says. "So, how does that get you to three unless maybe one of them got remarried and you consider that person your parent also? But that's not so uncommon, right?"

"No, I don't think it is, but that's also not my story. When Mom got pregnant with me, she was having an affair with Dad's good friend, who as it turns out is my biological father. It's alternately polite and messy and unpleasant and pretty healthy. I don't know. I don't tell people, although my friends tend to know my mom and at least one of my dads."

Harry looks at her. "That's nuts."

"Little bit. Anyway, now you see why I asked if we could just have your parents there. I can ask only my mom, but I think that would hurt my dads' feelings. There's no way I could choose between my dads, and having both of them . . ."

"Is the rest of the events in your life, Poppy." Harry takes her hand. "It's just homecoming. Invite your parents for the love of Pete. I don't care if you don't care."

"Will your parents care?" she asks, worried.

"Are you kidding?" he says with a wide smile. "Mom will think she found the goose that laid the golden egg."

Poppy isn't sure about any of this, but she's willing to go along. All she has to do now is find a dress.

## 15. Physical and Cognitive Development in Emerging/Early Adulthood

> ### Today you will practice the following:
>
> 15.1  Describe the features and characteristics of emerging and early adulthood.
>
> 15.2  Summarize the physical developments of emerging and early adulthood.
>
> 15.3  Analyze physical and sexual health issues in emerging and early adulthood.
>
> 15.4  Compare postformal reasoning, pragmatic thought, and cognitive-affective complexity.
>
> 15.5  Explain how attending college influences young adults' development, and identify challenges faced by first-generation and nontraditional students.
>
> 15.6  Discuss vocational choice and the transition to work.

Poppy telephones each of her parents from her bio-dad's house. She doesn't want to have the coming conversation, but the uptick in migraines tells her it's time. Once she gets it out of the way, she'll go back to the monthly headache she gets with her period and the handful that always follow her attempts to reconnect with Clover or Leaf. Her dad—with whom she still lives—agrees to let her have her other parents over to dinner so they can all talk. She knows she can always count on his support.

At 5:45 p.m., she orders two pizzas, vegetarian for her mom and herself and all the meats for her dads. Pizza is easy to order and easy to clean up. She pulls out paper plates, a bottle of wine for Mom, and a couple beers. She gets herself a cream soda and waits. Mom and Dad arrive together, which she knew would happen. Dad told her he'd pick up Mom on his way over from his house. Her bio-dad comes in carrying the pizza, having met the delivery lady in the driveway.

"Did you tip her well?" Poppy asks.

He gives her the evil eye and sighs. "Yes, Poppy, I tipped her well. You'll break me just in tipping."

"The service industry is the working poor in this country," she reminds him, taking the boxes and throwing them on the table where her other parents wait. "Dig in, everyone. I don't know about you, but I'm starved." The statement isn't quite true. She's too nervous to be hungry, but she can eat. The smell of pizza makes everyone hungry so far as she knows.

Her dads open their beers, and she pours her mom's wine. Her parents comment on the little luxuries being afforded them, and she smiles. After their second slice, she says, "You might've guessed there's more to this dinner than pizza and the pleasure of one another's company."

Dad, not her bio-dad, says, "I hope so," making everyone else frown.

Poppy bites back tears. Nodding, she rushes on. "I asked you to come over because I have some important news to share and some important considerations to go through with you."

Her bio-dad clears away the pizza boxes, and Poppy reaches behind herself for the folder she's been waiting to pull out. There are several paperclipped stacks inside. She lays them one at a time except for the last two on the table. She closes the folder with the others still inside.

"These are acceptance packages from Arizona State, Georgia Tech, Tufts, Cornell, and Virginia Tech," she tells them. It's ridiculously difficult to keep the pride from her voice.

All three of her parents stare slack jawed at the stacks of paper and then at her. Mom speaks first. Poppy expected that.

"Oh, honey. I didn't even know you were applying anywhere. This is amazing. What validation for all your hard work! I'm so proud of you."

"Yes," her dads agree. "So proud of you, sweetheart."

"Thanks. That means a lot." And it does.

Dad—her bio-dad—counts and asks, "How did you pay for all the admissions applications? That had to be close to $500, Poppy."

She nods. "It was. I used money I've saved from working at the grocery store and birthday and Christmas money from you guys and the grands."

"You didn't have to do that," her other dad said. "We would've been happy to pay for you."

"I know," she tells him. "This isn't an indictment. I just wanted to show you my options."

"They're all far away," Mom says, but she doesn't sound like she's complaining. "Were they specific choices?"

"Yes, they were. I'm going to study ergonomics. Human factors," she clarifies when she sees their blank looks. "You know, man and the machine."

"Wow. That's—" Bio-dad gropes for a good word. "Impressive," he says at last.

"I don't know about that," Poppy says. "I just find it interesting. Remember when we hiked the Moonshine Trail last summer, and you showed me how to use a drone for conducting global positioning surveys?"

"Sure. That was a great trip."

"It was!" Poppy agrees. "I was so interested in those drones. I was dating that boy then, Harry. I don't know if you remember that, too, but we used to go to the park and fly kites when the wind was right. He had such pretty kites. Anyway, I started thinking about it then, how to create the perfect machines to assist humans in the human–machine interaction. It seemed really cool."

"I think it does, too," her other dad says. "So, which lucky school did you choose?"

"Oh, none of those," she tells him. Stacking all the packages into a neat pile, she puts them back into the folder and brings out the two remaining ones. "I'm going to West Point. Here's my acceptance," she says, pushing one to the center of the table, "and here's all the financial information." She pushes the second to sit beside the first.

"West Point?" Mom asks, sounding faint.

"Yes, Mom, West Point. Try to find it in you somewhere to be glad for me."

"Poppy," her dad says, "we are. We just didn't expect . . . West Point," he repeats.

Her bio-dad comes around the table and hugs her. "I'm proud of you, Poppy. This is an amazing achievement."

"Thanks, Dad."

"You said financials," he reminds her. "How much is this going to cost us?"

Poppy shakes her head. "Nothing. The U.S. Military Academy pays for everything.

My tuition, room, board—all of it's covered—and they give me a small stipend every month, too. I'm no longer on your dime."

Mom tries to interrupt, but Poppy holds up her hand. All of her parents look stricken. She knew this would be the difficult part, but there's nothing for it now but to plow through.

"Again, not an indictment, but kids are expensive. I know that."

"You've got it all planned out," Mom says, pale and uncertain.

"I do," Poppy tells her. "Try to be happy for me," *especially because you never even asked if I wanted to go to college.*

## 16. Socioemotional Development in Emerging/Early Adulthood

### Today you will practice the following:

*16.1 Summarize psychosocial development in emerging and early adulthood.*

*16.2 Discuss influences on friendship and mate selection and interactions in emerging and early adulthood.*

*16.3 Analyze the diverse romantic situations that may characterize emerging and early adulthood, including singlehood, cohabitation, marriage, and divorce.*

*16.4 Compare the experiences of young adults as stepparents, never-married parents, and same-sex parents.*

Poppy sits at one of the four small tables in the room dedicated to student clubs in the wing where psychology is housed at West Point. Her roommate and best friend Colleen Pierce sits adjacent to her as they plan the annual spring Psi Chi induction. She's participated in several events honoring cadets for this accomplishment or that achievement, but Psi Chi is close to her heart. The national honor society for psychology, while thriving, had a fairly defunct chapter at the U.S. Military Academy until a future ergonomist and future counselor decided to revive it last fall. Now they're days away from inducting the first group of cadets in more than six years.

"I still can't believe the registrar gave us all the names of cadets who qualify," Colleen says with a wide grin.

Poppy looks over the list and thinks about her classmates. "Well, when you think about requirements, it's really down to majors who have enough psych credits, right? I mean who here isn't going to have the GPA? All we needed was faculty sponsorship."

On cue, Major Wolfe sticks his graying head into the doorway, and they stand. Wolfe is the new Psi Chi faculty sponsor, for which both cadets are immensely grateful. "Bell, Pierce, how go the plans?"

"Almost finalized, Major Wolfe. Thank you again for supporting us," Colleen answers with a dimpled smile. She almost looks feminine when she smiles, but Poppy knows what lurks behind the benign façade. Colleen puts most of the male second-year cadets to shame in their physical training.

"Excellent." Major Wolfe turns to go. "Remember to let me know if you need anything."

"Thank you, sir," they both say before resuming their seats once he's gone.

"That man," Colleen whispers, "could make me forget I'm gay."

Poppy snorts in laughter. "That man," she rejoins, "is inappropriately named. He shouldn't be Major Wolfe but Major Fox because he is one major fox."

Colleen rolls her eyes. "Like he's never heard that one before."

"I never said I was a creative genius."

"Good thing," Colleen says, laughing, "or I'd have to call you out for false advertising."

Poppy stares at the empty doorway. "Do'ya think he's married?"

"Major Wolfe?" Geez, you do have some daddy issues, don't you? Not that it's terribly unexpected given your, ah, childhood situation."

"Har-dee-har, Anna Freud."

One week later, in a club room in Cullum Hall, Major Wolfe stands between Colleen Pierce (announcing cadet names at the podium) and Poppy (shaking hands and snapping photos). As each cadet walks past Colleen, Major Wolfe hands him or her a folder with a certificate recognizing the cadet as a lifetime member of Psi Chi, after which he shakes the cadet's hand and smiles in a roguish way for Poppy's camera—17 times. It's wonderful!

The adjoining club room holds the usual array of social niceties, passed by plebes hopeful of induction next spring. Once all cadets have their certificates, Poppy thanks Major Wolfe and the assembled guests and then directs them to the reception next door. The string quartet she'd wrangled from friends she knew casually plays in a corner, and she barely needs to do anything at all for the evening to continue on its path to success.

"We did it," Colleen breathes in her ear.

"We did!" Poppy grabs a flute of sparkling grape juice. "I'm so proud of the whole event. Aren't you?"

"I am actually. I'm glad we did it."

"Me, too." Beaming, she sips the drink, pinkened by the raspberries she suggested be dropped in the bottoms of all the glasses, and watches everyone chatting, eating, and enjoying the night they'd made. She never even notices Colleen slipping away to speak to someone across the room or the arrival of another second-year cadet she shares several classes with.

"Poppy, hi."

She looks around from her lazy watching of the crowd. "Nick Caldwell as I live and breathe. What brings you here tonight?"

He shifts the plate of cake and psi-shaped breadsticks into his other hand and smiles at her. "Jody Aitken is my roommate. I came to see him get inducted."

"Oh, cool! Jody's great. It's nice of you to come."

"It's nice of you to do all this. Jody said it's mostly been you and Colleen?"

"Pretty much," she admits. "Major Wolfe gave the club seed money we'll have to pay back with a fund-raiser. That'll have to happen soon. But yeah, I guess we did."

"I hope you're proud of yourselves. This is amazing."

She can feel herself blush, which annoys her. Compliments annoy her because she never knows quite what to do with them. Self-deprecate as usual, she supposes. "Thanks, but it's not like I'm off fighting a war or anything."

"It takes real leadership to engage a group of other leaders to pull off something like this."

"Careful, Nick. I'll start to think you care."

"Come to dinner with me tomorrow, and let's find out."

## 17. Physical and Cognitive Development in Middle Adulthood

> Today you will practice the following:
>
> *17.1* Summarize age-related physical changes during middle adulthood.
>
> *17.2* Discuss common health conditions and illnesses and the roles of stress and hardiness on health during middle adulthood.
>
> *17.3* Contrast the findings of cross-sectional and longitudinal studies of crystallized and fluid intelligence over adulthood.
>
> *17.4* Analyze changes in cognitive capacities during middle adulthood, including attention, memory, processing speed, and expertise.

Poppy's five-year service requirement as a result of attending West Point turns into ten years. Once she realizes she doesn't want to quit until she makes captain and that making captain will take her at least eight years, well, re-upping is the only real option open to her. It's fine. For the first five years, she and Nick (who knew it would be so easy to fall in love in the end?) manage the long-distance relationship pretty well. Neither of them has any say in whether they go, and they both know this is both the jobs and the lives they've chosen. It's hard, harder than anything Poppy's ever done, she thinks. Losing Clover's affection might've been worse, but she never lets herself think about that at all.

After they both reenlist, they have a slight amount of say in where they go. They get to prioritize a handful of tours, always with the acknowledgment that they could end up somewhere else entirely. Knowing this and knowing what they both want to do with their careers, Nick has a reversible vasectomy just before he does his first tour in Syria and she does her first in Afghanistan. It's not that they don't both like kids; they do. They just don't see kids of their own in their future, and they're both okay with that.

Working in Afghanistan gives Poppy new purpose, a direction focusing her so completely on the now that she sees nothing other than the job and the distance between when she sees Nick and when she'll see him again. Over a noisy, crackling phone line, she tries to talk to him about it.

"We're patrolling in the hills, protecting a school," she yells.

"Did you say school? It's hard to hear you."

"Yes! A school for girls! Nick, I need you to be here. I need you to help me on this project. Can you get some time?"

He manages four days, during which she shows him the school, the photos she's taken of it from every angle, and tells him her idea. She's the integrative person, the one to make the product work in conjunction with the persons using it. She needs Nick's physics expertise to bring it to life first.

"Can we do it?"

He nods. "If we can get the materials, we can do it. Let me talk to my CO."

"Thank you." She hugs him tightly. "How long do we have left?"

Nick checks his watch. "Seventeen hours until my chopper leaves. What do you have in mind?"

"Wanna get hitched? Chaplain's on duty. I already checked."

He doesn't look scared or angry—possibly a little amused, which helps her relax. "Think we need a marriage license for some period of time?" he asks.

Poppy shakes her head. "No. Not here. Just someone to recognize the ceremony and two witnesses." She squints at him. "You're sure?"

"I'm sure, and the sooner we get it done, the sooner we can design your cloak of invisibility for the girls' school."

"That's true," she agrees. "Just let me brush my teeth or something."

Nick grabs her hand and pulls her from the barracks. "You're a rock star, Bell. Leave everything for ten minutes, and come make us the Bell-Caldwells, would you?"

"I will," she says, and she says it again a few minutes later in front of the army chaplain, a first lieutenant, and a green beret—best day of her life.

## 18. Socioemotional Development in Middle Adulthood

### Today you will practice the following:

*18.1 Summarize the theories and research on psychosocial development during middle adulthood.*

*18.2 Describe the changes that occur in self-concept, identity, and personality during middle adulthood.*

*18.3 Analyze relationships in middle adulthood, including friend, spousal, parent–child, and grandparent relationships.*

*18.4 Discuss influences on job satisfaction and retirement planning during middle adulthood.*

It isn't perfect, but it's awfully close.

Poppy and Nick appear for the unveiling, oxymoronic at best, of their brainchild wearing dress uniforms. She wears a hijab in deference to the Afghani officials who will be present. The demonstration is partial; she and Nick plan to show how the cloaking mechanism works on a small segment of one wall inside the building being used for the ceremonial event. Military proprietary contracts as well as simple security precludes them doing a live demonstration on any real schools.

After prolonged introductions and much bowing and bestowing of honors backward and forward among leaders of both militaries, Poppy explains to the room how she came to think of the idea and the barest bones of Nick's design. Every couple sentences, she pauses and allows the translator to catch up. She tells the small room of people that she envisioned a tool that would essentially drop like a net over any portion of the school—all four outer walls of the school she's protecting, for instance—with hundreds of tiny cup-shaped mirrors attached to the web. The cups, facing outward, would reflect back to a viewer anything from the surrounding environment—sand, shrubbery, or mountains—while obscuring the structure behind the net.

As she explains, Nick moves into position and, at the appropriate pause, drops the small net of sample materials over the wall. The room of people draws a collective breath as the wall disappears and the room seems to take on a larger open space to the left of their seating area. As far as small demonstrations go, it's a success. They answer questions from the gallery, one of which comes from a small Afghani woman Poppy is surprised to learn is from America originally. Recently arrived to help with the same school, she has many questions about the cloaking tool, and Poppy makes an appointment to sit with her, Aminah Mohammed she says her name is, the following week.

Waiting for Aminah, Poppy's attention is stolen by a major in her unit. He's playing with a dirty child of indeterminate age and sex. She asks the store's proprietor about the boy—she thinks he's a boy—when he brings her coffee and learns that four-year-old Ismail was found wandering two days before after his village was bombed and his mother killed. His father fights with the Americans, she's told, but no one has seen him in months. Poppy hands the proprietor all the money she has and tells him to feed Ismail. Aminah arrives moments after the child receives a plate of strew, and Poppy shakes her head at the woman's look of understanding.

"The embassy is making short work of adoptions to Western families," Aminah tells her.

"He's a lovely boy," Poppy says, "but I'm clearly in no position to adopt any child, much less one living in an international war zone."

"No? My mistake. I thought for sure you had the look."

Poppy finds herself wanting to hide entirely inside her hijab. Maybe these women were onto something. "The look? What look?"

"The wounded mother look. The I've-see-you-and-now-you're-mine look." Aminah shrugs. "It happens and to far more stalwart souls than yours. What's his name?"

"Ismail," she says.

"I love that name."

Poppy nods. "Me, too."

## 19. Physical and Cognitive Development in Late Adulthood

### Today you will practice the following:

19.1  Discuss age-related changes in brain and body systems in late adulthood, and identify ways that older adults may compensate for changes.

19.2  Identify risk and protective factors for health in late adulthood.

19.3  Summarize common dementias including characteristics, risk and protective factors, and treatment.

19.4  Analyze patterns of cognitive change in late adulthood.

"*Ahbk ya amy,*" Ismail tells Poppy, leaning over her bed and kissing her cheek.

Poppy gives her son the evil eye. "If you loved me, you'd bring me a pad of paper and some pencils."

"It's because I love you that I don't do that," he counters. "Now sleep. You're sick."

"I have a cold!" she yells as he closes the door behind himself, leaving her alone to think thoughts she can't use productively. It's the worst sort of day she can have, an unproductive one, and her son knows it. Maybe he'll at least bring her soup—or whiskey. Whiskey is an acceptable substitute.

If she can't keep busy, she misses Nick, and that's too much to ask of her. She tries to think of going home with Ismail instead, of that long-ago visit from Afghanistan to see him settled and safe.

She makes it out of Afghanistan and returns home with a terrified but beautiful Ismail in tow. Against her better judgment and with no reason why she should, she takes him to Clover's. Her sister has a three-year-old son, and she knows Clover will guard her new nephew with her life. She visits the grave of her biological father, who'd died the previous year when she was in the Middle East and couldn't get home, and on her last day, she visits her mom and dad. Mom, as always, seems so frail and guilt ridden. Poppy hugs her and tells her she's forgiven. She and her dad do their awkward dance, and even though she suspects she won't see him again, it's the best she has.

"You should go meet your grandson," she says as she leaves. "He needs family now."

She returns to Afghanistan, detouring to Syria to spend a two-day furlough with Nick. The missile strikes the army base only hours after she leaves. All 31 soldiers inside when the missile hits die, including Nick. She tries mourning by throwing herself into her work in Afghanistan. Aminah is a wonderful friend and colleague, but it's never the same again. When her tour's up, she returns home, finishes her last year stateside, and gets out.

Poppy does an array of ergonomics contract jobs after her stint in the military. Mostly, she works for the Department of Defense, making enough money to buy a small house in Alexandria and raise Ismail on her own without worrying about going bankrupt. Now, here he is bullying her into bed when he knows what her memories do to her if she's idle. She finds it's like choosing a photo album to peruse. She can pick her first date with Nick, their wedding, the day she first saw Ismail, or the day she brought him home, the last day she spent with Nick, or the day she returned home for good without him. She understands mourning. People mourn losses every day. But she and Nick weren't even married a decade, and they'd never lived together in all the years they were wed. It doesn't seem fair.

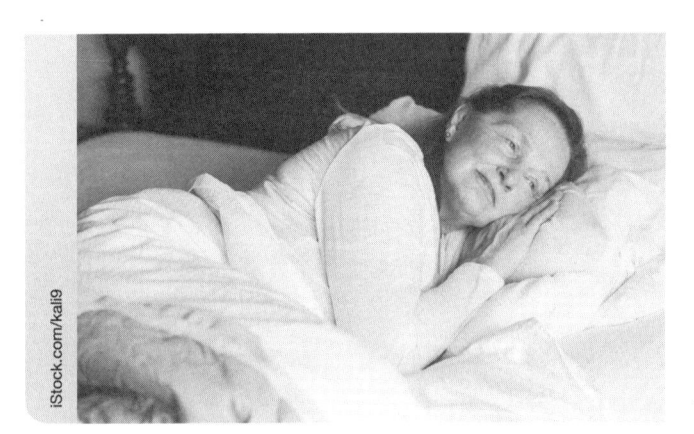

"*Úmi?*" Ismail asks, sticking his head back in the door.

"Yes, love?"

"I know you said it's just a migraine, but do you want to go to the doctor?"

Poppy shakes her head. "No, Ismail. Just find my medicine if you would. I'll be fine."

"Promise?"
"I do, yes."
So many promises. She can't remember now how many she's kept.

## 20. Socioemotional Development in Late Adulthood

*Today you will practice the following:*

*20.1 Examine the contributions of self-concept, personality, and religiosity to older adults' well-being.*

*20.2 Identify social contexts in which older adults live and their influence on development.*

*20.3 Summarize features of older adults' relationships with friends, spouses, children, and grandchildren, and identify how these relationships affect older adults' functioning.*

*20.4 Discuss influences on the timing of retirement and adaptation to retirement.*

Poppy is 60 when she begins attending the mosque with Ismail and his wife. She's never been particularly religious, and she's always allowed Ismail to know his heritage and find his own way. Going to the mosque with him reminds her of her years in Afghanistan, which were some of her best, and she slips into the hijab easily even if sitting behind a partition with the other women irritates her. She prays beside her daughter-in-law, Shalini, of whom she is fond, and some days she even forgets she's old, widowed, and nearly irrelevant.

"Don't say those things," Ismail chides whenever she says them aloud.

"It's true," she reminds him without any rancor.

"I'm glad you come with us, Ma," Shalini says, always with a gentle hand squeeze. "I don't like to think of you here alone."

"I don't like to be alone!" Poppy admits.

One day, Ismail traps her after this confession. "Good," he says, "then it's settled. You'll move in with us this week."

"What?"

She's glad of the insistence and the move. Although half of her feels like a burden, it's nice not to be lonely and to have her grandchildren climbing over her and begging for stories. She might have a year or a decade left. No matter, she's loved and only wistful for Nick, who so would've loved all this.

"I miss you every day, Nick," she tells him before going to sleep at night. "It won't be too long now."

## 21. Experience With Death and Dying

> Today you will practice the following:
>
> 21.1 Identify ways in which death has been defined and end-of-life issues that may arise.
>
> 21.2 Contrast children's, adolescents', and adults' understanding of death.
>
> 21.3 Discuss the physical and emotional process of dying as it is experienced over the lifespan.
>
> 21.4 Summarize typical grief reactions to the loss of loved ones and the influence of development on bereavement.

As Poppy slides into her 70s, she feels the approach–avoidance conflict of old age. She loves every minute with her family, but her grandchildren have grown and started college. They're no longer small toddlers needing bedtime stories or boo-boo kisses from Granny. She's a drain on Ismail and Shalini's resources. She's tired, so tired. The days seem so long without Nick and without fruitful work. Her doctor tells her at every checkup that she's depressed, a diagnosis Poppy rejects out of hand. She's not depressed; she's old. The doctor reminds her those two aren't mutually exclusive.

Poppy figures as much, which she tells Ismail and Shalini over dinner. Although she continues to be active as she always has been, the doctor's words stay with her. No one is surprised when she falls ill a few weeks after the doctor's appointment and claims vague ailments and an inability to get up and do her normal tasks. Worried, Ismail calls the doctor. Despite everyone's best efforts, Poppy passes away at age 79 from natural causes exacerbated by depression and loneliness.

# CASE DISCUSSION QUESTIONS

1. Before Poppy is born, her three parents decide that it will be in her best interests to know her biological father Sam. This is accomplished through an informal visitation and child support arrangement and shared decision-making for big issues that affect her. Brian will be her legal father because he and Wendy are married when Poppy's born. Wendy and Brian don't have to allow Sam visitation unless he takes them to court. How might Poppy's life have been different both positively and negatively across any and all domains (biological, cognitive, and socioemotional) if Sam had not been involved in her life? Be specific.

2. In early childhood, Poppy spends a morning in bed with her sister Clover. Both girls are sad because Brian has left on one of his many short trips away from the house. He leaves because he's still coping with Wendy's infidelity. Often, Poppy reminds him of this. Clover tells Poppy in a vague way that the situation with their dad is Poppy's fault, and she indicates that their brother Leaf feels this way, too. Poppy's prior life experiences suggest Clover is gentle and understanding with Poppy. This conversation will have additional impact on Poppy because she feels her sister's anger and hurt more than she might since they've been close in the past. How can we expect Poppy's perspective of their shared experiences to shape her future interactions with her siblings and her parents? Why?

3. In early adulthood, Poppy informs her parents of the colleges that have accepted her and the choices she's made about her future. Her parents are stunned; they didn't know she'd applied anywhere, even less that she had a plan. Why is this not an unexpected behavior from Poppy? If Poppy intended to keep her parents out of her decision-making process, what developmental domain factors (biological, cognitive, and socioemotional) best explain her decision to pursue the next step in her life on her own?

4. Poppy's entire life occurs over many decades that are, loosely, contemporary. Cars, telephones, televisions, and so on exist, but era-specific technology isn't presented (e.g., cell phones, space shuttles, and artificial intelligence). Would Poppy's life have been different if she were born in a specific period, earlier or later? If so, how? Be specific.

# 12   Aminah Mohammed

## Introduction

Welcome to your case study!

Congratulations! You will follow the lifespan of baby girl Aminah Mohammed. Try to use your best judgment, textbook, classmates, instructor, and supplementary resources to make the best decisions to help her grow.

This semester you will observe Aminah as she grows from infant to child to teen to adult. Who will she become in your care? Will you understand and agree with all decisions available within her circumstances? How will you feel about the tough decisions that forever shape her path in life?

## Meet Aminah Mohammed

Aminah is the first daughter and second child of Munya and Riad Mohammed. Munya is a 22-year-old Muslim American housewife who has a couple years' worth of college credits. Riad is 44; he has a master's degree and is the owner of several small businesses in their urban community. Riad's business concerns generate significant income for the family. Although they

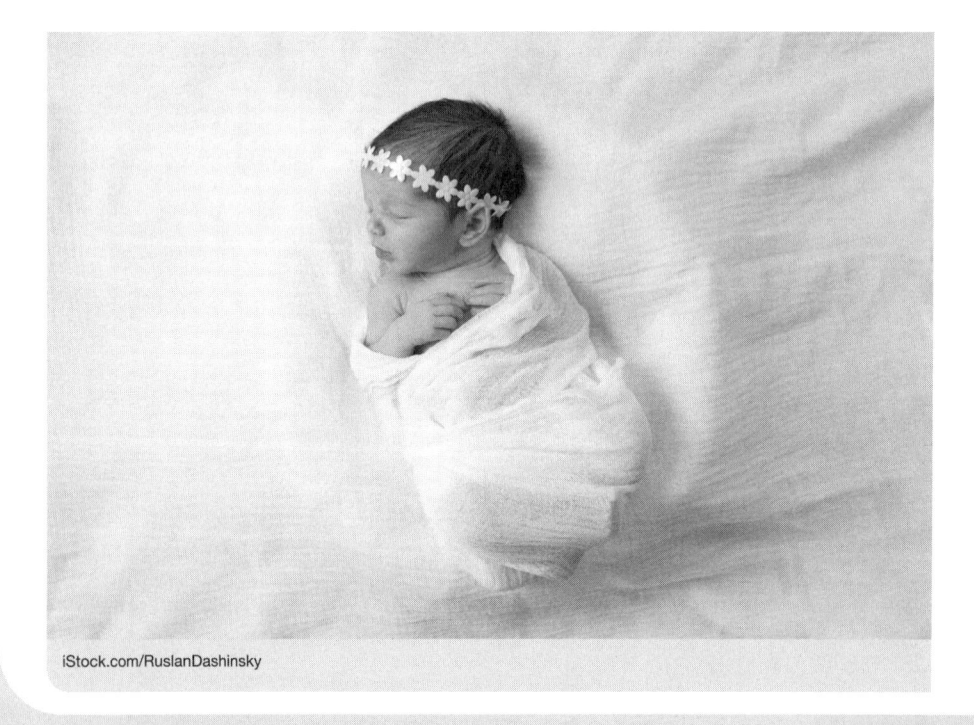

iStock.com/RuslanDashinsky

have this money, they live in an urban apartment building comprising all social classes but one that is primarily Muslim. Theirs is a small, close-knit community. The Mohammads have one other child, their son Naveed; Navi is two years old when Aminah is born.

Through this case study and your lifespan course, you will be asked to consider decisions regarding Aminah's physical, emotional, and cognitive growth and development from several perspectives: her parents', her brother's, and her grandparents' as well as those of her potential spouse, her potential children, other potential family members, friends, teachers, doctors, and supervisors.

Now let's get started.

## 1. Development and Its Influences

### Today you will practice the following:

1.1 Outline five principles of the lifespan developmental perspective.

1.2 Explain three theoretical controversies about human development.

1.3 Summarize five theoretical perspectives on human development.

1.4 Describe the methods and research designs used to study human development.

As a leader in their community, Riad can afford for Munya to receive the best prenatal care available to them. He hires Farah Abbas, the most experienced and well-regarded midwife in the community. Ms. Abbas has a master's degree in nursing with a postgraduate certificate in midwifery, and although she didn't deliver Naveed, this is because she lived in another location and not because she didn't want to or couldn't. Munya enjoyed a home birth when she delivered Navi and wants the same with Aminah. Ms. Abbas tells her that's fine as long as no complications arise during her labor and delivery. Aminah arrives after 36 weeks gestation with her father and brother waiting in the living room and two local women Munya trusts in the bedroom with her.

## 2. Biological and Environmental Foundations

### Today you will practice the following:

2.1 Discuss the genetic foundations of development.

2.2 Identify examples of genetic disorders and chromosomal abnormalities.

2.3 Discuss the choices available to prospective parents in having healthy children.

2.4 Describe the interaction of heredity and environment, including behavioral genetics and the epigenetic framework.

Aminah, conceived when Munya is just barely 22, is a mystery to her parents. Both decide not to learn the sex of their coming child, just as they chose with Navi. Riad, who wed Munya in an arranged ceremony five years before and has grown to love her deeply, doesn't hold that his wife should bear only boys into the world. He does believe it's better for her to be at home raising whatever children they have than it is for her to be, say, in one of his convenience stores cashing out sales. It's not an equitable trade for her time—the eight dollars he pays a high school kid to do that job versus the invaluable job she does raising children. If Munya wants to know Aminah's sex, she doesn't want to know enough to go against Riad. She's a peaceful, agreeable woman who generally lets others have their wishes because it makes her happy to do so and not out of any sense of duty. The baby will come out the same regardless of sex and will eat and cry and sleep the same, too. She can wait.

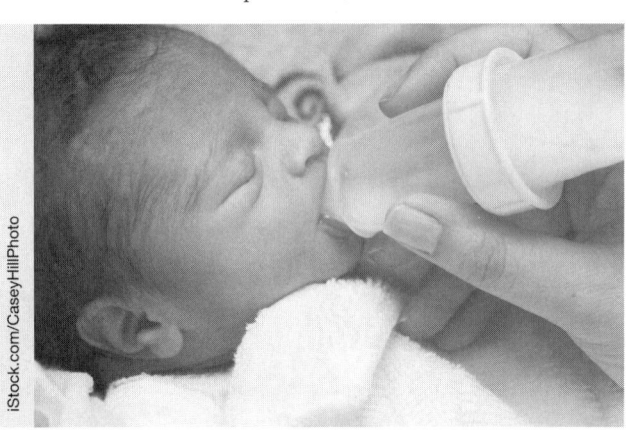

What cannot wait, Ms. Abbas scolds her, is Munya's need to control her morning sickness. It wasn't like this with Navi. The first trimester passing of nausea and occasional vomiting proves a myth, and Munya continues to feel wretched well past the halfway point of her pregnancy. She can barely tolerate any food at all, which Ms. Abbas worries over. Eventually, she prescribes a medicine to help with nausea and tells Riad to bring home a case of Gatorade from one of the stores. Munya improves after that, but Ms. Abbas remains concerned. Playing with Navi on the floor of their apartment, Munya waves off her worries. She feels her child moving with clockwork regularity. There's no trouble; she's sure of it.

## 3. Prenatal Development, Birth, and Newborn Experience

### Today you will practice the following:

3.1 *Describe the three periods of prenatal development that begin with conception.*

3.2 *Identify how exposure to teratogens can influence the prenatal environment.*

3.3 *Explain the process of childbirth.*

3.4 *Discuss the neonate's physical capacities, including development in low-birth-weight infants.*

When Munya is 36 weeks pregnant, she feels her labor begin. Having Navi so recently, she waits a bit to make certain this isn't false labor, and when she knows her child really will be born in the next day, she telephones Riad at the store where he's working that day. Riad calls Ms. Abbas, who arrives within half an hour and checks Munya's progress. She tells Munya that, yes, her baby will be born in the next eight or ten hours probably and, settling her on the birthing mat, makes lunch for Naveed and tea for herself.

Riad arrives and sits in the living room to wait with Navi. They play games and watch television, then, assured by Ms. Abbas that the baby won't be born very soon, they go out for a quick dinner. Riad bathes his son and puts him to bed on the sofa beside him when they return. Two local women he recognizes as being part of Munya's prayer circle and close friends of hers have arrived by this time and are in attendance in the bedroom where Munya struggles to deliver their baby. Ms. Abbas comes into the living room to tell him that Munya is fine, and his child should be arriving soon.

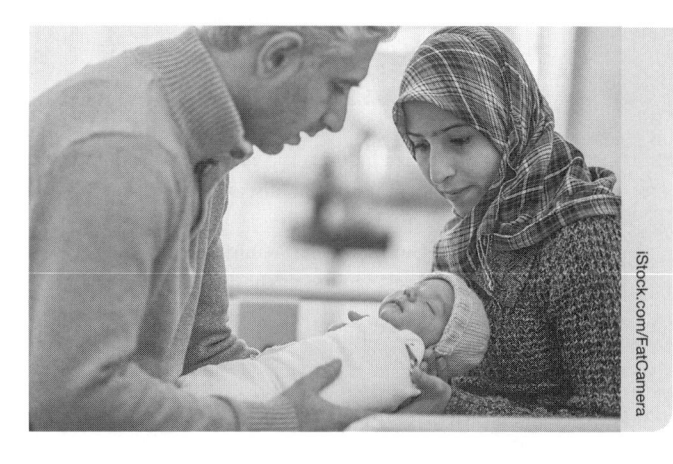

It seems to take forever and in fact takes two and a half hours longer than her first labor, but Munya delivers Aminah just after midnight. Aminah is small, 5.4 pounds; although she's technically full term, she seems frail to her parents. The midwife says she has good tone, color, and lusty cries, and they should try not to worry too much. Dr. Ramanujan, the local pediatrician for almost everyone's children, will be by in the morning to check her out thoroughly, but Ms. Abbas sees only a healthy, if rather tiny, baby. She removes the soiled linens from the birthing mat and helps Munya into her own bed. Checking everyone over once more and finding them in tip-top shape, she says good night, promising to return in the morning.

## 4. Physical Development in Infancy and Toddlerhood

### Today you will practice the following:

*4.1*  Discuss growth and the role of nutrition in development during infancy and toddlerhood.

*4.2*  Summarize brain development during infancy and toddlerhood.

*4.3*  Compare infants' early learning capacities for habituation, classical conditioning, operant conditioning, and imitation.

*4.4*  Describe infants' developing sensory abilities.

*4.5*  Analyze the roles of maturation and contextual factors in infant and toddler motor development.

Munya holds Aminah while an active Navi plays at her feet. Dr. Ramanujan, whose pediatric practice is run from the first floor of his two-story home, speaks to Navi now and then while examining the baby. Munya strokes her head and asks the worried questions she committed to memory before coming.

"Ms. Abbas said she was 'small-for-date,' you remember?"

Dr. Ramanujan nods. "I do, but do you remember when we talked about that the day Aminah was born?"

"Yes. I just don't understand. I read about this condition, small-for-date, and I don't know why my Aminah was born so. I didn't have any of the risk factors I read about."

Dr. Ramanujan raises one eyebrow at her. Riad does the same sometimes, and he usually follows the expression with a comical rebuke of some sort. So does the doctor. "My patients," he says, "always reading, reading, reading. Why don't you read a good novel? Or the *New York Times*? Don't read about illness and disease. Please. You make my job so much harder when you do."

They both laugh.

"But then why?" Munya pushes. She's assertive regarding the children's health.

"Well," he says, "she was just on that line between full term and premature. A few days earlier and we would've said she was preterm and a healthy weight for her gestational age. These are the best definitions and guidelines we have, Mrs. Mohammed, but they're not as specific as we like to believe. For instance, does it make sense to you that on one day, Aminah is premature and of good size and the next day is not premature and of insufficient size? We draw a line, and 98 percent of the time it works."

"I see," Munya says, nodding. She thought she did, too.

"Good, because this little girl is happy and clearly healthy. She's hitting all her milestones and shows nothing to worry about that I can see. Shall we make her cry now with a couple vaccinations?"

Munya laughs. "Yes. I think that would be good for both of them. Then I can take Navi for an ice cream and put this little one down for a long nap." She looks at Dr. Ramanujan in complete gratitude. "Thank you."

"That's what I'm here for," he replies.

## 5. Cognitive Development in Infancy and Toddlerhood

### Today you will practice the following:

5.1 *Discuss the cognitive-developmental perspective on infant reasoning.*

5.2 *Describe the information processing system in infants.*

5.3 *Discuss individual differences in infant intelligence.*

5.4 *Summarize the patterns of language development during infancy and toddlerhood.*

Munya stands at the stove cooking. Dinner takes a long time. They're eating lemon-garlic steak, eggplant, and rice tonight, and she likes a tender steak. She doesn't want to overcook or end up steaming it. Keeping focused on this delicate task is a challenge with little miss distraction at her feet. Glancing down, she laughs at Aminah, sitting in front of the children's cabinet full of plastic bowls and cups. She has two cups, one in each hand, banging them together like some musical instrument and singing along with her own song.

"Pretty," Munya tells her, and Aminah looks up and smiles. She scoots on her diapered bottom and bangs some more. "Don't get carried away there."

Navi runs into the kitchen, sliding on his socks. "What's pretty?"

"Aminah's music," she says, pointing with a spoon.

On his knees, Navi walks to his sister and holds out a hand. "Can I play?"

Aminah hands him a cup and gets another from the cabinet. Together, they sit and sing while Munya returns to cooking. She thinks back over Aminah's short life. It's hard for her to remember when her baby went from a smiling, inquisitive but largely passive recipient of her world to this interactive model, learning and squirreling away that knowledge for future use. Glancing back at Navi and Aminah, she smiles again. If they were any cuter, she might die of baby overload.

## 6. Socioemotional Development in Infancy and Toddlerhood

### Today you will practice the following:

6.1 Summarize the psychosocial tasks of infancy and toddlerhood.

6.2 Describe emotional development in infancy, and identify contextual and cultural influences on emotional development in infants and toddlers.

6.3 Identify the styles and stability of temperament, including the role of goodness of fit in infant development.

6.4 Describe how attachment develops in infancy and toddlerhood.

6.5 Differentiate the roles of self-concept, self-recognition, and self-control in infant development.

Riad, who works hard to have no favorite child, is beloved by Aminah. Although Munya has no trouble with the baby ever and Aminah responds rapidly and with pleasure to any overtures Navi makes, she absolutely shines when Riad returns home each night. Munya jokes that if they opened the big dictionary on the bookshelf and turned to the entry for "daddy's girl," it would read simply *Aminah Mohammed*. Navi displays no jealousy. Munya believes this is because the baby is passed so frequently among them when Riad is home. Aminah also self-soothes better than her brother did, lying in her basket in whatever room Munya is in, babbling to herself or sucking her thumb. She shows no hesitance with strangers, not yet anyway, and she's the current darling at the mosque nursery. Munya, always striving to be a good mother and wife, loves the family she's building and can't help smiling whenever she sees either child but particularly when she catches sight of them together.

# 7. Physical and Cognitive Development in Early Childhood

## Today you will practice the following:

7.1 *Discuss physical development in early childhood.*

7.2 *Compare Piaget's cognitive-developmental and Vygotsky's sociocultural perspectives on cognitive development in early childhood.*

7.3 *Describe information-processing abilities during early childhood.*

7.4 *Summarize young children's advances in language development.*

7.5 *Contrast social learning and cognitive-developmental perspectives on moral development in early childhood.*

7.6 *Identify and explain approaches to early childhood education.*

Aminah is four the first time she gets into trouble with her parents. The unfairness of it makes her even angrier, because it's all Naveen's fault, Naveen who took her abacus and told her she didn't need it because she was a girl. First, *wrong*. Second, so what if she hit him? He's *wrong*. She uses the abacus as well as he does, and he's six. They're both sent to their rooms by *Al'umu*, Mommy, and told to wait for *Baba*, Daddy, to get home. That's fine, Aminah thinks, let's just wait for *Baba*.

She hears him come in and sits quietly to listen to him talk to *Úmi*. She doesn't say much. Navi took the abacus, and Aminah hit him. Yes, that's the story. *Baba* doesn't come to her right away. *Úmi* calls for her to eat, and she sits at the table with *Baba* while Navi has a talk with *úmi*. Then everyone switches places.

"Your mother tells me you hit your brother today, *hubibi*," *Baba* says to her, sitting on the edge of her bed where she's lying. He holds her hand, so she thinks maybe she's not in too much trouble.

Aminah nods. "Yes, *Baba*, but—"

He holds up a hand. "I know what Naveen did and what he said to you."

"He was mean!"

"Those were not nice words, and he shouldn't have taken your abacus."

Aminah risks a glance at his face. "Can I have it back?"

*Baba* moves his head side to side, thinking about it. "I should bring you a new one. Yours is probably best left in your brother's coarse boy hands now."

"Okay?" Aminah isn't finished. "What about what Navi said? He said I didn't need it because I was a girl! That's so mean, *Baba*!"

"I asked *Úmi* to talk to him about that," he says.

"Why *Úmi*? He's afraid of you. At least a little," she adds quickly, not wanting to hurt his feelings.

"*Úmi* is better because she, too, is a girl, yes? I want Naveen to be reminded that ours is a family where girls are not only allowed but expected to excel. Your mother, she is bright and eager to learn constantly. It's one of the things I love best about her."

Aminah smiles a little, feeling better. "Did she tell him he's *wrong*? Because he is *wrong*."

He does his head thing again, and she fights the urge to put her hands on his ears and hold it still. "She did, yes, but she was more interested in learning why he said those things to you, where he learned to think that."

"The mosque," she whispers.

*Baba* frowns at her. "How do you know that? Our mosque doesn't teach such things, and our imam doesn't lead us to believe them either."

"I know because I've heard other boys say it." Aminah, indignant, frowns at him. "They're *wrong*, too."

"Yes," *Baba* agrees, "they're wrong, too. You can do anything academically your brother can, and if he doesn't learn to think better, you'll be doing more than he will because I'll ground him until he's 40." She laughs at that. "Not so fast, *hubibi*. You still did a very bad thing. What does the Quran say? You know this well."

Aminah says softly, "Compete with one another in doing good."

"Yes," her father says, "and is striking your brother in anger doing good?"

"No," she replies, shaking her head, "but he—"

"Aminah," *Baba* warns, "this isn't about Naveen, and he will be dealt with. This is only about you."

"Okay, *baba*."

"Good. Thank you, *hubibi*. Now, how shall we settle the matter?"

"I can give up rice pudding for the week?" Aminah whispers. She loves rice pudding, and *Úmi's* is the very best.

*Baba* shakes his head. "No, I think not. I prefer not to punish you. In this house, we don't hit, and we don't act in anger. I would rather you think of a positive—good, I mean—way to make this right, as will Naveen," he promised.

"Okay. Can I think about it tonight?"

"Sure." Standing, he bends to kiss her head. "I love you, *hubibi*."

"I love you, too, *Baba*."

In the morning, Aminah and Navi sit in the kitchen discussing their bargain. When *Baba* enters for his morning coffee, Aminah tells him proudly, "I'm going to make Navi's bed for one week to say I'm sorry for hitting him, and to say sorry for taking my abacus, he's going to teach me the parts of the *abjad* I don't already know so I can write the whole Arabic alphabet."

*Baba* nods. "I think those sound like excellent compensations. Good. No more mischief. Your mother doesn't need the hassle."

"Yes, *Baba*," they promise, and the world resumes its turning for the Mohammed household.

## 8. Socioemotional Development in Early Childhood

Today you will practice the following:

*8.1 Discuss young children's emerging sense of initiative, self-concept, and self-esteem.*

*8.2 Summarize the development of emotional understanding, regulation, and behavior in early childhood.*

8.3 Identify four parenting styles and their associations with child outcomes.

8.4 Compare biological, cognitive, and contextual theoretical explanations of gender role development.

8.5 Explain the function of play and the form it takes during early childhood.

Aminah's day, fairly structured, includes lots of time with *Úmi* helping her learn things she'll need to know for Kindergarten. They do math and spelling, read storybooks, color, and craft. Some things they do only on certain days (Monday is music day), and some things they do every day (math and prayers). Aminah has lots of breaks in between things, too. *Úmi* has to clean the house (Aminah helps sometimes), and she has to walk to get Navi from school (Aminah goes with her), and they make dinner together for the family before *Baba* comes home. Her favorite part of most days is going to the big city park two blocks from their apartment. When the weather is nice, they go every day for a little while before walking to Navi's school.

At the park, Aminah gets to play with lots of other children, including girls, which are woefully lacking in her apartment building. They have so much fun! The park has beautiful trees to climb or dance under, and there's a tree fort built around one of them that all the children like to play in when they can find space. There are two spinny things one of the moms calls a witch's hat. Aminah loves those; she can stand and hold on while *Úmi* or someone else starts it spinning. Sometimes she goes so fast that she gets dizzy.

On quiet days, some of the children like to play school. Aminah is always the teacher. On a warm day just before Navi's school gets out for summer, a new girl comes to the park with her mother. She calls herself Samira Saab, and Aminah asks her to play school with some of the other kids. Samira shakes her head no and runs away to the tree fort. Following, Aminah climbs up behind her and asks why she doesn't want to play. She promises that all the children are nice, and she never plays a mean teacher. Refusing still, Samira explains that she isn't allowed to do things like read and write, and she doesn't want to get into trouble. Aminah doesn't know how to feel about Samira's announcement or how to respond. After backing down the tree fort's ladder, she returns to her friends, but she asks her parents about it at dinner.

"Did you see her mom didn't speak to Mrs. Ali either? Why?"

*Baba* says, "I can only guess, Aminah, but Mrs. Ali doesn't wear the hijab. If your new friend Samira has such restrictions imposed on her, then Mrs. Ali is probably of a very strict behavior code. I don't know this name, Munya. Saab, you said, Aminah?" She nods. "They must go to the old mosque just outside the city."

"Probably," *Úmi* agrees. "Do you understand why I wear the hijab, Aminah?"

"Because the Quran tells you to cover your head?"

Her mother smiles but shakes her head. "Actually, no, it doesn't, and actually Islam isn't the only religion in which women choose to cover their heads. The important thing for you to understand, and you—" she says, turning to Navi for a second and then back to Aminah, "is that I do choose to wear it. All women of Islam choose whether or not to cover their heads and how. Mrs. Ali doesn't. That's her choice."

"But I thought the Quran—" Aminah says and stops.

"No, *hubibi*. The Quran only tells us to be modest of dress, and how we choose to do that is up to us. What do you see Mrs. Ali wear every day?"

This one was easy. Aminah says, "Long sleeves and long pants or skirts. She doesn't cover her head or hands, but everything else is covered. She probably covers more than you do!" she adds, thinking hard about it.

"She might," her mother says. "So, you see, the head is important, but it isn't the only way to be modest. Clearly, this is a very important point for Mrs. Saab, and it's a less important one for Mrs. Ali. Most of us? We just choose. I like the hijab. It makes me freer to be me in so many ways, but you may choose differently."

"I don't think so," Aminah says seriously.

"Well, I hope not, but we have a long time to see about that." *Úmi* points her fork at Aminah's plate. "Now, finish your peas, please."

## 9. Physical and Cognitive Development in Middle Childhood

### Today you will practice the following:

9.1 *Identify patterns of physical and motor development during middle childhood and common health issues facing school-age children.*

9.2 *Discuss school-age children's capacities for reasoning and processing information.*

9.3 *Summarize views of intelligence including the uses, correlates, and criticisms of intelligence tests.*

9.4 *Examine patterns of moral development during middle childhood.*

9.5 *Summarize language development during middle childhood.*

9.6 *Discuss children's learning at school.*

In elementary school, Aminah is allowed more responsibility at home. Some of this she wishes she could shirk (who really gets excited about cleaning bathrooms?), but some of it she enjoys (being in the kitchen with *Úmi* is always fun). One of the coolest skills she develops at her mother's side is what *Baba* calls "creative food planning." Aminah doesn't think their menu strays much from the normal, but she becomes invested intellectually in seeing how she can divest the week's groceries to maximize the family's consumption. Naveen calls her a nerd, of course, but she knows he's secretly impressed. She also knows part of his being impressed comes from the fact that she doesn't care that he's impressed. *Úmi* on the other hand? Yeah, she wants her mother's approval. Every week, she attacks the groceries from more and more daring angles, seeing how far she can push their traditional recipes to make the best use of ingredients. The day in sixth grade that her mom tells her she's proud of her is probably the best day in all of Aminah's life.

## 10. Socioemotional Development in Middle Childhood

### Today you will practice the following:

10.1 *Describe school-age children's self-conceptions and motivation.*

10.2 *Examine the roles of friendship, peer acceptance, and peer victimization in school-age children's adjustment.*

10.3 *Discuss family relationships in middle childhood and the influence of family structure on adjustment.*

10.4 *Analyze the role of resilience in promoting adjustment to adversity, including characteristics of children and contexts that promote resilience.*

Aminah sits on the lower landing of the fire escape allocated to her family, the Abdulrashids below them, and the El-Amins below them. She can see into the El-Amins' living room from her vantage point and is glad Mr. El-Amin agreed to the garden in exchange for half the harvest from his landing. The Abdulrashids had, too, and *Baba* told her she was a shrewd negotiator. Aminah doesn't know about that; she's just so happy to be able to try out her idea that she would give all the food away.

Today, she's building the big planters. Thanks to Naveen, she has better sketches with good measurements. Mr. Nejem cut all the lumber for her, and Naveen collected it from Mr. Najem's store two days before. Now, Saturday, Aminah's starting. She has a power drill, screwdrivers, screws, and a cast-off pair of plastic safety glasses. Everything works perfectly for the first half hour, and she's three-quarters of the way through the planter outside the El-Amins' living room when Samira Saab wanders by.

She stops and points at Aminah's work. "What are you doing?"

"Building a planter so I can plant a garden," Aminah replies after turning off the drill and lifting the safety glasses from her face.

"Why?"

This is the silliest question Aminah's ever heard. "Because I want to. Why are you walking down the street?"

"Because my mother needs milk from your father's store."

Oh. Maybe hers was the silliest question. "Sorry." She gestures to the building supplies around her. "Hang around if you want. I'm planning a really good time today."

"Maybe next time," Samira says, but her face tells Aminah she does want to stay. Aminah nods. "Sure. Anytime."

Samira walks away in the direction of one of *Baba*'s stores, and Aminah replaces the safety glasses. In no time, the box is built, and after giving it the once over, she moves up a floor to the landing outside the Abdulrashids' apartment. Her goal for the day was to build the three planters and fill them with potting soil. At the rate she's going, she might even be able to hang the pots in their places.

She glances down the street where Samira has disappeared and feels a tug. It seems like they're on opposite sides of an invisible line, and if one of them could cross over, they could be good friends. Like Samira said, maybe next time.

## 11. Physical and Cognitive Development in Late Childhood

### Today you will practice the following:

*11.1 Describe school-age children's self-conceptions and motivation.*

*11.2 Examine the roles of friendship, peer acceptance, and peer victimization in school-age children's adjustment.*

*11.3 Discuss family relationships in middle childhood and the influence of family structure on adjustment.*

*11.4 Analyze the role of resilience in promoting adjustment to adversity, including characteristics of children and contexts that promote resilience*

"*Úmi?*"

"Aminah?" her mother replies when she slips into the kitchen late at night. She's interrupted her mother's tea; that's clear. "Can I help?"

"Maybe. I wanted to ask a favor."

"Go ahead. I make no promises, but I think you know that if it's within my power, I'll try to make whatever it is happen."

"I know." Aminah sits at the table across from her mother. It never occurred to her that Munya could age, but a handful of gray hairs thread their way through the long, black ponytail. She stares a minute, wanting this picture of *Úmi* to be the one she never forgets. Her mom is so beautiful. "Ah, sorry. I want to know if you care if I plant a garden."

*Úmi* laughs. "And where do you plan to plant it? We're in a third-floor walk-up, and there's no dirt anywhere around us."

"I did think about that before coming to you, you know." She pulls a handful of pretty terrible sketches from the pocket of her bathrobe. An artist she would never be, but the drawings get the point across. She hopes. "I want to use the fire escape. See how I've got different sorts of planters all the way down? We've got two landings where I can set bigger planters for things that can't go in pots or rail boxes. Then I can use hanging pots for vines like beans and stuff and the rail boxes for everything in between. I think, if I stagger the seeding just right, I can have a really good cycle of crops over several months."

*Úmi* raises her brows and scrutinizes the sketches. "I'm impressed, Aminah. You've done a lot of work on this project."

"I have," she says, proud of herself. "What do you think? It won't be cheap. I priced the potting soil and sand as well as the materials to make the big planters. No reason to buy those. Also, the hanging pots will have to be bought, but I think I can figure out how to make the rail planters, too. All the supplies totaled come to just over $300." Aminah cringes, wondering if this will be a deal breaker.

"I assume," her mother says, "that this does not include any plants or seeds."

"That would be correct."

They sigh together, but *Úmi* collects the sketches and taps them into a neat rectangle. "I'll talk to *Baba* about what can be exchanged from his store with Mr. Nejem at the home improvement store. Nejem may also have some plants or seeds available. I'm sure we can cut the costs in half, and I'd like to see what you can do with this, Aminah."

Beaming, she jumps up from the table and runs to the other side. She throws her arms around *Úmi* and squeezes. "Thank you. Thank you so much. This is going to be great!"

## 12. Socioemotional Development in Late Childhood

> ### Today you will practice the following:
>
> 12.1 Summarize the processes by which self-concept, self-esteem, and identity change during adolescence.
>
> 12.2 Discuss the nature of parent–child relationships in adolescence.
>
> 12.3 Examine the developmental progression of peer relations in adolescence.
>
> 12.4 Analyze patterns of adolescent sexual activity including sexual orientation.
>
> 12.5 Identify common psychological and behavioral problems in adolescence.

Aminah's studying for her last test in elementary school when her father comes home early on a Thursday. *Baba* never comes home early. She can hear the lowered voices of her parents talking in the kitchen and carefully cracks her bedroom door to listen. Across the hall, Navi looks at her through a similar crack in his door. The conversation comes to her in disjointed sentences, but the significance is easy to understand.

"The bank turned us down for the mortgage," *Baba* says quietly.

*Al'umu* replies in a voice Aminah recognizes as confused and a little disbelieving. Bad things don't happen to them. "I don't understand, Riad. How is that even possible? With the money we have saved, we could buy the house outright. Your credit is perfect, and you have exemplary business records for how many years?"

"Enough years," he says.

"What did they say? Did they give a reason?"

"Presumably there was 'an issue with the appraisal,'" *Baba* tells her with a lot of sarcasm in his voice.

Aminah closes her door. She's heard all she needs to. They're not going to move into the house her parents want to buy. It's like the one day she went to school and someone had slipped a note inside her locker. When she found it, she didn't understand why the person had written

"TERRORIST" in black magic marker. The guidance counselor tried to explain it to her but only confused her more. The principal said he would try to find the person responsible, but only when her dad came to the school to meet with the principal did Aminah really feel like anything would get done. At home, her mother explained to her about the World Trade Center attack and how easy it is to put all people of a certain type into a basket.

"Remember when Samira Saab's mother wouldn't speak to Mrs. Ali because she didn't wear a hijab?" Aminah nodded. "Same thing. Some Muslim women think 'no hijab, no morals' when that's obviously not true. Mrs. Ali is as pious as any woman you could meet."

Aminah thought that made a little sense.

"And think of all the followers of Islam," *Baba* added. "Many people think Muslims look like we look, and they do; that's true, but only maybe 25 percent, yes? Just as many are African, and even more are from the Southern Asian nations. If everyone's looking at us, they're really not learning much about Islam, are they?"

"That's sad," Aminah remembers saying.

"It is," her mother agreed.

Her principal didn't make any effort, even though he assured her father he would, to find the jerk who left the note in Aminah's locker. The boy was caught only because he bragged about it in the gym locker room, and Navi heard him and told the teacher. Listening to her parents talk about the house they aren't buying anymore, Aminah is reminded of that incident and learning the lessons of how easy it is to pigeonhole people. Everyone does it, but it's easy to feel like you're the only target when you actively are a target. She thinks about Mrs. Ali, who is whispered about behind her back because she doesn't cover her head, and she wonders if people who aren't Muslim know that the Torah and the Gospels of Jesus are two of Islam's four holy books. She wishes she could tell them.

## 13. Physical and Cognitive Development in Adolescence

### Today you will practice the following:

13.1  Evaluate the "storm and stress" perspective on adolescence in light of research evidence.

13.2  Summarize the physical changes that occur with puberty and the correlates of pubertal timing.

13.3  Discuss brain development during adolescence and its effect on behavior.

13.4  Identify ways in which thinking changes in adolescence and how these changes are reflected in adolescent decision-making and behavior.

13.5  Discuss moral development and influences on moral reasoning.

13.6  Describe the challenges that school transitions pose for adolescents and the role of parents in academic achievement.

"Samira," Aminah breathes, sliding into the booth at the back of the desolate coffee house. They always meet here instead of the trendier Starbucks or Panera, where Samira might be recognized, which could lead to her mother finding out. Here, at Mr. Kader's shop that he artfully named Qahua (coffee), they can meet in obscurity, and Mr. Kader is a long-standing supplier of Aminah's father. It's unlikely he will tattle. "I'm glad you're here. I thought maybe you wouldn't come."

Samira laughs. "You always think I won't come, and I'm always here when you arrive."

"Very true," she agrees, reaching for the notebook Samira secrets with her to their semi-weekly rendezvous. "Where did we leave off last time?"

"You were teaching me basic algebra, I think. I've also finished reading two of the books you leant me, shorter ones, but I finished."

"That's great!"

Aminah and Samira started meeting on Mondays and Thursdays so that Aminah could teach Samira how to read and write, but Samira is so clever and quick that they moved beyond the basics sooner than either expected. Instead of quitting, they decide to risk the wrath of Samira's parents to keep going. Aminah wants to get Samira caught up with her own level by the time she starts high school next year, and she thinks she can if they both work hard.

## 14. Socioemotional Development in Adolescence

### Today you will practice the following:

14.1 *Summarize the processes by which self-concept, self-esteem, and identity change during adolescence.*

14.2 *Discuss the nature of parent–child relationships in adolescence.*

14.3 *Examine the developmental progression of peer relations in adolescence.*

14.4 *Analyze patterns of adolescent sexual activity including sexual orientation.*

14.5 *Identify common psychological and behavioral problems in adolescence.*

"*Baba, Úmi,*" Aminah says, entering the kitchen and laying kisses on her parents' cheeks. "Good morning."

"Good morning, *hubibi*," *baba* replies. As Aminah prepares her breakfast, *Baba* looks at her, squinting. "There's something different about you this morning. What is it?"

"She's wearing the hijab, Riad," *Úmi* tells him.

"Ah! So you are." He picks up the travel mug of coffee her mother fixes for him every morning. "Good day, ladies."

"Bye, *Baba*."

"Good-bye, darling," *Úmi* says. Then she turns to Aminah. "Why today, sweetheart?"

Aminah fingers the edges of the deep blue hijab she bought herself a couple weeks before from Mrs. Nejem's tailoring shop. At least half the girls her age already wear the hijab to school and the mosque. "Why not today?"

"Good point." Her mother smiles. "That color is nice on you."

"Thank you, *Úmi*." Finishing her breakfast, she grabs her backpack and heads out the door for school feeling confident and secure in who she is. She'll get stared at, but so do girls with pimples. It'll be okay.

## 15. Physical and Cognitive Development in Emerging/Early Adulthood

### Today you will practice the following:

15.1 Describe the features and characteristics of emerging and early adulthood.

15.2 Summarize the physical developments of emerging and early adulthood.

15.3 Analyze physical and sexual health issues in emerging and early adulthood.

15.4 Compare postformal reasoning, pragmatic thought, and cognitive-affective complexity.

15.5 Explain how attending college influences young adults' development, and identify challenges faced by first-generation and nontraditional students.

15.6 Discuss vocational choice and the transition to work.

Aminah wants to go away to college. *Baba* doesn't want her to go to college. "Your husband will surely let you attend classes once you're married, as I did your mother until Navi was born," he points out.

She rolls her eyes.

"Navi went to college, and you told me I could do anything my brother could."

*Úmi* smiles and sets a pot of tea to steep on the table between them. "She has a point, Riad. Times are different now."

So, they compromise.

Aminah goes to college, but she doesn't leave home. Her parents agree that the local state university campus offers sound education, and when she marries, Aminah can continue classes there if she chooses.

"What if I don't want to get married?" she asks. *Baba* gives her an evil eye, and she holds up her hands in defeat. "Okay, okay. It was just a question. Do you have candidates in mind?"

Her father tells her about three sons of business acquaintances and members of the mosque he favors, one of whom Aminah favors as well. She has objections to none and leaves her parents to make final decisions. She's always known she'll be married by 19 or 20, and although she might prefer it otherwise, she doesn't disagree with her culture's customs. She knows too many marriages that were arranged and are loving and affectionate—marriages like her parents'—to ever complain.

With thoughts of marriage planning pushed to the back of her mind, Aminah concentrates on school. She graduates from high school and begins her studies at university, performing well in all her courses but doing exceptional work in science-based ones. After a year of indecision, she selects agricultural science as her major and throws herself completely into her studies. The campus is large, and she's no longer "the girl in the hijab;" she's just a student spending too many hours in the library and eating bad vending machine food between classes. When she stays late, *Baba* comes in the car to bring her home, and despite a couple social clock interruptions along the way (like getting married), she receives her degree in four and a half years, walking across the stage with a belly ripe with her first child.

## 16. Social Development in Emerging/Early Adulthood

### Today you will practice the following:

*16.1 Summarize psychosocial development in emerging and early adulthood.*

*16.2 Discuss influences on friendship and mate selection and interactions in emerging and early adulthood.*

*16.3 Analyze the diverse romantic situations that may characterize emerging and early adulthood, including singlehood, cohabitation, marriage, and divorce.*

*16.4 Compare the experiences of young adults as stepparents, never-married parents, and same-sex parents.*

When she's 20, Aminah marries Yusef El-Amin in a traditional contracted ceremony at the mosque. If they hadn't gone to high school together and she hadn't grown vegetables on his fire escape for ten years, they might not know one another nor see one another at their own wedding. As it is, they do know one another well and share a fondness that her parents feel offers benefits to the match. *Baba* agrees to a rather elaborate ceremony and reception, for which Aminah is grateful. He's a good father, and he works hard to blend their traditions with those of their adopted land. She had wanted a beautiful dress; thanks to *Baba* she has one.

Yusef, like most of the mosque's men, is progressive. Not only does he encourage Aminah to finish college, but he's also in favor of their use of birth control until she decides she wants a child. This gift of bodily autonomy, so rare in her culture, is the first jewel in the crown of her marriage. She believes in her marrow there will be many more and is happy to begin honoring her marriage with them. If any of the women in the prayer circle wonder that she doesn't conceive right away—or at all—in the first year, no one speaks of it, and Aminah keeps her own counsel. What lies beneath the marriage blanket is between a man and his wife.

Six months or so into her marriage, Aminah seeks out her mother after prayers one evening. This makes twice she's come to the mosque and hasn't seen Samira, who is faithful as the lamb. Touching her mother's shoulder, Aminah whispers in her ear, "*Al'umu,* have you seen Samira Saab? It's been three weeks or more since I've seen her. Her mother's here, but I haven't seen Samira nor heard anything about her. Usually the women gossip, at least a little . . ."

*Al'umu* clucks her tongue and steers Aminah to a bench beneath a live oak dancing in a light breeze. "I didn't tell you before, darling, because I wasn't sure. *Baba* only learned last night to be certain. Samira's gone."

"Gone?" Alarm causes Aminah to flush. She feels the heat just below the surface of her skin. "What is 'gone,' Mother? I don't understand."

"Her family sent her to stay with relatives in Afghanistan. I believe they live near your aunt Hannah."

"In Kabul?" This is madness. "Why did they send her away, and why there?"

*Al'umu* shrugs. "Aminah, *hubibi,* you have to calm down. The Saabs' business is not our concern."

"But, Mama, you know she didn't do anything wrong. Someone has to help her. We have to bring her back, or she's going to die over there."

"Ah, child, don't be so dramatic," her mother says, drawing her close. "We mustn't look too closely sometimes. You know that. Come along. Let's have a sweet before Yusef takes you home, no?"

"No," she says as she pulls away. "*Al'umu,* it's when we want to look away that we *must* look more closely. If you won't help me, I'll find someone who will."

Aminah left her mother and went in search of her husband. She was, technically, of the El-Amins now, and Yusef's family was as well off as her own and had more relatives left in Afghanistan. If her parents wouldn't help Samira, maybe her new family would.

## 17. Physical and Cognitive Development in Middle Adulthood

### Today you will practice the following:

*17.1* Summarize age-related physical changes during middle adulthood.

*17.2* Discuss common health conditions and illnesses and the roles of stress and hardiness on health during middle adulthood.

*17.3* Contrast the findings of cross-sectional and longitudinal studies of crystallized and fluid intelligence over adulthood.

*17.4* Analyze changes in cognitive capacities during middle adulthood, including attention, memory, processing speed, and expertise.

Just as Aminah begins her maternity leave with their second son, a White House initiative from the First Lady's office rolls out. She wants to encourage better, healthier school lunch options for children nationally, and part of that will be sustainable gardening at the local level. Aminah sits in the rocker Yusef sent for from his grandmother's house in Kandahar when Avi was born four years before and nurses little Farouq. Avi, such a good boy, sits at his *úmi's* feet with a pot of lotion, massaging each toe one by one. Aminah smiles at him. Who says only women can serve?

Rereading the article about the First Lady's school lunch agenda, Aminah has an idea. When Farouq's head falls off her breast and he's fast asleep as well as sated, she lays him gently in his Moses basket and sends Avi to play in the living room. "*Úmi* will be there in just a minute," she promises him. Digging around in the directories they keep in the drawer that will never be cleaned out, she finds the telephone number for the elementary school she and Navi once attended. It surprises her to learn, once the receptionist answers, that her old principal retired a decade ago, and she wonders if adult children always believe the people from their childhoods remain forever fixed as they were—probably.

A young woman, Martha Holmes, is the new principal, and Aminah asks to speak to her. They discuss the new initiative, and Aminah explains to the principal some ideas she has for sustainable gardening at the elementary school. She tells her she'd like to work on this project with the school if there's going to be money for it, and Ms. Holmes promises to get back to her, which she does the following day. She asks Aminah how she would feel about being the project manager for sustainable gardening for the city school district. Aminah agrees to take the job without even asking the salary, but she tells Holmes it may be some time before she can begin. She needs to complete her maternity leave and then work an appropriate notice at her current position for the county.

Nine months into the new job, with Avi in Kindergarten at the elementary school where she's working two days each week and Farouq nearly walking, Aminah loves what she's doing. She has almost everything she's ever wanted. Her family are all close by and healthy. Her husband is wonderful, kind, passionate, and successful. Her children are the most beautiful in the state at least, even if she is a little bit biased. If she wants any one thing, it's to know what happened to Samira all those years ago. She tries not to dwell on that.

After a particularly grubby day at the elementary school, Aminah puts the boys in a warm bath to get clean while she fixes dinner, which entails telephoning Yusef at work and asking him to bring home takeout from Mr. Sultan's. Then she pours a glass of wine and turns on the radio just loud enough to hear but soft enough that the children are louder still. When she hears the car door slam, she moves to the front door to help Yusef inside with the food and his briefcase. Yusef isn't at the door. A policeman is—no, a policeman and a policewoman. Not once in all her life have the police stood on her doorstep.

"Mrs. El-Amin?"

"Yes," she says, straining still to hear the boys upstairs. "Can I help you? Is something wrong?"

The policewoman steps forward. She has red hair and freckles. For a half second, Aminah thinks how out of place she looks in their neighborhood and wonders if this is how she looks anywhere else.

"Mrs. El-Amin," the woman whose nametag proclaims her to be Officer Agnes Lane says, "Officer Harding and I are here because there's been an accident."

No, her parents. One of them? Naveen maybe or one of his kids.

"An accident?" she echoes, listening to her own voice waver.

"Yes, ma'am. I'm terribly sorry. There was a hit and run accident on Lux and Ninth—" Lux and Ninth? That's where Mr. Sultan's takeaway is. No, it can't be Yusef. It can't be.

" —and pushed into the electricity post. I'm sorry, Mrs. El-Amin, but he died at the scene."

Aminah shakes her head to clear it. "Died? Who did you say?"

"Your husband, ma'am. Mr. El-Amin."

"No," she says quietly, shaking her head. "That's not possible. I just spoke to Yusef 15 minutes ago—less even. I asked him to get takeaway and—"

"Ma'am, is there someone we can call for you?"

"No. No, thank you." The man, Officer Harding, she thinks, looks toward the hallway where Farouq is squealing with his brother. "My children," she whispers, "in the bath." She turns back to Officer Lane. "Yusef?" she asks. "Are you sure? Are you positive it was my husband Yusef?"

"Yes, ma'am. I'm sure. I'm terribly sorry. Please allow me to call someone," Officer Lane repeats, but Aminah shakes her head.

"I'll do it." She looks at both of them. "Hit and run, you said?"

"Yes, ma'am."

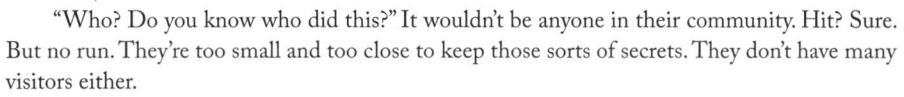

"Who? Do you know who did this?" It wouldn't be anyone in their community. Hit? Sure. But no run. They're too small and too close to keep those sorts of secrets. They don't have many visitors either.

"Sorry, ma'am, we don't, but we're checking all possible leads."

Officer Harding steps forward and looks down at her. He doesn't remove his hat even though Officer Lane has held hers the entire time since Aminah opened the door.

"Important for you to understand, Mrs. El-Amin, that hit and runs don't get solved very often. No witnesses, no evidence, the cases just go cold."

He's telling her they're not even going to try. Officer Lane shoots him a look, but Aminah understands hierarchies. Officer Lane is a small, young woman to Officer Harding's tall, experienced man. He'd get his lieutenant's sign-off and file the report before the younger woman ever got her jacket off.

"Thank you, Officer Harding. I understand." She does, and she will be at the station every day until something's done about her husband's death or until they arrest her for trying. "If you don't mind," she says, turning back to the woman, "I need to call my husband's parents now, and I need to get my children out of the bath."

"Of course." Officer Lane hands her a business card. "If you need anything," she says.

"Thank you," and as she closes the door, holding herself together by the web of her grief alone, she thinks she might actually telephone the woman—but first, family.

## 18. Socioemotional Development in Middle Adulthood

### Today you will practice the following:

*18.1  Summarize the theories and research on psychosocial development during middle adulthood.*

*18.2  Describe the changes that occur in self-concept, identity, and personality during middle adulthood.*

*18.3  Analyze relationships in middle adulthood, including friend, spousal, parent–child, and grandparent relationships.*

*18.4  Discuss influences on job satisfaction and retirement planning during middle adulthood.*

Aminah buries Yusef quietly in the traditions of Islam. She wraps his body, a body she loved for far too brief a time, in the burial shroud she embroidered before and after classes during their engagement. The edges have bluebells and yellow daisies, and among the leaves she's stitched the tiniest of crosses and hearts to send her beloved to paradise. In the quiet of a house devoid even of the children her mother takes so she can be alone with her grief, she writes Yusef's eulogy. When they reach the mosque, she doesn't want to deliver it. She stands before his casket and touches her fingers to her lips, then to the polished wood, and says, "The Quran beseeches us to compete with one another in doing good. Yusef, my beloved, set the bar against which we all measured ourselves. In only ten years he became my everything. Allah—may He be glorified—will place balm on our grief. Let us pray Yusef is now accepted into *Jannat al Firdus,* where his sins will be forgiven and he will find himself in the company of the prophets. Ameen." The actual eulogy she slips into the wooden box that holds their silver after she returns home. It's enough that she wrote it.

Years pass as Aminah continues the sustainable gardening work she began with the local schools. She expands this to other nearby districts, fretting each time she leaves a post that she will impoverish her children. This must be her chosen work, for the ends always work out. Her parents and Yusef's, even as they age, are her rock. She knows how fortunate she is. Widows such as herself have few rights in Afghanistan, and many face social isolation or worse. In America, it doesn't matter that she's Muslim; she's a mourning mother, and her community cares for her. Often, she thinks about Samira and what may have happened to her; she wonders whether or not their hidden lessons played any role in the girl's disappearance. She tries to teach her boys to regard people as people and to accept their own responsibilities in creating a just world, and she wonders if she's done enough to do that herself.

When Farouq leaves for college and Avi has married, she lobbies a nonprofit international nongovernmental organization in New York, Equality Now, to send her to Afghanistan. It's not their mission—sending workers to such dangerous places—but the work she wants to do is part of their mission. Somehow, she succeeds and, after tearful and perhaps permanent good-byes to her sons and her parents, including Yusef's, she embarks on her trip. With the visas, money for bribes, local transport papers, miscellaneous costs, she budgets $5,000 for the two-and-a-half-month trip. The plane ticket from Reagan National to Harmid Karzai International Airport in Kabul is $3,000 round-trip, but she only purchases the flight to Afghanistan. *Baba* tells her the borders close and open with extreme irregularity, and she doesn't want to waste money on a ticket that may not be good the particular day she's due to return when she could leave the very next day, even if it costs her slightly more money to buy it when she's ready to leave. She travels light, only a heavy canvas backpack and thin wallet she keeps in her pocket like a man. Whatever she didn't bring that she needs, she can buy there.

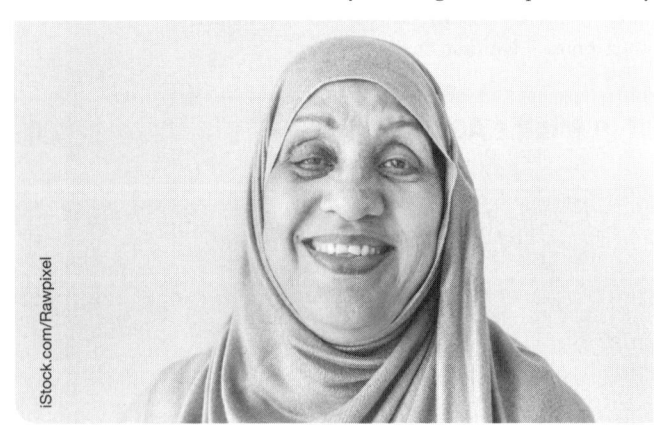

Her guide and translator meets her at the airport. Rokhshana Abdulla is slight with serious eyes and a frightening sense of competence in the way she ignores the rifle slung across her back. She wears a simple white linen hijab that makes Aminah feel shabby in her costly gold-threaded burgundy one. They shake hands before

Rokhshana motions toward a waiting car. It's a battered and dusty Ford Fiesta, and Aminah has a moment's hesitation. Staring at the gun hanging between Rokhshana's shoulder blades, she hitches her backpack and pushes her graying hair out of her face. This isn't about her.

Beside her, Rokhshana glances over from time to time as they drive. "I'll take you first to your guest house. You can leave your bag there. Then we'll go see the school if you like."

"Oh, yes!" Aminah came to work with local organizations to help advance girls' education. Of course, she wants to go to the school. "I want to see it as soon as possible."

Rokhshana gives her a cryptic look. "Don't get excited, American." She points to a low adobe building in the distance. "There's a meeting after lunch I think you'd like to attend if we can get you there on time and if you're not too tired."

"I'm not too tired," she assures the guide. "What's the meeting?"

"The army. The *United States* Army," she clarifies, "is conducting a demonstration of new technology they claim will enhance security at your school. Because their forces are responsible for security right now, they have an interest in developing anything that will help. It sounds interesting, some sort of blanket of invisibility."

Aminah chuckles. "Sounds like something my boys would've watched on television as children."

"Superheroes?" Rokhshana asks.

"Yes."

"Half the locals think the Americans are."

"And the other half?"

Rokhshana glances at her again. "Don't ask, and stay close to me."

## 19. Physical and Cognitive Development in Late Adulthood

### Today you will practice the following:

*19.1  Discuss age-related changes in brain and body systems in late adulthood, and identify ways that older adults may compensate for changes.*

*19.2  Identify risk and protective factors for health in late adulthood.*

*19.3  Summarize common dementias including characteristics, risk and protective factors, and treatment.*

*19.4  Analyze patterns of cognitive change in late adulthood.*

When Aminah approaches her 65th birthday, she takes stock of the years since she started traveling to Afghanistan. She spends six months of every year in the more remote villages of Kandahar, Kabul, and Helmand Provinces. Her work with schools and girls' education rewards her in a way her earlier agricultural positions never quite reached. She's able to speak to village elders about their valid reasons for keeping daughters home from school and creating solutions for excising those concerns one by one. In doing so, she's also able to work with village women in creating plans for their own cottage industries, sustainable farming, and market sales.

During her first trip, Aminah met and formed an instant friendship with another American, then army captain Poppy Bell. Poppy worked on the "blanket of invisibility" Rokhshana mentioned in her drive from the airport to her lodgings, and Aminah, loving the technology on sight, took the opportunity of the small meeting to introduce herself. All these years later, they're still the best of friends, early widowhood and a shared love of her homeland binding them tightly. Every time Aminah returns to Afghanistan, Poppy implores her not to go, but the mountains and its people are in her veins now. Avi has come with her a time or two, and Farouq enlisted in the U.S. Marine Corps, volunteering every tour for Afghanistan and bordering nations. She doesn't want her children in danger, but she's so pleased to see their sense of history and family propelling their choices.

During her stateside months, Aminah spends all her time with her children and grandchildren. She's a happy and fit—if aging—sexagenarian, and one of her favorite activities is sitting on the living room pallet while her two small granddaughters style her hair and decorate it with jeweled pins and combs. Her own mother, who barely looks older than she does in her 80s, always looks on with pleasure, but like Poppy, she's grown weary of Aminah's continued travels. *Baba* passed away when Aminah was abroad, and she nearly missed the funeral with her difficulties getting out of southern Asia. She probably should retire and stop causing her mother worry.

## 20. Socioemotional Development in Late Adulthood

### Today you will practice the following:

*20.1 Examine the contributions of self-concept, personality, and religiosity to older adults' well-being.*

*20.2 Identify social contexts in which older adults live and their influence on development.*

*20.3 Summarize features of older adults' relationships with friends, spouses, children, and grandchildren, and identify how these relationships affect older adults' functioning.*

*20.4 Discuss influences on the timing of retirement and adaptation to retirement.*

At 67, Aminah makes her final journey to Afghanistan. She selects an outlying village in Jālālābād that has one school in what can generously be called a building. She's worked with worse. After a week in the village, she ventures with her new guide Zaina Nagi to the school. The walk is three miles, more than an hour in the chill of coming snow, but Aminah enjoys every step. When they reach the path to the school, Zaina says they should wait until dismissal in a quarter hour. Aminah wanders the nearby creek bank while waiting but comes quickly when Zaina whistles the end of the school day.

Children of all ages from the small to near college age tumble through the door and head in several directions. Aminah watches them go until the last one leaves. Zaina motions for her to come through the doorway, and together they enter the dim recess of the school, built without electricity but serving dedicated students with a dedicated teacher. The teacher looks up at Aminah and Zaina's arrival. Aminah's breath stops. She thinks surely she's wrong. It's been more than 40 years after all.

"Samira? Samira Saab?"

Zaina turns to Aminah. "You know our teacher here? But you said this is your first time in Jālālābād."

She nods. "It is."

Samira walks toward her, arms open. They embrace, and Aminah doesn't want to let her go. She feels 19 again and terrified of what befell her friend.

"What happened to you?" she asks. "I asked, but no one would say."

"My family sent me to live with relatives here. I was rebelling." Samira smiles sadly in recollection. "I think I was meant to either submit or die as an example of what happens when one is wicked."

"Oh, Samira," she says, hand over her heart. "Did I do this? Teaching you to read and write?"

"No." She shakes her head. "This was of my own making, but teaching me to read and write gave me purpose here. I think my parents perhaps overestimated the degree to which I would bring dishonor on the house by being literate and refusing an ill match. This has been a good place for me. My marriage is one of love, and I contribute to the welfare of my village. *Allāh akbar*," she finishes.

Aminah hugs her again. "*Allāh akbar. Subhanallah.*"

God is great. Glory to God.

"*Subhanallah*," Samira echoes. Zaina clears her throat, and Samira laughs. "Yes, we should discuss the school before your guide is due to have you back. It's good, Aminah. Today, we strategize, and tomorrow you dine with my family, yes?"

She smiles and nods. "Yes!"

## 21. Experience With Death and Dying

### Today you will practice the following:

*21.1 Identify ways in which death has been defined and end-of-life issues that may arise.*

*21.2 Contrast children's, adolescents', and adults' understanding of death.*

*21.3 Discuss the physical and emotional process of dying as it is experienced over the lifespan.*

*21.4 Summarize typical grief reactions to the loss of loved ones and the influence of development on bereavement.*

The school in Jālālābād is a grand achievement for Aminah. The building, constructed by men and women in the village, is ramshackle by design. The Taliban destroy houses of learning when they come upon them, but so do other oppressive sects. A substandard structure is easier to replace quickly than a permanent one.

Aminah offers Samira one of Poppy's remaining webs of invisibility. It will be easy to install before she leaves and may provide additional protection in the future by reflecting to patrolling men the trees and tracks around them while obscuring the school itself. Samira is thrilled. Aminah also marks off and helps plow a small area for the school's first garden. What grows in Jālālābād differs wildly from what grows in her temperate American town, but she's brought appropriate seeds. Once the students start planting and tending, the garden will do the hard work. Students invariably invest their all in the process, and the learning they gain from it equals the harvest.

Near the end of her stay, she and Samira divide the students into groups of varying ages so that each has at least one older student. The groups are sent into the woods surrounding the school to collect vegetative examples and materials for making the Afghan version of a scarecrow. Samira trails them, keeping watch, while Aminah puts the finishing touches on the garden. When she's done, she rinses her hands in the creek and carries the gardening supplies into the schoolhouse.

The drone drops its small payload on the building when Aminah is two steps from clearing the door on her way to rejoin the others. With the students and Samira scattered and digging in the woods, none is harmed. Aminah dies in the explosion. Samira immediately reaches out to Poppy, whose information she now has because of the cloak they hadn't put into place yet, and Poppy contacts Aminah's family. The boys, Poppy, and Poppy's son Ismail, an Afghan national adopted as an orphaned child, travel to Jālālābād for the funeral. Samira decides, and the family agrees, that Aminah would want to be buried there. She is wrapped in the shroud Yusef brought to her at their marriage, and Samira swears the cedar tree growing mere yards from her grave appeared the spring after they buried her. She calls it the Prophet's Tree after her first friend Aminah Mohammed.

# CASE DISCUSSION QUESTIONS

1. Aminah is born small-for-date. At an early checkup with the pediatrician, her mother Munya asks about this, what being small-for-date might mean for Aminah's development. The pediatrician explains that although Aminah was technically full term, she was just on the cusp, and if she'd been born a couple days earlier, she would've been both premature and a healthy weight. Discuss the different developmental trajectories for Aminah across any and all domains (biological, cognitive, and socioemotional) for a full-term/low-birth-weight beginning versus a premature, healthy-weight one.

2. Aminah's parents support her development (and her brother's) across a range of interests, including those that are gender and possibly cultural atypical. How does this parental perspective change how Aminah views her own future?

3. In adolescence, Aminah visibly adopts many of the behaviors of her culture, including wearing a hijab. She also forges a compromise with her parents regarding college and marriage, being willing and even happy to make a marriage in the traditional fashion but also eager to study beyond high school. How do Aminah's childhood experiences across any and all domains (biological, cognitive, and socioemotional) lead naturally to these outcomes for her, and what would we predict about the stability of her future?

4. Aminah's entire life occurs over many decades that are, loosely, contemporary. Cars, telephones, televisions, and so on exist, but era-specific technology isn't presented (e.g., cell phones, space shuttles, and artificial intelligence). Would Aminah's life have been different if she were born in a specific period, earlier or later? If so, how? Be specific.

# Appendix A: Domain Mapping

## Biological Domain

Biological Beginnings (moments 01, 02)

Albert, James (45–46); Archer, Edward (143–144); Bell, Poppy (235–236); Dennel, London (119–120); Everett, Riley (71–72); Jones, Jamal (3–4); McCallen, Bliss (213–214); Mohammed, Aminah (263–264); Morris, Aiza (164–165); Park, Zack (187–188); Ramirez, Leonardo (97–98); Rowe, Naomi (25–26)

Pregnancy and Childbirth (moment 03)

Albert, James (47); Archer, Edward (144); Bell, Poppy (236); Dennel, London (121); Everett, Riley (72); Jones, Jamal (5); McCallen, Bliss (215); Mohammed, Aminah (264); Morris, Aiza (166); Park, Zack (189); Ramirez, Leonardo (99); Rowe, Naomi (27)

Infancy and Toddlerhood (moment 04)

Albert, James (49); Archer, Edward (145); Bell, Poppy (237); Dennel, London (122); Everett, Riley (73); Jones, Jamal (6); McCallen, Bliss (216); Mohammed, Aminah (265); Morris, Aiza (167); Park, Zack (191); Ramirez, Leonardo (100); Rowe, Naomi (28)

Early Childhood (moment 07)

Albert, James (52); Archer, Edward (148); Bell, Poppy (240); Dennel, London (126); Everett, Riley (76); Jones, Jamal (9); McCallen, Bliss (218); Mohammed, Aminah (268); Morris, Aiza (169); Park, Zack (194); Ramirez, Leonardo (103); Rowe, Naomi (31)

Middle and Late Childhood (moment 09)

Albert, James (54–56); Archer, Edward (152–153); Bell, Poppy (243–245); Dennel, London (128–130); Everett, Riley (79–81); Jones, Jamal (10–12); McCallen, Bliss (220–222); Mohammed, Aminah (271–273); Morris, Aiza (171–172); Park, Zack (196–198); Ramirez, Leonardo (105–106); Rowe, Naomi (32–34)

Adolescence (moment 11)

Albert, James (58); Archer, Edward (154); Bell, Poppy (247); Dennel, London (131); Everett, Riley (82); Jones, Jamal (13); McCallen, Bliss (224); Mohammed, Aminah (275); Morris, Aiza (174); Park, Zack (200); Ramirez, Leonardo (108); Rowe, Naomi (35)

Emerging/Early Adulthood (moment 13)

Albert, James (61); Archer, Edward (156); Bell, Poppy (251); Dennel, London (133); Everett, Riley (84); Jones, Jamal (15); McCallen, Bliss (226); Mohammed, Aminah (277); Morris, Aiza (177); Park, Zack (203); Ramirez, Leonardo (110); Rowe, Naomi (37)

Middle Adulthood (moment 15)

Albert, James (63); Archer, Edward (158); Bell, Poppy (255); Dennel, London (135); Everett, Riley (88); Jones, Jamal (17); McCallen, Bliss (228); Mohammed, Aminah (279); Morris, Aiza (180); Park, Zack (206); Ramirez, Leonardo (112); Rowe, Naomi (39)

Late Adulthood/End of Life (moment 17)

Albert, James (66); Archer, Edward (160); Bell, Poppy (257); Dennel, London (137); Everett, Riley (92); Jones, Jamal (19); McCallen, Bliss (229); Mohammed, Aminah (283); Morris, Aiza (182); Park, Zack (208); Ramirez, Leonardo (115); Rowe, Naomi (41)

Death and Dying (moment 19)

Albert, James (68); Archer, Edward (162); Bell, Poppy (260); Dennel, London (139); Everett, Riley (94); Jones, Jamal (21); McCallen, Bliss (231); Mohammed, Aminah (285); Morris, Aiza (184); Park, Zack (210); Ramirez, Leonardo (116); Rowe, Naomi (43)

## Cognitive Domain

Biological Beginnings (moments 01, 02)

Albert, James (45); Archer, Edward (143); Bell, Poppy (235); Dennel, London (119); Everett, Riley (71); Jones, Jamal (3); McCallen, Bliss (213); Mohammed, Aminah (263); Morris, Aiza (164); Park, Zack (187); Ramirez, Leonardo (97); Rowe, Naomi (25)

Pregnancy and Childbirth (moment 03)

Albert, James (47); Archer, Edward (144); Bell, Poppy (236); Dennel, London (121); Everett, Riley (72); Jones, Jamal (5); McCallen, Bliss (215); Mohammed, Aminah (264); Morris, Aiza (166); Park, Zack (189); Ramirez, Leonardo (99); Rowe, Naomi (27)

Part II: Appendix

Infancy and Toddlerhood (moment 05)

    Albert, James (50); Archer, Edward (145); Bell, Poppy (239); Dennel, London (124); Everett, Riley (74); Jones, Jamal (7); McCallen, Bliss (217); Mohammed, Aminah (266); Morris, Aiza (168); Park, Zack (193); Ramirez, Leonardo (101); Rowe, Naomi (29)

Early Childhood (moment 07)

    Albert, James (52); Archer, Edward (148); Bell, Poppy (240); Dennel, London (126); Everett, Riley (76); Jones, Jamal (9); McCallen, Bliss (218); Mohammed, Aminah (268); Morris, Aiza (169); Park, Zack (194); Ramirez, Leonardo (103); Rowe, Naomi (31)

Middle and Late Childhood (moment 09)

    Albert, James (54–56); Archer, Edward (152–153); Bell, Poppy (243–245); Dennel, London (128–130); Everett, Riley (79–81); Jones, Jamal (10–12); McCallen, Bliss (220–222); Mohammed, Aminah (271–273); Morris, Aiza (171–172); Park, Zack (196–198); Ramirez, Leonardo (105–106); Rowe, Naomi (32–34)

Adolescence (moment 11)

    Albert, James (58); Archer, Edward (154); Bell, Poppy (247); Dennel, London (131); Everett, Riley (82); Jones, Jamal (13); McCallen, Bliss (224); Mohammed, Aminah (275); Morris, Aiza (174); Park, Zack (200); Ramirez, Leonardo (108); Rowe, Naomi (35)

Emerging/Early Adulthood (moment 13)

    Albert, James (61); Archer, Edward (156); Bell, Poppy (251); Dennel, London (133); Everett, Riley (84); Jones, Jamal (15); McCallen, Bliss (226); Mohammed, Aminah (277); Morris, Aiza (177); Park, Zack (203); Ramirez, Leonardo (110); Rowe, Naomi (37)

Middle Adulthood (moment 15)

    Albert, James (63); Archer, Edward (158); Bell, Poppy (255); Dennel, London (135); Everett, Riley (88); Jones, Jamal (17); McCallen, Bliss (228); Mohammed, Aminah (279); Morris, Aiza (180); Park, Zack (206); Ramirez, Leonardo (112); Rowe, Naomi (39)

Late Adulthood/End of Life (moment 17)

    Albert, James (66); Archer, Edward (160); Bell, Poppy (257); Dennel, London (137); Everett, Riley (92); Jones, Jamal (19); McCallen, Bliss (229); Mohammed, Aminah (283); Morris, Aiza (182); Park, Zack (208); Ramirez, Leonardo (115); Rowe, Naomi (41)

Death and Dying (moment 19)

    Albert, James (68); Archer, Edward (162); Bell, Poppy (260); Dennel, London (139); Everett, Riley (94); Jones, Jamal (21); McCallen, Bliss (231); Mohammed, Aminah (285); Morris, Aiza (184); Park, Zack (210); Ramirez, Leonardo (116); Rowe, Naomi (43)

## Socioemotional Domain

Biological Beginnings (moments 01, 02)

    Albert, James (45–46); Archer, Edward (143–144); Bell, Poppy (235–236); Dennel, London (119–120); Everett, Riley (71–72); Jones, Jamal (3–4); McCallen, Bliss (213–214); Mohammed, Aminah (263–264); Morris, Aiza (164–165); Park, Zack (187–188); Ramirez, Leonardo (97–98); Rowe, Naomi (25–26)

Pregnancy and Childbirth (moment 03)

    Albert, James (47); Archer, Edward (144); Bell, Poppy (236); Dennel, London (121); Everett, Riley (72); Jones, Jamal (5); McCallen, Bliss (215); Mohammed, Aminah (264); Morris, Aiza (166); Park, Zack (189); Ramirez, Leonardo (99); Rowe, Naomi (27)

Infancy and Toddlerhood (moment 06)

    Albert, James (51); Archer, Edward (147); Bell, Poppy (240); Dennel, London (125); Everett, Riley (75); Jones, Jamal (8); McCallen, Bliss (217); Mohammed, Aminah (267); Morris, Aiza (168); Park, Zack (193); Ramirez, Leonardo (102); Rowe, Naomi (30)

Early Childhood (moment 08)

    Albert, James (53); Archer, Edward (151); Bell, Poppy (242); Dennel, London (127); Everett, Riley (78); Jones, Jamal (10); McCallen, Bliss (219); Mohammed, Aminah (270); Morris, Aiza (170); Park, Zack (195); Ramirez (104), Leonardo; Rowe, Naomi (31)

Middle and Late Childhood (moment 10)

    Albert, James (55–57); Archer, Edward (152–154); Bell, Poppy (243–244); Dennel, London (128–130); Everett, Riley (79–81); Jones, Jamal (10–12); McCallen, Bliss (220–222); Mohammed, Aminah (271–273); Morris, Aiza (171–172); Park, Zack (196–198); Ramirez, Leonardo (105–106); Rowe, Naomi (32–34)

Adolescence (moment 12)

    Albert, James (59); Archer, Edward (155); Bell, Poppy (249); Dennel, London (132); Everett, Riley (84); Jones, Jamal (14); McCallen, Bliss (225); Mohammed, Aminah (276); Morris, Aiza (175); Park, Zack (201); Ramirez, Leonardo (109); Rowe, Naomi (36)

Emerging/Early Adulthood (moment 14)

    Albert, James (62); Archer, Edward (157); Bell, Poppy (253); Dennel, London (135); Everett, Riley (86); Jones, Jamal (16); McCallen, Bliss (227); Mohammed, Aminah (278); Morris, Aiza (179); Park, Zack (204); Ramirez, Leonardo (111); Rowe, Naomi (38)

Middle Adulthood (moment 16)

Albert, James (64); Archer, Edward (159); Bell, Poppy (256); Dennel, London (136); Everett, Riley (89); Jones, Jamal (18); McCallen, Bliss (228); Mohammed, Aminah (281); Morris, Aiza (181); Park, Zack (207); Ramirez, Leonardo (113); Rowe, Naomi (40)

Late Adulthood/End of Life (moment 18)

Albert, James (67); Archer, Edward (160); Bell, Poppy (259); Dennel, London (138); Everett, Riley (93); Jones, Jamal (20); McCallen, Bliss (230); Mohammed, Aminah (284); Morris, Aiza (183); Park, Zack (209); Ramirez, Leonardo (116); Rowe, Naomi (42)

Death and Dying (moment 19)

Albert, James (68); Archer, Edward (162); Bell, Poppy (260); Dennel, London (139); Everett, Riley (94); Jones, Jamal (21); McCallen, Bliss (231); Mohammed, Aminah (285); Morris, Aiza (184); Park, Zack (210); Ramirez, Leonardo (116); Rowe, Naomi (43)